State of the Art in Computer Graphics

Fractal if by land, Gaussian if by sea

This seascape shows the result of combinations of deterministic and stochastic models. The land is modeled by an interactively designed height field, which was then modified by fractal displacement generated by stochastic interpolation. The sea is a modification of a Rankine wave model, with random elements added to the distribution of wave heights, periods, and a random small scale texture added to the surface reflection. The wave model was developed by Alain Fournier and Bill Reeves; the picture was rendered by the Pixar's *reyes* renderer.

David F. Rogers   Rae A. Earnshaw
Editors

State of the Art in Computer Graphics

Visualization and Modeling

With 171 Figures in 186 Parts, 17 in Color

Springer-Verlag
New York Berlin Heidelberg London
Paris Tokyo Hong Kong Barcelona

David F. Rogers
Aerospace Engineering Department
U.S. Naval Academy
Annapolis, MD 21402
USA

Rae A. Earnshaw
University of Leeds
Leeds LS2 9JT
United Kingdom

Cover illustration: A radiosity rendering of an interior scene, Michael F. Cohen
©Cornell University Program of Computer Graphics and Michael F. Cohen

Library of Congress Cataloging-in-Publication Data
State of the art in computer graphics : visualization and modeling /
    David F. Rogers, Rae A. Earnshaw, editors.
        p. cm.
    Includes bibiliographical references and index.
    ISBN 0-387-97560-8
    1. Computer graphics.   I. Rogers, David F., 1937-
II. Earnshaw, Rae A., 1944- ,
T385.S73   1991 91-17348
006.6–dc20   CIP

Printed on acid-free paper.

Typeset by Nancy A. Rogers using TₑX. Photocomposition on a Chelgraph IBX-2000.
Printed and bound by R.R. Donnelley and Sons, Harrisonburg, Virginia.
Printed in the United States of America.

9 8 7 6 5 4 3 2 1

ISBN 0-387-97560-8 Springer-Verlag New York Berlin Heidelberg
ISBN 3-540-97560-8 Springer-Verlag Berlin Heidelberg New York

Contents

Introduction

State of the Art in Computer Graphics –
Visualization and Modeling

This is the third volume derived from a State-of-the-Art in Computer Graphics Summer Institute. The current volume represents a snapshot of a number of topics in computer graphics. These topics include: parallel processing, image generation including radiosity, textures and fractals, modeling including pioneering work in n-manifold geometry and an excellent survey of rational B-spline curves and surfaces (NURBS), graphical user interfaces, and a survey of scientific visualization techniques.

Many of the papers first present a background introduction to the topic followed by a discussion of current work in the topic. The volume is thus equally suitable for nonspecialists in a particular area, and for the more experienced researcher in the field. It also enables general readers to obtain an acquaintance with a particular topic area sufficient to apply that knowledge in the context of solving current problems.

The volume is organized into five chapters as follows: Hardware/Parallel Processing, Image Generation, Modeling, Graphical User-Computer Interfaces, Visualization.

In the first chapter Frank Crow and Turner Whitted address graphics algorithms suitable for parallel processing and development of hardware architectures to take advantage of these algorithms. Although many graphics algorithms nicely lend themselves to parallelization, Crow shows that a number of pitfalls exist. He also looks at a number of architectural paradigms including Local Area Networks (LAN), Single Instruction Multiple Data (SIMD), and Multiple Instruction Multiple Data (MIMD). Whitted points out that although the high performance of the current generation of graphics systems owes much to VLSI technology, architectural considerations are equally, if not more, important.

The second chapter discusses image generation in computer graphics. The first paper by Michael Cohen provides a thorough and insightful survey of radiosity. He provides an excellent discussion of techniques for increasing the efficiency of the radiosity calculations, including combined radiosity and ray tracing and efforts to parallelize the algorithm.

The second paper by Paul Heckbert and Henry Moreton points out several errors resulting from using linear interpolation in screen space with Gouraud and Phong shading and especially texture mapping. They show that *rational* linear interpolation yields 'correct' results. They present an 'easy' algorithm for performing rational linear interpolation.

The third paper in the chapter by Alain Fournier looks at random processes in computer graphics, especially fractals and in particular fractional Brownian motion as used for modeling terrain. He also discusses stochastic interpolation and Fourier synthesis.

The third chapter contains three papers on modeling. In the first paper in this chapter Roy Hall discusses some fundamental questions about supporting complex modeling environments. He advances the notion that the resulting geometry and the environment used to generate it is, in fact, an abstraction of nongeometric decisions made during the design process. An approach for addressing and preserving these nongeometric decisions is presented.

In the second paper of this chapter, Mike Muuss and Lee Butler present techniques for representing nonmanifold geometries that result from complex intersections of CSG primitive solids as surface tessellations. They discuss the details of Weiler's radial-edge data structure as applied to nonmanifold geometries. They point out that, using this data structure, Boolean operations as well as other powerful modeling operations are easily implemented. Further, they discuss system design level issues, e.g., tessellation accuracy, associated with implementation.

Rational B-splines (NURBs) have become the industry standard for representing and designing sculptured surfaces. In the third paper in this chapter Les Piegl surveys the important properties of NURBs. The result is a set of algorithmic tools that can be used to design and visualize complex models.

In the fourth chapter, Jim Foley discusses a topic of considerable current interest—user interfaces. He surveys and describes interactive toolkits and user-interface management systems for developing and implementing user interfaces. He emphasizes the importance of providing both data models and control models in designing and implementing user interfaces.

Finally, in the fifth chapter Craig Upson surveys techniques for scientific visualization. Noting that the visualization cycle consists of computation or experimentation followed by analysis, he presents examples of several techniques for visualizing scientific data, including point clouds, markers, tracer particles, contouring, vector nets, continuous tone color and pseudocolor renderings and volumetric visualization.

Computer graphics is now both endemic and generic. Today excellent computer graphic capabilities are considered standard on workstations and even personal computers. Graphical user interfaces are becoming both more acceptable and more useful. Powerful graphics, coupled with ever increasing computational power at either constant or decreasing cost, makes a typical workstation an exceptional design and analysis tool. For example, engineers typically have sitting on their desk more computational power than was used to design the Concord! Further, if required, they can connect with even more powerful computers via a network. However, at least two important problems of current and critical importance remain—modeling and interpretation.

Today one of the hardest parts of computer aided design or analysis is first modeling the design, then recording and verifying it. For example, a typical vehicle such as a tank, automobile, ship or aircraft might be composed of tens of thousands of individual parts. Many of these parts are composed of cylinders, flats, and simple conic curves and surfaces such as are amenable to modeling using a constructive solid geometry (CSG) approach. However, especially with the increasing use of composite materials, many parts are designed using sculptured surfaces. A marriage of these two techniques in now critical to continued development of computer aided design and analysis. Further, the graphical user interfaces used in most modeling systems are at best barely adequate to the required task. Critical work on these interfaces is required to continue pushing back the frontiers. Similarly, once the design is modeled, how are the varied and diverse pieces stored, retrieved, and modified? How are physical interferences prevented or eliminated? Although considerable progress has been made, there are still more questions and frustrations than answers. One of the fundamental problems of the 1990s is and will continue to be modeling.

The second problem is interpretation. With the ever increasing computational power available, our ability to generate data far exceeds our ability to interpret, understand, and utilize that data. For example, a typical computational fluid dynamics program yields literally millions of pieces of information in a few hours of computation. How does the scientist or engineer interpret and understand that data? Although scientists and engineers have always used graphical techniques for interpretation and understanding, computer graphics techniques for scientific visualization are now crucial for interpreting and understanding these vast amounts of data. Fundamentally, if you do not have the tools to interpret and understand the data, there is little sense in generating it!

Both computer modeling and computer graphics techniques for scientific visualization are in their infancy. Their development will place ever increasing demands on both computational and graphical resources. These demands will far exceed current capability.

Acknowledgements. The papers in this volume formed the basis of an International Summer Institute on The State of the Art in Computer Graphics held at the Edinburgh Conference Centre, Heriot Watt University, Edinburgh, United Kingdom, in the summer of 1990. We are very grateful to our co-sponsors: the British Computer Society (BCS) Computer Graphics and Displays Group, the Computer Graphics Society (CGS), and Springer-Verlag. We also thank the Association for Computing Machinery (ACM) for their co-operation and support. Our thanks and appreciation go to Mrs. Frances Johnson of Concilia for all her help and support with the practical arrangements for the Institute. Our thanks and appreciation also to all those delegates who attended from many countries and contributed by their discussion, interaction, and inspiration. The following countries were represented: Australia, Austria, Belgium, Bulgaria, Canada,

Federal Republic of Germany, Finland, France, Hong Kong, Israel, Italy, Netherlands, Norway, Portugal, Saudi Arabia, Sweden, Switzerland, the United Kingdom, and the United States.

Special thanks and appreciation go to Gerhard Rossbach of Springer-Verlag, Computer Science Editor, USA West Coast Office, Santa Barbara, California for his continued support of this series of Summer Institutes. Thanks are certainly due Nancy A. Rogers, who computer typeset the book using TeX.

A volume such as this is the result of many months of planning and preparation, and we thank all those who have assisted us. Colleagues, students, contributors, and publisher—we thank you all for your forbearance and patience, and for enduring our persistence in seeking to bring this project to a successful conclusion.

David F. Rogers
Annapolis, Maryland, USA

Rae A. Earnshaw
Leeds, United Kingdom

1 Hardware/Parallel Processing

Graphics Algorithms for Parallel Machines

Franklin C. Crow

Abstract

State-of-the-art computer graphics has been increasing its demand for computer cycles at least as fast as computer technology has been increasing their availability. An obvious solution to faster state-of-the-art graphics is parallelism. Most aspects of existing algorithms for computer graphics are easily parallelized. However, a close look shows some pitfalls. After looking at conventional rendering algorithms with an eye to parallelization, some existing architectural paradigms—Local Area Network (LAN), Single Instruction Multiple Data (SIMD), Multiple Instruction Multiple Data (MIMD)—are examined for their utility to computer graphics.

Looking to the future, it is quite clear that we have years of continuing exponential increase in the computing power available to us. Furthermore, radically different computing technologies promise to open new possibilities as existing integrated circuit technologies push against physical limits. Algorithms which it seems absurd to propose today may seem quite reasonable in a different world to come.

Introduction

The exponential increase in instructions required to produce state-of-the-art computer graphics has more than kept pace with the similar growth in availability of computing cycles to execute them. Although dedicated graphics hardware provides a way to produce imagery more rapidly, massively parallel computing is the obvious route to fast production of state-of-the-art imagery. The economies of scale inherent in producing microprocessors by the millions make it relatively impractical to use special-purpose hardware. Furthermore, annual increases in speed via processor upgrades are virtually guaranteed. Similar constant speedups for custom hardware require a great deal more development effort.

There are increasing numbers of parallel computing engines devoted to computer graphics. Flight simulator architectures, initially made in very purposefully specialized ways [Roug69; Scha83], have yielded to more general architectures [Schu80; Zyda88]. Current graphics workstations exhibit highly parallel approaches although still highly specialized for graphics [Torb87; Akel88; Apga88; Potm89; Haeb90]. Furthermore, there are a few experimental graphics machines built using general-purpose, massively parallel approaches [Nish83; Fuch85; Fuch89]. At the same time, general-purpose massively parallel machines are becoming more widely available [Haye86; Hill86; Rett86] and are occasionally being used for graphics [Crow89]. Finally, proliferating networked workstations provide a simple approach to parallel graphics, which is seeing increasing use [Crow86; MMG87; Muus90a].

Here, ways in which existing approaches to computer graphics can be adapted for parallel execution are examined. Then, three fundamental approaches to massive parallelism are investigated for their applicability to graphics and for the difficulties they may impose. Finally, a look to the future attempts to suggest how current trends in graphics may couple with the possibilities for future computer technologies.

Parallelizing Existing Graphics Algorithms

THE TRADITIONAL RENDERING PIPELINE

Taking clues from special-purpose graphics architectures, it makes sense to parcel out the stages of rendering into a pipeline. At the same time, the pipeline stages requiring the heaviest computation are replicated in order to smooth the pipeline flow. In an ideal larger system, all stages of the pipeline are heavily replicated with computation flowing to the least heavily loaded appropriately coded processor.

Given the wide variety of parallel architectures possible, it is clearly necessary to look more closely at the nature of the computation involved in the pipeline stages to see what kinds of algorithms map easily on to what kinds of architectures. For most purposes, the conventional rendering pipeline is broken down into the following stages: (1) data input, (2) coordinate transformation, (3) clipping, (4) visible surface determination, (5) scan conversion, and (6) pixel shading.

Different algorithms place different emphases on these operations. For example, ray tracing does not require a conventional clipping process. Current very expensive images devote so much computation to pixel shading that the other elements of the pipeline are relatively insignificant in cost. However, future images depending on very complex data will find that all stages of the pipeline need attention. Furthermore, no stage of the pipeline can be ignored where real-time animation is the goal.

Data Input

Models of very complicated scenes remain painful to produce. This has helped avoid the issue of data input for most applications, the primary exceptions being in flight simulator applications. However, data exists which can swamp any existing system. For example, large amounts of terrain data for visual simulation are available on tape from the United States Defense Mapping Agency.

Complex construction projects are depending on computer-aided design and manufacturing to ever greater extent. Thus, immense data bases are being created for large buildings, airplanes, spacecraft, etc. There are abundant reasons for making imagery from such databases. For example, an application such as an interactive repair manual based on computer generated imagery could require instant access to immense amounts of data.

Massively parallel machines and supercomputers in general have massive I/O problems. If the data rendered is relatively constant, then it is reasonable to consider storing it in a distributed manner in the primary memory of the machine. Remember, the primary memory of a multi-thousand processor machine is of necessity huge. However, constantly changing data, more typical of today's use, require staging the data through secondary storage.

The advent of smaller, less expensive disk drives has led to an innovative disk usage strategy known as the Redundant Array of Inexpensive Disks (RAID) [Patt88], similar to the 'disk striping' techniques used in supercomputers. Clearly, greater bandwidth is achieved by reading from many disks simultaneously. Thinking Machines developed the 'DataVault' for its Connection Machine following this principle.

The DataVault is an array of 39 disk drives, providing 32 bits in parallel with single-bit error correction (the data can be reconstructed if one drive fails). The bandwidth matches that of a Connection Machine I/O port, 40 megabytes/second. Clearly, innovative I/O of this or a similar nature is necessary for large data bases. For really large machines, it is likely that I/O must be distributed over the processor interconnection network, perhaps physically as well as logically.

Coordinate Transformation

Coordinates are transformed to (1) assemble primitive shapes into complex articulated objects, (2) locate and orient objects in a scene, (3) orient the scene to a particular view, and ultimately (4) provide locations on the display. Happily, this is a very straightforward computation requiring a single simple data structure. It needs no interaction between different coordinate vectors, and does not even involve conditional branches. The basic operation is a matrix multiply.

The simple nature of the computation makes it ideally suited for SIMD machines, or anything else for that matter. Vector units and SIMD machines exhibit a 'sawtooth' or 'staircase' performance profile for applications like these (Figure 1). If there are n execution units, then execution speed is proportional to the ceiling of c/n, where c is the number of coordinate vectors transformed. For most efficient utilization of such a machine, the number of coordinate vectors should be many times the number of execution units.

MIMD machines run with maximum efficiency on coordinate transformations, since no communication is required between processors, and the work may be parceled out in chunks of arbitrary size. The only communication problem lies in getting the coordinate vectors into the memory of the processors executing the transformations.

Transformations traditionally involve multiplying a sequence of matrices representing the operations described above and then applying the result to a large number of coordinate vectors. However, for less than four vertices per processor,

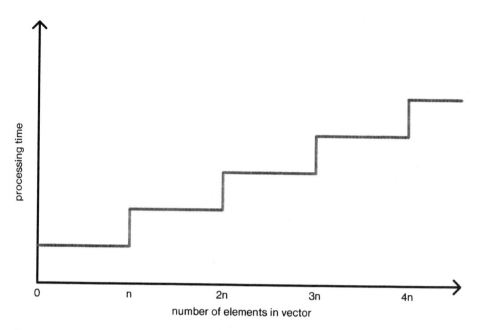

Figure 1. The sawtooth curve for SIMD and vector machine performance, where n processing elements are available.

it is more efficient to apply each matrix in turn to the vertices (16 multiplies, 12 adds for a 4 × 4 matrix) than to concatenate the matrices (64 multiplies, 48 adds). Therefore, where the number of processors available falls in the same order of magnitude as the number of coordinate tuples to be transformed, it is prudent to rethink the way in which transformations are computed.

Clipping

Clipping, where required, involves determining whether surfaces lie wholly inside or wholly outside the image or need to be divided at the boundary of the image. Techniques for polygons are well established, but higher order surfaces and algorithmic shapes require specialized methods.

In any event, clipping starts with determining the state (inside or outside) of the defining points of the surface elements (e.g., vertices, in the case of polygons). Like transformations, these operations are carried out straightforwardly on almost any parallel architecture.

Given the state of all the defining points, some surface types are trivially accepted or rejected. If all vertices of a polygon lie within the image, then the entire surface of the polygon lies within the image. If all control points of a bicubic Bézier patch lie within the image, then the entire surface of the patch lies within the image. Similarly, if all points lie off the image across the same edge, polygons and some curved patches are trivially rejected.

Clipping requires gathering all the information about a surface element together at one processing element. However, defining points are usually shared between neighboring surface elements. For example, in a shape defined as a mesh of quadrilaterals each vertex is shared by four polygons. Operating on the vertices polygon by polygon takes four times the effort as operating on just the vertices in an unduplicated list. Thus, transformations and initial determination of the clipping state are best done on an unstructured list of vertices.

On the other hand, to find out if a polygon, for example, lies within the image, it is necessary to retrieve transformed vertices from wherever the transformation process left them. This is very demanding on the processor interconnect if it is done for thousands of polygons simultaneously.

For machines designed with an interconnect intended for use in this way, such as the Connection Machine, interdependent data structures like this work successfully. However, in a machine intended for coarser-grained programming styles it is clearly preferable to keep all the information about a surface element together, even at the expense of having to replicate some computations.

The process of actually dividing polygons which cross the bounds of the image is traditionally done with algorithms involving substantial numbers of conditional branches. These clearly do not run very efficiently on SIMD machines. Only a small portion of the polygons in a complicated image are clipped by an image boundary. Of these, a smaller percentage is clipped by a corner of the image. Furthermore, polygons have different numbers of vertices.

All this nonuniformity suggests that clipping is best done on an architecture with independently executing processors. Furthermore, the clipped polygons are not evenly distributed, requiring more use of the interconnect to balance the load.

Happily, clipping is an insignificant expense in images where the surfaces are elaborately shaded. Therefore, inefficiencies are often tolerable. However, where extremely complicated scenes or high frame rates are involved, clipping must be considered carefully. Furthermore, if image subdivision is used for increased parallelism, a greatly increased clipping load results.

Visible Surface Determination

Visible surface determination is, at root, a sorting problem. Sorting here is reduced to finding the closest opaque surface. Similarly, a ray tracer based on space division needs only to traverse the space until the first opaque surface is reached. A true sort is needed where multiple transparent surfaces are involved or, equivalently, where surface colors are blended for purposes of antialiasing. In simpler cases, the closest surface is simply culled from a list.

Traditional hidden-surface algorithms are heavily dependent on global sorting schemes [Suth74]. However, most of these schemes are impractical for very complicated scenes. Furthermore, only certain fine-grained parallel architectures, such as the Connection Machine, are very good at global sorting, since heavy communication overhead is involved. Generally, parallel algorithms probably work better by replacing global sorting with local or at least distributed sorting.

Distributed sorting is done by calculating object priorities and then sorting within objects [Suth74; Clar76; Crow82]. If a scene is easily modeled as a reasonably uniform hierarchy of shapes, this approach is successful. In such a hierarchy shapes are collected into articulated objects, which in turn are collected into object clusters, which in turn make up the scene. The hierarchy has to be uniform enough that no step in the hierarchy requires significantly more time to sort than the others.

Local sorting handles the problem at the pixel level. All surfaces are scan converted independently. Each pixel collects the color, depth, and other salient information on each surface affecting it. Once all surfaces are processed, the surfaces at each pixel are sorted independently; the proper color is computed from the resulting order. This general method is trivially adapted to parallel environments of all kinds.

This form of sorting adds expenses which are not present in conventional serial algorithms. It is now necessary to do a full sort of all surfaces covering each pixel. Traditional algorithms use pixel-to-pixel coherency to avoid this for most pixels. On the other hand, most images have very few surfaces per pixel, making trivial sorting schemes possible. For scenes with significant *depth complexity*, several overlapping surfaces occur for most pixels, and storage becomes a potential problem. All the necessary information for each surface overlapping each pixel must be stored, whether visible or not.

The simplest form of local sorting, of course, is the *depth buffer* algorithm. As each surface arrives at a pixel, it is compared with any previous surface and only the closer is retained. This is the first thing one expects to try in a parallel environment. The depth buffer has deficiencies for antialiasing and transparency, of course, since only a single surface is handled. However, given adequate memory, more robust techniques which retain a record of the amount and location of surface coverage over the pixel can be employed [Carp84].

Scan Conversion

Scan conversion offers a more difficult challenge than other stages of the pipeline. The obvious algorithms are woefully inefficient or lead to poor load balancing. For example, if processors are assigned to one or more pixels, it is straightforward to broadcast each surface element to all processors and let each determine what pixels are affected. However, as scenes become more complicated, putting all surface elements through a single broadcast process creates a bottleneck.

Similarly, surface elements can be parceled out, one or more to a processor. However, a large bicubic patch takes much longer to scan convert than does a small triangle. Therefore, unless there are many more surface elements than processors and a way is provided of dynamically allocating work to the less busy processors, then the larger or otherwise more difficult surface elements dominate the execution time.

Even where the entire scene is composed of a single surface element type, such as polygons, there is enough variance among polygon sizes and shapes to cause load balancing problems. Especially in SIMD architectures, scan conversion is inefficient without substantial additional algorithmic complexity to smooth out the computational flow [Crow89].

Other suggestions for distributing the computation include assigning a processor to each scanline (or group of scanlines) or other subimage. All such simplistic task assignments fall heir to the same flaw. The computation is not uniformly distributed over any aspect of the image or the shapes from which it is derived. This argues heavily for a more loosely structured architecture, in which a pool of processors are assigned work as required and all tasks are small enough that none takes a significant portion of the total frame time.

Efforts at splitting larger polygons and subdividing patches to more uniform sizes may pay dividends in better performance. However, the best results come from making sure that task times are short relative to the time needed to make the image, and that tasks are distributed over the processors dynamically in quick response to changes in processor loading .

Patch subdivision makes a good example of another kind of parallel algorithm. Instead of parceling out surface elements and having a processor convert the whole thing to pixels, each processor subdivides its patch, spawning new patch tasks to be handed to other processors. The process then recurses on each of the newly created subpatches until the patches are small enough to be scan converted as polygons, or until some other termination criterion is met.

In this case an exponentially expanding number of tasks is generated very quickly. This turns out to be a very successful way in which to use the Connection Machine, since its interconnect is well matched to this kind of algorithm. However, other architectures have difficulty with the communications overhead inherent in the rapid spawning of new tasks. Furthermore, if the splitting process consumes significant time, then one must consider that most processors will be idle for all but the last split step.

Pixel Shading

Even after determining which surfaces contribute to which pixels, calculating the color for each pixel consumes the vast majority of the total computation in scenes with textured or reflective objects, or otherwise nontrivial shading requirements.

For simpler shading, as noted above, the similarity of neighboring pixels is used to reduce the computation to very inexpensive incremental operations. Under these circumstances, it is clear that neighboring pixel shades should be calculated in a single process which can take advantage of the much faster algorithms based on area coherence. Organizations that devote a processor to each polygon make sense.

On the other hand, expensive shading algorithms often use little or no coherence between neighboring pixels. Therefore, the shading computation for pixels proceeds completely independently, making the application of massively parallel architectures relatively straightforward. A processor is devoted to a pixel or group of pixels.

However, images with surfaces with widely varying shading characteristics (the expected case) greatly complicate the task of programming for SIMD machines. To avoid idling the majority of the processors on conditional branches, pixel shading tasks with similar requirements are accumulated until there are enough to compute efficiently. In contrast, an MIMD machine proceeds more efficiently by executing many different shading algorithms in parallel, as needed. The more straightforward algorithms already in existence for serial use need not be changed.

Textured surfaces offer some interesting cases to consider. Generally, texture is considered in two classes, texture mapped from an image, and texture computed as a function. Computed texture is generated from parametric coordinates over a surface or other two-dimensional basis, or by intersecting a space-filling function with a surface. Example functions are either space-filling based on simple trigonometry [Peac85] or perturbed random noise [Perl85; Lewi89], or surface-covering based on fractal expansions [Haru84] or statistical properties of natural phenomena [Gaga85].

The color of a pixel is found by computing the shade of the surface(s) represented at that pixel. It is usually a simple matter to recover the three-dimensional coordinates of the point on the surface represented at the pixel. A space-filling function applied to these coordinates defines a scalar value, a color, a transparency, a displacement vector, or any number of other quantities affecting the ultimate color of the pixel.

The advantage of function-based texture is that the functions generally require insignificant storage and are computed independently for each pixel. Therefore, they are well-suited to most parallel architectures. Algorithms using area coherence to speed up these functions may be discovered, but none have been published as yet.

The more problematic texturing techniques are those which require an image to define the texture. These techniques (image mapping [Catm74], environment mapping [Blin76], bump mapping [Blin78], displacement mapping [Cook84]) are very successful, primarily because photographs of natural textures are far easier to come by and more successfully realistic than computed texture functions.

However, image-based texture maps pose some severe problems for massively parallel execution environments. Images require substantial memory. In order to avoid losing all detail when the surface is seen close up, the texture image must be as large as a substantial portion of the intended display, at least a significant portion of a megabyte. If they are replicated for every processor, they take up unacceptably large amounts of storage. If they are not replicated, then they become bottlenecks in a parallel system as many processors try to access them at once. Clearly, successful use of texture maps in parallel environments will require a careful balance of replicated maps and orchestrated access patterns. This is an area in which innovations are needed.

Two recent applications have shown uses of texture images that might better fit a massively parallel situation. Kajiya and Kay [Kaji89] used very small 3D texture images, which they replicated very frequently to achieve the appearance of fur. The 3D texture images were actually volumes which were filled with an approximation to hair. In spite of that, their method points out the fact that fine-grained textures are successfully achieved with clever use of quite small texture images (Plate 1b). Furthermore, there is the possibility of using different texture images at different scales. This has received little exploration. Multiple texture images for multiple levels of detail provide a way to see fine detail on a surface without having to store an immense texture image.

Another approach is seen in work published by Williams [Will90] and Pentland [Pent90]. Here, a large image is used to displace a simple surface to produce a more interesting shape. In this case a single displacement image covers the whole surface. Therefore, the displacement image can be split up. Only those parts of the image which affect a given part of a surface need to be stored with it. By contrast, a typical texture image is replicated many times over the surface (Plate 1). On the other hand, the single large image cannot offer the finer detail that conventional texturing methods do. Here again, a hierarchy of textures might offer a solution which is ultimately more space-efficient in a massively parallel environment.

Summary of the Traditional Rendering Pipeline

The traditional graphics rendering pipeline poses few problems to massively parallel implementation. SIMD architectures pose more difficulties than MIMD, as might be expected by their more specialized nature. In general, the algorithms which cause the greatest trouble are typical of those known to be difficult for parallel implementation. They involve substantial intercommunication, resource sharing, or other interdependencies. Solutions to these difficulties are likely to be applied to other fields as well. Similarly, general systems research in parallel processing continues to address issues such as these and may well provide the answers for us.

Graphics is traditionally in the forefront of demanding applications and inspires much work in computer architecture and operating systems. With massive parallelism, we find ourselves once again needing more than is provided. However, so much of traditional graphics is so easily parallelized that the remaining parts can be allowed proportionally more effort.

RAY TRACING

Ray tracing in its simplest form [Whit80] is claimed to be inherently suited to parallel application, and indeed it is, at a superficial level. Every pixel is truly calculated independently of all others, so no interprocessor communication is required. However, each pixel's process must have available to it the entire description of the scene being rendered, in order to evaluate reflecting and refracting rays. The arguments of the previous section say that the scene description must therefore be small to avoid excessive storage costs or contention for shared instances. This is fine for images of a few glass spheres suspended above a plane but is too constrained for anything very visually rich.

Truly complex scenes are generally considered intractable for straightforward ray tracing anyway, so the various methods for accelerating ray tracing must be considered. One class of acceleration algorithms involves using primitive bounding shapes to speed up ray-object intersection tests. A second approach subdivides space and propagates rays from cell to cell, after distributing object descriptions through the space.

The use of primitive bounding shapes increases the size of the scene description and therefore appears to make things worse for a parallel implementation. However, these techniques do allow a multilevel scene description. A very small top-level description could be replicated everywhere, and the most detailed description could be distributed over the processors. It might even be reasonable to have an intermediate-level description broken into subdescriptions and replicated over subsets of the processors.

Such an organization allows top-level ray-object intersection tests to proceed on any processor but sends more detailed tests to progressively smaller subsets of the processor array, until a single processor is ultimately responsible for all rays hitting some part of the surface of a given object. Obviously, the ray distribution has to be carefully monitored. A close-up of a single surface might force all computation on to a single processor. Furthermore, scenes must be organized with the hierarchy in mind.

The second basic approach, subdividing space and propagating rays from cell to cell [Glas84; Kapl85; Fuji86], has actually been used for a massively parallel implementation [Dela88]. The space division techniques require a good deal more storage than conventional ray tracing. However, the storage is distributed across the processors without being replicated everywhere.

Delaney's implementation of space division ray tracing on the Connection Machine, described below, depends on a uniform cubic tessellation of space. This appears to be necessary for an SIMD implementation to keep the computation regular enough. However, the object descriptions end up more uniformly distributed if space is adaptively subdivided. An MIMD implementation might do better with such a strategy.

General Parallel Architectures Applied to Graphics

Computer graphics traditionally needs more resources than are available at any given time. When a deadline looms, those trying to finish a project are likely to cast about for any source of useable computing cycles. This leads to informal methods for manually commandeering multiple machines, carrying tapes back and forth, etc., before machines were so universally networked. Now we see a range of possibilities, from commercial products containing anywhere from four to dozens of intimately connected processors, to student software projects, remotely controlling collections of workstations. The following presents some examples of parallel architectures used for graphics. It is not intended to be an exhaustive survey.

NETWORKED WORKSTATIONS

The local area network connecting a group of workstations is the dominant computing paradigm in most places where more than one computer is used. The whole notion of personal workstations guarantees that most of the power of most of the machines goes to waste when considered on a 24-hour-a-day basis. Therefore, there are virtually unlimited resources available for intensive computing if the unused workstation cycles are captured.

An obvious application for this situation is animation. Each frame of an animation can be computed independently, in nearly all cases. In general, computing a frame takes considerably longer than transmitting it to a centralized storage facility. Furthermore, personal workstations spend long periods idling. Those idle periods allow guest computations to run uninterrupted for 8 to 14 hours on a typical night.

Animation lovers calling themselves the Midnight Movie Group at Apollo have made movies by distributing the computation over as many as a few hundred idle computers at a time. Their frames were done using ray tracing algorithms on relatively small workstations. Where a frame took too much time to compute in the available time (usually overnight), frames were divided, each computer getting a subset of the scan lines to compute. At the SIGGRAPH 87 conference they presented a film entitled 'Fair Play', with frames "computed on a network of 1958 Apollo DOMAIN workstations" [MMG87].

Many others run animations similarly on groups of workstations or even using networked mainframes. However, there is an important difference between using few or even a few tens of machines this way and using a few hundred or a few thousand. It is not possible to go visit all the machines to see that they are running and not being used for something else. It is extremely difficult to manually keep track of all the computations underway at a given time. When using hundreds of machines, the whole process must be automated.

In principle, automating the use of hundreds of machines is not difficult. Networked file systems allow all the workstations to retrieve the necessary scene descriptions from a common source and to store the resulting frames to conventional disk storage or a video disk. Remote login and system monitoring utilities allow one workstation to monitor the state of any other workstation on the network and to control programs remotely. The difficulties lie in the robustness, or rather the lack thereof, in the required system utilities, and in the control program needed to keep track of the animation.

Operating systems for current workstations are not bug-free. For example, there are many conditions which cause a machine to crash or to wait indefinitely when trying to access information from a workstation or file server which is not responding, or when trying to write to storage with no available space. In a large shared environment, the conditions causing the crash may well have been corrected by the time the crash is discovered, making diagnosis very difficult indeed.

The difficulties with operating systems and hardware failures are to be expected and can be fixed. However, there is another source of difficulty which is inherently social. The advent of the personal workstation often brings with it a

sense of personal propriety. When a person has control over the utilization of
the disk space on a machine, he expects to have all the resources of the machine
at any given moment, and he may keep sensitive information on the machine.
It is possible that the person will feel violated when a large computation moves
in. Moreover, if the large computation leaves behind evidence of its presence
in the form of temporary files which saturate the disk space, or leaves the operating system in a nonrecoverable state, the primary user of the machine will
undoubtedly be displeased.

The social side of distributed computation cannot be ignored. It is necessary to have a clear understanding that the networked workstations are a shared
resource. It is also necessary to take extreme measures ensuring that the remotely run programs are tidy, leaving behind as little evidence of their presence
as possible.

Most workstations now run Unix or some variation, and there is a rapid movement toward 'RISC' processors ('Reduced Instruction Set Computers'). These
forces, combined with relatively slow disk drives, make task switching ponderous
on the typical workstation. If a remote task takes over your computer while
you are thinking between keystrokes, it takes an apparently enormous time to
get the machine's attention again once you resume typing. It is important to
be able to detect that a machine is truly idle before unleashing a multihour
compute-intensive graphics task upon it.

True idleness is hard to detect. The operating system does not generally have
utilities to detect idleness over the space of more than a minute or two. That
is insufficient for determining whether there is someone sitting at the keyboard
or not. Many workstation environments are used by collections of people who
keep irregular or otherwise unconventional hours. It is entirely possible for the
primary user of a workstation to show up in the middle of a remote computation.
At such times the remote computation should gracefully shut down. In any given
environment it may be possible to detect the arrival of someone at the keyboard
by a change in the balance of foreground and background tasks. The remotely
initiated computation is assumed to run in the background.

A perhaps more challenging task than computing frames remotely overnight
is to try to use the idle resources on a network during the normal working day.
When trying to design a scene, test an algorithm, or otherwise develop graphics,
the difference between a minute or less and a few tens of minutes makes enormous
productivity improvements. Here the problem becomes slipping in and grabbing
a few seconds or tens of seconds of time to get part of a frame computed.

The author tried some experiments along this line in the mid 80s [Crow86].
The general result was that the technique was useful although speedups were
modest, under a factor of five except for very expensively shaded images. Improvements were limited to an extent by contention for the relatively slow network and the cost of assembling the completed image on the controlling workstation. However, the primary limitation is believed to be due to the author having
chosen an overly large task size. If any task was delayed, the time to completion
was substantially affected.

As networks get faster and workstation operating systems become more sophisticated, this sort of resource-sharing should become more popular and therefore easier to implement. It clearly is a waste to have millions of instructions per second spilling on the floor while users chat with their colleagues, especially while other users sit impatiently waiting for results from their overtaxed machines.

SIMD MACHINES

The nature of SIMD machines (Figure 2) forces more radical changes from conventional algorithms than MIMD approaches. Two existing SIMD architectures have attracted graphics applications, the Connection Machine [TMC87], a commercial product, and Pixel Planes [Fuch85], a research prototype. Although the two architectures are radically different, Pixel Planes being much more a single-purpose machine, the same algorithm was among the first things to be tried on both machines.

When one hears 'massively parallel' and 'computer graphics' in the same sentence, the usual first reaction is to think in terms of a processor per pixel. That is a large part of the architectural notion behind the Pixel Planes project. Similarly,

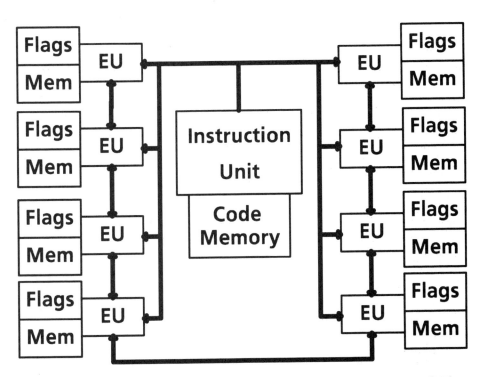

Figure 2. SIMD architecture: instructions are executed by all execution units (EU) simultaneously. Flags may be set to disable instruction execution, among other purposes.

some early applications of the Connection Machine to graphics concentrated on a mapping of the processors to the pixels in the image.

Pixel Planes is an ongoing project name. Currently, a Pixel Planes 5 is under construction which bears little resemblance to the earlier generations. Pixel Planes 4 and earlier are conceived as some dedicated memory (72 bits in PP 4) and part of a one-bit processor. The processing is done in a tree organization, which solves a linear equation as calculation moves down the tree. The parameters A, B, and C are delivered to the input stream, and $F(x, y) = Ax + By + C$ is computed for every pixel [Fuch82].

Clearly, the whole calculation of F need not be done at every processor. For example, the calculation $Ax + C$ is needed but once per column, and By but once per row. Calculations are done bit serially. Therefore, By is calculated by flowing the bits of B through circuits which add delayed copies of B to the developing sum, depending on whether the corresponding bits of y are set or not. One such circuit is needed for the most significant bit of y, two circuits for the next bit, four for the next, etc. Finally, an adder for each scanline acts on the least significant bit of y, shifting the incoming sum to the left by delaying it for a cycle, then adding in B if y is odd and passing it through unchanged if y is even. By is then broadcast to all pixels on row y, where adders sum the similarly calculated values for Ax and then add C.

Additional control paths allow comparison of the result of the linear expression with a stored value at each pixel, enabling depth comparisons. Also, a disable bit allows the pixel to ignore cycles until it is reset. With a total of 72 bits of storage for each pixel, quite a number of interesting algorithms are possible. While the initial intent was to do the scan conversion, depth comparisons, and smooth shading for convex polygons, many additional schemes have been hatched. Algorithms for shadows, texture, transparency, and sphere-like shading have been proposed, as well as various methods for image processing [Fuch85].

Straightforward polygonal scenes are generated by calculating the linear equation describing each edge of a convex polygon. All pixels are enabled, then each polygon edge equation is passed to the evaluation tree. Pixels with negative results assume they are outside the polygon and set their disable flags until the next polygon. Each successive edge disables more pixels until, after the final edge, only the pixels inside the polygon remain active (Figure 3).

To ensure that only visible pixels are shaded, the equation describing the plane of the polygon is then evaluated. Each of the active pixels compares the result with its currently stored depth value; it disables itself if the new value is larger. Finally, the remaining active pixels are sent a constant value for red, green, and blue, or additional plane equations are used to calculate linearly varying shading for smoother surfaces.

One of the first attempts to use the Connection Machine for computer graphics used much the same strategy as Pixel Planes. Polygon descriptions were delivered in the instruction stream, and each processor calculated the inclusion or exclusion of a given pixel. However, in the Connection Machine the computation is done completely at each pixel. The result is a rather inefficient use of the machine.

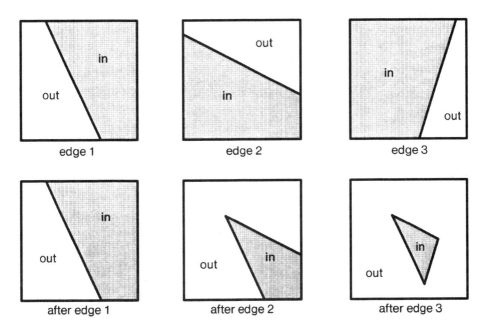

Figure 3. Scan conversion by clipping off successive half-spaces.

Part of the concept behind the Connection Machine is that one should not worry too much about the efficiency with which the processors are used. However, if one makes an economic decision based on cost vs. performance, utilization efficiency determines whether the Connection Machine is a better choice than a comparably expensive minisupercomputer. At the time of its announcement, and perhaps still, the Connection Machine CM2 with floating point option (a Weitek floating point chip for every 32 processors) offered easily the best price for peak performance.

However, consider that an interesting image may contain tens of thousands to millions of polygons. At that level, each polygon is quite small. Many cover only a handful of pixels. With 16k to 64k processors, a Connection Machine is using only 0.1 percent of its processors much of the time, using the processor per pixel algorithm. The rest of the time is spent in discovering which 0.1 percent of the processors to use. Subsequent algorithmic explorations took a different direction, trying to discover ways of using a processor per polygon to do scan conversion [Crow89].

Ray-traced images were one of the first applications of the 16k-processor Connection Machine at the MIT Media Lab. Sims implemented an algorithm [Crow89] in which each processor handles a pixel. A simple scene description is repeatedly delivered to the processors in the instruction stream. Each processor goes idle when its initial or reflected ray fails to hit anything. Therefore, processors with simple pixels spend a good deal of time idle while waiting for the most complex pixel to complete. Grayscale nonantialiased images of a few spheres over a plane take a few minutes to produce.

More recently, Delaney built a space division ray tracer [Dela88] in which space is divided by a cubic tessellation with tags for objects intersecting each cube. Objects are also stored one per processor, and chains of tags associate all the objects intersecting a cube. Each processor traces a ray through the subdivided space. Scenes with many thousands of spheres and polygons are ray-traced in minutes.

Even more recently, Sims used the Connection Machine to build images using particles. The result was animations of waterfalls, snow, and other natural phenomena. Combining these techniques with polygon rendering resulted in some very successful imagery [Sims90].

Approaches to tiling triangles on the Connection Machine make an enlightening study. One approach takes a conventional scan conversion algorithm and tries to make it work straightforwardly [Crow89]. In this approach each edge of a triangle is converted to an incremental form. Then the top two edges are walked scanline by scanline to produce endpoints for scanline segments. The segment endpoints are used to get incremental descriptions for scanline segments, which are then walked to produce pixel values. The following algorithm tries to capture the flavor of the code needed.

```
for <each triangle> {
    top ← GetUppermostVtx[triangle]
    leftEdge ← MakeEdge(triangle[top],triangle[top-1])
    rightEdge ← MakeEdge(triangle[top],triangle[top+1])
    botEdge ← MakeEdge(triangle[top-1],triangle[top+1])
    while not (leftFinished and rightFinished) {
        scanSeg ← MakeEdge(leftEdge,rightEdge)
        while not scanFinished {
            x ← scanSeg.x; y ← leftEdge.y
            if(scanSeg.z < image[x,y].z) {
                image[x,y].color ← scanSeg.color
                image[x,y].z ← scanSeg.z
                }
            ---- Increment to next pixel ----
            scanFinished ← Increment(scanSeg)
            }
        ---- Increment to next scan line ----
        leftFinished ← Increment(leftEdge)
        if (leftFinished) leftEdge ← botEdge
        rightFinished ← Increment(rightEdge)
        if (rightFinished) rightEdge ← botEdge
        }
    }
```

Here it is assumed that the number of triangles is comparable to the number of processors, and that pixels are allocated some number to each processor. Note that the meaning of the **while** loops is that those processors finishing the loop go idle while the others continue. Thus, the time to compute all the triangles is determined by the tallest triangle and, for each scanline segment, the widest triangle. Clearly, it is a good idea to try to preprocess polygons to a fairly uniform size.

Another approach is described by Salem [Sale88], in which a smaller number of polygons is reasonable. In Salem's algorithm the height of each polygon is determined, and then a processor is allocated for each scanline segment. Now each processor has a scanline segment to work on. Each segment processor queries its parent polygon's processor for information about where it is and what color to use. Then all segment processors allocate a processor for each pixel on the segment.

Now we have a processor for every pixel to be written. The pixel processors all try to write their pixels to z-buffer processors representing frame buffer pixels. The Connection Machine interconnect allows collisions in the network to be resolved arithmetically. Thus, the depth of all pixels is written to the frame buffer, with the proviso that the smallest one always gets through. This automatically stores the minimum depth at the pixel; the proper accompanying color follows.

This method requires enough storage for all pixels in the scene simultaneously, so it has very different characteristics from the first approach. Salem's algorithm is clearly better for simpler images with a smaller number of polygons. The more conventional approach may be better for a large number of polygons which overlap a great deal.

MIMD MACHINES

A number of MIMD machines have been commercially available for the last few years. These range from multiprocessors sharing memory over a common bus, through multiprocessors sharing memory on a multistage network, to multicomputer message-passing systems based on either 2D mesh interconnections or an n-dimensional hypercube interconnect. Some vendors have offered display subsystems with direct connections into the network, making interesting graphics possible. However, the direct connections have not generally brought enough computing power close enough to the display to allow substantial real-time graphics. These are not large companies, and we have yet to see any really helpfully innovative graphics architectures from them.

A number of offerings have allowed a handful of processors (usually four) to work together on an image [Levi84; Torb87]. Furthermore, Very Long Instruction Word (VLIW) architectures are available which achieve comparable throughput by executing a number of low-level operations in a single instruction [Engl88]. These architectures are not designed to scale to massively parallel configurations. However, considerable low-level parallelism exists which is easy to find. For example, these systems are often used to calculate red, green, blue, and depth or coverage values simultaneously.

We have seen at least two concepts of the notion of a distributed frame buffer realized. One idea is to associate subsets of pixels with particular processors. The memory for such pixels is dual-ported, so that it may be used to refresh the display from one side while it is being read and written by the processor from the other side. This concept is offered by AT&T Pixel Machines and by NCube. The other idea is to compute sets of pixels in general-purpose memory and transmit those pixels to the display memory when completed. This is offered by Stellar (now Stardent) [Apga88].

Examples of more ambitious attempts to use parallelism are growing. Early attempts, however, were often hampered by woefully inadequate communications bandwidth between processors, and to input and output channels. A project at Bell Labs [Potm87] used an early 64-node message-passing system with hypercube interconnect, supplied by Intel Scientific, to scan convert polygons. Each processor ran a z-buffer tiler on a 64×64 pixel subimage. Performance was limited to about 300 triangles/second by input/output constraints. A coarser-grained algorithm would have been more appropriate for the particular machine used. However, it took the implementation of a simple algorithm to demonstrate that fact conclusively.

A machine using a 2D mesh-connected architecture, supplied by Meiko, is used to compute ray-traced images using up to 300 processors simultaneously. Full-color antialiased images are produced in the order of a minute. Each computer holds the scene description and program in its own memory, and a supervisory processor distributes small blocks of pixels to be computed. A short queue of pixel blocks is kept at each processor to avoid forcing a processor to request and then wait for its next task. This method keeps the processors quite busy through most of the time an image is generated.

Watching this system run is quite interesting. Blocks of pixels appear in increasingly random order but with a general top to bottom trend. The scene being depicted is of necessity simple, usually the requisite transparent spheres over a checkerboard. In such scenes the time taken to compute the image for a block of pixels varies considerably, the most expensive blocks being toward the center of the image where the transparent spheres are found. With hundreds of processors involved, the last few pixel blocks to be completed at the bottom of the image are those enqueued behind very expensive blocks closer to the middle of the image.

An enhancement to this approach, used by Muuss [Muus90b], smooths the arrival of the final pixels by redistributing tasks when some processors go idle. Idled processors are given the tasks which remain enqueued at busy processors. The busy processors then have their enqueued tasks revoked.

If the size of the pixel blocks is kept constant, then the ragged nature of the arrival of the last pixel block is more extreme with greater numbers of processors, and the speedup of image generation is less than linear. In the limit, the image is made no faster than the time taken for the most expensive block of pixels. Ideally, the size of the pixel blocks is adjusted with the number of processors. This serves to illustrate what should be recognized as a fundamental in multiple instruction stream parallel computation. The task size must always be small enough so that the longest task takes only a small portion of the total time to completion.

Real-time graphics on truly massively parallel machines requires a great deal of attention to the problem of interconnecting the display pixels with the massive numbers of sources for those pixels. It is clearly easy to distribute scan conversion tasks over as many processors as you have polygons or other primitive surface elements. However, getting almost a hundred million pixels (or a greater number of subpixel samples, when antialiasing) through the interprocessor links to a frame buffer every second is a problem that has not yet been adequately addressed.

Assuming a depth buffer is used, to keep up with 10^8 pixels a second requires a highly distributed frame buffer. A pixel store takes several cycles. A pixel must arrive with an (x, y) coordinate pair, a depth value, and at least an rgb color triple. Say that two cycles are required to pick up the coordinates, two more to get the depth and color, two to calculate the pixel location, one to fetch the previously stored depth, one to compare the two depths, and, conditionally, at least two cycles to store the new depth and color. That adds up to an average of ten cycles. Assuming a frame buffer processor can do 20 million operations/second, it requires fifty of them just to keep up with depth buffering and storing pixels.

Consider the problem of delivering pixels to the fifty frame buffer fragments (Figure 4). Elaborate networks such as hypercubes as used in the Connection Machine, NCube, and Intel machines, or multistage networks such as used in the Butterfly [Rett86], remain rather expensive for large configurations. The Connection Machine currently is the most potent hypercube interconnect. It is capable of delivering 250 million 32-bit messages a second [TMC87], almost enough for our 100 million pixels. However, that figure is for ideally organized communications patterns (no collisions). The figure of 80 million is used for more random patterns, such as those generated by our pixel storage problem.

Neither the Pixel Machine nor the Stellar described above has the right organization for handling the pixel distribution problem. Any one of perhaps hundreds of pixel-producing processors must be able to send a pixel to any of fifty or more frame buffer processors, with a minimum amount of overhead due to collisions and poor load balancing. This appears to be one of the more interesting architectural problems which must be addressed in order to realize real-time graphics on massively parallel machines.

Possible Scenarios for the Future

As we have seen, there is a great deal of activity moving inevitably in the direction of parallel computation and commodity processors. There seems to be no fundamental limit keeping an institution with enough resources from building, with today's technology, a general-purpose machine capable of a peak rate in excess of a trillion operations/second. At the same time, there are still supercomputer manufacturers trying to build the fastest possible scalar processor.

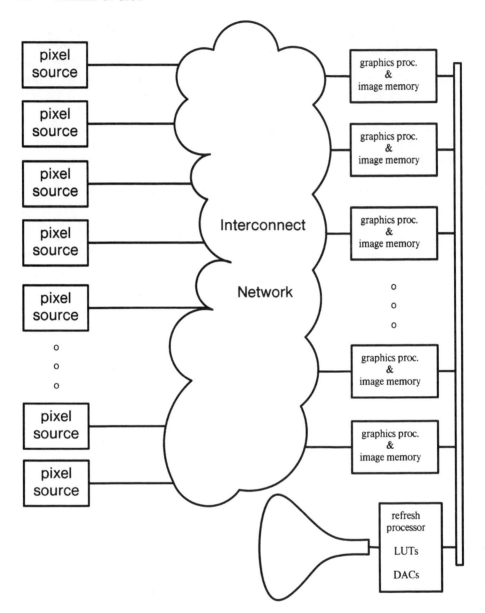

Figure 4. Mapping pixel sources to pixel sinks.

They are pushing towards a billion operations/second in the next few years. What do technological trends tell us that the scenario will be in another five to ten years? What are the limits on current technologies?

Existing computer technologies are based on writing thin lines on various substrates to produce circuits. How thin a line can be made by the kinds of focused-energy technologies in use today? At this writing, commercial processes are hovering around one micron (a millionth of a meter) feature size. One projection says that the limit lies at the resolution of electron-beam lithography [Joy87], which is generally considered to be something larger than 100 angstroms, that is, 0.01 microns, or about 40 atoms across. To put this in perspective, integrated circuits started with feature sizes around 25 microns in the 1960s [Mohs79]. Sizes are decreasing at about 11 percent a year, so it appears there are another 20 years or so to go with the same general fabrication techniques.

Using completely different technology, IBM researchers recently placed individual atoms of xenon on a nickel substrate to spell out 'IBM' 50 angstroms high, using a five-dot-high matrix [Eigl90]. It took 22 hours. However, the basic feature size is on the order of 10 angstroms, or 0.001 microns, i.e., a nanometer. There is much recent talk of nanotechnology, building things with features measured in nanometers. Drexler [Drex87] proposes a mechanical computing paradigm on a molecular scale that provides for 15 bits of storage in a cubic nanometer. This means that storage for an entire one MByte frame buffer fits in the space occupied by the smallest dot made in today's technology. On the other hand, Drexler predicts the equivalent of a gate delay to be not much under a nanosecond, not all that much faster than today's electronic technology.

A project called 'TF1' was proposed by researchers at IBM a few years back [Denn88]. This was to be a 32k processor behemoth capable of a teraflop/second. It would have been 80 feet in diameter, 12 feet high, with 4000 miles of wire in it, used 256 disk drives (and a 24-hour-a-day technician to replace failed drives), consumed 4.5 megawatts, and cost 0.012 TeraCents in 1988 dollars. Clearly, the massively parallel computer of the future will not have statistics such as these. It is likely to be quite small.

One of the barriers to massively parallel machines at the moment lies in slow interchip communication. Two factors will tend to reduce this problem: Chips are getting larger, and a higher percentage of communication takes place on-chip; and better interconnection technologies are coming. Fabrication techniques for large numbers of very small laser diodes promise extremely fast and numerous communication lines connected merely by proximity. Furthermore, the same technology allows three-dimensional packaging since, in theory at least, components can be sandwiched together mechanically and then later disassembled for repair.

With much larger computing resources available, one is tempted to consider the sort of algorithms which might arise. As we saw in the introductory section, the field of computer graphics has had no trouble keeping pace with the availability of increasing computing power thus far. We have seen occasional hints of what might yet come. In 1981 Moravec [Mora81] proposed achieving the ultimate in realism by working with light at the level of wave theory. More recently Kochevar [Koch90] proposed an algorithm based on directly propagating wavefronts through space, using a combination of the methods used for space subdivision ray tracing and those used for radiosity.

Consider the implications of trying to completely ape reality by storing the details of a scene description to the level required to properly implement effects such as iridescence and diffraction, which are caused by features near the wavelength of visible light. Assume the region of interest was stored in a cubic grid with a cell size of 100 nanometers on a side. Drexler's model of the future suggests that such a model could indeed be stored. However, the space to store it could not have dimensions much less than a tenth of those of the reality being represented. That would limit such a technique to pretty small volumes. Thus, by being only a little outrageous we can see the way to waste any conceivable level of technology on an adequately profligate algorithm.

CONCLUSION

It is clear that parallel processing already has a substantial presence in computer graphics through its inclusion in the architecture of the contemporary graphics workstation. Furthermore, as more reasonable system software develops for general-purpose massively parallel machines, we can expect more applications to migrate to them. The applications that have been seen so far have generally been those that are easily parallelized and so badly in need of cycles that their proponents were willing to do almost anything necessary to get greater cost effectiveness.

Forecasts such as seen in the previous section indicate that processor speeds will continue to increase at the present rate for some time to come. At any given time, one is tempted to guess that factors such as the limited resolution of the human visual system, or the limits of less rapidly developing display technology, will eventually mean that we can manufacture any image that can be displayed as quickly as we might like. However, we keep inventing new standards for image richness and fidelity to accompany our increasing processor resources. The end of the current match of increasing demand and increasing processor power is not yet in sight.

REFERENCES

[Akel88]
Akeley, K., and Jermoluk, T., High-performance polygon rendering,, *Comput. Graph.*, Vol. 22, 1988, pp. 239–246 (SIGGRAPH 88).

[Apga88]
Apgar, B., Bersack, B., and Mammen, A., A display system for the Stellar[TM] Graphics Supercomputer Model GS1000[TM] *Comput. Graph.*, Vol. 22, 1988, pp. 255–262 (SIGGRAPH 88).

[Blin76]
Blinn, J.F., and Newell, M.E., Texture and reflection in computer generated images, *CACM*, Vol. 19, 1976, pp. 542–547.

[Blin78]
Blinn, J.F., Simulation of wrinkled surfaces, *Comput. Graph.*, Vol. 12, 1978, pp. 286–292 (SIGGRAPH 78).

[Carp84]
Carpenter, L., The a-buffer, an antialiased hidden surface method, *Comput. Graph.*, Vol. 18, 1984, pp. 103–108 (SIGGRAPH 84).

[Catm74]
Catmull, E.E., A subdivision algorithm for computer display of curved surfaces, UTEC-CSc-74-133, Dept. Computer Science, Univ. of Utah, Salt Lake City, UT, Dec. 1974.

[Clar76]
Clark, J.H., Hierarchical geometric models for visible surface algorithms, *CACM*, Vol. 19, 1976, pp. 547–554.

[Cook84]
Cook, R.L., Shade trees, *Comput. Graph.*, Vol. 18, 1984, pp. 223-231 (SIGGRAPH 84).

[Crow82]
Crow, F.C., A more flexible image generation environment, *Comput. Graph.*, Vol. 16, 1982, pp. 9–18 (SIGGRAPH 82).

[Crow86]
Crow, F.C., Experiences in distributed execution: A report on work in progress, *ACM SIGGRAPH 86 Course Notes #15* Aug. 1986.

[Crow89]
Crow, F.C., Demos, G., Hardy, J., McLaughlin, J., and Sims, K., 3D image synthesis on the Connection Machine, in *Parallel Processing for Computer Vision and Display*, Dew, P.M., Earnshaw, R.A., and Heywood, T.R., Eds., Reading, MA: Addison-Wesley, 1989, pp. 254–269.

[Dela88]
Delaney, H.C., Ray tracing on a Connection Machine, *Proc. Int. Conf. on Supercomputing*, St. Malo, France, July 1988, pp. 659–667 (available from ACM, Order No. 415881).

[Denn88]
Denneau, M.M., Hochschild, P.H., and Shichman, G., The switching network of the TF-1 Parallel Supercomputer, *Supercomputing Magazine*, Winter 1988, pp. 7–10.

[Drex87]
Drexler, K.E., Molecular machinery and molecular electronic devices, in *Molecular Electronic Devices II*, Carter, F.L., Ed., New York: Marcel Dekker, Inc., 1987, pp. 549–571.

[Eigl90]
Eigler, D.M., and Schweizer, E.K., Positioning single atoms with a scanning tunneling microscope, *Nature*, Vol. 344, pp. 524–526, April 1990.

[Engl88]
England, N., Application acceleration: Development of the TAAC-1, *Sun Technology*, Winter 1988, pp. 34–41.

[Fuch82]
Fuchs, H., et al., Developing PixelPlanes: A smart memory-based raster graphics

system, *Proc. Conf. on Advanced Research in VLSI*, 1982, pp. 137–146 (also in *Selected Reprints on VLSI Technologies and Computer Graphics*, Fuchs, H., Ed., IEEE Computer Society Press, 1983, pp. 371–380).

[Fuch85]
Fuchs, H., et al., Fast spheres, shadows, textures, transparencies and image enhancements in Pixel-planes, *Comput. Graph.*, Vol. 19, 1985, pp. 111–120 (SIGGRAPH 85).

[Fuch89]
Fuchs, H., et al., Pixel Planes 5: A heterogeneous multiprocessor graphics system using processor enhanced memories, *Comput. Graph.*, Vol. 23, 1989, pp. 79–88 (SIGGRAPH 89).

[Fuji86]
Fujimoto, A., Tanaka, T., and Iwata, K., ARTS: Accelerated ray-tracing system, *IEEE Comput. Graph. and Appl.*, Vol. 6, Apr. 1986, pp. 16–26.

[Gaga85]
Gagalowicz, A., and DeMa, S., Model driven synthesis of natural textures for 3-D scenes, *Proc. Eurographics 85*, pp. 91–108, New York: North Holland, September 1985.

[Glas84]
Glassner, A.S., Space subdivision for fast ray tracing, *IEEE Comput. Graph. and Appl.*, Vol. 4, Oct. 1984, pp. 15–22.

[Haeb90]
Haeberli, P., and Akeley, K., The accumulation buffer: Hardware support for high-quality rendering, *Comput. Graph.*, Vol. 24, 1990, pp. 309–318 (SIGGRAPH 90).

[Haru84]
Haruyama S., and Barsky, B.A., Using stochastic modeling for texture generation, *IEEE Comput. Graph. and Appl.*, Vol. 4, Mar. 1984, pp. 7–19.

[Haye86]
Hayes, J.P., Mudge, T., Scott, Q.F., Colley, S., and Palmer, J., A microprocessor-based hypercube supercomputer, *IEEE Micro*, Vol. 6, No. 5, 1986, pp. 6–17.

[Hill86]
Hillis, W.D., and Steele, G.L., Jr., Data parallel algorithms, *CACM*, Vol. 29, 1986, pp. 1170–1183.

[Joy87]
Joy, D.C., The ultimate spatial resolution of electron beam lithography, in *Molecular Electronic Devices II*, Carter, F.L., Ed., New York: Marcel Dekker, Inc., 1987, pp. 367–380.

[Kaji86]
Kajiya, J.T., The rendering equation, *Comput. Graph.*, Vol. 20, 1986, pp. 143–150 (SIGGRAPH 86).

[Kaji89]
Kajiya, J.T., and Kay, T.L., Rendering fur with three dimensional textures, *Comput. Graph.*, Vol. 23, 1989, pp. 271–280 (SIGGRAPH 89).

[Kapl85]
Kaplan, M.R., The uses of spatial coherence in ray tracing, *ACM SIGGRAPH 85 Course Notes #11*, July 1985.

[Koch90]
Kochevar, P., Ph.D. Dissertation, Cornell Univ., Ithaca, New York, 1990.

[Levi84]
Levinthal, A., and Porter, T., Chap—A SIMD graphics processor, *Comput. Graph.*, Vol. 18, 1984, pp. 77–82 (SIGGRAPH 84).

[Lewi89]
Lewis, J.P., Algorithms for solid noise synthesis, *Comput. Graph.*, Vol. 23, 1989, pp. 263–270 (SIGGRAPH 89).

[MMG87]
Midnight Movie Group (contact: Michael Sciulli), Apollo Computer Co., Fair Play, *ACM SIGGRAPH 87 Film and Video Show*, July 1987.

[Mohs79]
Mohsen, A., Device and circuit design for VLSI, *Proc. Caltech Conf. on VLSI*, Jan. 1979, pp. 31–54.

[Mora81]
Moravec, H.P., 3D graphics and the wave theory, *Comput. Graph.*, Vol. 15, 1981, pp. 289–296 (SIGGRAPH 81).

[Muus90a]
Muuss, M.J., Workstations, networking, distributed graphics, and parallel processing, in *Computer Graphics Techniques, Theory and Practice* (State of the Art in Computer Graphics, Exeter, UK, July 1988), Rogers, D.F., and Earnshaw, R.A., Eds., New York: Springer-Verlag, 1990, pp. 409–472.

[Muus90b]
Muuss, M.J., Ballistics Research Laboratory, MD, personal communication, July 2, 1990.

[Nish83]
Nishimura, H., Ohno, H., Kawata, T., Shirakawa, I., and Omura, K., Links-1: A parallel pipelined multimicrocomputer for image creation, Proc. Ninth Symposium on Computer Architecture, *ComputerArchitecture News*, Vol. 11, June 1983, pp. 387–394.

[Patt88]
Patterson, D.R., Gibson, G., and Katz, R.H., A case for redundant arrays of inexpensive disks (RAID), *Proc. ACM SIGMOD Conf.*, Chicago, IL, 1–3 June 1988, pp. 109–116.

[Peac85]
Peachey, D.R., Solid texturing of complex surfaces, *Comput. Graph.*, Vol. 19, 1985, pp. 279–286 (SIGGRAPH 85).

[Pent90]
Pentland, A., Essa, I., Friedman, M., Horowitz, B., and Sclaroff, S., The Thingworld modeling system: Virtual sculpting by modal forces, Proc. 1990 Symposium on Interactive 3D Graphics, *Comput. Graph.*, Vol. 24, Mar. 1990, pp. 143–144.

[Perl85]
Perlin, K., An image synthesizer, *Comput. Graph.*, Vol. 19, 1985, pp. 287–296 (SIGGRAPH 85).

[Potm87]
Potmesil, M., and Hoffert, E.M., FRAMES: Software tools for modeling ren-

dering and animation of 3D scenes, *Comput. Graph.*, Vol. 21, 1987, pp. 85–93 (SIGGRAPH 87).

[Potm89]
Potmesil, M., and Hoffert, E.M., The Pixel Machine: A parallel image computer, *Comput. Graph.*, Vol. 23, 1989, pp. 69–78, (SIGGRAPH 89).

[Rett86]
Rettberg, R., and Thomas, R., Contention is no obstacle to shared memory multiprocessing, *CACM*, Vol. 29, 1986, pp. 1202–1212.

[Roug69]
Rougelot, R.S., The General Electric computer color TV display, in *Pertinent Concepts in Comput. Graph.*, Faiman, M., and Nievergelt, J., Eds., Urbana, IL: Univ. Illinois Press, 1969.

[Sale88]
Salem, J.B., *Render: A data parallel approach to polygon rendering, Tech. Report VZ88-2, Thinking Machines Corp., Jan. 1988.

[Scha83]
Schachter, B.J., *Computer Image Generation*, New York: John Wiley & Sons, 1983.

[Schu80]
Schumaker, R.A., A new visual system architecture, *Proc., 2nd Interservice/Industry Training Equipment Conference*, Salt Lake City, UT, 16–20 November 1980, pp. 94–101.

[Sims90]
Sims, K., Partical animation and rendering using data parallel animation, *Comput. Graph.*, Vol. 24, 1990, pp. 405–413 (SIGGRAPH 90).

[Suth74]
Sutherland, I.E., Sproull, R.F., and Schumaker, R.A., A characterization of ten hidden-surface algorithms, *Computing Surveys*, Vol. 6, No. 1, Mar. 1974, pp. 1–55.

[TMC87]
Connection Machine Model CM-2 Technical Summary, Tech. Report HA87-4, Thinking Machines Corp., Apr. 1987.

[Torb87]
Torborg, J.G., A parallel processor architecture for graphics arithmetic operations, *Comput. Graph.*, Vol. 21, 1987, pp. 197–204 (SIGGRAPH 87).

[Whit80]
Whitted, T., An improved illumination model for shaded display, *CACM*, Vol. 23, 1980, pp. 343–349.

[Will90]
Williams, L., 3D paint, Proc. 1990 Symposium on Interactive 3D Graphics, *Comput. Graph.*, Vol. 24, Mar. 1990, pp. 225–233.

[Zyda88]
Zyda, M.J., McGhee, R.B., Ross, R.S., Smith, D.B., and Streyle, D.G., Flight simulators for under $100,000, *IEEE Comput. Graph. and Appl.*, Vol. 6, Jan. 1988, pp. 19–27.

Evolution of 3D Graphics Architectures

Turner Whitted

Abstract

The high performance of modern display systems is a direct result of the revolution in VLSI technology. However, current and future high performance 3D graphics systems rely as much on structural innovations as on the raw speed and storage capacity of components.

Introduction

Support for graphics functions in special purpose processors is in some ways advancing as rapidly as computing in general, but in other ways has reached technical and economic roadblocks that make further increases in performance a challenge. A major factor of previous advances has been the magic of faster and less expensive hardware components [Engl89]. However, the course of future enhancements is more likely to be related to the structure, or architecture, of the graphics systems.

At the lowest level, the hardware in high performance graphics systems is not, by itself, very interesting. The cleverness of how it is used is what determines how effective a particular set of components is in a graphics application. Furthermore, the requirement of increased flexibility in display systems, coupled with the high performance of new general purpose processors, makes the term 'graphics hardware' nebulous. Users, and even programmers, are rarely aware of the specifics of the underlying implementation, whether it is a hardwired function, a microcoded function, or a program in a general purpose CPU. Other than to note that fixed function hardware still retains some speed advantage over general purpose computing elements for a given function, this review ignores the hardware itself and describes instead the structural and algorithmic aspects of high performance 3D display systems. Furthermore, the discussion is limited to graphics systems which are imbedded in, or can be imbedded in, workstation class computers.

High performance display systems obtain their speed from both parallelism and specialization. As general purpose CPU's become more powerful, the relative advantage of a processor optimized for one function diminishes. However, there remain major differences between a graphics display system and a generic parallel processor.

What we discover in reviewing new developments is a trend toward flexibility and new features, in addition to the traditional obsession with speed. Where interactive systems were once limited to a style of graphics that used only trivial shading, we now see the increased performance of graphics processors devoted to improved lighting, transparency, and antialiasing. To achieve this, designers are turning away from highly optimized, hard-wired, single-function elements, and towards carefully constructed elements which, while not always general purpose, perform operations which are common to several functions. We also see, in some recent systems, a tendency to rely on the processing power of a general purpose CPU to perform floating point operations at the front end of the graphics pipeline.

This paper explores the evolution of graphics architectures, those which are proposed as well as those which are in use, in terms of structural and algorithmic innovations. After a review of the gross properties of popular architectures, it describes individual developments, including footprint processors, interpolation schemes, and multipass algorithms, and it concludes by examining the role of general-purpose components in high performance systems.

Elementary Display Systems

Graphics-display hardware traditionally includes a pipeline with at least two parts: a geometry element, and a raster element. There are three commonly used classes of rendering algorithm, as diagramed in Figures 1–3. Each of these represents a unique combination of geometric and raster processing.

Scanline algorithms sweep the image plane from top to bottom, forming spans of visible surfaces along each scanline. A shading operation is performed at each pixel along a visible span. As Figure 1 illustrates, edges in the scene are accumulated in a *y-sort* buffer to permit all display primitives to be scan converted simultaneously. The size of this buffer is a function of the scene complexity.

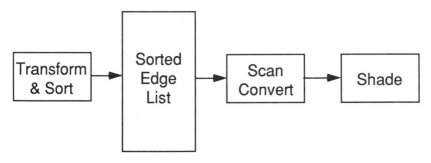

Figure 1. Scanline pipeline.

Internally, the scan conversion process also maintains an *x-sort* buffer, whose size is a function of the local complexity in the scene. The classic example of a hardwired scanline renderer is given by Watkins [Watk70], although more recent examples are also found [Niim84; Deer88; Ghar88]. Because allocation of a fixed amount of memory to either of these buffers opens the possibility of overflow for complex scenes, hardware implementations of scanline algorithms have not become mainstream workstation graphics processors. Scanline-based rendering software, on the other hand, continues to be the first choice among high-end commercial packages running on virtual memory machines.

Image buffer-based algorithms process one surface element at a time and ac-cumulate an image in an augmented frame buffer (Figure 2). In this respect, the buffer-based algorithms mimic earlier line drawing displays, a fact that en-ables painless switching from a line drawing to a shaded display. Typically, a shader computes a color for each polygon vertex, and the polygon is then scan-converted and drawn into the frame buffer as the color is interpolated over the surface of the polygon in a relatively simple process called *tiling*. The most common form of this class of algorithm uses a *z-buffer* and determines visibility on a pixel-by-pixel basis. Variations include the *A-buffer* algorithm [Carp84], an advanced tiler which supports antialiasing and transparency. For the special case of a fixed scene and a varying viewpoint, e.g., flight simulators, *list priority* algorithms which pre-sort the scene in either front-to-back or back-to-front order are used. If back-to-front sorting is done, then the image buffer need only store color intensity values, since nearer surfaces simply overwrite pixels tiled from far surfaces. With front-to-back sorting, a single bit per pixel indicates that the pixel has already been written. The pipeline for any of these is simple, which partly explains the popularity of this class of algorithm in hardware.

The third category, ray tracing, performs an elaborate series of calculations for each pixel. It supports a recursive shading method, which alternately computes the intersection of a ray with surfaces and invokes the shader at each point of intersection. This cycle may be repeated several times for a single pixel. The heart of any ray tracer is the intersection processor, which must access the entire scene (Figure 3) each time it is invoked. The distinction between geometric and raster processing is indistinct in ray tracers. This explains why most hardware implementations have been parallel arrays of general purpose

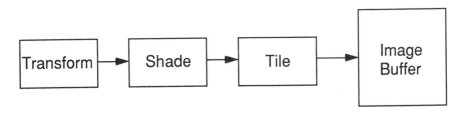

Figure 2. Buffer based pipeline.

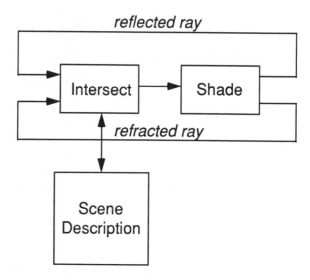

Figure 3. Ray traced display processor.

CPUs [Nish83; Potm89], although some research has been done on specialized ray tracing processors [Ulln83; Gaud88].

For practical purposes, the most significant difference between the three popular rendering architectures is in the way they use memory. The scanline renderer must accumulate the geometry for the entire scene between the transformer and the scan converter in order to sort the display elements. Similarly, the intersection procedure of the ray tracer must have access to the entire scene database. In both cases, the amount of memory required depends on scene complexity. The image buffer renderer, on the other hand, accumulates the scene one element at a time in a frame buffer. While the frame buffer may be large, its size is fixed and depends only on the resolution of the image. For this reason, the buffered renderer is the dominant architecture for workstation hardware.

The emphasis for the remainder of this paper is on image buffer renderers. Although this architecture has not been the first choice for high quality, realistic rendering, much of the work reviewed and proposed here focuses on the type of high end extensions that produce high quality images.

Conventional Geometry/Raster Pipelines

The simplest special-purpose display processor contains a geometric element for transformation and clipping, and a raster element for tiling or line drawing.

The lack of floating point performance in typical workstation CPUs forced designers to use dedicated floating point processors [Clar82]. The recent introduction of workstation CPU's with respectable floating point performance gives designers the opportunity to leave the entire geometric element in the host CPU

[Bord89; Apga88]. In both instances, the geometric operations in the pipeline occur in roughly the sequence shown in Figure 4.

For the common case of transformation of polygons the performance of the transformation stage is easy to predict, since the costs are directly proportional to the number of vertices. Scenes which contain polygons that are clipped from the image complicate the analysis, because the cost of clipping is less when a polygon is completely off the screen than for the case of a polygon which straddles the boundary of the screen. As a consequence, the rate at which vertices emerge from the clipping stage varies according to scene content. This means that a pipeline in which the performance of each stage is evenly balanced for one scene may be grossly imbalanced for another. Designers alleviate this problem by inserting FIFOs between stages. Alternatively, the designer can eliminate the pipelined hardware altogether by using a parallel array of geometry elements which is wide rather than deep, so that no one stage blocks the operation of any other [Torb87].

The simplest raster processor is a forward different engine, with one part for setup and one or more other parts for incrementing values along edges and then along spans between edges (Figure 5). High performance is obtained by incrementing different vector components in parallel. However, since the incremental computations are inherently sequential, an alternative for highly parallel implementations is to build large arrays of linear expression evaluators [Fuch85].

Setup for a DDA (Digital Differential Analyzer) requires a reciprocal calculation and multiplies, while incremental steps involve only adds. For large polygons the expense of setup is amortized over many pixels, but for large collections of small polygons the setup cost is a bottleneck [Whit81]. Many designers are attracted to Bresenham's algorithm because of its negligible setup costs [Swan86]. Bresenham's algorithm, however, is a method of interpolating a single linear function of an independent variable, where the slope is less than one and the independent variable is incremented by one at each step. Bresenham's algorithm does not generalize gracefully to a drawing function which interpolates multiple linear functions with slopes greater than one.

For direct display of curved surfaces and the display of polygonal approximations of curved surfaces, higher-order forward differencing is useful, particularly for shading. However, the requirements of higher precision and costlier setup complicate the design of quadratic or cubic difference engines [Shan87; Kirk90].

As is the case with stages within the geometry processor, balance between the raster and geometry elements is an important design consideration. In the

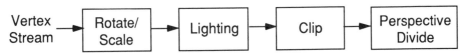

Figure 4. Stages of geometric processing.

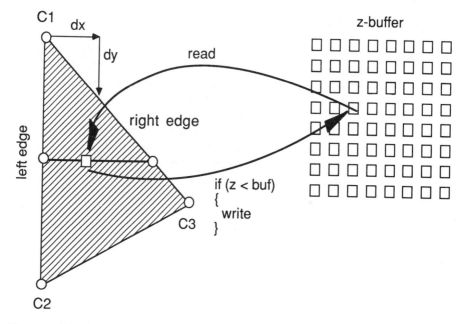

Figure 5. Z-buffer tiling engine.

conventional forward differencing tiler shown in Figure 5, the cost of tiling an individual polygon is affected by the number of edges, the number of spans, and the number of pixels covered by the polygon. A pipeline balanced for small polygons chokes on large polygons. Designers generally optimize for an average expected polygon size.

Pixel Level Processing: Footprints

In the typical workstation graphics pipeline with trivial shading operations done at each polygon vertex, per pixel computation dominates the processing costs. The incremental calculations for interpolation of color and depth, and the comparison needed for the visibility test, are performed once per pixel. While these operations are pretty mundane, the sheer number of pixels leads to a bottleneck for both computation and memory access. Hardware designers attack this bottleneck with parallel arrays of pixel processors, each of which is dedicated to some portion of the image.

Footprints describe the way that individual pixel processors map to regions of the screen. In the case of a single tiling processor which accesses one pixel at a time, the footprint covers a single pixel. At the other extreme is Pixel Planes 4 [Fuch85], in which each pixel is assigned an individual processor. In this case, the footprint covers the entire screen.

The issues which affect the relative performance of different footprint configurations are memory contention and processor utilization. To understand memory contention, consider a 512×512 pixel frame buffer constructed from $256K \times 1$ memory chips. In a low performance graphics system, the speed of display update is limited by contention between the display processor and the video refresh circuitry, both of which must share a single data line into and out of each memory chip [Whit84]. The addition of a separate and more efficient data port for the video channel in VRAM memory reduces this contention somewhat, but the memory access bottleneck remains. For example, assuming an access time of 100 ns, a display processor can write no more than ten million pixels per second. While this barely allows the display processor to redraw the screen 30 times a second (assuming no overhead for video refresh), it is not sufficient for real time z-buffered rendering, which requires that each pixel in the screen be cleared and potentially redrawn several times for a single image.

The data path bottleneck for frame buffer memories is relieved by partitioning the screen and storing different partitions in different memory chips. The obvious partitioning of the screen into adjacent, fixed regions (Figure 6a) does not work well, because access to the regions is not typically balanced [Park80]. If the display system tries to tile a single small primitive that falls entirely within a single region, the memory and processors of the other regions remain idle. In the worst case, the entire scene falls into one region and parallelism is all for naught. One popular alternative is to interleave memory in a pattern that stores adjacent pixels in different memory chips and assigns pixels in each memory chip to a different processor, as shown in Figure 6b. With interleaved organization, a small display primitive that covers several pixels is much more likely to make use of all the processor and memory bandwidth. A second alternative is to partition the screen into many small adjacent regions, with no fixed assignment of processors to screen regions (Figure 6c). The regions are made small enough that the number of regions far exceeds the number of processors. Display primitives which map to a particular region of the screen are sent to a single processor, which draws the entire region. Processors are assigned to screen regions in a round robin fashion. Making the regions small reduces the chance that all of the scene falls within one region. However, by not making the processor-to-memory assignment fixed, the processors are more evenly utilized.

To fully understand the effect of footprints on the efficiency of multiprocessor raster engines, consider the range of scenes which the rendering engine is likely to encounter, as well as the type and size of the screen partition. A fine-grained, fixed-map partition, such as Pixel Planes 4, is extremely efficient for scenes consisting of a few large polygons. However, if scenes are expected to consist of a large number of small polygons, a one-to-one processor-to-pixel assignment leaves all but a few of the processors doing little useful work. An interleaved array is subject to the same problems. Beyond a certain size, a rectangular array of pixel processors begins to yield diminishing returns. In both cases, the trade-off pits the desire to tile each polygon in a single cycle against the need to obtain nearly full utilization for all processors. Deering et al. [Deer88]

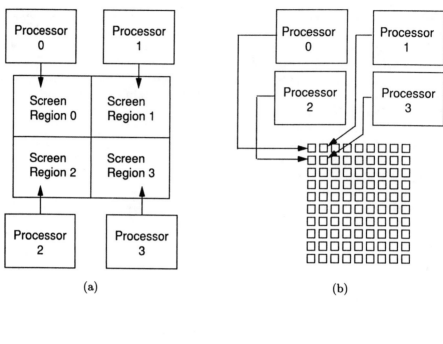

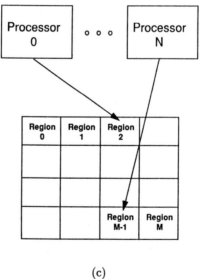

(c)

Figure 6. Alternative partitioning schemes for parallel raster engines. (a) Fixed partition with fixed processor assignment; (b) interleaved, with fixed processor assignment; (c) round robin processor assignment.

make the argument that diminishing returns result if the footprint is larger than 8×8. (Note that balanced utilization and full utilization are very different criteria. Obviously, a fully utilized array is evenly balanced, but the reverse is not necessarily true.) Characterizing the performance of partitions without fixed processor assignments is a bit more complicated. A discussion of the problems of this configuration is given below in the description of Pixel Planes 5.

While the characterizations presented above are simple and easy to understand, they do not really present an accurate indication of the inner workings of actual systems. A case by case exposition provides a better appreciation of the advantages of each design.

The Stellar GS-1000 footprint engine [Apga88] is a 4×4 SIMD (Single Instruction Multiple Data) array of linear expression evaluators, a mini-Pixel Planes (see Figure 7). For each polygon tiled by the processor array, for the initial position of the array, the linear expressions for the polygon are evaluated for one corner of the array. The linear expression is evaluated for every other processor in the array, using adds and shifts. To completely draw the polygon, the footprint array is stepped through all of the 4×4 cells that contain the bounding rectangle for the polygon. As the array is stepped to a new location, the linear expressions are incremented by either of two precomputed values, depending on whether the step is vertical or horizontal.

The Silicon Graphics raster processor (Figure 8) has four stages, consisting of a single polygon processor, a single edge processor, five span processors, and a 5×4 array of pixel processors [Akel88]. The pixel processors are interleaved with each processor, accessing every fifth pixel along a row and every fourth pixel in a column. The pixel processors are simple, fast devices whose functions are limited to z-buffer comparisons, alpha blending, and memory control. The 5×4 array does not participate in the scan conversion, which is relegated to the first three stages in which the polygon processors decompose polygons into edge pairs

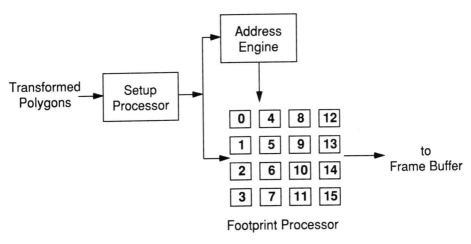

Figure 7. Footprint processor mapping for Stellar GS-1000.

(trapezoids); the edge processor slices the region between edge pairs into spans, and each span processor steps through a span generating pixel information. The polygon processor also performs the setup of forward differences for the edge processor, and the edge processor sets up forward differences for each span. Span processors are horizontally interleaved, so that each span processor connects to one column of four pixel processors. For purposes of scan conversion, the Silicon Graphics footprint dimension is 5×1; for memory access, the footprint dimension is 5×4.

Note that as the scan conversion proceeds the number of edge pairs is greater than the number of polygons, the number of spans is greater than the number of edge pairs, and the number of pixels is greater than the number of spans. The raster hardware tracks this growth in number of data elements with one, five, and finally twenty processors. Furthermore, the use of a separate forward-differencing setup for edges and spans means that the raster processor is more robust than one which deals only with planar polygons and performs setup only once per polygon.

Pixel Planes 5 has multiple 128×128 raster processors which, like the Stellar processor, stamp out rasters across the screen [Fuch89]. Unlike other dedicated

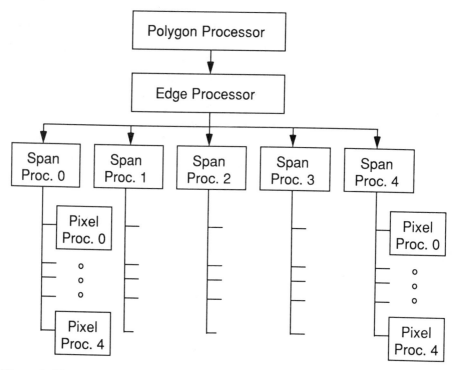

Figure 8. Silicon Graphics raster processor.

graphics systems, Pixel Planes 5 is intended to serve as a test vehicle for architectural experimentation. Consequently, it can be programmed to take on several configurations, including some of those described here.

At the component level, Pixel Planes 5 consists of one or more independent geometry processors with completely flexible connection, through an ultra high speed token ring network, to one or more independent raster processors, each of which in turn can be mapped to any 128×128 region of a virtual frame buffer. The geometry processors contain general purpose CPU and local memory. The raster processors contain special purpose linear and quadratic expression evaluators and local memory.

While the connectivity in Pixel Planes 5 is completely flexible, some data transfer mechanisms are faster than others. In particular, the path from raster engines to and from the virtual frame buffer is through block copies. While the transfer is very fast, it should be executed as seldom as possible. This leads to a preferred algorithm which completes all processing for a screen region in a single pass. To accomplish this, all primitives for a given region must be accumulated prior to scan conversion in buffers dedicated to each region. This process is a crude two-dimensional sort, which amounts to a generalization of the y-sort step in scanline algorithms. Consequently, the algorithm is susceptible to buffer overflow in the same way as a scanline technique. In practice, this problem has not affected the usefulness of Pixel Planes 5.

A special case of footprint is the horizontal array proposed by Deering et al. [Deer88] and Gharachorloo et al. [Ghar88]. Because both of these processors are intended for scanline architectures, there is no reason for the footprint to extend vertically beyond the current scanline. As noted in a previous section, however, the problems of scanline architectures are related to the sorted edge list, not the pixel processing.

As we see in each of these cases, the footprint of a parallel raster processor enhances the performance of the display system by providing a high bandwidth data path into the display memory, and by applying multiple processors in a balanced manner.

Geometric Processing: Interpolation

Interpolation receives almost no attention from graphics researchers, even though both the scanline and z-buffer algorithms spend much of their time doing interpolation. This section reviews two common methods of interpolation and suggests that a hybrid of the two may be most effective in interactive applications. Table 1 lists examples of interpolants which are part of the rendering process.

The two common interpolation mechanisms are forward differencing and recursive subdivision. Generally speaking, forward differencing is most efficient for interpolants which have a lot of coherence, i.e., those situations in which the setup costs of forward differencing are small compared to the total number of incremental computations.

Table 1. Common rendering interpolants.

Interpolant	Domain(s)	Context
surface position	surface,edge,span	tiling
surface normal	surface,edge,span	shading
texture index	surface,edge,span	shading
color	surface,edge,span	tiling
color	pixel	compositing

Use of recursive subdivision in graphics applications is usually limited to the display of parametric surfaces, fractal surfaces, and other procedural shapes. While subdivision all the way to pixel-sized primitives is an elegant approach to display [Catm74], it is not always the most efficient approach. In practice, procedural shapes are subdivided to a level at which a polygonal approximation is sufficiently accurate, and thereafter forward differencing is employed to tile the polygonal approximation (Figure 9).

A strategy for interpolation is especially important in the case of realistic rendering. The critical issue of choosing a rendering architecture which fits the parallel computing environment supplied by graphics workstations may conflict with the algorithms employed for realistic rendering. For example, most algorithms for realistic image synthesis defer shading until the very end of the pipeline. This insures that only visible surfaces are shaded, and that each visible surface is shaded once per pixel. However, there is no compelling reason for linking the rate at which the shader is invoked to the pixel sampling rate. For some portions of a scene, shading once per pixel is too often; for other, such as a region of narrow highlights, it may be too seldom. Furthermore, shading at the end of the pipeline means that the renderer must interpolate all shading variables in the raster processor, an expensive operation.

Current workstation hardware places all of the general purpose cycles at the front of the display pipeline with high speed tilers at the back, dictating that shading be performed prior to tiling. For polygonal object descriptions, this calls for shading to be computed at polygon vertices and polygons to be passed to a color-interpolating tiler. This type of display is inadequate for realistic rendering, because color-interpolated shading produces visible errors in polygons which cover more than a few pixels. Since shading at each pixel does not fit the workstation hardware structure, a new solution is needed to support realistic shading in workstation display pipelines.

A reasonable compromise is a hybrid interpolation scheme, whose first stage interpolates in the geometric domain by dicing surfaces into sufficiently small

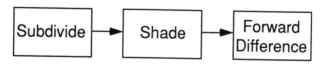

Figure 9. Hybrid interpolation: subdivision cascaded with forward differencing.

polygons. Each small polygon is then shaded at the vertices and passed to a color-interpolating tiler. The first interpolation step should be adaptive, to insure that the resulting fragments are too small to show shading artifacts. One advantage of this solution is that the shader is invoked only as often as needed. Note that this is the same hybrid shown in Figure 9 for procedural surfaces, but in this case the decision to terminate the subdivision is based on shading parameters, not geometric accuracy. Note also that polygons are split into smaller polygons if the size of the polygon is such that it might exhibit shading artifacts.

The Reyes rendering system follows this general approach, but dices polygons into fragments which are no larger than half a pixel in size and does no color interpolation in the tiler [Cook87]. Presumably this eliminates all detectable shading artifacts, but such a fine degree of subdivision is overkill for many types of shading.

Since color interpolation is faster than geometric interpolation, a more fruitful approach is to use adaptive geometric interpolation prior to shading, followed by color interpolation in the tiler. With currently available hardware, the best quality still requires a software implementation, since hardware tilers do not provide all of the functions needed. However, workstations with general purpose coprocessors present an opportunity to program high quality tilers. For previews, a fast but simple tiler can be substituted. The preview might not be antialiased, it might not show transparency or shadows, but other shading features will be apparent. If the shader presents a preview bottleneck, then the dicing can be coarser. Keep in mind that this range of performance is accommodated in a single architecture. With several VLSI tiling engines now in commercial production and more being developed, it seems safe to assume that hardware tilers that offer transparency, shadows, and antialiasing will become available sooner or later.

The efficiency of a hybrid interpolation scheme is very much a function of the type of shading performed. The hybrid interpolation scheme does its shading prior to the visibility tests, with the assumption that shading at vertices rather than pixels overcomes the cost of potentially shading invisible surfaces. As pointed out in an earlier section, tiling of large numbers of small polygons is limited at some point by setup costs. For many simple shading functions, the size of polygons can remain large without introducing visible shading errors. However, shaders which produce features with high spatial frequencies can destroy the performance of the display system by overloading the tilers with huge numbers of tiny polygons.

Multipass Algorithms

The traditional graphics pipeline passes each display primitive once and presents a completed image when it has completed a single pass through all primitives. The high end of graphics display has produced algorithms which desperately need hardware support in the form of a path from the end of the pipeline back to the front. For example, all global illumination models use some form of multiple visibility calculation. A prime example is progressive refinement radiosity, which recomputes rather than stores form factors [Cohe88]. Each form factor array is computed by tiling a single polygon at low resolution. Efficient use of workstation tiling hardware requires a fast data path from the image buffer back to the host CPU, as diagramed in Figure 10.

While this example leads one to view the display pipeline as a component within a complex rendering algorithm, one could just as easily view a looped pipeline as a way to extend the features of an algorithm that resides entirely within the display processor. This section describes some cases in which multiple passes provide the only means of adding advanced features to the standard pipeline. With this view, however, the mismatch in performance is so heavily weighted toward the graphics pipeline that putting the host in the middle of a loop kills performance. The typical approach is to leave the host out of the loop and accumulate intermediate results at the back of the pipeline rather than the front.

The advent of multipass algorithms is a direct result of the improved speed of display systems. Since the speed of display processors continues to rise, there are, for some simple scenes, cycles to spare. At this point the designer can start to trade off speed for features. Examples of features that were missing in previous raster engines are antialiasing, transparency, and advanced shading effects. To achieve these effects in the standard graphics pipeline requires multiple passes of the scene through the pipeline. If a display processor passes 500K polygons in a second, and a scene contains only 10K polygons, then the update rate is 50 frames per second. Good interactive performance requires only about 10 updates per second. The 5:1 excess performance can be translated into additional features.

Antialiasing is an example that has been demonstrated on Pixel Planes 4, the Stellar GS-1000, and others. Jitter sampling at each pixel has been used for antialiased ray tracing, with good results. The scheme is to cast multiple rays for each pixel, with slightly perturbed directions for each ray. This approach is not directly possible with buffer-based rendering algorithms, since they sample on a regular grid. What can be done, however, is to jitter the origin of the grid for each of several passes through the rendering pipeline and accumulate weighted sums from the multiple passes.

One of the more impressive examples of multipass algorithms used for shading effects is texture and environment mapping in the Silicon Graphics VGX series [Haeb90]. One way to explain the unit's operation is to make a slight generalization of the standard color-indexed frame buffer, as shown in Figure 11. The generalization is to pass two indices from the frame buffer instead of one. If texture map indices are interpolated by the tiler instead of color index, and if the color look-up table contains the texture map itself, then the RGB outputs of the pipeline are texture-mapped images of the frame buffer contents.

The second step (not shown in a figure) is to consider that the color look-up table is fed directly from the tiler itself, to eliminate the need to store texture indices in the frame buffer. The result is a very fast way to display texture-mapped

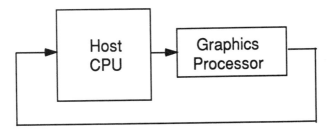

Figure 10. Multipass using a conventional display processor.

polygons without interrupting the pipeline. If the texture map indices are re-placed with reflected ray directions in spherical coordinates, then the same hard-ware will support environment mapping. The only disadvantage of the scheme is that it does not allow simultaneous texture mapping and environment mapping, or combinations of more than one color texture on a single surface. The way around this limitation is to use multiple passes through the pipeline and com-bine results in a deep image store called an *accumulation buffer* (Figure 12). The multipass scheme permits complex combinations of shading effects to accumu-late before being passed to the video refresh buffer. Examples demonstrated by Silicon Graphics include texture mapping, environment mapping, antialiasing, and motion blur.

Another example is multipass transparency. Ordinarily, transparency requires a complete depth-ordered sort of the transparent elements of a scene. However, sorting of any kind just does not fit the framework of the z-buffer algorithm. An old trick for transparency in z-buffers is to make a pass through all opaque surface elements with the z-buffer enabled, and to make a second pass through just the transparent surface elements with the z-buffer memory write-protected.

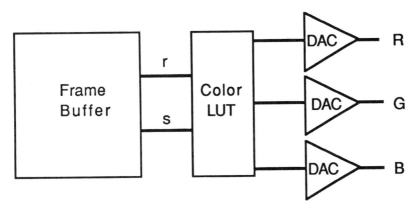

Figure 11. Texture map as a generalization of color look-up tables.

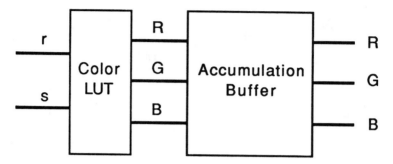

Figure 12. Texture mapping in Silicon Graphics VGX, with accumulator at the end of the pipeline.

In the second pass, all transparent surface elements in front of the current opaque z-value are blended with the current frame buffer color, with the result returned to the frame buffer. Obviously, the lack of ordering of the transparent surfaces yields errors in the final image, but the errors are not horribly noticeable if there are few transparent layers. However, with more than two passes transparency can be rendered accurately using a scheme described by Mammen [Mamm89].

Shading in Conventional Hardware

As noted previously, shaders are called upon for interpolation, normalization, inner products, and table look-up. In the absence of hardware assists for the shading process, it remains relegated to the general purpose segment of the display pipeline. With the exception of the superworkstations mentioned previously, shading in the host CPU is a bottleneck.

The transformation engine at the front end of a display pipeline contains most of the elements needed to perform some shading calculations. The most widely used model for calculating reflected intensity is the Phong shading model

$$\text{Intensity} = C_{\text{ambient}} + C_{\text{diffuse}}(\mathbf{N} \cdot \mathbf{L}) + C_{\text{specular}}(\mathbf{R} \cdot \mathbf{L})^n$$

where

$$\mathbf{R} = 2(\mathbf{N} \cdot \mathbf{V})\mathbf{N} - \mathbf{V}$$

and $\mathbf{N}$ is the surface normal, $\mathbf{L}$ is the direction of a light source, and $\mathbf{V}$ is the direction to the viewpoint [Phon75]. Each of the vectors in the above expressions is constrained to be unit length. If the vectors are not unit length, they must be normalized by dividing each vector component by the square root of the sum of the squares of the components. In hardware, this operation is usually implemented as a reciprocal square root followed by multiplies.

The Phong model with a single light source is a special case of a reflection model, which is expressed as a sum of functions of inner products [Cook84]

$$\text{Intensity} = \sum_i k_i f(\mathbf{A} \cdot \mathbf{B})$$

where $\mathbf{A}$ and $\mathbf{B}$ are vectors of the sort found in the simple equations above. The easiest implementation of an arbitrary function of an inner product is to precompute the function and store it in a look-up table indexed by the inner product. Since transformation engines generally operate on floating point numbers, a conversion from floating point to fixed point must precede the table look-up. This conversion normally costs a shift in hardware but presumably could be done with no cost at all, by disabling normalization of the mantissa after computing the inner product.

A simple display pipeline can compute reflected light intensity for each vertex of a polygonal mesh, transform and clip the mesh, and then feed the mesh to a color-interpolating tiler. If the shading is done once and not modified while the scene is transformed, the result is not very interesting. In general, the shading calculation must be performed once per vertex, every time the transformation changes.

Typically, the most time consuming part of shading in software is the vector normalization step. However, if the polygon vertex normal vectors are unit length to begin with, then they remain unit length after passing through the transformation pipeline. Evaluating the intensity value at polygon vertices means that no normalization is required. In some cases the cost of shading is further reduced by assuming that both the viewpoint and the light source are infinitely distant from the point of reflection [Akel88].

Evaluating the shading model at each vertex and interpolating the result across the face of the polygon yields adequate quality for a mesh of small polygons. For larger polygons, the deficiencies of color interpolation become apparent in the distortion of the specular reflection. As noted previously in the section on interpolation, the common antidote for this distortion is to evaluate the shading expression once per pixel rather than once per vertex. Common shading implementations ignore some simple facts. The number and size of polygons needed in a model are a function of the model's shape. The rate at which a shader must be evaluated when rendering the model is a function of the spatial frequency content of the shading function. Failure to decouple the shading rate from the number of vertices or the number of pixels results in inefficient use of the shader.

Reflection from explicit light sources is not the only function of a shader. Additional effects, such as texture mapping or reflection mapping, are common features of high quality graphics systems. Since the geometry hardware is not particularly suited to texture mapping, this function is usually deferred until tiling and is done at the pixel level. However, the full power of elaborate shading models, such as those described by shade trees [Cook84], needs a more elaborate engine.

Specialized Shading Processors

The graphics literature has little to say about specialized shading hardware. This is surprising, in view of the fact that shading dominates the cost of high quality rendering. There have been attacks on the problem. Duff [Duff79] shows a second-order interpolant which produces a better approximation for the diffuse component of the Phong reflection model than that achieved with interpolated normals. Bishop and Weimer extend this approach to the specular term as well [Bish86]. While these methods are clearly directed toward hardware realizations, there have been few descriptions of dedicated hardware for shading. An exception is the Normal Vector Shader described in the next section.

The Normal Vector Shader

The NVS (Normal Vector Shader) chip [Deer88] implements the Phong shading model in a straightforward manner. Vector normalization uses a look-up table for the inverse square root, and another look-up table for the specular distribution function. The remainder of the chip is comprised of the arithmetic elements needed for the shading operations.

While conventional hardware shading is limited to simple Phong shading, the NVS chip also supports environment mapping. Simulations of the chip's operation, run prior to its fabrication, demonstrated the use of one-dimensional environment mapping, in which the y component of the $\mathbf{R}$ vector is used to index a look-up table of colors.

The NVS chip requires 16 50 ns. clock cycles to shade a pixel. The design of the system in which the chip operates calls for multiple chips allocated to successive pixels in round robin fashion in order to maintain video rates.

The important feature of the NVS chip is its departure from fixed-shading functions. One hopes that this marks a trend toward display systems which contain dedicated shading hardware that implements general shading functions.

A Generalized Shading Processor

Given a shift toward more sophisticated shading in specialized display processors, it is instructive to dissect the portion of a display system which does the actual shading. It also helps to recast the shading process itself into distinct geometric and raster operations, to better fit the framework of conventional display systems [Abra88]. Shading takes place at the boundary between geometric and raster processing. The normalization and inner product steps clearly belong in the geometric domain. Other operations such as texture mapping clearly belong in the raster domain.

In this section we propose a simple framework for a shading processor and discuss its suitability for an accelerated implementation. The shader diagramed in Figure 13 performs its operations in a fixed order. All geometric interpolation is completed first, so that the steps that follow deal with a single polygon vertex at a time. Streams of vertices are passed from the interpolator to the vector math calculator. The vector math stage computes a reflected vector based on the vertex's normal vector and its position relative to the viewer. If bump maps are applied to the surface normal they are added here. At this point inner products used by the final stage are also computed, and environment map indices are derived from the reflection vector. Scalar values produced by the vector math unit are passed to the combiner stage, which accumulates color intensity values for each vertex. (It is tempting to let the combiner scale and clamp intensity values prior to tiling, but this produces shading artifacts.) Finally, the vertex colors along with the vertex coordinates are passed to the tiler. To support user-defined shading functions, both the vector math unit and the combiner are programmable.

The table sampler is responsible for antialiasing of textures. The most common tables are texture maps, indexed by texture indices attached to each vertex,

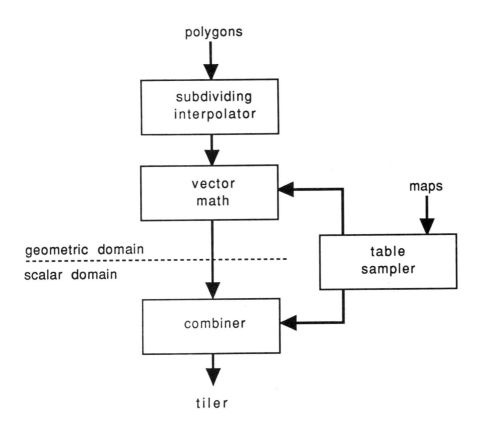

Figure 13. Generalized shading processor.

and environment maps, indexed by values derived from the reflection vector. Texture maps are used for setting vertex colors or for perturbing the surface normal. Whether the geometric operations can be vectorized, whether the memory bandwidth available to the table sampling stage will present a bottleneck, and whether a balance can be maintained between the throughput of the shader and the performance of the tiler are all open questions. This shading processor does fit nicely into a pipeline of independent processors. The entire shader can be programmed into a general purpose accelerator, provided the accelerator has enough memory for the texture and environment maps. Finally, because of its modularity, the design of a hardware implementation can be broken into a few simple elements.

General Purpose Processors for High Performance: the i860

The Intel i860 CPU has generated much excitement because of its potential as a building block for high performance graphics systems. While some see it as a complete graphics workstation on a chip (just add memory) [Grim89], it looks more like the pieces of the standard graphics pipeline brought together in a single package. Studying the i860 also yields some insight into the problems encountered in using general purpose CPUs in the display pipeline.

Viewed as a platform for a graphics pipeline, the i860 includes a RISC core for address calculation, a floating point unit for geometric operations, and the z-buffer unit as the raster engine, all clocked at 40 MHz. The major computational elements and data paths are shown in Figure 14. While the chip has high internal bandwidth, it requires a high percentage of instruction overlap to achieve full performance. Critics of the chip claim that it would be excellent base for a graphics processor if it had been produced as separate chips. The root of this criticism is that it is extremely difficult to program the i860 in such a way that all components of all three sections are fully utilized. Current compilers are incapable of such optimization, and assembly coding so many simultaneous operations for a machine with so many data paths is a programmer's nightmare. Producing the i860 as a chip set, however, would have greatly increased the price of systems incorporating the chip set. Furthermore, the bandwidth of the on-chip data paths is much higher than could be sustained if the data paths were to pass off-chip.

Because the i860's floating point section can be configured as a pipelined multiplier/accumulator, inner product calculations for transformations are in the range of 500,000 vertices per second. The performance of the dedicated graphics unit depends on the number of bits used for depth and color. With 16 bits of depth and 16 bits of color, the graphics unit processes four pixels per 11 clock cycles, or about 14.5 million pixels per second with a 40 MHz clock. This rate is for the inner loop and excludes setup, which means that the performance asymptotically approaches this rate as polygon sizes become large. Assuming unconnected triangles are the display primitives, the floating point stage achieves

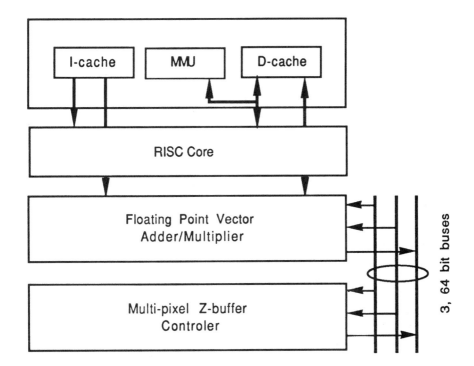

Figure 14. Intel i860 block diagram.

a throughput of 167,000 triangles per second. Ignoring tiling setup costs, a balance between the geometric and raster engines occurs for triangles that cover less than 100 pixels each. A more thorough analysis [Grim89] predicts a throughput of only about 40,000 triangles of 100 pixels each per second, indicating that the chip as a whole is only able to maintain about 25 percent of the raw throughput of its components.

Parallelism in the i860 is seen in the pipelining in its single floating point unit, and in the ability of the graphics unit to compute interpolated depth and intensity for four pixels simultaneously. This degree of parallelism is less than that seen in the highest performance workstation graphics pipelines. There is no obvious way to gain greater degrees of parallelism with multiple i860 chips.

The i860, in spite of the difficulty of getting all of its units to operate simultaneously at full efficiency, is the main computing engine of several commercial graphics systems, as well as the experimental Pixel Planes 5. However, it is not always used as an all-in-one graphics engine. In the case of Pixel Planes 5, for example, the i860 performs only geometric processing with separate specialized tiling processors. A number of plug-in boards for personal computers are based on the i860. In these cases the entire graphics pipeline is implemented in the i860. For these PC systems, an i860-based graphics coprocessor represents an enormous leap in performance compared to what was previously available at the low end.

Summary

The design of high performance workstation display systems is an exercise in connecting powerful pieces together in such a way that they do not slow each other down. The high speed of modern graphics pipeline components provides designers the opportunity to add new features without seriously changing the structure of the pipeline. Moreover, there is some promise that graphics of the very highest quality with realistic shading can be provided within the framework of the traditional pipeline.

Acknowledgements. I thank Kurt Akeley of Silicon Graphics, Brice Tebbs of Numerical Design Limited and the University of North Carolina, and Nick England of Sun Microsystems for providing materials used to prepare this paper.

REFERENCES

[Abra88]
Abram, G.D., Westover, L., and Whitted, T., Accelerated rendering, Proc. Ausgraph 88, Melbourne, Australia, pp. 93–98, July 1988.

[Akel88]
Akeley, K., and Jermoluk, T., High-performance polygon rendering, *Comput. Graph.*, Vol. 22, pp. 239–246 (SIGGRAPH 88).

[Akel89]
Akeley, K., The Silicon Graphics 4D/240GTX superworkstation, *IEEE Comput. Graph. and Appl.*, Vol. 9, No. 4, pp. 71–83, July 1989.

[Apga88]
Apgar, B., Bersack, B., and Mammen, A., A display system for the Stellar Graphics Supercomputer Model GS1000, *Comput. Graph.*, Vol. 22, pp. 255–262 (SIGGRAPH 88).

[Bish86]
Bishop, G., and Weimer, D.M., Fast Phong shading, *Comput. Graph.*, Vol. 20, pp. 103–106 (SIGGRAPH 86).

[Bord89]
Borden, B.S., Graphics processing on a graphics supercomputer, *IEEE Comput. Graph. and Appl.*, Vol. 9, No. 4, pp. 56–62, July 1989.

[Carp84]
Carpenter, L.C., The A-buffer, an antialiased hidden surface method, *Comput. Graph.*, Vol. 18, pp. 103–108 (SIGGRAPH 84).

[Catm74]
Catmull, E.E., A Subdivision Algorithm for Computer Display of Curved Surfaces, Ph.D. dissertation, University of Utah, December 1974.

[Clar82]
Clark, J.H., The geometry engine: A VLSI geometry system for graphics, *Comput. Graph.*, Vol. 16, pp. 349–355 (SIGGRAPH 82).

[Cohe88]
Cohen, M.F., Chen, S.E., Wallace, J.R., and Greenberg, D.P., A progressive refinement approach to fast radiosity image generation, *Comput. Graph.*, Vol. 22, pp. 75–84 (SIGGRAPH 88).

[Cook84]
Cook, R.L., Shade trees, *Comput. Graph.*, Vol. 18, pp. 223–231 (SIGGRAPH 84).

[Cook87]
Cook, R.L., Carpenter, L.C., and Catmull, E.E., The Reyes image rendering architecture, *Comput. Graph.*, Vol. 21, pp. 95–102 (SIGGRAPH 87).

[Deer88]
Deering, M., et al., The triangle processor and normal vector shader: A VLSI system for high performance graphics, *Comput. Graph.*, Vol. 22, pp. 21–30 (SIGGRAPH 88).

[Duff79]
Duff, T., Smoothly shaded renderings of polyhedral objects on raster displays, *Comput. Graph.*, Vol. 13, pp. 270–275 (SIGGRAPH 79).

[Engl89]
England, N., Evolution of high performance graphics systems, Proc. Graph. Interface 89, June 1989.

[Fuch85]
Fuchs, H., et al., Fast spheres, shadows, textures, transparencies, and image enhancements in Pixel-Planes, *Comput. Graph.*, Vol. 19, pp. 111–120 (SIGGRAPH 85).

[Fuch89]
Fuchs, H., et al., Pixel-Planes 5: A heterogeneous multiprocessor graphics system using processor-enhanced memories, *Comput. Graph.*, Vol. 23, pp. 79–88 (SIGGRAPH 89).

[Gaud88]
Gaudet, S., Hobson, R., Chilka, P., and Calvert, T., Multiprocessor experiments for high-speed ray tracing, *ACM TOG*, Vol. 7, pp. 151–179, 1988.

[Ghar88]
Gharachorloo, N., et al., Subnanosecond pixel rendering with million transistor chips, *Comput. Graph.*, Vol. 23, pp. 41–49 (SIGGRAPH 89).

[Grim89]
Grimes, J., Kohn, L., and Bharadhwaj, R., The Intel i860 64-bit processor: A general-purpose CPU with 3D graphics capabilities, *IEEE Comput. Graph. and Appl.*, Vol. 9, No. 4, pp. 85–94, July 1989.

[Haeb90]
Haeberli, P., and Akeley, K., High speed high quality antialiased vector generation, *Comput. Graph.*, No. 24, pp. 309–318 (SIGGRAPH 90).

[Kirk90]
Kirk, D., and Voorhies, D., The rendering architecture of the DN10000VS, *Comput. Graph.*, Vol. 24, pp. 299–307 (SIGGRAPH 90).

[Mamm89]
Mammen, A., Transparency and antialiasing algorithms implemented with the Virtual Pixel Maps Technique, *IEEE Comput. Graph. and Appl.*, Vol. 9, No. 4, pp. 43–55, July 1989.

[Niim84]
Niimi, H., et al., A parallel processor system for three-dimensional color graphics, *Comput. Graph.*, Vol. 18, pp. 67–76 (SIGGRAPH 84).

[Nish83]
Nishimura, H., et al., LINKS-1: A parallel pipelined multimicrocomputer system for image creation, *Proc. 10th Symposium on Computer Architecture* (Stockholm), New York: ACM, pp. 387–394, 1983.

[Park80]
Parke, F.I., Simulation and expected performance analysis of multiple processor z-buffer systems, *Comput. Graph.*, Vol. 14, pp. 48–56 (SIGGRAPH 80).

[Phon75]
Phong, B.T., Illumination for computer generated pictures, *CACM*, Vol. 18, No. 3, pp. 311–317, July 1975.

[Potm89]
Potmesil, M., and Hoffert, E., The pixel machine: A parallel image computer, *Comput. Graph.*, Vol. 23, pp. 69–78 (SIGGRAPH 89).

[Shan87]
Shantz, M., and Lien, S.L., Shading bicubic patches, *Comput. Graph.*, Vol. 21, pp. 189–196 (SIGGRAPH 87).

[Swan86]
Swanson, R., and Thayer, L., A fast shaded-polygon renderer, *Comput. Graph.*, Vol. 20, pp. 95–101 (SIGGRAPH 86).

[Torb87]
Torborg, J.G., A parallel architecture for graphics arithmetic operations, *Comput. Graph.*, Vol. 21, pp. 197–204 (SIGGRAPH 87).

[Ulln83]
Ullner, M.K., Parallel machines for computer graphics, Ph.D. dissertation, California Institute of Technology, Pasadena, 1983.

[Watk70]
Watkins, G., A real time hidden surface algorithm, Ph.D. dissertation, Computer Science Dept., University of Utah, 1970.

[Whit81]
Whitted, T., Hardware enhanced 3-D raster display systems, Proc 7th Canadian Man-Computer Communications Conf., Waterloo, Ont., pp. 349–356, June 1981.

[Whit84]
Whitton, M.C., Memory design for raster graphics displays, *IEEE Comput. Graph. and Appl.*, Vol. 4, No. 3, pp. 48–65, March 1984.

2 Image Generation

Radiosity

Michael F. Cohen

Abstract

The goal of image synthesis is to create realistic images of nonexistent scenes. Achieving this goal involves simulating the way light propagates about an environment. One such technique, the radiosity method, is particularly suitable for environments with primarily diffuse surfaces. This paper begins with a short discussion of background material related to local light reflection models, and global image synthesis algorithms such as ray tracing. The paper then focuses on the derivation of the radiosity method and algorithmic approaches which have been taken to solve the radiosity equation. Recent improvements in the efficiency of the basic radiosity approach are described, ending with hybrid rendering schemes and opportunities to parallelize the algorithms. A bibliography is included as a further reference for the reader.

Realistic Image Synthesis

The radiosity method is an algorithmic approach designed to solve the realistic image synthesis problem. *The goal of realistic image synthesis is to create an image of a nonexistent environment which when viewed appears exactly like the real environment.* The environment is generally created with a geometric modeling system which provides a complete description. This must include both the geometry of the objects which comprise the environment and the material properties of objects and surfaces which affect the way in which light is reflected or emitted from surfaces and/or the medium, e.g., the air. In more familiar terms, we must know the objects' color(s) and texture(s) as well as have a full description of light sources in the environment. Finally, the position, direction, and field of view of an observer must be provided to create a specific image.

A Modified Goal

In general, the goal stated above is impossible to achieve in full. Some assumptions allow us to modify the goal to one which is more attainable. First, the final computer generated image is created on a cathode ray tube (CRT) which allows only a limited range of brightness values for a finite number of picture elements, or pixels. The use of a CRT immediately limits the final image to a small subset of the brightness values we encounter in the real world.

Furthermore, we restrict ourselves to a pinhole camera model of a viewer. This assumption is not absolutely necessary but permits us to confine ourselves to determining the intensity of light arriving at the viewer position, the hole in the pinhole camera, from the set of directions represented by each pixel of the image.

The limited nature of the brightnesses which can be displayed, the fact that pixel colors are ultimately constructed from red, green, and blue phosphors, and the discrete nature of the pixels all cause their own set of difficulties. These difficulties are not discussed in this paper. They are each treated at length elsewhere.

Given the above assumptions and restrictions, the remainder of this paper discusses a set of realistic image synthesis techniques designed to determine the intensity and spectral content of light arriving from all directions in an environment at a given viewpoint.

The goal defined above can be restated as the problem of fully determining the propagation of light within an environment, and of displaying the results of this analysis. This involves understanding how light interacts with a specific surface, i.e., the *local reflection model*, as well as how one surface affects other surfaces through interreflection and shadowing, i.e., the *global illumination model*.

LOCAL ILLUMINATION MODELS

Local illumination models seek to explain how a single ray of light from some direction is scattered back into the environment after hitting a single surface. There has been, and continues to be, a great deal of work done on this subject [Blin77; Phon75; Cook81].

Lambertian Diffuse Reflection

The simplest type of reflection is Lambertian diffuse, which characterizes a dull surface. In this model, the energy E of a ray of light, after some fraction is absorbed, is scattered back into the environment with equal intensity I in all directions. The amount of energy reflected per unit area is proportional to the cosine of the angle between the normal to the surface at that point, $\vec{N}$, and the direction to the light source, $\vec{L}$.

Lambertian reflection can be written as

$$I_d = I_i K_d \cos \theta \tag{1}$$

where I_i is the intensity of the light source;

         K_d is a constant of reflection dependent on the surface material;

         θ is the angle between the incident light direction, $\vec{L}$, and the surface normal, $\vec{N}$.

This can be rewritten as a dot product

$$I_d = I_i K_d \left(\vec{L} \cdot \vec{N} \right) \qquad (2)$$

where $\vec{L}$ is a unit vector in the direction of the light source;

$\vec{N}$ is a unit normal vector.

Although the intensity is equal in all directions, the energy is not. Intensity is energy per unit *projected area*, and projected area is inversely proportional to the cosine of the angle off the normal (Figure 1). Energy, therefore, is reflected from the surface in quantities proportional to the cosine. Thus, *the intensity the viewer sees reflected off a diffuse surface is independent of the viewer position*, while energy is not.

Specular Reflection

Specularity refers to that portion of the reflection that is due to the shininess of a surface. In contrast to diffuse reflection, specular reflection is highly dependent on the relationship between the direction to the light source and to the viewer *at each point on the specular surface*.

The simplest specular reflection model is *mirror specular*. As the name implies, this is the reflection from a perfect mirror. A ray of incident light is reflected back as a single ray in one direction, the *mirror direction* $(\vec{R})$, which is exactly opposite the normal from the incident direction (Figure 2).

More complex specular reflection occurs at surfaces which are shiny but not mirror-like. Here, the specular reflection is scattered about the mirror direction.

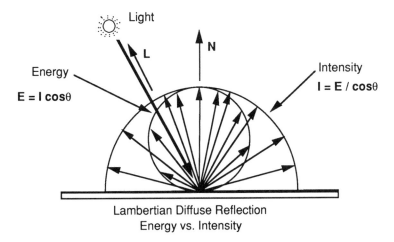

Figure 1. Lambertian diffuse reflection: Energy vs. intensity.

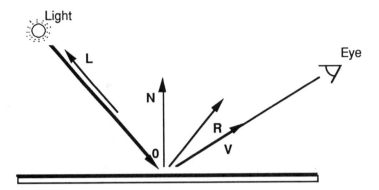

Figure 2. Unit vectors.

The Phong Model

Phong suggested an empirical model for specular reflection (Figure 3), in which the intensity of specular reflection is proportional to the cosine (raised to some power) of the angle between the mirror direction, $\vec{R}$, and viewer direction, $\vec{V}$

$$I_s = I_i K_s \left(\vec{R} \cdot \vec{V} \right)^n \tag{3}$$

where K_s is a constant representing the fraction of energy reflected specularly, which is a function of the surface properties;

      $\vec{R}$ is a unit vector in the mirror direction;

      $\vec{V}$ is a unit vector in the viewer direction;

      n is the specular exponent, also a function of the surface properties.

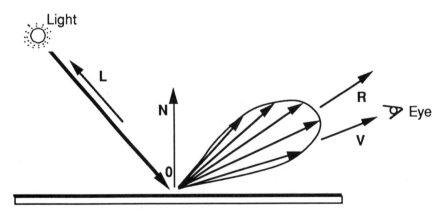

Figure 3. Specular reflection.

The power n represents a material property of the surface. Small values of n denote a not very shiny surface, while large values denote a very shiny surface. At the limits, one returns to a Lambertian diffuse reflectance ($n = 0$) and a mirrored surface ($n = $ infinite).

The Ambient Term

Finally, there is a third term, the *ambient term*, which is added to most local reflection models. Since all the models above deal only with light arriving directly from a light source, a simple global term is added to account for any light which arrives indirectly. If it is assumed that this light arrives equally from all directions, then a constant term, K_a, times the ambient intensity, I_a, can be added to account for this light source.

Transmission

Not all light arriving at a surface is either reflected or absorbed. Some portion may be transmitted through the surface, as in the case of transparent or semi-transparent materials. The transmission itself may be diffuse, e.g., frosted glass, or specular, e.g., clear glass. We simply state that some portion, K_t, of the incident illumination is transmitted.

COLOR

To this point there has been no mention of color. Color is typically specified as a set of wavelength bands, or simply as red, green, and blue components. It can be assumed that there is no interaction between color bands except for fluorescent materials. Thus, the above equations are independently repeated for each color band of interest.

PHYSICALLY BASED MODELS

The models for local illumination have been presented without discussing the physical nature of the surface, except to define a number of empirical constants used to simulate a variety of surface types. A closer look at surfaces in the real world reveals that even flat surfaces are made up of a large number of small imperfections. Looking closer, in particular at plastics, shows that the material is in fact a composite (Figure 4).

In this microscopic view of the surface of a piece of plastic it is seen that, although the average normal is straight up, the surface actually has a large number of small facets, each with its own normal. This microscructure produces the scattering of light seen from real materials. The smoother the surface, i.e., the more horizontal and smaller the facets, the more mirror-like the reflection. In addition, the potential exists for two types of reflection, surface reflection from the microfacets, and scattering from the pigment fragments after some of the light penetrates the surface. The scattering from the pigment is typically diffuse

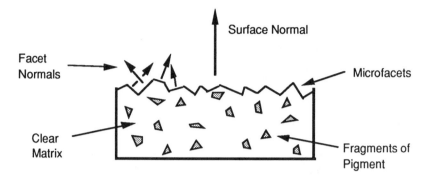

Figure 4. Microfacets.

and takes on the color of the pigment, while the surface scattering is specular in nature and carries the color of the light source.

Local illumination models have been developed to capture all the aspects of reflection and transmission implied by such a physical model. These are not discussed here. The major points to understand are the separation of diffuse and specular reflection, and the fact that diffusely reflected intensity is independent of viewer position, while specular reflection is highly dependent on where the viewer is located.

Global Illumination

Once a local illumination model is selected, one must determine the intensity and directionality of light which arrives at each surface. Unfortunately, knowledge of the location of light sources alone is insufficient. One surface might shadow another, or may in fact reflect some of the light arriving at it to another surface and, in essence, become a light source itself. The air which fills the spaces between objects may participate by absorbing and/or scattering light. These aspects of the problem must be addressed by a global illumination model.

Tracing Light from the Source to the Camera

Conceptually the simplest (and perhaps most accurate) model is to begin with a unit of light (a photon) leaving a source in the environment and to trace its path through the environment according to the local reflection model, until it is absorbed (Figure 5). If it passes through the pinhole of our 'camera', then it is recorded as contributing to the final image.

Unfortunately, unless we are extremely lucky the photon does not pass through the pinhole and consequently is not recorded. In fact, the odds of it happening are nearly nil, and the algorithm chases photons around forever before a complete image is formed.

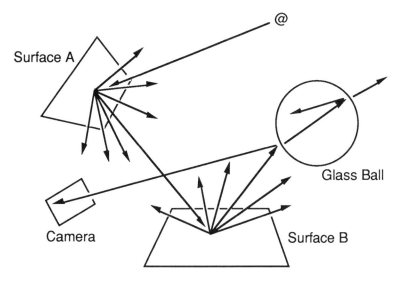

Figure 5. Following light from source to camera.

TRACING LIGHT FROM THE CAMERA TO THE SOURCE

Recognizing that the only photons of interest are those with paths that end up in the camera, 'rays' are traced backwards from the camera through the environment until they hit a light source (Figure 6). Unfortunately, this does not help either, since there are again an infinite number of paths to trace.

RAY TRACING

Finally, recognizing that only paths starting from the camera which reach the light are important, we cheat a little and arbitrarily send a shadow ray towards the light at every intersection between the ray and an object (Figure 7). The process stops when the ray hits a diffuse surface, since there are an infinite number of directions to select for the reflected ray. This causes some quantity of diffusely interreflected light to be missed, which is captured by an arbitrary ambient term. This is the basis for the *ray tracing* algorithm [Whit80; Cook84; Glas89].

This algorithm does in fact solve the global illumination problem to a great extent. A large body of literature exists devoted to efficient computational methods for the ray tracing algorithm. These techniques generally seek to reduce the number of ray intersections. It should be noted that Surface A plays no role in the ray tracing shown in Figure 7, although we said earlier that it does in fact play a role in the more complete (if inefficient) models. This interreflection between diffusely reflecting surfaces plays a major role in many environments. An attempt to capture this process led to the development of the radiosity method, which is the main topic of this paper.

Radiosity

The radiosity method was first developed in the context of heat transfer. A more complete description of the underlying theory is found in many radiative heat transfer texts [Sieg81; Spar63; Spar78]. It was introduced in the context of image synthesis by Goral et al. in 1984 [Gora84]. The radiosity method takes a very different approach to the global illumination problem. Rather than starting from the light source or the camera, the radiosity method models the intensity of light leaving each point in the environment as a function of the light leaving all other points. As expected, a number of assumptions are required to make the problem tractable.

THE RADIOSITY EQUATION

We will begin the discussion by assuming all surfaces are Lambertian diffuse reflectors or emitters. This assumption will be removed later.

The underlying assumption of Lambertian diffuse reflection allows a single nondirectional intensity value per wavelength band to fully describe the light leaving a surface. We also restrict ourselves to a monochromatic description of the light, with exceptions to this pointed out where relevant.

The terms used in deriving the radiosity equations are

Radiosity: (B) the basic quantity we want to compute for each surface (energy per unit area per unit time);

Emission: (E) energy which a surface emits itself, as in the case of a light

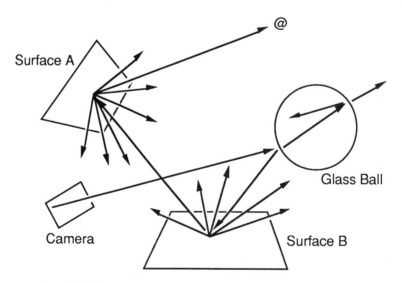

Figure 6. Following light from camera to source.

source (energy per unit area per unit time);

Reflectivity: (ρ) a number between 0 and 1 which indicates the fraction of the light arriving at a surface which is reflected (unitless); absorption = 1 − reflectivity;

Form factor: (F) the fraction of the light leaving one surface which arrives at another surface (a unitless number between 0 and 1).

The radiosity, if any, of a differential surface area, dA_i, depends on light which it emits directly, plus light which is reflected. Some fraction of the light leaving every other surface may arrive at the surface in question and be reflected back into the environment. This fraction depends on the geometric relationship between the surfaces and the reflectivity of the differential area. Putting this together results in the interrelationship

$$B_{dA_i} dA_i = E_{dA_i} dA_i + \rho_{dA_i} \int_j B_{dA_j} F_{dA_j - dA_i} dA_j \tag{5}$$

where B_{dA_i} = radiosity of differential area dA_i;

dA_i = differential area i;

E_{dA_i} = emission of differential area dA_i;

ρ_{dA_i} = reflectivity of differential area dA_i;

$F_{dA_j - dA_i}$ = form factor from dA_j to dA_i, the fraction of energy leaving dA_j which arrives at dA_i.

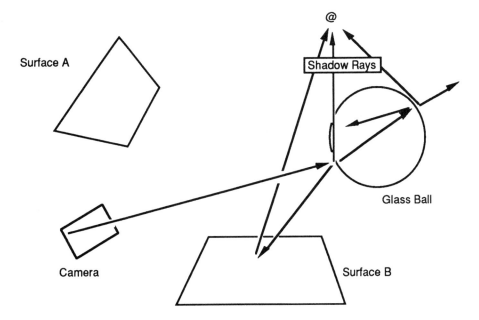

Figure 7. Ray tracing.

Discretization

Since there are an infinite number of differential areas and thus an infinite number of unknown radiosities, we cannot hope to find a separate radiosity for each differential area. The problem must be made tractable by discretizing the surfaces of the environment into finite areas or patches. The integral equation above is then recast as the summation

$$B_{A_i} A_i = E_{A_i} A_i + \rho_{A_i} \sum_j B_{A_j} F_{A_j - A_i} A_j \tag{6}$$

Reciprocity

Using the reciprocity relationship between emitters and receivers of light, the dependence of the equations on the areas of the patches is eliminated. If we switch the roles of equally sized emitters and receivers, the fraction of the energy emitted by one and received by the other is identical to the fraction of energy going the other way. Thus, the form factor between area i and area j is simply related by the ratio of their areas, i.e.

$$F_{A_i - A_j} A_i = F_{A_j - A_i} A_j \tag{7}$$

Thus

$$F_{A_i - A_j} = F_{A_j - A_i} \frac{A_j}{A_i} \tag{8}$$

Given the relationship in Eq. (8), the summation in Eq. (6) is divided by A_i to yield the basic radiosity relationship for finite area patches

$$B_{A_i} = E_{A_i} + \rho_{A_i} \sum B_{A_j} F_{A_i - A_j} \tag{9}$$

Participating Media

Although we do not generally consider air to play a role in the global illumination problem, it clearly has an influence. This is seen in the shift in color when looking at distant objects ('the purple mountains majesty'). It is more evident in foggy or smoky environments. Rushmeier and Torrance examined the role of the participating medium within the context of a radiosity algorithm [Rush87].

MATRIX FORMULATION AND SOLUTION

Equation (9) represents N linear equations of the form given above, where N is the number of patches in the environment. In matrix form these linear relationships are written as

$$\begin{bmatrix} 1 & -\rho F_{1,2} & -\rho F_{1,3} & \cdots & -\rho F_{1,N-1} & -\rho F_{1,N} \\ -\rho F_{2,1} & 1 & -\rho F_{2,3} & \cdots & -\rho F_{2,N-1} & -\rho F_{2,N} \\ \vdots & \vdots & \vdots & \vdots & \vdots & \vdots \\ -\rho F_{N-1,1} & -\rho F_{N-1,2} & -\rho F_{N-1,3} & \cdots & 1 & -\rho F_{N-1,N} \\ -\rho F_{N,1} & -\rho F_{N,2} & -\rho F_{N,3} & \cdots & -\rho F_{N,N-1} & 1 \end{bmatrix} \times$$

$$
\begin{bmatrix} B_1 \\ B_2 \\ \vdots \\ B_{N-1} \\ B_N \end{bmatrix} = \begin{bmatrix} E_1 \\ E_2 \\ \vdots \\ E_{N-1} \\ E_N \end{bmatrix}
\tag{10}
$$

This set of linear equations can be solved with most linear equation solvers. It should be noted, however, that special properties of this matrix allow more efficient solutions. In particular, since the sum of the form factors across a row are, by definition, equal to unity, and the reflectivity is less than one, the matrix is strictly *diagonally dominant*. This means that an iterative Gauss-Siedel solution method is guaranteed to converge to a solution [Horn75].

The iterative Gauss-Siedel algorithm begins with a guess for the solution vector of radiosities. The emission vector serves as a reasonable starting point. Each step in the Gauss-Siedel process involves performing an inner product of a row in the matrix with the current guess at the radiosity solution. This product produces a new guess for a single radiosity value. This new value is then used in successive steps. The algorithm continues until the change in the radiosity values between guesses is below some threshold. If the initial guess is set to be the emission values, then each step can be thought of as projecting the illumination of the current guess onto a patch, resulting in an updated estimate for that patch. The solution process is greatly enhanced through reordering of the rows in the matrix, as described in a later section.

The reflectivity value is typically defined for a discrete number of color bands, e.g., red, green, and blue. This implies that the matrix must be formed and solved for each such band. Note that *the form factors remain constant, as they are solely a function of geometry.*

THE FORM FACTOR

The form factor between patches defines the fraction of energy (light) leaving one patch which arrives at another. Computation of form factors is the most expensive part of the radiosity computation for complex environments. The form factor is purely a function of the geometric relationship between patches and thus does not depend on viewer position or reflectivity attributes (color) of the surfaces. This is an important aspect of the radiosity method, in that it allows rapid changes to viewing and attribute parameters once the form factors have been computed.

The Form Factor Equation

Between differential areas, the form factor depends on the distance between the areas, r, and their orientation towards one another, θ_i and θ_j (Figure 8). The form factor follows the familiar $1/r^2$ drop-off as the distance between differential areas grows. The form factor is also proportional to the projected area of one differential area as seen from the other; thus, it is related to the *cosine* of the

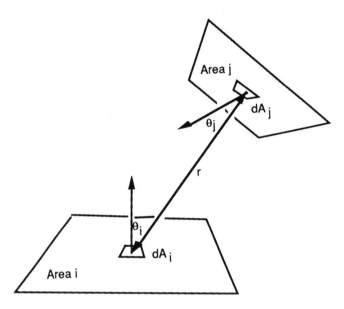

Figure 8. Geometric interpretation of the individual terms.

angle between the area's normal and the line connecting them. In other words, the form factor is proportional to the differential *solid angle* subtended by one area. This relationship is expressed as

$$F_{dA_i - dA_j} = \frac{\cos\theta_i \cos\theta_j}{\pi r^2} \, dA_j \qquad (11)$$

The form factor between discrete patches is found by integrating over *area j* and taking the area average over *area i*. Thus, the form factor is expressed as a double area integral over the two patches. The inner integral represents the form factor from a differential area to a finite patch, and the outer integral and division by area *i* provides area averaging

$$F_{A_i - A_j} = \frac{1}{A_i} \int_{A_i} \int_{A_j} \frac{\cos\theta_i \cos\theta_j}{\pi r^2} \, dA_j dA_i \qquad (12)$$

In general, there is no analytical solution for this integral equation. However, a set of analytic formulae for specific patch shapes and orientations can be found in the appendices of a number of radiative heat transfer texts [Sieg81; Spar63]. For more complex shapes and relationships, a number of numeric and analog approaches have been developed.

Hidden Surfaces

The form factor derivation given above assumes that patch *i* and patch *j* have an unobscured view of each other. This is, in general, not a valid assumption for complex environments. To be complete, an additional term, δ_{ij}, taking on the value of 1 or 0 depending on the visibility between differential areas dA_i and dA_j, must be included in Eq. (12). Including this factor, Eq. (12) becomes

$$F_{A_i-A_j} = \frac{1}{A_i} \int_{A_i} \int_{A_j} \frac{\cos\theta_i \cos\theta_j}{\pi r^2} \delta_{ij}\, dA_j dA_i \qquad (13)$$

Although the δ_{ij} term does not appear further in the discussion, it must be understood to be an inherent part of the problem of determining form factors for general environments.

Contour Integral

A numerical approach to solving the integral is obtained by converting the double area integral into a double contour integral using Stokes Theorem [Spar78; Gora84]. Unfortunately, this method is computationally expensive and *does not lend itself readily to complex environments containing hidden surfaces*, since intervening surfaces in essence change the apparent contour of one patch when viewed from the other.

Nusselt's Analog

Nusselt's analog, although not directly useful for image synthesis, provides a starting point for development of other algorithmic techniques to compute the form factors. The inner integral of the form factor in Eq. (13) is found by surrounding a differential area with an imaginary hemisphere oriented about the differential area's normal (Figure 9). A finite patch is then radially projected onto the hemisphere, and from the hemisphere orthogonally projected onto the base of the hemisphere. The fraction of the base area covered by this projection is equal to the form factor.

Why does this analogy work? The projection onto the hemisphere accounts for the $\cos\theta_j$ as well as the $1/r^2$ term in Eq. (13). The projection onto the base accounts for the $\cos\theta_j$ term, and the π in the denominator is the area of a unit circle. This analog is performed photographically on real models using a fisheye lens and manually measuring the area covered on the resulting photograph.

The Hemicube

The Nusselt analog illustrates the fact that *any patch which covers the same projected area on the hemisphere has the same form factor*, since it occupies the same solid angle. This leads to the use of a *hemicube* [Cohe85] rather than a hemisphere (Figure 10). A hemicube (half of a cube) is placed around a differential area, with the sides subdivided into small grid cells. Each grid cell defines a particular direction and solid angle. Thus, a specific *delta form factor* associated with each of these grid cells can be precomputed and stored in a lookup table. Although *the delta form factors of the grid cells are independent of the size of*

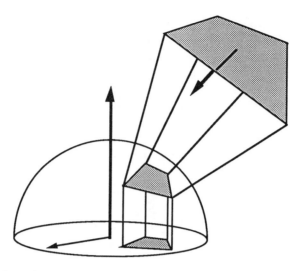

Figure 9. Nusselt analog.

the imaginary hemicube, it is easiest to think of it as a unit hemicube similar to the unit hemisphere in Nusselt's analog.

Each face of the hemicube represents a 90° viewing frustum from the point of view of the differential area at the center of the hemicube. This type of frustum is well known in computer graphics, i.e., all the technology which has been developed for projecting environments within a frustum can be taken advantage of. Patches are projected onto the five hemicube surfaces and the hidden surfaces

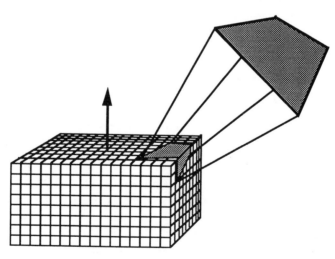

Figure 10. The hemicube.

determined using standard scanline Z-buffer techniques. Rather than recording a surface intensity at each grid cell, an ID referring to the projected patch is saved. Hidden surface algorithms are now embedded in silicon on many graphics workstations, which provides hardware assistance for this algorithm.

Once all patches have been projected onto the hemicube, the ID contained in each grid cell represents the patch visible in that direction. The form factor to a specific patch is determined simply by summing the precomputed delta form factors for each grid cell containing the patch's ID

$$F_{ij} = \sum_q \Delta F_{qj} \tag{14}$$

where q represents the delta grid cells covered by patch j.

DATA REPRESENTATIONS AND RENDERING

The result of the form factor calculations and matrix solution is a set of radiosity values for the patches. Rendering an image from these values involves selecting an eye point and other viewing parameters. The patches are then displayed as polygons in screen space (Figure 11). This results in a very blocky looking image, since each patch is shaded as a single color. In reality, shading generally varies continuously across a surface. To create a continuous shading across patches, the patch values must be interpolated to the vertices of the patch. An alternative approach which computes radiosities directly at the patch vertices is discussed later.

Winged-edge Data Structure

Subdivision of surfaces into patches and recapturing patch radiosities at the vertices requires a data structure which maintains connectivity information between patches. A *winged-edge data structure* has been used successfully for this purpose [Weil85].

DISPLAY

With the radiosity values residing with the vertices, the patches are displayed as Gouraud shaded polygons, either through software or by utilizing the hardware shading and hidden surface capabilities of current workstations. In a workstation environment, reasonably complex environments of 5–10K patches can be displayed in subsecond time, allowing dynamic walk throughs simply by varying the view position and orientation. This is in sharp contrast to ray tracing methods which are inherently view-dependent. Since the form factors are purely geometric quantities, lighting or reflectivity parameters can also be changed quickly.

ADAPTIVE SUBDIVISION OF THE ENVIRONMENT

So far the assumption has been made that the radiosity of a patch is either constant across its surface or continuous after interpolation to its vertices. This

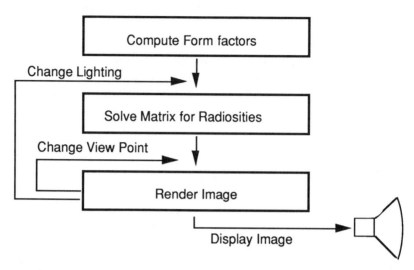

Figure 11. Radiosity pipeline.

assumption is adequate for areas in which the radiosity varies very little, i.e., has a low gradient, or patches are very small. Unfortunately, large gradients occur in many places, particularly at shadow boundaries. Making the patches small enough to capture this makes the $O(N^2)$ form factor computation prohibitive.

Patches and Elements

When localized areas with large gradients occur in the scene, the efficiency of the computation is aided by adopting a two-level hierarchy to the subdivision of the environment [Cohe86] (Figure 12). Patches perform two functions, as a receiver of light from other patches, and as a light source when reflecting light back into the environment. The assumptions that patches act as a reflecting *light source* with constant shading is, with few exceptions, adequate for large areas. On the other hand, more detailed information about the *received* illumination is required to accurately display the radiosity gradients. For this reason, each patch is further subdivided into smaller *elements*.

Each element acts as an individual receiver of light with its own radiosity value. The patch radiosity is simply the area average of the element radiosities. A form factor is now required from each element to each patch. In this case, the radiosity equations become

$$B_e = E_e + \rho_e \sum_j B_j F_{ej} \qquad (15)$$

where B_e = radiosity of element e;

B_j = radiosity of patch j (average of its element radiosities);

E_e = emission of element e;

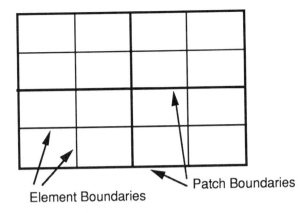

Figure 12. Patches and elements.

ρ_e = reflectivity of element e;
F_{ej}= form factor from element e to patch j.

The patch radiosity is now the area average over its elements' radiosities

$$B_i = \sum_{ei} B_e \frac{A_e}{A_i} \qquad (16)$$

and the patch-to-patch form factor is simply

$$F_{ij} = \sum_{ei} F_{ej} \frac{A_e}{A_i} \qquad (17)$$

where the summation is over those elements e (or vertices) which are part of patch i (Figure 13).

Element Radiosity Solution

The solution process now consists of 5 steps

determine element-to-patch form factors;
sum form factors to determine patch-to-patch form factors;
solve for patch radiosities;
determine element radiosities directly from patch radiosities;
display elements.

Adaptive Subdivision

The subdivision process described above has two advantages. First, more accurate form factors between patches result from the averaging of element-to-patch

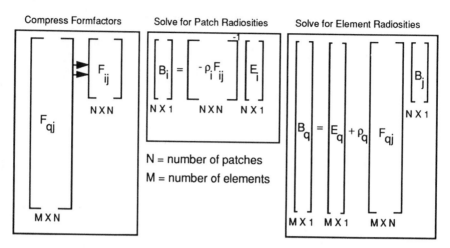

Figure 13. Patch subdivision and radiosity solution.

form factors. Second, the matrix to be solved remains small, while at the same time large gradients are found and displayed within patch boundaries.

Once the patch radiosities are determined and a set of element radiosities derived from them, large radiosity gradients within patches are found by examining neighboring elements. These elements can be further subdivided into new, smaller elements (Figure 14). The only new computation which is necessary

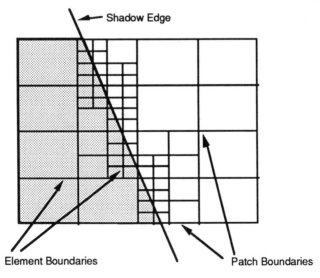

Figure 14. Adaptive subdivision.

are the small number of new element-to-patch form factors. Since the patches remain unchanged, their radiosity solution is still valid and is used to directly determine the new element radiosities. This *adaptive subdivision* process continues to any desired level of refinement. Intermediate images are generated, since they contain information for the whole environment.

PROGRESSIVE REFINEMENT

A number of limitations are still inherent in the algorithms described above. The radiosity method as outlined is still $O(NM)$, where N = number of patches and M = number of elements. This is due to the fact that all of the element-to-patch form factors must be computed before the matrix solution is started.

A more appealing algorithmic approach is to compute only a single row of form factors, to compute a single step in the solution, and to display results as the solution process continues. This *progressive refinement approach* is described in detail by Cohen et al. [Cohe88].

Examination of the Gauss-Siedel iterative matrix solution provides a different way to approach the radiosity solution. Each row i of the matrix represents the effect of all other patches on patch i. Each step in the standard solution forms an inner product of this row and the current guess for the radiosity solution vector to determine a single new radiosity value for patch i. This new value is then included in the current solution vector when proceeding to the next row, and so on.

Shooting versus Gathering

In essence this process *gathers in* the light from all patches to determine a new radiosity for one patch (Figure 15). (Note: we refer to patches, although depending on the context this might mean elements if a subdivision scheme as described earlier is used.)

For the gathering technique, the iterative step is given by

$$[X] = [X] + [X \quad X \quad X \quad X \quad X \quad X] \begin{bmatrix} X \\ X \\ X \\ X \\ X \\ X \end{bmatrix}$$

$$B_{i_{new}} = B_i + \rho_i \sum B_j F_{ij} \tag{18}$$

The progressive refinement goal is achieved by converting the row of form factors to a column. Since it is known from the reciprocity principle that $F_{ij} A_i = F_{ji} A_j$, the row of F_{ij}'s is converted into the column of F_{ji}'s given the areas of the patches. This allows the selection of one patch to *shoot the light* to all other patches (to all *elements* if the patches are subdivided). The new shooting iterative step is given by

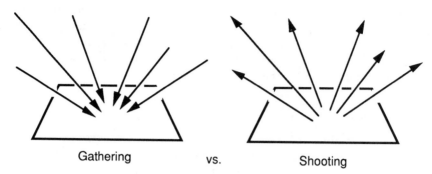

Figure 15. (a) Gathering vs. (b) shooting.

$$\begin{bmatrix} X \\ X \\ X \\ X \\ X \\ X \end{bmatrix} = \begin{bmatrix} X \\ X \\ X \\ X \\ X \\ X \end{bmatrix} + B_i \begin{bmatrix} X \\ X \\ X \\ X \\ X \\ X \end{bmatrix}$$

For all j

$$B_{j_{\text{new}}} = B_j + \rho_j B_i F_{ji} \tag{19}$$

where $F_{ji} = F_{ij} \, {}^{A_i}/_{A_j}$. In each iterative step, all patches (elements) are incrementally updated, simultaneously allowing display of a meaningful image after each step (Figure 16).

Sorting by Unshot Radiosity

Selecting the patch to shoot next is of great importance. We like to achieve the maximum improvement in quality in the minimum amount of time. Clearly, the patch with the most energy $(B_i A_i)$ has the best chance of having the greatest effect on the solution by shooting its energy. Thus, after each iteration the patch with the maximum *unshot energy* is selected for the next iteration. Unshot energy is used to avoid reshooting energy which has already been distributed to the environment. It is possible that a patch will receive significant new energy after it has been selected once. This new energy is considered in future iterations.

In practice, it is found that the progressive refinement algorithm produces an image almost as accurate as the complete solution after only a small fraction of the rows of form factors are computed. This represents a significant saving over the original algorithm.

Addition of Ambient Energy

A more accurate image is produced at each iteration by adding some *ambient energy* to each patch based on the sum of unshot energy. This unshot energy, and thus the ambient term, diminishes after each iteration. Adding ambient energy provides more illumination in the early stages of the solution convergence.

MORE ABOUT FORM FACTORS

Problems with the Hemicube Form Factor Algorithm

Because the hemicube divides the hemisphere into discrete regularly spaced small solid angles, a number of *aliasing problems* occur (Figure 17). Very small patches may 'fall between the cracks'. Others may be sampled by only one or two grid cells, causing accuracy problems when determining the form factors. The coherence of the errors, due to the regular grid of the hemicube beating against the grid of the patches, often results in a quilt-like pattern of illumination. This problem is further exacerbated during adaptive subdivision, since the elements get smaller and the sampling gets sparser and more uneven.

In addition, the hemicube approximates only the inner integral of the form factor equation. This approximation is justified if a patch is small compared to the distance to other patches, but causes serious inaccuracies if patches are close to each other.

The sampling problems are ameliorated to some extent by increasing the hemicube resolution. However, alternate methods are eventually necessary as the environment complexity increases. The size-to-distance approximation is ameliorated by selecting a number of sample points on each patch at which to

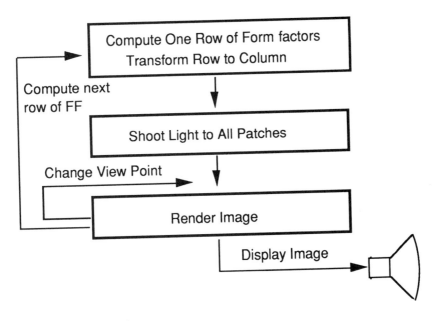

Figure 16. Progressive refinement.

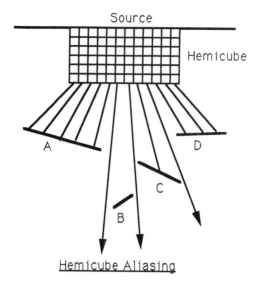

Figure 17. Hemicube aliasing.

place a hemicube, and averaging the resulting form factor estimates. However, this is an expensive proposition and does not solve the problem in all cases.

The two problems in the hemicube algorithm discussed above are examined, and suggestions for alternate algorithms are presented by Wallace et al., Sillion and Puech, and by Baum et al. [Wall89; Sill89; Baum89].

Ray Tracing Form Factors

Ray tracing from a differential area outwards to sample the environment is an attractive alternative. Two such methods are described by Wallace et al. and Sillion and Puech [Wall89; Sill89]. They differ primarily with respect to how the sample directions are selected. Although one does not get the type of coherence as in a scanline method used with the hemicube, ray tracing does not necessarily suffer from the aliasing problems created by a regular sampling pattern.

It is advantageous to replace the visibility sampling which takes place in the hemicube algorithm with a set of rays between pairs of patches. There is no restriction that rays must be distributed in a regular pattern, so long as a delta form factor can be computed for each ray. As discussed above, the final rendering requires radiosity values at the *vertices* of the patches. This leads to a simple decision to cast a ray from each patch to every other patch vertex.

The form factor now takes on a slightly different form, since we are computing a form factor from an area to a differential area at each vertex

$$dF_{A_i - dA_j} = dA_i \frac{\cos \theta_i \cos \theta_j}{\pi r^2 + A_2} \tag{20}$$

This form allows for a solution of the radiosity values directly at the vertices which, for a number of reasons, is a great advantage. There is *no need to perform an interpolation step*. It is also possible to *use a different normal at each vertex to allow inclusion of subdivided curved surfaces*.

Hybrid Form Factor Calculation

Baum et al. suggest a means to avoid the problems induced when patches are close together relative to their sizes [Baum89]. By transforming the inner integral of the form factor equation to a contour integral based on Stokes Theorem, it is possible to analytically determine accurate form factors. However, as Goral et al. found, this is only applicable to environments with no obscuring surfaces [Gora84]. In the new hybrid approach, the hemicube (or ray tracing) is used to estimate visibility, and analytic methods are used to determine the total unobstructed form factor.

Combining Radiosity and Ray Tracing

At the very beginning of the discussion of the radiosity method, all surfaces were assumed to exhibit diffuse reflection and emission. The restrictions on light sources is easily dealt with in the context of ray tracing form factors. However, extending the radiosity method to nondiffuse reflecting surfaces presents more difficulty. The major difficulty lies in the fact that specular surfaces do not allow their intensity to be represented by a single value, since the intensity varies depending on direction. If the matrix solution techniques are extended by discretizing the directions, we quickly get an intractable problem, as discovered by Immel et al. [Imme86]. For example, if 1000 patches are each discretized in 1000 directions, we have 1,000,000 unknowns and 10^{12} form factor coefficients! In addition, even this level of discretization is insufficient to capture the rapidly varying specular reflection function.

FOUR MECHANISMS OF LIGHT TRANSPORT

A better solution consists of combining the best aspects of both ray tracing and radiosity [Wall87]. Once a local reflection model is accepted which separates diffuse and specular reflection, four mechanisms of light transport can be identified

Diffuse	$\rightarrow$	Diffuse
Diffuse	$\rightarrow$	Specular
Specular	$\rightarrow$	Diffuse
Specular	$\rightarrow$	Specular

Clearly, radiosity is well designed to handle the first case. Ray tracing is able to account for diffuse to specular, as in the case where one surface is visible in the reflection off another shiny surface. By creating a recursive tree of rays, ray tracing also accounts for the specular to specular reflection. Unfortunately, neither method directly accounts for the third case, in which light bounces off a specular surface onto a diffuse one. Some methods have been suggested to handle this with varying degrees of success. These include 'The Rendering Equation' by Kajiya [Kaji86] and 'Backward Ray Tracing' by Arvo [Arvo86]. Special cases of specular reflection from flat mirrors are also handled well by algorithms described by Rushmeier.

A Two-pass Solution

The solution to combining ray tracing and radiosity as outlined by Wallace et al. involves performing a two pass solution. The first is a standard *view-independent* radiosity solution for diffuse interreflection. This is followed by a *view-dependent* solution for the specular component via ray tracing. In this case, the ray tracing algorithm does not have to perform any shadow ray testing when encountering a diffuse surface, since this process is inherent in the radiosity preprocess. The radiosity solution is simply determined from the location of the ray intersection.

The result of the two-pass image contains both diffuse interreflection and specular reflection. Unfortunately, the view-dependent step removes the view independence of the radiosity techniques described in earlier sections.

Parallelization of the Radiosity Algorithm

The above discussion did not include any reference to the computational architecture on which the radiosity computations are performed. In recent years, a great deal of emphasis has been placed on the ability to conduct parallel computations to solve large numerical problems. The radiosity algorithm, particularly in the progressive refinement form, is very amenable to parallelization.

The greatest portion of work must be devoted to form factor computation. Fortunately, each row of form factors is independent. In addition, the order in which the rows are computed affects efficiency, but not accuracy. Thus, the form factor computations can be conducted independently under the control of a central process.

In a coarse-grained system in which it is assumed that the description of the environment is available to each process, a single master processor selects patches to shoot energy. Other available processors are assigned to compute the form factors from the given patch to the rest of the environment. As each form factor processor completes its job, it returns the form factors to the central process, which 'shoots out' the energy of the patch. Finally, the incremental solution is delivered to another specialized processor for display (Figure 18).

Three groups have implemented systems such as the one described above. They reported efficiencies in the range of 0.5 to 0.9, depending on the number of processors [Reck90; Baum90; Puec90]. Clearly, as the number of processors increases the communication bottlenecks begin to overwhelm the processing. A number of solutions to this problem are possible and need to be developed.

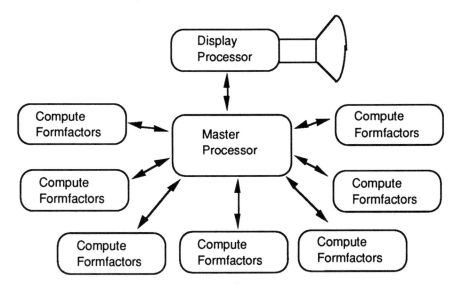

Figure 18. Parallel form factor computation.

Alternative architectures, such as fine-grained systems, should also be investigated for their ability to accelerate the radiosity solution process.

Conclusion

Most of the literature available for studying and understanding the radiosity algorithm exists as original papers. This paper is meant to provide an outline from which one can continue on to the finer points contained in the references. A bibliography is also included for the reader who is interested in a particular aspect of the problem.

It is clear that the radiosity method can provide a number of advantages for creating realistic images. In particular, when dealing with diffuse environments the radiosity method can achieve a high level of realism very quickly, with the added benefit of allowing dynamic walks through a virtual environment due to its view independence. If single images of highly specular environments are required for an application, then a ray tracing approach may be more efficient.

Realistic image synthesis techniques now provide the capability to explore worlds created from our imagination. It is left to the future to discover how this technology will impact our lives.

REFERENCES

[Arvo86]
    Arvo, J., Backward ray tracing, (SIGGRAPH 86) Developments in Ray Tracing course notes, August 1986.

84   Michael F. Cohen

[Baum89]
Baum, D.R., Rushmeier, H.E., and Winget, J.M., Improving radiosity solutions through the use of analytically determined form-factors, *Comput. Graph.*, Vol. 23, pp. 325–334, 1989 (SIGGRAPH 89).

[Baum90]
Baum, D.R., and Winget, J.M., Real time radiosity through parallel processing and hardware acceleration, *Comput. Graph.*, Vol. 24, No. 2, pp. 67–75, 1990.

[Blin77]
Blinn, J.F., Models of light reflection for computer synthesized pictures, *Comput. Graph.*, Vol. 11, pp. 192–198, 1977 (SIGGRAPH 77).

[Cohe85]
Cohen, M.F., and Greenberg, D.P., A radiosity solution for complex environments, *Comput. Graph.*, Vol. 19, pp. 31–40, 1985 (SIGGRAPH 85).

[Cohe86]
Cohen, M.F., Greenberg, D.P., Immel, D.S., and Brock, P.J., An efficient radiosity approach for realistic image synthesis, *IEEE Comput. Graph. and Appl.*, Vol. 6, No. 2, pp. 26–35, March 1986.

[Cohe88]
Cohen, M.F., Chen, S.E.,Wallace, J.R., and Greenberg, D.P., A progressive refinement approach to fast radiosity image generation, *Comput. Graph.*, Vol. 22, pp. 75–84, 1988 (SIGGRAPH 88).

[Cook81]
Cook, R.L., and Torrance, K.E., A reflectance model for computer graphics, *Comput. Graph.*, Vol. 15, pp. 307–316, 1981 (SIGGRAPH 81).

[Cook84]
Cook, R.L., Porter, T., and Carpenter, L., Distributed ray tracing, *Comput. Graph.*, Vol. 18, pp. 137–145, 1984 (SIGGRAPH 84).

[Glas89]
Glassner, A.S., *Ray Tracing*, New York: Academic Press, 1989.

[Gora84]
Goral, C.M., Torrance, K.E., and Greenberg, D.P., Modeling the interaction of light between diffuse surfaces, *Comput. Graph.*, Vol. 18, pp. 213–222, 1984 (SIGGRAPH 84).

[Horn75]
Hornbeck, R.W., *Numerical Methods*, New York: Quantum Publishers, 1975.

[Imme86]
Immel, D.S., Cohen, M.F., and Greenberg, D.P., A radiosity method for nondiffuse environments, *Comput. Graph.*, Vol. 20, pp. 133–142, 1986 (SIGGRAPH 86).

[Kaji86]
Kajiya, J.T., The rendering equation, *Comput. Graph.*, Vol. 20, pp. 143–150, 1986 (SIGGRAPH 86).

[Phon75]
Phong, B.T., Illumination for computer-generated pictures, *CACM*, Vol. 18, No. 6, pp. 311–317, June 1975.

[Puec90]

Puech, C., Sillion, F., and Vedel, C., Improving interaction with radiosity-based lighting simulation programs, *Comput. Graph.*, Vol. 24, No. 2, pp. 51–57, 1990.

[Reck90]

Recker, R.J., George, D.W., and Greenberg, D.P., Acceleration techniques for progressive refinement radiosity, *Comput. Graph.*, Vol. 24, No. 2, pp. 59–66, 1990.

[Rush87]

Rushmeier, H.E., and Torrance, K.E., The zonal method for calculating light intensities in the presence of a participating medium, *Comput. Graph.*, Vol. 21, pp. 293–302, 1987 (SIGGRAPH 87).

[Sieg81]

Siegel, R., and Howeol, J.R., *Thermal Radiation Heat Transfer*, Washington, DC: Hemisphere Publishing Corp., 1981.

[Sill89]

Sillion, F., and Puech, C., A general two-pass method integrating specular and diffuse reflection, *Comput. Graph.*, Vol. 23, pp. 335–344, 1989 (SIGGRAPH 89).

[Spar63]

Sparrow, E.M., A new and simpler formulation for radiative angle factors, *Trans. ASME, Jour. Heat Transfer*, Vol. 85, No. 2, pp. 81–88, 1963.

[Spar78]

Sparrow, E.M., Radiation Heat Transfer, Washington, DC; Hemisphere Publishing, 1978.

[Wall87]

Wallace, J.R., Cohen, M.F., and Greenberg, D.P., A two-pass solution to the rendering equation: A synthesis of ray tracing and radiosity methods, *Comput. Graph.*, Vol. 21, pp. 311–320, 1987 (SIGGRAPH 87).

[Wall89]

Wallace, J.R., Elmquist, K.A., and Haines, E.A., A ray tracing algorithm for progressive radiosity, *Comput. Graph.*, Vol. 23, pp. 315–324, 1989 (SIGGRAPH 89).

[Weil85]

Weiler, K., Edge based data structures for solid modeling in curved surface environments, *IEEE Comput. Graph. and Appl.*, Vol. 5, No. 1, pp. 21–40, January 1985.

[Whit80]

Whitted, T.J., An improved illumination model for shaded display, *CACM*, Vol. 23, No. 6, pp. 343–349, June 1980.

BIBLIOGRAPHY

[Aire90]

Airey, J.M., Rohlf, J.H., and Brooks, F.P. Jr., Towards image realism with interactive update rates in complex virtual building environments, in *Proc. Symposium on Interactive 3D Graphics*, Snowbird, UT, Vol. 24, pp. 41–50, March 1990.

[Aman84]
Amanatides, J., Ray tracing with cones, *Comput. Graph.*, Vol. 18, pp. 129–135, 1984 (SIGGRAPH 84).

[Aman87]
Amantides, J., A fast voxel traversal algorithm for ray tracing, in *Proc. Eurographics 87*, 1987.

[Appe68]
Appel, A., Some techniques for shading machine renderings of solids, *AFIPS 1968 Spring Joint Computer Conf.*, Vol. 32, pp. 37–45, 1968.

[Arvo87]
Arvo, J., and Kirk, D., Fast ray tracing by ray classification, *Comput. Graph.*, Vol. 21, pp. 55–64, 1987 (SIGGRAPH 87).

[Baum86]
Baum, D.R., Wallace, J.R., Cohen, M.F., and Greenberg, D.P., The back-buffer algorithm: An extension of the radiosity method to dynamic environments, *The Visual Comput.*, Vol. 2, No. 5, pp. 298–308, September 1986.

[Bouv85]
Bouville, C., Bounding ellipsoids for ray-fractal intersection, *Comput. Graph.*, Vol. 19, pp. 45–52, 1985 (SIGGRAPH 85).

[Bron84]
Bronsvoort, W.F., van Wijk, J.J., and Jansen, F.W., Two methods for improving the efficiency of ray casting in solid modeling, *CAD*, Vol. 16, No. 1, January 1984.

[Buit75]
Phong, B.T., Illumination for computer-generated pictures, *CACM*, Vol. 18, No. 6, pp. 311–317, June 1975.

[Chat87]
Chattopadhyay, S., and Fujimoto, A., Bi-directional ray tracing, in *Proc. CGI 87*, Kunii, T., Ed., Tokyo: Springer-Verlag, 1987.

[Chen89]
Chen, S.E., A progressive radiosity method and its implementation in a distributed processing environment, Master's thesis, Cornell Univ., Ithaca, NY, January 1989.

[Clea87]
Cleary, J.G., and Wyvill, G., An analysis of an algorithm for fast ray-tracing using uniform space subdivision, Research Report 87/264/12, Dept. Computer Science, Univ. of Calgary, Alberta, Canada, 1987.

[Cook86]
Cook, R.L., Stochastic sampling in computer graphics, *ACM TOG*, Vol. 5, pp. 51–72, 1986.

[Dipp84]
Dippé, M.E., and Swensen, J., An adaptive subdivision algorithm and parallel architecture for realistic image synthesis, *Comput. Graph.*, Vol. 18, pp. 149–158, 1984 (SIGGRAPH 84).

[duMo85]
du Montcel, B.T., and Nicolas, A., An illumination model for ray-tracing, in *Proc. Eurographics'85*, September 1985.

[Farr76]
Farrell, R., Determination of configuration factors of irregular shapes, *Jour. of Heat Transfer*, pp. 311–313, May 1976.

[Fole82]
Foley, J.D., and van Dam, A., *Fundamentals of Interactive Computer Graphics*, Reading, MA: Addison-Wesley, 1982.

[Fuji85]
Fujimoto, A., Accelerated ray tracing, in *Computer Graphics: Visual Technology and Art*, Tokyo: Springer-Verlag, 1985, pp. 41–65.

[Fuji86]
Fujimoto, A., Tanaka, T., and Iwata, K., ARTS: Accelerated ray-tracing system, *IEEE Comput. Graph. and Appl.*, Vol. 6, No. 4, pp. 16–26, April 1986.

[Glas84]
Glassner, A.S., Space subdivision for fast ray tracing, *IEEE Comput. Graph. and Appl.*, Vol. 4, No. 10, pp. 15–22, October 1984.

[Glas87]
Glassner, A., Spacetime ray tracing for animation, Introduction to Ray Tracing SIGGRAPH 87 course notes #13, Anaheim, CA, July 27–31, 1987.

[Glas88]
Glassner, A.S., Spacetime ray tracing for animation, *IEEE Comput. Graph. and Appl.*, Vol. 8, No. 2, pp. 60–70, March 1988.

[Gold87]
Goldsmith, J., and Salmon, J., Automatic creation of object hierarchies for ray tracing, *IEEE Comput. Graph. and Appl.*, Vol. 7, No. 5, pp. 14–20, May 1987.

[Gour71]
Gouraud, H., Continuous shading of curved surfaces, *IEEE Trans. on Comput.*, Vol. C-20, No. 6, pp. 623–628, June 1971.

[Hain86]
Haines, E.A., and Greenberg, D.P., The light buffer: a shadow testing accelerator, *IEEE Comput. Graph. and Appl.*, Vol. 6, No. 9, pp. 6–16, September 1986.

[Hain87]
Haines, E.A., A proposal for standard graphics environments, *IEEE Comput. Graph. and Appl.*, Vol. 7, No. 11, pp. 3–5, November 1987.

[Hall83]
Hall, R.A., and Greenberg, D.P., A testbed for realistic image synthesis, *IEEE Comput. Graph. and Appl.*, Vol. 3, No. 8, pp. 10–20, November 1983.

[Hall89]
Hall, R.A., *Illumination and Color in Computer Generated Imagery*, New York: Springer-Verlag, 1989.

[Hanr83]
Hanrahan, P., Ray tracing algebraic surfaces, *Comput. Graph.*, Vol. 17, pp. 83–90, 1983 (SIGGRAPH 83).

[Hanr86]
Hanrahan, P., Using caching and breadth-first search to speed up ray-tracing, *Proc. Graphics Interface 86*, pp. 56–61, May 1986.

88   Michael F. Cohen

[Heck84]
Heckbert, P., and Hanrahan, P., Beam tracing polygonal objects, *Comput. Graph.*, Vol. 18, pp. 119–127, 1984 (SIGGRAPH 84).

[Heck86]
Heckbert, P., Filtering by repeated integration, *Comput. Graph.*, Vol. 20, pp. 315–321, 1986 (SIGGRAPH 86).

[Jans86]
Jansen, F., Data structures for ray tracing, in *Data Structures for Raster Graphics*, Kessener, L.R.A., Peters, F.J., and van Lierop, M.P.L., Eds., New York: Springer-Verlag, 1986, pp. 57–73.

[Kaji82]
Kajiya, J.T., Ray tracing parametric patches, *Comput. Graph.*, Vol. 16, pp. 245–254, 1982 (SIGGRAPH 82).

[Kaji83]
Kajiya, J.T., New techniques for ray tracing procedurally defined objects, *ACM TOG*, Vol. 2, pp. 161–181, 1983.

[Kaji84]
Kajiya, J.T., and Von Herzen, B.P., Ray tracing volume densities, *Comput. Graph.*, Vol. 18, pp. 165–174, 1984 (SIGGRAPH 84).

[Kaji88]
Kajiya, J.T., An overview and comparison of rendering methods, ACM SIG-GRAPH Course Notes, No. 10, pp. 249–264, 1988.

[Kalr89]
Kalra, D., and Barr, A.H.. Guaranteed ray intersections with implicit surfaces, *Comput. Graph.*, Vol. 23, pp. 281–287, 1989 (SIGGRAPH 89).

[Kapl85]
Kaplan, M.R., Space-tracing, a constant time ray-tracer, SIGGRAPH 85 State of the Art in Image Synthesis seminar notes, San Francisco, CA, July 1985.

[Kay79]
Kay, D., and Greenberg, D.P., Transparency for computer synthesized images, *Comput. Graph.*, Vol. 13, pp. 158–164, 1979 (SIGGRAPH 79).

[Kay86]
Kay, T.L., and Kajiya, J.T., Ray tracing complex scenes, *Comput. Graph.*, Vol. 20, pp. 269–278, 1986 (SIGGRAPH 86).

[Lee85]
Lee, M.E., Redner, R.A., and Uselton, S.P., Statistically optimized sampling for distributed ray tracing, *Comput. Graph.*, Vol. 19, pp. 61–67, 1985 (SIGGRAPH 85).

[Maxw86]
Maxwell, G.M., Bailey, M.J., and Goldschmidt, V.W., Calculations of the radiation configuration factor using ray casting, *CAD*, Vol. 18, pp. 371–379, 1986.

[Meye80]
Meyer, G.W., and Greenberg, D.P., Perceptual color spaces for computer graphics, *Comput. Graph.*, Vol. 14, pp. 254–261, 1980 (SIGGRAPH 80).

[Meye86a]
Meyer, G.W., Rushmeier, H.E., Cohen, M.F., Greenberg, D.P., and Torrance,

K.E., An experimental evaluation of computer graphics imagery, *ACM TOG*, Vol. 5, pp. 30–50, 1986.

[Meye86b]
Meyer, G.W., Tutorial on color science, *The Visual Computer*, Vol. 2, pp. 278–290, 1986.

[Meye88]
Meyer, G.W., Wavelength selection for synthetic image generation, *Computer Vision, Graph., Image Processing*, Vol. 41, pp. 57–79, 1988.

[Nish85]
Nishita, T., and Nakamae, E., Continuous tone representation of three-dimensional objects taking account of shadows and interreflections, *Comput. Graph.*, Vol. 19, pp. 23–30, 1985 (SIGGRAPH 85).

[Pain89]
Painter, J.S., and Sloan, K., Antialiased raytracing by adaptive progressive refinement, *Comput. Graph.*, Vol. 23, pp. 281–287, 1989 (SIGGRAPH 89).

[Port84]
Porter, T., and Duff, T., Compositing digital images, Vol. 18, pp. 253–259, 1984 (SIGGRAPH 84).

[Roth82]
Roth, S.D., Ray casting for modeling solids, *Comput. Graph. Image Processing*, Vol. 18, pp. 109–144, 1982 (SIGGRAPH 82).

[Rubi80]
Rubin, S.M., and Whitted, T., A three-dimensional representation for fast rendering of complex scenes, *Comput. Graph.*, Vol. 14, pp. 110–116, 1980 (SIGGRAPH 80).

[Rush88]
Rushmeier, H.E., Realistic image synthesis for scenes with radiatively participating media, Ph.D. thesis, Cornell Univ., June 1988.

[Rush90]
Rushmeier, H.E., and Torrance, K.E., Extending the radiosity method to include specularly reflecting and translucent materials, *ACM TOG*, Vol. 9, pp. 1–27, 1990.

[Sede84]
Sederberg, T.W., and Anderson, D.C., Ray tracing of steiner patches, *Comput. Graph.*, Vol. 18, pp. 159–164, 1984 (SIGGRAPH 84).

[Shao88]
Shao, M.Z., Peng, Q.S., and Liang, Y.D., A new radiosity approach by procedural refinements for realistic image synthesis, *Comput. Graph.*, Vol. 22, pp. 93–102, 1988 (SIGGRAPH 88).

[Shin87]
Shinya, M., Takahashi, T., and Naito, S., Principles and applications of pencil tracing, *Comput. Graph.*, Vol. 21, pp. 45–54, 1987 (SIGGRAPH 87).

[Shir90]
Shirley, P., A ray tracing method for illumination calculation in diffuse-specular scenes, *Proc. Graphics Interface 90*, pp. 205–212, May 1990.

[Spee85]
Speer, L.R., DeRose, T.D., and Barsky, B.A., A theoretical and empirical analysis

of coherent ray-tracing, in *Proc. Graphics Interface 85*, May 1985.

[Toth85]
Toth, D.L., On ray tracing parametric surfaces, *Comput. Graph.*, Vol. 19, pp. 171–179, 1985 (SIGGRAPH 85).

[Wijk84]
van Wijk, J.J., Ray tracing objects defined by sweeping planar cubic splines, *ACM TOG*, Vol. 3, 223–237, 1984.

[Wang90]
Wang, Y., and Davis, W.A., Octant priority for radiosity image rendering, in *Proc. Graphics Inteface '90*, pp. 83–91, May 1990.

[Ward88]
Ward, G.J., Rubinstein, F.M., and Clear, R.D., A ray tracing solution for diffuse interreflection, *Comput. Graph.*, Vol. 22, pp. 85–92, 1988 (SIGGRAPH 88).

[Watt89]
Watt, A., *Fundamentals of Three-Dimaensional Computer Graphics*, Wokingham, UK: Addison-Wesley, 1989.

[Wegh84]
Weghorst, H., Hooper, G., and Greenberg, D.P., Improved computational methods for ray tracing, *ACM TOG*, Vol. 3, pp. 52–69, 1984.

[Wyvi86]
Wyvill, G., Kunii, T.L., and Shirai, Y., Space division for ray tracing in CSG, *IEEE Comput. Graph. and Appl.*, Vol. 6, No. 4, pp. 28–34, April 1986.

Color Plates

(a)

(b)

Plate 1. Texture (a) used conventionally; (b) as microtexture; (c) and to cover the whole surface.

(c)

Plate 1. (cont.)

Plate 2. Marble texture.

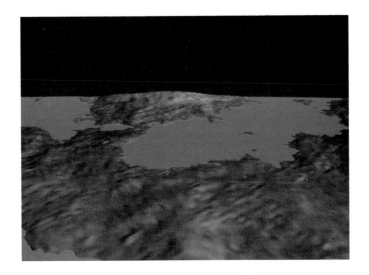

Plate 3. A fractal terrain model.

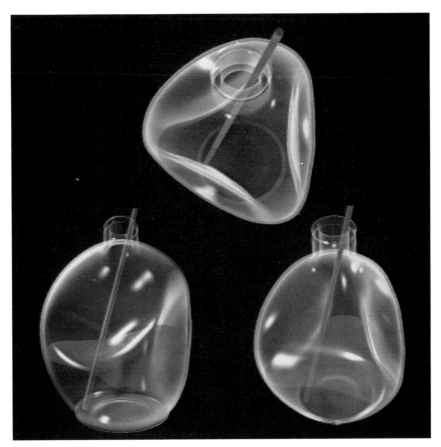

Plate 4. Scotch bottle obtained by using three warping operations (Courtesy of University of Utah).

Plate 5. Large scale structure in a turbulent mixing layer. This image is from a numerical simulation of the same phenomena as Figure 4.

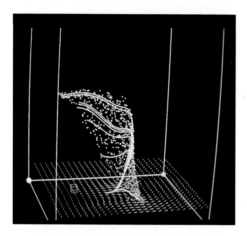

Plate 6. Particle traces from a numerical simulation of a severe thunderstorm.

Plate 7. Flow visualization of Jupiter for '2010'.

Plate 8. Dot surface of benzene's electron density field.

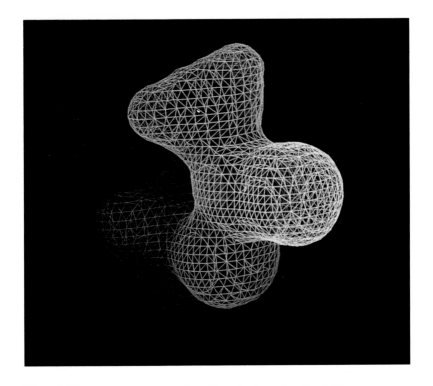

Plate 9. Vector net representation of an electron density field.

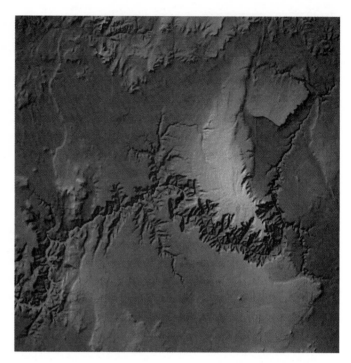

Plate 10. 'Pseudo-Illuminated' digital elevation map of the Grand Canyon region in Arizona.

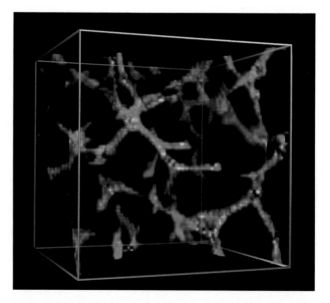

Plate 11. Stacked texture map image of a supercluster of galaxies. The simulated data was computed on a 64 by 64 by 64 grid, thus each texture map is interpolated up from 64 by 64 pixels to almost full screen size, resulting in a fuzzy image.

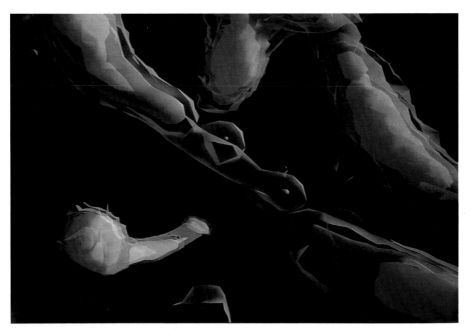

Plate 12. Polygonal surface derived from the matter density field. The blue surface corresponds to the lowest level of density, the inner salmon colored one to the highest.

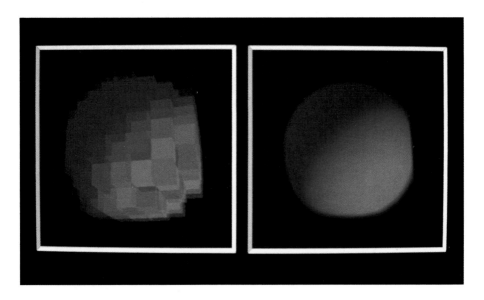

Plate 13. Two volume rendering techniques for a simple dataset. The representation on the left is voxel-based, the one on the right is cell-based.

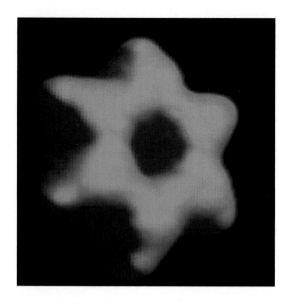

Plate 14. Voxel rendered image of benzene's electron density function.

Plate 15. Cell-based image of turbulence. The pressure field, as displayed here, is an indication of the distribution of vortices in the domain. This numerically simulated data is defined on a 67 by 50 by 55 cell domain.

Interpolation for Polygon Texture Mapping and Shading

Paul S. Heckbert

Henry P. Moreton

Abstract

A simple, fast method is presented for the interpolation of texture coordinates and shading parameters for polygons viewed in perspective. The method has application in scan conversion algorithms like z-buffer and painter's algorithms that perform screen space interpolation of shading parameters, such as texture coordinates, colors, and normal vectors. Some previous methods perform linear interpolation in screen space, but this is rotationally variant and, in the case of texture mapping, causes a disturbing 'rubber sheet' effect. To correctly compute the nonlinear, projective transformation between screen space and parameter space, we use rational linear interpolation across the polygon, performing several divisions at each pixel. We present simpler formulas for setting up these interpolation computations, reducing the setup cost per polygon to nil, and reducing the cost per vertex to a handful of divisions.

Introduction

We first define our terminology, then summarize a naive, linear method for interpolating shading parameters during scan conversion. After examining the flaws of linear interpolation, we describe the new method and prove its correctness. Readers uninterested in the proofs may want to read just the sections titled 'Polygon Rendering with Linear Interpolation' and 'New Algorithm'.

DEFINITIONS

We define the following coordinate systems: *Object space* is the 3D coordinate system in which each polygon is defined. There can be several object spaces. *World space* is a coordinate system that is related to each object space by 3D modeling transformations (translations, rotations, and scales). *3D screen space* is the 3D coordinate system of the display, a 'perspective space' with pixel coordinates (x, y) and depth z. It is related to world space by the camera parameters. Finally, *2D screen space* (or 'screen space' for short) is the 2D subspace of 3D screen space without z.

To facilitate affine and projective (perspective) transformations, we use homogeneous notation [Maxw46] in which, for example, the 2D real point (x, y) is represented by the 3D homogeneous vector $[p] = [xw \quad yw \quad w]$, where w is an arbitrary nonzero number. We are cavalier about the case where $w = 0$. In homogeneous notation, 2D points are represented by 3-vectors and 3D points are represented by 4-vectors.

We use the notation

Coordinate System	Real	Homogeneous
3D object space	(x_o, y_o, z_o)	$[p_o] = [x_o w_o \quad y_o w_o \quad z_o w_o \quad w_o]$
3D screen space	(x, y, z)	$[p_\sigma] = [xw \quad yw \quad zw \quad w]$
2D screen space	(x, y)	$[p_s] = [xw \quad yw \quad w]$

Projective and Affine Mappings

We use two classes of mapping (transformation), affine and projective. The 3D forms of these mappings are ubiquitous in computer graphics [Newm76]. The 2D *projective mapping* (or perspective mapping) from (u, v) to (x, y) has the general form [Maxw46]

$$x = \frac{au + bv + c}{gu + hv + i} \qquad y = \frac{du + ev + f}{gu + hv + i}$$

The mapping is more simply represented in homogeneous matrix notation

$$[xw \quad yw \quad w] = [uq \quad vq \quad q] \begin{bmatrix} a & d & g \\ b & e & h \\ c & f & i \end{bmatrix}$$

Affine mappings include scales, rotations, translations, and shears. They are linear mappings plus a translation. A 2D projective mapping is affine $\iff g = h = 0$ and $i \neq 0$.

These mappings are trivially generalized to map an m-dimensional space to an n-dimensional space. The homogeneous matrix for such a mapping is $(m + 1) \times (n + 1)$. Unlike affine mappings, projective mappings do not preserve parallel lines or equispaced points along a line. But like affine mappings, projective mappings preserve lines, that is, lines transform to lines. Projective mappings are closed under composition: they may be composed by concatenating their matrices. Projective mappings between spaces of equal dimension are invertible, using the inverse or adjoint matrix.

We call a parameter or space *X-affine* when it is an affine function or transform of space X, and *X-projective* when it is a projective function or transform of space

X. For example, in texture mapping, texture space is typically object-affine, but screen-projective.

Polygon Rendering with Linear Interpolation

Scan conversion algorithms such as z-buffer, painter's, and scanline methods [Roge85] typically use a set of interpolated shading parameters at each pixel. This set might include: texture coordinates (u, v) for texture mapping [Blin76; Heck86], (r, g, b) for Gouraud shading, a normal vector for Phong shading, and world space position for per-pixel shading. Polygons are described by listing these parameter values along with the object space coordinates (x_o, y_o, z_o) at each vertex. During scan conversion, both the parameters and the screen coordinates (x, y, z) are interpolated along the edges of the polygon from scanline to scanline, and then interpolated across each scanline for use at each pixel.

The steps of the linear interpolation algorithm are

Associate a record containing the parameters of interest with each vertex of the polygon.

For each vertex, transform object space coordinates to homogeneous screen space, using the 4×4 object to screen matrix, yielding the values $[xw \quad yw \quad zw \quad w]$.

Clip the polygon against the plane equations for each of the six sides of the viewing frustum, linearly interpolating all the parameters when new vertices are created.

Perform a homogeneous division to compute $x = xw/w$, $y = yw/w$, $z = zw/w$.

Scan convert in screen space by linear interpolation of all parameters, using the parameter values at each pixel for shading.

C code is available for such a generic polygon clipper and scan converter [Heck90].

FLAWS OF LINEAR INTERPOLATION

Linear interpolation algorithms like the above are generally used for Gouraud shading, Phong shading, and often for texture mapping as well. It is wrong, however, to perform linear interpolation in screen space of parameters that are not screen-affine. We assume that the only perspective in the transformation pipeline lies between world space and screen space. That is, world space, object space, and the parameters are mutually affine, but they are screen-projective. The above algorithm is correct only when the parameters are screen-affine, which occurs only for parallel projection or for perspective projection of a plane perpendicular to the line of sight.

The flaws are most visible in texture mapping. Figure 1 shows the artifacts that result for linear, screen space interpolation of texture coordinates. Note that this image does not exhibit the foreshortening we expect from perspective. The texture also shows disturbing discontinuities along horizontal lines passing through the vertices. In animation, the horizontal ripples move distractingly as the camera rolls, since the ripples are rotation variant; and the lack of foreshortening makes the texture appear to slide across the surface like a rubber sheet. Figure 2 shows the correct image.

The above problems occur because the texture transformation effected by our linear parameter interpolation is inconsistent with the geometry transformation used to transform the vertices to screen space. Linear interpolation computes a piecewise bilinear mapping[†] from screen space to parameter space, while the actual mapping defined by affine transformations and a perspective camera is projective.

Similar errors occur when colors, normals, or positions are linearly interpolated in a space to which they are not affine, but these errors are much less noticeable than the errors for texture mapping. The flaws in Gouraud and Phong shading are so subtle, in fact, that they went unnoticed for several years in the production renderer at the New York Institute of Technology. Actually, it is hard to say what 'correct' interpolation means for Gouraud and Phong shading, since they are approximations.

The rubber sheet effect occurs for polygons with any number of sides, but rotational variation occurs only for polygons with four or more sides. Linear interpolation across triangles in screen space effects an affine mapping, which is rotation invariant. Rotation invariance does not imply correctness, however: if the scene employs affine texture-to-object parameterization and a perspective camera, then texture space is screen-projective, not screen-affine, and linear interpolation is incorrect. Although triangulation is usually inappropriate, it is often used to solve the rotational variation problem.

The correct solution described later involves several divisions per pixel. A cheap alternative that avoids divisions at each pixel is polygon subdivision, where parameter values at the new vertices are computed using linear interpolation in object space. The Silicon Graphics VGX workstation currently does texture mapping this way. In Figure 3 we see how splitting a polygon into a number of smaller polygons improves the approximation. Others approximate the nonlinear function with quadratic or cubic polynomials [Wolb90]. But note that rational linear functions have poles (behaving like $f(x) = 1/x$) at the horizon of an infinite plane, near which they are not well approximated by linear functions or other polynomials. If subdivision is used, it should be adaptive. We do not recommend subdivision or approximation, however, as they increase the number of polygons, and the results are never exact. The per-polygon and per-vertex cost of transformation, clipping, and scan conversion may even cancel the advantages of faster pixel rendering.

[†]A bilinear mapping from (x, y) to (u, v) is one of the form $u = axy + bx + cy + d$, $v = exy + fx + gy + h$.

Figure 1. Image produced by texture mapping a checkerboard onto a rectangle in perspective, using linear interpolation of u, v. Note the horizontal lines of discontinuity passing through the vertices on the left.

Figure 2. Correct image produced by the new algorithm using rational linear interpolation of the texture coordinates. Note the proper foreshortening.

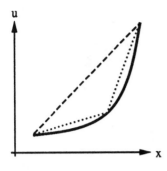

u

x

Figure 3. An object-affine parameter u is a rational linear function of screen x. Solid curve: correct function $u(x) = (ax + b)/(cx + d)$; dashed curve: piecewise-linear approximation for one polygon; dotted curve: linear interpolation with two polygons.

Polygon Rendering with Rational Linear Interpolation

The 'correct' solution requires *rational linear interpolation*: independent interpolation of a linear numerator and linear denominator, followed by division at each pixel. In previous work, Newman and Sproull found the rational linear formula relating a linear interpolation factor (between 0 and 1) for screen space to the interpolation factor for eye space [Newm76, p. 362]. Smith applied a similar technique to texture mapping, showing that a divide was needed at each pixel [Smit80].

Rational Linear Interpolation the Hard Way

In previous work, the first author described incremental interpolation of texture coordinates with a per-pixel cost of three additions, two divisions, and a texture access [Heck83]. Along each scanline, texture coordinate u has the form $u(x) = (ax + b)/(cx + d)$, and $v(x)$ is similar.

The method employed for computing the homogeneous texture coordinates (uq, vq, q) at each vertex was quite involved [Heck89]. First, it required inference of the affine texture-to-object parameterization from the correspondence at three vertices of the polygon. This mapping was then concatenated with the object-to-screen mapping, to arrive at the 3×3 projective mapping matrix. The screen coordinates of each vertex of the clipped polygon were transformed by the inverse of this matrix to compute the homogeneous texture coordinates, which were linearly interpolated across the polygon. The cost of texture mapping setup with this method was 133 arithmetic operations (multiplies and adds) per polygon, plus 12 arithmetic operations per vertex. Transformation and clipping are usually done in floating point, but scan conversion will work in 32-bit integer arithmetic if done carefully.

The Easy Way: Derivation

However, there is a much simpler alternative! As observed by the second author, the homogeneous texture coordinates suitable for linear interpolation in screen space can be computed simply by dividing the texture coordinates by screen w, linearly interpolating $(u/w, v/w, 1/w)$, and dividing the quantities u/w and v/w by $1/w$ at each pixel to recover the texture coordinates. Any object-affine parameter can be interpolated in this fashion. To demonstrate this, we need the following theorem:

Theorem:

   Given

   n parameters $r_1, r_2, \cdots, r_n$ that are object-affine,

   a 3D object space that is 3D-screen-projective, and

   a plane in object space that is not 'edge-on' to screen space;

   then the parameters are screen-projective on this plane.

Proof:

   We write the homogeneous parameter space as $[p_r] = [r_1 w_r \quad \cdots \quad r_n w_r \quad w_r]$, the homogeneous object space as $[p_o] = [x_o w_o \quad y_o w_o \quad z_o w_o \quad w_o]$, homogeneous 3D screen space as $[p_\sigma] = [xw \quad yw \quad zw \quad w]$ and homogeneous (2D) screen space as $[p_s] = [xw \quad yw \quad w]$. Let $[M_{ab}]$ denote the transform matrix from a space to b space. Then the parameters are $[p_r] = [p_o][M_{or}]$ for some $4 \times (n+1)$ parameterization matrix $[M_{or}]$. Since the parameters are object-affine, the last column of this matrix is $[0 \quad 0 \quad 0 \quad 1]^T$, so $w_r = w_o$. Similarly, since object space is 3D-screen-projective, we have $[p_o] = [p_\sigma][M_{\sigma o}]$ for some 4×4 matrix $[M_{\sigma o}]$.

   Since projective mappings preserve planes, a plane in object space transforms to a plane in screen space; and since the plane is not edge-on, the plane has a unique depth z at each (x, y). Thus, $z = \alpha x + \beta y + \gamma$ for some α, β, and γ. On this plane

$$[x \quad y \quad z \quad 1] = [x \quad y \quad 1] \begin{bmatrix} 1 & 0 & \alpha & 0 \\ 0 & 1 & \beta & 0 \\ 0 & 0 & \gamma & 1 \end{bmatrix}$$

or $[p_\sigma] = [p_s][M_{s\sigma}]$.

   Since the screen-to-3D-screen, 3D-screen-to-object, and object-to-parameter mappings are all projective, their composition is projective. Thus, the screen-to-parameter mapping is projective, and $[p_r] = [p_s][M_{sr}]$, where $[M_{sr}]$ is a $3 \times (n+1)$ matrix

$$[M_{sr}] = [M_{s\sigma}][M_{\sigma o}][M_{or}] = \begin{bmatrix} a_1 & a_2 & & a_n & A \\ b_1 & b_2 & \cdots & b_n & B \\ c_1 & c_2 & & c_n & C \end{bmatrix}$$

for some a_i, b_i, c_i, A, B, and C.

   The parameter values on the plane are thus related to the screen coordinates via $[r_1 w_r \quad \cdots \quad r_n w_r \quad w_r] = [xw \quad yw \quad w][M_{sr}]$, so

$$[r_1 w_r / w \quad \cdots \quad r_n w_r / w \quad w_r / w] = [x \quad y \quad 1][M_{sr}] \tag{1}$$

is screen-affine on this plane. To solve for the parameter values at each pixel
we could simply compute the matrix multiply above, but that would be unnec-
essarily slow. A faster, incremental method is feasible if we can determine the
unknown function $w_r(x, y)$.

If we start with a point on the plane that has object space coordinates $[p_o]$
with $w_o = 1$, transform it through the mapping $[M_{o\sigma}] = [M_{\sigma o}]^{-1}$ and discard z,
we can compute homogeneous screen coordinates $[xw \quad yw \quad w]$. If this point is
then transformed back to object space, we recover $[p_o]$, of course; but most importantly, its homogeneous coordinate w_o is unchanged, since the concatenated
matrices annihilate each other and the point is on the plane. Transforming
further to parameter space, we find that $w_r = 1$, since $w_r = w_o$. And since
we transformed all the way back from screen space to parameter space, Eq. (1)
applies; thus

$$\frac{r_i(x, y)}{w(x, y)} = a_i x + b_i y + c_i$$

$$\frac{1}{w(x, y)} = Ax + By + C$$

The homogeneous parameter space so computed is screen-affine.

THE EASY WAY: SUMMARY

If the parameters are affine with respect to object space, and the homogeneous
screen coordinates are computed by transforming an object space point with
$w_o = 1$ (or any nonzero constant), then the homogeneous parameter vector
$[r_1/w \quad \cdots \quad r_n/w \quad 1/w]$ is screen-affine. Thus, it can be linearly interpolated
in screen space (Figure 4).

Setup for interpolation is much simpler with this method than with the previous method described in Heckbert [Heck89]. None of the matrices used in the
proof need to be computed, and no matrix multiply to transform from screen
space to homogeneous parameter (or texture) space is needed. The only setup
required is that each parameter value be divided by the screen w at that point,
and an extra parameter with value $1/w$ be added to the interpolated-variable
list. To compute n parameters, $n + 1$ divisions are needed per vertex; and $n + 1$
variables must be interpolated. At each pixel, we divide[†] the n interpolated
homogeneous parameters by the interpolated $1/w$ to compute each parameter
value

$$r_i(x, y) = \frac{r_i(x, y)/w(x, y)}{1/w(x, y)} = \frac{a_i x + b_i y + c_i}{Ax + By + C}$$

If it turns out that w is identical at all the vertices, then the parameters are
screen-affine for that polygon, and the division at each pixel can be avoided.

[†]Note that on most machines the fastest way to divide n numbers by a common value
is to compute the reciprocal of that value and then perform n multiplications.

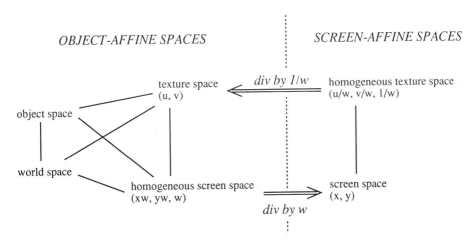

Figure 4. Interrelationship of the coordinate systems required for standard texture mapping. The parameter set is (u, v). Affine transformations relating two spaces are indicated by a solid line; projection transformations are indicated by a double arrow.

GENERALIZATIONS AND LIMITATIONS

Gouraud and Phong shading often require a renderer to interpolate parameters with arbitrary values at the vertices. If the interpolation method described here is used but the first condition of this algorithm is not met, that is, the parameters are not object-affine, then for polygons with four or more sides the results in general are rotation variant. Interpolation of arbitrary data over polygons with five or more sides requires mappings more complex than those discussed here, but for quadrilaterals, interpolation can be done using projective mappings. To do this, we assume that the parameters are object-projective, not object-affine. Our interpolation technique can be generalized further for the interpolation of parameters all of which are screen-projective, but some of which are not object-affine. For example, with a projective texture parameterization, $w_o = 1 \not\approx w_r = 1$. Therefore we cannot assume $w_r = 1$, as above. But if w_r were computed, we could linearly interpolate $[\, uw_r/w \quad \cdots \quad vw_r/w \quad w_r/w \,]$ to find the correct values of u and v at each pixel. A different homogeneous variable w_r/w must be interpolated for each mutually affine cluster of parameters in the parameter set. This generalization also allows perspective transformations to be used as modeling transformations in addition to camera transformations.

The new method cannot be used when there is no 3D information, as in image warping. In that case, warp inference techniques must be used [Heck89].

NEW ALGORITHM

The rational linear rendering algorithm is:

> Associate a record containing the n parameters of interest $(r_1, r_2, \ldots, r_n)$ with each vertex of the polygon.

For each vertex, transform object space coordinates to homogeneous screen space, using the 4×4 object to screen matrix, yielding the values $[\,xw \quad yw \quad zw \quad w\,]$.

Clip the polygon against the plane equations for each of the six sides of the viewing frustum, linearly interpolating all the parameters when new vertices are created.

At each vertex, divide the homogeneous screen coordinates, the parameters r_i, and the number 1 by w to construct the variable list $[\,x \quad y \quad z \quad s_1 \quad s_2 \quad \cdots \quad s_{n+1}\,]$, where $s_i = r_i/w$ for $i \leq n$, $s_{n+1} = 1/w$.

Scan convert in screen space by linear interpolation of this variable list, at each pixel computing $r_i = s_i/s_{n+1}$ for each of the n parameters; use these values for shading.

Conclusions

We have presented a new method for setup of parameter interpolation on polygons viewed in perspective. The previous method, when interpolating two parameters, cost 133 arithmetic operations per polygon and 12 operations per vertex. The new method allows interpolation of any number, n, of parameters. It is simpler than the old method, it has no per-polygon overhead, and its per-vertex cost is $n + 1$ divisions. The per-pixel cost of the new method is identical to the old rational linear cost: n divisions per pixel. For texture mapping, the dominant cost is thus three divisions per vertex and two divisions per pixel.

The ability to cheaply and correctly interpolate parameters is useful for a number of shading techniques. This interpolation technique is most helpful for texture mapping, however, where the flaws of linear interpolation are most visible.

Acknowledgements. The second author was supported by a fellowship from Silicon Graphics.

REFERENCES

[Blin76]
   Blinn, J.F., and Newell, M.E., Texture and reflection in computer generated images, *CACM*, Vol. 19, Oct. 1976, pp. 542–547.

[Heck83]
   Heckbert, P.S., Texture mapping polygons in perspective, NYIT Computer Graphics Lab, TM 13, April 1983.

[Heck86]
   Heckbert, P.S., Survey of texture mapping, *IEEE Comput. Graph. and Appl.*, Vol. 6, Nov. 1986, pp. 56–67.

[Heck89]
   Heckbert, P.S., Fundamentals of texture mapping and image warping, Master's thesis, UCB/CSD 89/516, CS Dept., UC Berkeley, May 1989.

[Heck90]
Heckbert, P.S., Generic convex polygon scan conversion and clipping, *Graphics Gems*, Glassner, A., Ed., Boston: Academic Press, 1990.

[Maxw46]
Maxwell, E.A., *The Methods of Plane Projective Geometry, Based on the Use of General Homogeneous Coordinates*, London; Cambridge Univ. Press, 1946.

[Newm79]
Newman, W.M., and Sproull, R.F., *Principles of Interactive Computer Graphics* (2nd ed.), New York: McGraw-Hill, 1979.

[Roge85]
Rogers, D.F., *Procedural Elements for Computer Graphics*, New York: McGraw-Hill, 1985.

[Smit80]
Smith, A.R., Incremental rendering of textures in perspective, (SIGGRAPH 80) Animation Graphics seminar notes, July 1980.

[Wolb90]
Wolberg, G., *Digital Image Warping*, Los Alamitos, CA: IEEE Computer Society Press, 1990.

Random Processes in Computer Graphics

Alain Fournier

Abstract

Random numbers and random processes have an important role to play in many areas of computer graphics. While they are mostly used to add variability to geometric models and textures, they can also be found associated with sampling techniques and illumination models.

After a brief survey of techniques used in the computer generation of random numbers with a given distribution, we look at some visualization techniques that can replace or supplement the standard tests. We then discuss relevant properties of stochastic processes.

Applications of random processes are examined through several case studies. Textures and texture mappings are powerful tools in modeling, and random textures have been used extensively. We examine the techniques used in their generation both 'from scratch' and from a given real texture. Fractals are a class of objects which have captured everybody's imagination, and random fractals are very popular in modeling. We describe and discuss various ways to generate random fractals, in particular fractional Brownian motion, mainly used in the modeling of terrain. A more general approach, generalized stochastic interpolation, is also discussed, and we show the wide range of its applicability.

Another useful approach to the generation of random processes is through spectral or Fourier synthesis. We present the basic principles and illustrate with examples of terrain, waves, and wind modeling using this method. Stochastic processes can also be used at the level of local shading, and we give some examples of the techniques that can be used there.

In conclusion we assess the benefits and drawbacks of using random processes, and we identify areas where further investigation is necessary and promising.

Introduction

In most of the modeling methods commonly used (geometric modeling, constructive solid geometry, procedural models, grammar-based models, etc.) the same objects are generated when applying the same rules the same number of times. The objects generated, while looking interesting and complex, are much too *regular* to convincingly model natural objects. We can keep the power of these techniques and introduce needed variations by using *stochastic* elements. 'Stochastic' is just a fancy word for *random*. What is meant by random is more difficult to explain, and volumes have been written about that. For our purposes we define as random a property that is unpredictable for a single occurrence, but whose average behavior after many observations can be quantified. To use an example relevant to natural phenomena, the exact height of the fir tree ahead of me in the middle of the forest cannot be predicted, but if the heights of many fir trees are measured and averaged, somebody knowledgeable about this particular species of tree can very confidently give limits within which this average should be found. Inversely, realistic heights for trees can be generated by creating 'random' heights, knowing the average obtained and knowing some facts about the distribution of the measured heights.

So the basic idea of stochastic modeling is very classic and, in fact, very simple. We therefore benefit from the wealth of knowledge and tools that have been acquired in mathematics, probability, statistics, and numerical methods. The new challenge is to integrate these techniques into the common tools and methods of computer graphics. The main questions are: what stochastic variables and processes are of interest, how do we compute them accurately and efficiently, and how do we introduce these stochastic elements to geometric models, textures, and illumination models so that they integrate well with our current systems?

Another interesting issue, which we only briefly mention, is that of perception. There is no reason in most applications to generate artefacts beyond the capabilities of human perception. In the context of the random processes used for visual purposes, an obvious question is how much of the statistics of a random process do we actually see, and with what 'resolution' do we see it? As an example, there is a well known conjecture by Julesz [Jule62] to the effect that humans cannot discriminate textures on the basis of third order statistics and beyond. The practical result of such a conjecture, if true, is that we only need model the first two orders of statistics to generate realistic textures. Counter-examples have been found [Prat81], but in practice it is safe to assume that this holds in most circumstances.

Generating Randomness

RANDOM NUMBER GENERATION

To be able to implement a given distribution in a computer program, one should be able to generate random numbers. In fact, this is not possible with an ordinary (deterministic) computer, and it is not even useful, so computer algorithms generate *pseudorandom* numbers (PRN). We refer you to a computer science textbook for a more thorough treatment of this topic. The unavoidable best is Knuth, Volume 2 [Knut81].

Uniformly Distributed PRN

The basic building block of most distributions is the *uniformly distributed random number* (UPRN). The basic one is when the variable is in the interval $[0, 1]$. The theoretical probability distribution function $F(x) = $ *Probability that random variable* $X \leq x$ is

$$F(x) = x$$

We denote U as an RN with such distribution. It is obvious that any uniformly distributed random variable over a finite interval is obtained from U by scaling. When the values are from a discrete set, one must be careful to handle the range correctly. Most programming languages have built-in functions for a uniformly distributed PRN; some have more flexibility than others in the choice of range. Sometimes the built-in function returns a number in the open range $(0, 2^n)$, where n is the integer word size in bits. In this case one has to divide by 2^n to obtain the open range $(0, 1)$; note that most methods do not give the closed range.

There are basically three true and tested methods to generate such pseudorandom numbers: *multiplicative congruential*, *shift-register*, and *lagged Fibonacci*. They all rely on a series of linear transformations of some algebraic structure.

Multiplicative Congruential Method

The most popular method is the so-called multiplicative congruential. It produces a sequence $X_0, X_1, X_2, \ldots$ from the iteration

$$X_n = (aX_{n-1} + b) \bmod m$$

The first term X_0 is called the *seed*. It generates uniformly distributed pseudorandom numbers within a given range. Most of the time m is chosen to be 2^n, where n is the word size in bits to simplify the modulo operation, and the term $b = 0$. With suitable choices of seeds and multiplicator, the maximum open range $(0, m)$ is achieved.

Shift-register Methods

A shift-register looks at the n-bit word of the computer as an n element binary vector $\vec{V}$ and uses an $n \times n$ binary matrix T to transform the vector into VT, VT^2, VT^3, etc. Each of the resulting vectors is taken as a pseudorandom integer. The computations are simple if T is of the form

$$T = (I + R^s)(I + L^t)$$

where I is the identity matrix, R a right shift operator, and L a left shift operator. The VT operation is then performed by shifting V right s times, exclusive-or'ing the result with V, then shifting the new vector left t times and exclusive-or'ing the result with it. It is easy to achieve the maximum period of $2^n - 1$ with a good choice of the matrix T. An important property of the method for our purposes is that any nonzero V can be used as a seed.

Lagged Fibonacci Methods

The lagged Fibonacci generators use a vector of r elements $X_1, X_2, X_3, \ldots, X_r$ and two lags, r and s $(r > s)$, and apply the formula for the new random element $X_i, i > r$

$$X_i = X_{i-r} \cdot X_{i-s}$$

where $\cdot$ is a bit operation. The usual operations are $+$, $-$, **and**, or **xor**. If we denote the generator by $F(r, s, \cdot)$, the most popular are $F(17, 5, +)$ and $F(17, 5, -)$ on integers $\mathrm{mod}\,2^n$, with a period of $(2^{17} - 1) \times 2^{n-1}$. From our point of view, the most serious problem of the lagged-Fibonacci generators is that their state needs to be defined by a vector of r words, making seeding a bigger problem.

Pseudorandom number generators yield only a finite sequence of numbers before they repeat. In practice, the length of the sequence is considerable. In some applications the number of different terms can be quite low without any visible consequences. At this point it is difficult to distinguish between a deterministic sequence of numbers and a pseudorandom sequence. In fact, in many applications the pseudorandom number generator is replaced by a lookup table which contains from 8 to 1024 numbers. The advantage of these tables is that any distribution can be precomputed and stored in the table. Then the numbers can be used only at the cost of a table lookup. It is often necessary to tie the outcome of the generators to some parameters of the object generated, especially for consistency when the object is regenerated in another frame and at another level of detail. The basic way to accomplish this is to relate the seed of the generators to the parameter(s) of the objects. See Fournier [Four82], Piper [Pipe84], Smith [Smit84], and Lewis [Lewi89] for more discussions of these issues. Note that not much is known about the distribution of the PRN under these conditions.

Random Distributions

A good book on probability and statistics (such as [Fras76]) should be consulted for the fundamental definitions and properties of random distributions. Here we just give examples of the simple ones which can also be used as building blocks for other distributions, and examples of where they would occur in modeling natural phenomena. The *binomial* distribution gives the number of successes in n independent Bernoulli trials (i.e., trials with two possible results, success or failure), where the probability of each success is p. Note that the same polynomials reappear as *Bernstein* polynomials in the context of *Bézier* parametric formulations. The *geometric* distribution is the distribution of the number of trials required to achieve the first success in a series of independent Bernoulli trials with probability of success p.

Assume a process where events occur uniformly distributed at a mean rate of λ per unit time. The number of events in a given time period follows a Poisson distribution (for the formula given in the table the time period is unity). The distribution of the length of time necessary to observe r occurrences of an event is a *gamma* distribution.

The *uniform* distribution is used to position objects in one or more dimensions such that the objects do not interfere with each other. For example, the position of falling raindrops on the ground within a given square area can be determined by selecting uniformly distributed x and y coordinates. The number of raindrops within subsquares of the preceding square follow a *Poisson* distribution. The distribution of trees in a forest is similar; but in this case the points are not independent, since the probability of a new tree grows smaller as it gets closer to an already existing tree. The *normal* distribution is the most useful of all continuous distributions, since it occurs when a phenomenon is the sum of many independent random variables. The distributions of heights of trees, of branching angles, of surface displacements on the ocean, are all normal. The normal, or *Gaussian*, distribution is also important as a component of more complex distributions. For example, the differences between successive positions in Brownian motion (see below) are normally distributed.

Tables 1 and 2 summarize the most useful probability laws and give some examples of their occurrences (see also *Stochastic Processes*, by E. Parzen, Holden-Day, 1962).

Generating Distributions from the Uniform Distribution

The general method to generate a uniform distribution is derived from the observation that a distribution function $F(x)$ is in the range $[0, 1]$ and is monotonically increasing. Therefore, there is an inverse function

$$F^{-1}(y) = x$$

If we compute the random variable X such that

$$X = F^{-1}(U)$$

the probability that $X \leq x$ is the probability that $F^{-1}(U) \leq x$, which is the probability that $U \leq F(x)$, which is $F(x)$ from the distribution function U. The only problem (and in general it is a serious numerical problem) is to know how to invert $F(x)$. Note that this is not always the best method.

Consider the distribution $F(x) = x^2$. The above method says that computing

$$X = \sqrt{U}$$

produces the required distribution. Knuth [Knut81] shows that if two independent uniformly distributed variables U_1 and U_2 are produced, then

$$X = \max(U_1, U_2)$$

also has the required distribution.

Table 1. Some discrete probability laws.

Probability Law	Mass Function		Mean	Variance
Binomial	$\binom{n}{x} p^x q^{n-x}$	$x = 0, 1, \ldots, n$	np	npq
$n = 1, 2, \ldots$	0	otherwise		
Poisson	$e^{-\lambda} \dfrac{\lambda}{x!}$	$x = 0, 1, 2, \ldots$	λ	λ
$\lambda > 0$	0	otherwise		
Geometric	pq^{x-1}	$x = 1, 2, \ldots$	$\dfrac{1}{p}$	$\dfrac{q}{p^2}$
$r = 1, 2, \ldots$	0	otherwise		

Table 2. Some continuous probability laws.

Probability Law	Density Function		Mean	Variance
Uniform	$\dfrac{1}{b-a}$	$a < x < b$	$\dfrac{a+b}{2}$	$\dfrac{(b-a)^2}{12}$
over interval $[a,b]$	0	otherwise		
Normal $\sigma > 0$	$\dfrac{1}{\sigma\sqrt{2\pi}}e^{-\frac{1}{2}(\frac{x-m}{\sigma})^2}$		m	σ^2
Gamma $r, \lambda > 0$	$\dfrac{\lambda}{\Gamma(r)}(\lambda x)^{r-1}e^{-\lambda x}$	$x > 0$	$\dfrac{r}{\lambda}$	$\dfrac{r}{\lambda^2}$

The Exponential Distribution

The exponential distribution is

$$F(x) = 1 - e^{-\frac{x}{\mu}} \qquad x \geq 0$$

Note that in the preceding tables $\lambda = 1/\mu$. Therefore

$$x = -\mu \ln(1 - y)$$

Since $(1 - U)$ is uniformly distributed when U is, we can compute the variable X with the exponential distribution by

$$X = -\mu \ln(U)$$

Note that since the UPRN is never 0 in most methods, problems with the previous formula are avoided.

The Normal Distribution

The normal, or Gaussian, distribution is the most important nonuniform distribution, theoretically as well as practically. The inversion is rather difficult here, and many methods have been devised (see Knuth [Knut81] for descriptions and analysis). I mention only one, because it is simple and elegant.

The algorithm starts by computing two uniform independent RN, U_1 and U_2. These RN are then scaled to be in the range $(-1, +1)$ by

$$V = 2U - 1$$

letting
$$S = V_1^2 + V_2^2$$

If $S \geq 1$, then two new U are chosen.

Then the two RN are computed, with

$$X_1 = V_1 \sqrt{\frac{-2 \ln S}{S}}$$

and similarly for X_2. Again, see Knuth [Knut81] for the proof that X_1 and X_2 are two independent normally distributed random variables. In practice, the cost of the square root and the logarithm may be high on some systems, but it is a clean and correct method.

VISUALIZATION OF DISTRIBUTIONS

It is very easy to use a bad method to generate a particular distribution and therefore obtain bad numbers for an application. Of course, the concept of badness depends on the needs of the application. There are many tests developed to assert various desirable properties of PRN, but often a visualization quickly eliminates the bad ones. In graphics applications the absence of visible problems can be a proof of adequacy in itself.

As in all visualizations, one can use the 'spatial' visual channels, as in scatter plots to illustrate the distributions, and one can use the intensity channels, either achromatic (strictly luminance) or in colour.

Using Intensity

Many UPRN generators which are supplied with computer systems generate numbers whose last few bits are quite far from random. It is easy to illustrate this by mapping the numbers in a frame buffer to an intensity scale (the easiest in most cases is to the semiopen range [0,256)). If we look at the resulting image, any pattern caused by the nonrandomness of the bits mapped is obvious (of course assuming the statistics of the deviations from randomness are visually noticeable; recall the remark in the introduction to this paper regarding the Julesz conjecture [Jule62]).

As an example, consider the three greyscale pictures in Figure 1. These pictures show the result when the last 1, 2, and 8 bits, respectively, of the UPRN output by rand() supplied with IRIX 3.2 are mapped to intensity in a 256×256 picture (with suitable scaling so that the mean is 128). It is easy to see that the last bit exhibits a pattern, and it is fair to say that the pattern would be hard to detect by standard tests. Another example has to do with forcing the seed each time an RN generator is used. In this case, a Gaussian PRN was generated with the seed computed from the row and column position of the relevant pixel in the picture (Figure 2).

In the first case (Figure 2a) the seeds were just a count of the pixel, in the second case (Figure 2b) the row and column number were multiplied by 'fudge' factors before being added together to give the seed, and in the third case (Figure 2c) the results of the multiplications were logically 'anded' instead of added. It is obvious that the first two methods generate a distribution that would be unacceptable for most applications, while the last one produces visually acceptable results.

In some cases, a good strategy is to try to generate scatter plots that give uniformly distributed 2D arrays of points. The human visual system is very good at detecting patterns. Viewing distance can be varied to inspect correlations at

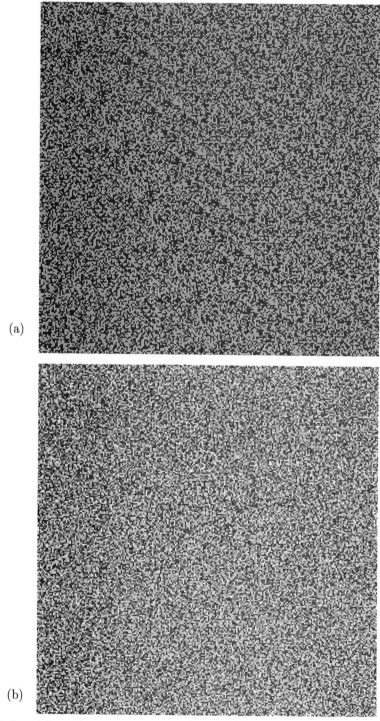

(a)

(b)

Figure 1. Last (a) 1, (b) 2, and (c) 8 bits of the output of rand().

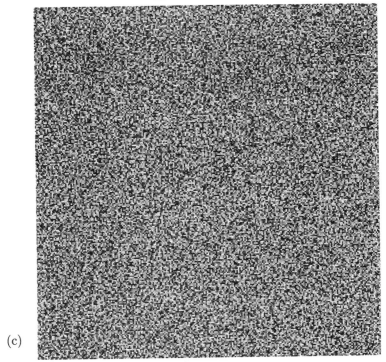

(c)

Figure 1. (*Continued*).

various scales. For example, Figure 3 shows 5,000 points normally distributed (Figure 3a) and exponentially distributed (Figure 3b) around the center of the circle. In Figure 3b the distance from the center is exponentially distributed and the angle is uniformly distributed; the standard deviation is equal to the radius of the circle. It is difficult to verify visually which distribution is close to normal. Figure 4 shows the same points remapped (by inverting the algorithm to generate a normal distribution from a uniform one) to be uniformly distributed within the unit circle if the original distribution is normal. One can see that the first distribution indeed passes this visual test.

Stochastic Processes

A *stochastic process* is any process that generates random variables. Therefore, the model for any phenomenon which includes random elements must include the simulation of a stochastic process. Fournier and Fussell called *stochastic modeling* the group of techniques which involve blending ordinary models and stochastic processes [Four82].

The techniques described earlier in this paper to simulate the position of falling raindrops or the positions of trees in a forest are simulations of stochastic processes. Some properties of stochastic processes are especially important in sim-

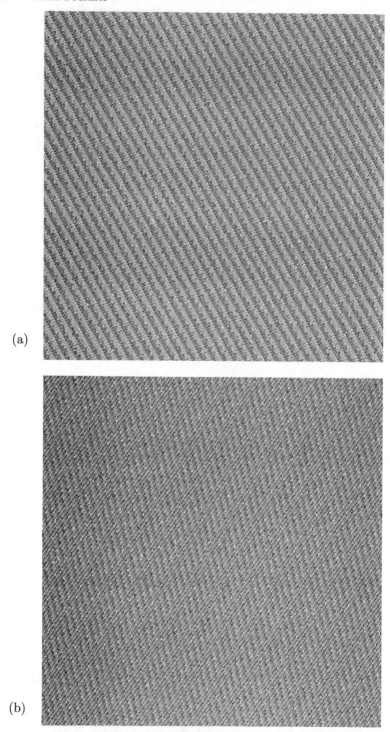

Figure 2. 'Gaussian' distributions with forced seeds (a) count; (b) multiplied; (c) anded.

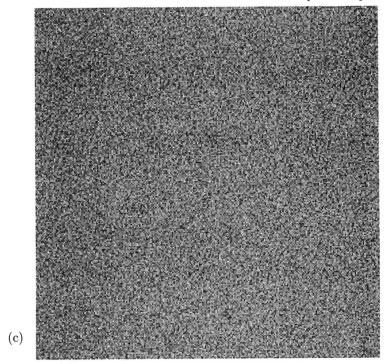

(c)

Figure 2. (*Continued*).

ulation. One is *stationarity*. It means that the characteristics of the process
are independent of the time at which they are sampled (or the space, for stationarity in space). The advantage of a stationary process is that it can be
simulated without worrying about the origin in time (or space). As stationarity
is to translation, *isotropy* is to rotation. A process is isotropic if its statistics
are invariant under rotation of the coordinate system. This is actually hard to
achieve in computer-generated processes, because the numbers are often tied to
the coordinate system and computed on a regular grid. It is easy to have the
statistics stationary, but to have them strictly isotropic requires paying close
attention to the real distances between neighbouring grid points.

Also important is the *Markov* property. A process is a Markov (or Markovian)
process if its state at a given time is enough to determine completely its distribution at later times. It is an important property for computations, because in
a time computation it means that only the current state (that is, the current
frame in animation) is needed to compute the following ones. It is then not
necessary to carry around large amounts of information. In space this means
that extrapolation or subdivision can be done with only boundary information,
again limiting the amount of information to be carried at each step.

The last important property is *ergodicity*. A process is ergodic if its statistics
are identical for all realizations of the process. There are more formal ways to
define ergodicity, but taking for example a time phenomenon like the distribution

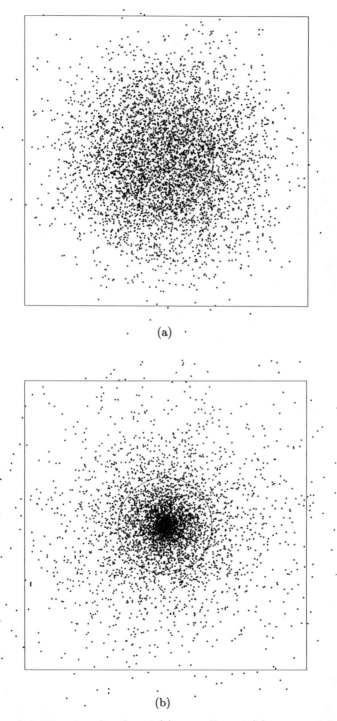

(a)

(b)

Figure 3. 5,000 points distributed (a) normally and (b) exponentially.

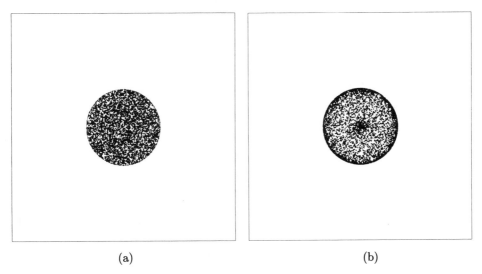

(a)   (b)

Figure 4. Same as in Figure 3, remapped within the unit circle. (a) Gaussian; (b) exponential.

of height of waves through space and time, ergodicity means that if we determine experimentally the statistics from a sea taken at an instant in time, we get the same results as if we determine the statistics through an average in time.

Covariance and Autocovariance

If we have two random variables X_1 and X_2, their *covariance* $\text{Cov}[X_1, X_2]$ is given by

$$\text{Cov}[X_1, X_2] = \mathbf{E}[X_1 X_2] - \mathbf{E}[X_1]\mathbf{E}[X_2] = \mathbf{E}[(X_1 - \mathbf{E}[X_1])(X_2 - \mathbf{E}[X_2])]$$

The *correlation coefficient* is the covariance relative to the variance of the two variables

$$\rho(X_1, X_2) = \frac{\text{Cov}[X_1, X_2]}{\sigma[X_1]\sigma[X_2]}$$

where $\sigma[X]$ is the standard deviation of the variable X. The two random variables are *uncorrelated* if either their covariance or their correlation is zero. Note that $\text{Cov}[X, X] = \text{Var}[X] = \sigma^2[X]$. You can easily show that if the two variables are uncorrelated then

$$\text{Var}[X_1 + X_2] = \text{Var}[X_1] + \text{Var}[X_2]$$

To simplify notation we consider a stochastic process with one parameter, t, denoted by $X(t)$. If we consider the process at two values of the parameter,

t_1 and t_2, we have two random variables; their covariance is now, in general, a function of t_1 and t_2 called the *autocovariance*

$$\text{Cov}[X(t_1), X(t_2)] = \mathbf{E}[X(t_1)X(t_2)] - \mathbf{E}[X(t_1)]\mathbf{E}[X(t_2)]$$
$$= \mathbf{E}[(X(t_1) - \mathbf{E}[X(t_1)])(X(t_2) - \mathbf{E}[X(t_2)])]$$

The *autocorrelation function* (it is too bad that the autocorrelation is not in general to the correlation what the autocovariance is to the variance) is given by

$$R(t_1, t_2) = \mathbf{E}[X(t_1)X(t_2)]$$

Autocovariance is an essential characteristic of a stochastic process and plays a central role in its appearance and synthesis. The relationship between the autocovariance and autocorrelation is obvious

$$\text{Cov}[X(t_1), X(t_2)] = R(t_1, t_2) - \mathbf{E}[X(t_1)]\mathbf{E}[X(t_2)]$$

If the process is stationary, $\mathbf{E}[X(t_1)] = \mathbf{E}[X(t_2)]$, and $R()$ is only a function of $\tau = t_2 - t_1$ (often called the *lag*, since it is the time distance between the variables). Intuitively, the autocorrelation describes the relationship between the process and a copy of itself with a time lag τ. For a totally uncorrelated process, such as *white noise*, the autocorrelation is everywhere zero, except when $\tau = 0$. When $\tau = 0$, the autocorrelation is one (if the process has been normalized to a variance of one, which is often the case). So the autocorrelation is a Dirac $\delta(0)$ function. At the other extreme, for a constant process $R(\tau) = 1$ for all τ.

For understanding the role of the autocorrelation function, as well as for its relevance to synthesis, the *Wiener-Khintchine* relation between the autocorrelaton function and the *power spectrum* of the process is very important. The power spectrum $S(\omega)$ is the square of the Fourier transform of the signal

$$S(\omega) = |F(\omega)|^2$$

where
$$F(\omega) = \int_{-\infty}^{\infty} X(t)\exp(-2\pi i \omega t)dt$$

For a physical signal, the power spectrum can be interpreted as the distribution of the power density as a function of the frequency ω.

The Wiener-Khintchine relation says that the autocorrelation function and the power spectrum are Fourier transform pairs

$$S(\omega) = \int_{-\infty}^{\infty} R(\tau)\exp(-2\pi i \omega \tau)d\tau$$

Therefore this ties together modeling a signal through its statistics (mainly the autocorrelation) and *spectral modeling*, that is, modeling its power spectrum or its frequency spectrum.

EXAMPLE: BROWNIAN MOTION

A simple example of Brownian motion is the simulation of the Brownian motion of a molecule in three-dimensional space. A mathematical model for Brownian motion was developed by N. Wiener and is usually called the *Wiener process*. The position of the molecule is $[P(t)] = [X(t), Y(t), Z(t)]$ at time t. For each increment of time Δt, the position at $t + \Delta t$ is given by

$$X(t + \Delta t) = X(t) + \overline{V}\sqrt{\Delta t} \times N(0, 1)$$

$$Y(t + \Delta t) = Y(t) + \overline{V}\sqrt{\Delta t} \times N(0, 1)$$

$$Z(t + \Delta t) = Z(t) + \overline{V}\sqrt{\Delta t} \times N(0, 1)$$

where $N(0, 1)$ is a normally distributed random variable with mean 0 and variance 1, and where $\overline{V}$ is the mean speed of the particle in the X, Y and Z directions (here assumed to be the same). Note that in this formulation the variance on the position is

$$\sigma^2 = 3 \times \overline{V}^2 \Delta t$$

It is easy to see that this process is stationary and Markovian.

In spite of its simplicity, it is an interesting case. The process is continuous, and the preceding formulae apply for any Δt, no matter how large. Having computed the molecule positions for t and $t + \Delta t$, if it becomes necessary to compute the position at $t + \Delta' t$, where $\Delta' t = k \times \Delta t$, $0 \leq k \leq 1$, then the expected value knowing these positions is

$$[P(t + \Delta' t)] = (1 - k)[P(t)] + k[P(t + \Delta t)]$$

and the variance at the midpoint ($k = 1/2$) is

$$\sigma'^2 = \frac{1}{2}\sigma^2$$

Textures and Randomness

A texture is simply a function of space, $F(x, y)$ in two dimensions, or $F(x, y, z)$ in three dimensions. The function can have a scalar value (a single value) or a vector value, for example a three-dimensional color vector. In most applications the coordinates x, y or x, y, z are discrete coordinates (in so-called *texture space*); we can look at the texture as a discrete array of values indexed by the coordinates.

The use of textures in computer graphics in general, and in the modeling of natural phenomena in particular, has two aspects: the modeling of textures, and their application, the latter usually known as *texture mapping*. Since we are mainly discussing modeling, we refer you to an excellent survey paper by Heckbert [Heck86] and his paper in this volume on the topic of texture filtering and texture mapping [Heck91].

When textures are used to model natural phenomena, the range of techniques used for other kinds of objects also applies to them. In this particular case, digitized pictures of real objects, or real textures, are easy to use as a source of texture, since both they and the texture are two-dimensional images. This is, of course, just an easier version of an empirical model. The ubiquitous mandrill is a classic example of this technique.

Procedurally generated textures are also very useful. Their main advantages are that they can be generated at controllable levels of detail, they can be *band-limited* to avoid aliasing problems, and they usually require few parameters. The papers by Perlin [Perl85], Peachey [Peac85], Norton et al. [Nort82], Gardner [Gard85], Perlin and Hoffert [Perl89], Lewis [Lewi89], and Kajiya and Kay [Kaji89] should be consulted for more details.

Perlin's Noise and Turbulence Functions

In his aforementioned 1985 SIGGRAPH paper, Perlin introduced two functions to generate random textures that are probably the most 'borrowed' pieces of code in computer graphics. The first one is a noise function. `Noise()` maps 3D points to a scalar value; the main characteristics of the pseudorandom values produced are that they are

> invariant under translation and rotation (in other words isotropic and stationary);
>
> narrowly limited within a band in frequency (in terms of spatial frequencies, this means that the objects produced have a narrow range of sizes).

These properties are important for `Noise()` to be used as a stochastic 'primitive', since various scaled and weighted versions of it can then be used to 'construct' more complex stochastic primitives. To achieve a reasonable approximation of the ideal noise function, Perlin suggested the following algorithm:

> to each point (i, j, k) on the integer lattice, associate a pseudorandom value d and a gradient (a, b, c);
>
> if a given point (x, y, z) is such that the coordinates are all integers, return `Noise` $(x, y, z) = d(x, y, z)$;
>
> if (x, y, z) is not on the lattice, interpolate the neighbouring ds.

The random values associated with lattice points can be precomputed and stored in a hash table which is addressed by the point integer coordinates taken with a suitable modulo to make the table finite (and not too large). It is important to note that the samples produced are not strictly isotropic, since the basic frequency in the diagonal direction is lower than in the direction of the grid axes, and they are not very well band-limited (see [Lewi89] for a sample spectrum).

A turbulence function is generated from `Noise()` by adding several noise terms, each scaled by a term proportional to the inverse of their main frequency. One thus obtains a fast approximation of a $1/f$ signal by adding several noise terms of frequency doubled and amplitude halved (seven in the code given below:

the number of terms should be related to the limit in spatial frequency imposed by the pixels).

The following code shows the implementation of these concepts within a ray tracer, *optik*, written at the University of Toronto and the University of British Columbia by John Amanatides, Andrew Woo, Pierre Poulin, John Buchanan, and a few others. This particular code is mostly the work of John Amanatides. The texture Marble uses a turbulence function (built-in) and adds a sine wave for the main signal.

```
*  ----------------------------------- Module Macros ------------ */

#define HASH_3D(a,b,c)  (hashTable[hashTable[hashTable[(a) & 0xfff] ^
                        ((b) & 0xfff)] ^ ((c) & 0xfff)])
#define SCURVE(a)       ((a)*(a)*(3.-2.*(a)))

/* ---------------------------------- Imported Variables -------- */
/*
 * Initialize table of random numbers.  All random
 * calls loop through this array for random numbers.
 */
void InitTextureTables()
        {
        register int i, j;

        int temp;
        hashTable= (short int *) GetMem(4096*sizeof(short int));
        for(i=0;i<4096;i++)
                hashTable[i]= i;
        for(i=4095;i > 0;i--)
                {
                j= Random()*(i-1);
                temp= hashTable[i];
                hashTable[i]= hashTable[j];
                hashTable[j]= temp;
                }

        randTable= (double *) GetMem(259*sizeof(double));
        for(i=0;i<259;i++)
                randTable[i]= Random()*2. -1.;
        Init_D_Machine();
        }

/*
 * Noise Mapping: Solid texture.
 */

double Noise(point)
        Point3D point;
        {
        register int i;
        int ix, iy, iz;
        int jx, jy, jz;
        int hash;
        double fraction;
        double sx, sy, sz;
```

```
double tx, ty, tz;
double sum;
double weight;

/*
 */

ix= point.x;
if(point.x < 0.) ix--;
iy= point.y;
if(point.y < 0.) iy--;
iz= point.z;
if(point.z < 0.) iz--;

fraction= point.x - ix;
sx= SCURVE(fraction);
fraction= point.y - iy;
sy= SCURVE(fraction);
fraction= point.z - iz;
sz= SCURVE(fraction);

tx= 1. - sx;
ty= 1. - sy;
tz= 1. - sz;

sum= 0.;
for (i=0; i<8; i++)
        {
        switch(i) {
                case 0:
                        weight= tx*ty*tz;
                        jx= ix;
                        jy= iy;
                        jz= iz;
                        break;
                case 1:
                        weight= sx*ty*tz;
                        jx= ix+1;
                        jy= iy;
                        jz= iz;
                        break;
                case 2:
                        weight= tx*sy*tz;
                        jx= ix;
                        jy= iy+1;
                        jz= iz;
                        break;
                case 3:
                        weight= sx*sy*tz;
                        jx= ix+1;
                        jy= iy+1;
                        jz= iz;
                        break;
                case 4:
                        weight= tx*ty*sz;
                        jx= ix;
                        jy= iy;
```

```
                            jz= iz+1;
                            break;
                    case 5:
                            weight= sx*ty*sz;
                            jx= ix+1;
                          ( jy= iy;
                            jz= iz+1;
                            break;
                    case 6:
                            weight= tx*sy*sz;
                            jx= ix;
                            jy= iy+1;
                            jz= iz+1;
                            break;
                    case 7:
                            weight= sx*sy*sz;
                            jx= ix+1;
                            jy= iy+1;
                            jz= iz+1;
                            break;
                    }

            hash= HASH_3D(jx, jy, jz) & 255;
            sum += weight*(randTable[hash]*.5+randTable[hash+1]*(point.x-jx)
                    + randTable[hash+2]*(point.y-jy)
                    + randTable[hash+3]*(point.z-jz));
            }

        sum += .5;
        if (sum > 1.0) sum = 1.0;
        if (sum < 0.0) sum = 0.0;
        return(sum);
        }
/*
 * Marble mapping: Solid texture.
 */

Colour Marble(point, surfCol)
        Point3D point;  /* intersection point */
        Colour surfCol; /* surface rgb colour if no texturing */
        {
        Point3D v;      /* point x f */
        double s;       /* noise factor component */
        double t;       /* simulate a 1/f signal */
        double f;       /* frequency */
        register int i; /* index variable */

        s = t= 0.;
        f = 1.;

        /*
         * Simulating a 1/f signal over space (see Perlin's
         * paper [Perl89, p. 292]) by powers of 2 in frequency.
         */
        for(i= 0; i < 7; i++)
                {
```

```
        v.x= point.x * f;
        v.y= point.y * f;
        v.z= point.z * f;
        s= Noise(v) - .5;
        t += FABS(s)/f;
        f= 2.*f;
        }

/*
 * The marble look is supposed to come from turbulent forces
 * which create deformations before the layers solidify.
 * Unperturbed layers can be modeled by a sine wave.   Then
 * a frequency component is added to include the rgb value.
 */
t= sin(t*8. + 7.*point.z);
t= (t+1.)/2.;
f= t*t*t*t;
f *= f; f *= f; f *= f;

/* Combining marble with original rgb value */
surfCol.red= (f + (1.-f)*surfCol.red)*t;
surfCol.green= (f + (1.-f)*surfCol.green)*t;
surfCol.blue= (f + (1.-f)*surfCol.blue)*t;

return(surfCol);
}
```

Plate 2 shows an example of the Marble texture thus generated.

MA AND GAGALOWICZ' PARAMETERIZED TEXTURES

An important and powerful variation of the empirical approach consists in using
a parameterized texture model, and applying a fitting procedure to simulate
a given real texture with some minimum error criteria.   This technique was
developed by Ma and Gagalowicz [Ma85]. They first assume (from experimental
evidence about our ability to discriminate textures) that a small set of gray
levels is enough.   Then they assume that for most textures the domain where
the various statistics have to be approximated is rather small (in terms of field
of vision, corresponding to a few degrees of solid angle). N is the total number
of pixels in the source texture, k is one of the grey scale values, Δ is a distance,
N_Δ is the number of pixels at that distance, and $\delta()$ is the Kronecker delta. The
statistics they have used in various models are the histogram

$$H(k) = \frac{1}{N} \sum_{\text{all } ij \text{ pairs}} \delta(V_{ij} - k)$$

the autocovariance within a distance Δ

$$R(\Delta) = \frac{1}{N_\Delta} \sum_{\text{all } ij \text{ pairs}} \frac{(V_{ij} - \overline{V})(V_{ij\Delta} - \overline{V})}{\text{Var}(V_{ij})}$$

and the third order moment

$$M_3(\Delta_1, \Delta_2) = \frac{1}{N_{\Delta_1 \Delta_2}} \sum_{\text{all } ij \text{ pairs}} \frac{(V_{ij} - \overline{V})(V_{ij\Delta_1} - \overline{V})(V_{ij\Delta_2} - \overline{V})}{\text{Var}(V_{ij})^{\frac{3}{2}}}$$

$\overline{V}$ is the mean defined as

$$\overline{V} = \frac{1}{N} \sum_{\text{all } ij \text{ pairs}} V_{ij}$$

and $\text{Var}(V_{ij})$ is the variance

$$\text{Var}(V_{ij}) = \frac{1}{N} \sum_{\text{all } ij \text{ pairs}} (V_{ij} - \overline{V})^2$$

Note that these are only estimates of the right distribution; true statisticians would state them differently. Once those statistics are computed for a given texture, we generate white noise with the required histogram and then iteratively modify each pixel to minimize the error

$$\text{Err} = ||S - S_{Tx}||^2 - \alpha\, ||H - H_{Tx}||^2$$

where S is one of the statistics above for the generated texture (autocorrelation, second and/or third moment depending on the model), S_{Tx} is the corresponding statistic for the source texture, H and H_{Tx} are the histograms, and α is a multiplier (usually high, to more heavily weight the histogram). The models are very successful for most textures without strong macroscopic features. The main drawback is that the number of parameters is rather large (from 300 to 2000, depending on the model).

Fractal Models

The term and most of the concepts and methods of *fractals* were introduced by Benoit Mandelbrot during the last 20 years. Lately there has been a plethora of books and articles on the subject, but Mandelbrot's *The Fractal Geometry of Nature* [Mand82a], Peitgen and Richter's *The Beauty of Fractals* [Peit86], and Peitgen and Saupe's *The Science of Fractal Images* [Peit88] are the most useful.

Some natural objects seem to have details within details, and so on to (apparently) infinity. Another way to look at the phenomenon is to consider most classical mathematical functions. The definition of the derivatives of a function involves taking the limit of the tangent to the curve or surface representing the function. If we try this process with a curve representing a *coastline*, for instance, the 'limit' does not seem to go anywhere in particular. From such observations, and from the existence of rigorously defined mathematical objects that shared this paradoxical property, Mandelbrot [Mand82a] introduced the concept of *fractals*, and in so doing he introduced a whole new way to look at some mathematical objects and some natural phenomena that can be described by these objects.

To put it in ordinary terms, a fractal is an object with more details than seem possible for the dimension of the object. In fact, a new concept of dimension can be used for fractals, which is different from the dimension normally defined for them in classical geometry (see [Voss86] for more details on the definition and computation of fractal dimension). It is interesting to note that in many published methods the dimension of the generated surface is neither established nor discussed.

The universe of fractals is by now very large. But, for our purposes here, it can be divided into deterministic fractals, such as Koch curves and stochastic fractals, where the fractal properties apply to the various characteristics of random variables. We only discuss one such stochastic fractal process, *fractional Brownian motion* (fBm). It was introduced by Mandelbrot and Van Ness [Mand68] as a generalization of Brownian motion, which itself has fractal properties. It is relevant here because as a first approximation it is a useful model for terrain. How can we show this? There are at least three possible ways, and they illustrate the different kinds of models. We can compute samples of fBm and display them rendered to simulate terrain color and shading, and check visually if they are satisfactory. We can measure the statistical properties of real terrain and see if they correspond to fBm characteristics. The third way is to build a model for the creation of the terrain, which leads to a description of the surface in terms of fBm. For the first way, we will let you be the judge. For the second one, the results are mixed at best. Terrain certainly has fractal characteristics, but not through the whole measurable range. This is not very surprising. There are many forces and phenomena at work in the shaping of terrain, from plate tectonics to rainfall. It is too much to ask that one single mathematical process model the sum of their effects. As for the third one, there are no satisfactory models to date, for exactly the reasons just mentioned: there are too many factors at work. An interesting model, however, was given by Mandelbrot as a sum of randomly distributed faults.

There are various algorithms to compute approximations to fBm. One class, introduced by Voss [Voss86], consists in generating white noise and filtering it so the result has the frequency distribution characteristic of fBm. The other, used by Fournier et al. [Four82], uses *recursive subdivision* to successively add details with the required distribution (see Figure 5).

Fractal processes have been used not only to model terrain, but also to model clouds [Kaji84; Voss86], water, texture for trees, fire, etc. This has been done without first verifying by analysis if the statistics of the natural objects to be modeled are those of a fractal object.[†]

The main advantage of fBm as a model of terrain is a remarkable compactness of representation. Depending on how much deterministic data is included, the

---

[†]Also in the class of fractals are objects such as *Julia sets* and *Mandelbrot sets*, which model nothing but themselves.

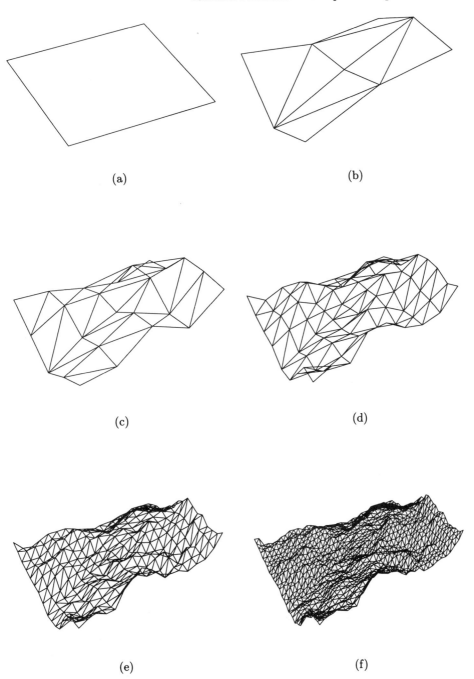

Figure 5. Generating fBm by recursive subdivision. (a) Original polygon; (b) one subdivision; (c) two subdivisions; (d) three subdivisions; (e) four subdivisions; (f) five subdivisions.

data base can be from two numbers to a few hundred, to represent terrain that ultimately contains thousands or million of polygons. The second big advantage, due to its fractal nature, is that unlimited amounts of details can be generated. The disadvantages include the fact that to generate a surface, pure recursive subdivision is not sufficient. This complicates the subdivision algorithms. The second disadvantage is that it has limited flexibility, with basically only one parameter to be adjusted to generate different terrains. As an example of the output of the algorithm, the terrain in Plate 3 was generated with recursive subdivision in 20 minutes on a 1 MIPS machine. Another example is Plate 2, where fractal interpolation was used to generate the terrain over which the waves roll [Four86a, Four86b].

STOCHASTIC INTERPOLATION TO APPROXIMATE FBM

There are numerous methods published for stochastic subdivisions. The criteria to evaluate them depends on what they claim to accomplish and their intended use. The techniques to approximate specifically fractional Brownian motion [Four82; Voss86] are well described. The paper by Fournier et al. [Four82] [†] puts their methods squarely into the context of computer graphics, and emphasizes the problems of integrating the generation of approximations to fBm with traditional graphics modeling.

The methods used in this paper are all based on *stochastic interpolation*, that is, an interpolation method where stochastic variables are used to approximate samples of a known stochastic process. They use recursive subdivision, which has the advantage of being a known and common method in computer graphics, especially in conjunction with parametric surfaces. Since, in the case of fBm, the expected position of the midpoint between two existing sample points is the arithmetic mean of these points, the only problem is to determine the variance. But the influence of scale (and therefore of level of subdivision) on the variance is given directly by the definition of fBm. As a function of one variable, this directly yields an acceptable algorithm to generate fBm. Note that it has most of the required properties: it is adaptive, it is fast, and the cost is proportional to the number of sample points actually generated. When applied to the two-variable case, that is, surfaces, we must deal with the non-Markovian properties of fBm. Straight recursive subdivision, especially on triangles (see pattern in Figure 6), has been used extensively. The obvious attraction is that most hardware/firmware/software rendering systems deal efficiently with triangles. The possible artefacts created by the nonstationarity of the samples generated (usually seen as 'creases', that is, boundaries where the slope changes are higher than in the neighbourhood) can be controlled. The easiest way to do this is to reduce the scale factor applied to the displacement value obtained. This is, however, conceptually unsatisfactory. In the same paper an alternate technique

---

[†] This was originally two distinct papers submitted to SIGGRAPH 80 by Carpenter and Fournier/Fussell, then merged to appear in *CACM*.

using interwoven quadrilateral subdivision is proposed and illustrated. In this scheme, the subdivision proceeds by using information not only from the boundaries but from neighbours across it; the distribution information is spread in a non-Markovian fashion (see Figure 7). Both the pictures and some analysis [Four80] show that it is an effective scheme. It also has the important advantage of fitting well with the use of bivariate parametric surfaces as geometric models.

An important concern with this scheme is the possibility that when only a small section of the object is seen a much larger number of sample points has to be computed. Fournier [Four80] shows that this is not the case, and that the number of external sample points to be computed is bounded by a constant times the number of sample points seen.

PROBLEMS AND FURTHER DEVELOPMENTS

Mandelbrot [Mand82b] stated some objections and criticisms of the method(s) used in the previously discussed paper by Fournier [Four82]. The most serious (and visible) ones have to do with the appearance of *creases*, slope discontinuities which are made much more visible by the shading of the surfaces. As pointed out above, since 2D fBm is non-Markovian we cannot hope to produce too good an approximation of it by 'context-free' recursive subdivision. This is why the 'meshed' subdivision using quadrilaterals was proposed and used. Various authors have subsequently addressed problems in this area, not always trying to solve the real problem.

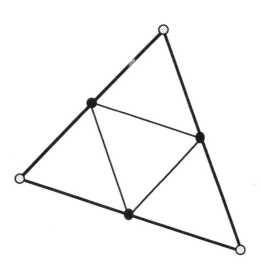

○ Points of generation i

● Points of generation i+1

Figure 6. Triangular recursive subdivision.

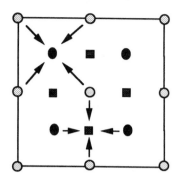

○   Points of generation i

●   Points of generation i+1, computed from corners

■   Points of generation i+1 , computed from sides

Figure 7. Quadrilateral recursive subdivision.

An important point, and the reason why we called the technique stochastic 'interpolation', is that one of the constraints is to not modify previously computed points at later stages of the subdivision. An important but under-studied question is how to make sure that intermediate stages of the recursions are truly representative of the fully detailed surface (as judged by the visible statistical properties of the shaded image).

Methods recently proposed by Voss [Peit88], Saupe [Peit88], and Musgrave et al. [Musg89] do not respect that constraint, although they try to be more flexible or more faithful to the process simulated (generally fBm). The latter is especially interesting as it uses *noise synthesis* in the spatial domain with Perlin-type noise functions. An interesting work by Szeliski and Terzopoulos [Szel89] describes how to use constrained splines to fit an initially discrete set of points, and then use the energy function used for minimization to derive the probability distribution of the stochastic element. This, when properly implemented, generates *constrained fractal* surfaces and seems a very useful modeling tool. Depending on the modalities of implementation, one can obtain varying levels of detail through a multigrid approach, and true interpolation by sacrificing some of the data-fitting aspects of the method.

To go back to stochastic interpolation proper, a paper by Miller [Mill86] proposes a solution which can be interpreted as smoothing over the already generated values with a small filter. Two papers [Pipe84; Four85] describe 'cheap' ways to implement stochastic subdivision and to render the resulting data in a 'near-real-time' environment. But the 'real' answer is *generalized stochastic subdivision* by Lewis, described in a later section of this paper.

SAMPLE CODE: FRACTIONAL BROWNIAN MOTION IN 3D

As mentioned previously, fBm is non-Markovian in spaces of even dimension, but Markovian in spaces of odd dimension. In 3D, therefore, it is easier to generate approximations to fBm by recursive subdivision. The following C-code shows an example of generation of 3D fBm but includes the flexibility to use meshed subdivision, with weights for neighbours given in a table. Another interesting aspect of the 3D fBm is that we can take time as one of the three dimensions and therefore get an animation of a 2D fBm out of the signal generated. To facilitate the 'looping' of such an animation, the procedure is implemented so that the 'front' and the 'back' of the cube are the same.

```c
#include <stdio.h>
#define TYPES 7
#define SIZE 129
#define MAXLEVEL 7 /* MAXLEVEL is to be log2(SIZE-1) */
/* At the beginning there are eight CORNERS. */
/* Then eight types of points are computed. The first type is CENTER, computed */
/* from the four CORNERS. The next three are FACE CENTERS, computed */
/* from two CENTERS and four CORNERS. There are three kinds of */
/* FACE CENTERS, in order, in the XY plane, in the XZ plane and in the */
/* YZ plane. Last are EDGE CENTERS, computed from two CORNERS and four */
/* FACE CENTERS. There are three kinds of EDGE CENTERS, in order */
/* Z//, X// and Y// */
double fbm [SIZE][SIZE][SIZE];
int start[TYPES][3]={1,1,1,1,1,0,1,0,1,0,1,1,0,0,1,1,0,0,0,1,0};
int neigh [TYPES]={8,6,6,6,6,6,6};
int offset[TYPES][8][3]={1,1,1,1,1,-1,1,-1,1,1,-1,-1,-1,1,1,-1,1,-1,-1,-1,1,
              -1,-1,-1,0,0,1,0,0,-1,1,1,0,1,-1,0,-1,1,0,-1,-1,0,0,0,0,
              0,0,0,0,1,0,0,-1,0,1,0,1,1,0,-1,-1,0,1,-1,0,-1,0,0,0,0,
              0,0,1,0,0,-1,0,0,0,1,1,0,1,-1,0,-1,1,0,-1,-1,0,0,0,0,0,
              0,0,0,1,0,0,-1,0,-1,0,0,1,0,1,0,0,-1,0,0,0,0,0,0,0,0,
              1,0,0,-1,0,0,0,0,-1,0,0,1,0,1,0,0,-1,0,0,0,0,0,0,0,0,
              0,1,0,0,-1,0,0,0,1,0,0,-1,1,0,0,-1,0,0,0,0,0,0,0,0};
/* The last point in the loops is U-start for each coordinate. */
/* The steps are 2*dist in every case. */
/* The order of the points is important, since some early */
/* data is subsequently used. */
double weight[TYPES][8]= {1.0,1.0,1.0,1.0,1.0,1.0,1.0,1.0,
               1.0,1.0,1.0,1.0,1.0,1.0,0.0,0.0,
               1.0,1.0,1.0,1.0,1.0,1.0,0.0,0.0,
               1.0,1.0,1.0,1.0,1.0,1.0,0.0,0.0,
               1.0,1.0,1.0,1.0,1.0,1.0,0.0,0.0,
               1.0,1.0,1.0,1.0,1.0,1.0,0.0,0.0,
               1.0,1.0,1.0,1.0,1.0,1.0,0.0,0.0};
/* For now, the weights are all one. They should be related to the distance. */
int fudge[3] = { 2514521, 891653, 8765142};
main(argc, argv)
    int argc;
    char *argv[];
{
double h,scale,std,ratio;
```

```
int level,seed,max,clevel,type,i,j,k,dist;
int inseed;
double atof(), gauss(), expect();
int scrseed();
char sum;
char *filename = "fbm3d.out";
char cbuf[100];
char dummy;
FILE *fpframe;
double pow();
/* default values */
h = 0.5;
level = 1;
scale = 80.0; /* to get a range 0-255 */
inseed = 12356719;

    while(argc > 1 && argv[1][0] == '-') {
        switch(argv[1][1]) {
        case 'l':
            level = atoi(argv[2]);
            argc--; argv++;
            break;
        case 'h':
            h = atof(argv[2]);
            argc--; argv++;
            break;
        case 's':
            scale = atof(argv[2]);
            argc--; argv++;
            break;
        case 'f':
            filename = argv[2];
            argc--; argv++;
            break;
        default:
            fprintf(stderr, "unknown arg %c" , argv[1][1]);
            fprintf(stderr, " Known arguments: -l for level, -h for h,
              -s for scale, -i for (in)seed, -f for filename. );
            break;
        }
        argc--; argv++;
    }
if (level < 0 || level >MAXLEVEL) {
   fprintf(stderr, " Level (%d) out of range." ,level);
   exit();
   };
if ( h>1.0 || h<0.0) {
      fprintf(stderr, " h (%f) out of range." ,h);
      exit();
   };
if ( scale< 0.0) {
   fprintf(stderr, " Scale (%f) out of range." ,scale);
   exit();
   };
```

```
/* Determine max. */
max = 1 << level;
std = scale;
dist = max;
ratio = pow ( 2.0, -h);
/* Compute corners (all eight of them). */
seed = scrseed(0,0,0,inseed,max);
fbm [   0][   0][   0] = gauss(0.0,std,&seed);
seed = scrseed(max,0,0,inseed,max);
fbm [ max][   0][   0] = gauss(0.0,std,&seed);
seed = scrseed(0,max,0,inseed,max);
fbm [   0][ max][   0] = gauss(0.0,std,&seed);
seed = scrseed(0,0,max,inseed,max);
fbm [   0][   0][ max] = gauss(0.0,std,&seed);
seed = scrseed(max,max,0,inseed,max);
fbm [ max][ max][   0] = gauss(0.0,std,&seed);
seed = scrseed(0,max,max,inseed,max);
fbm [   0][ max][ max] = gauss(0.0,std,&seed);
seed = scrseed(max,0,max,inseed,max);
fbm [ max][   0][ max] = gauss(0.0,std,&seed);
seed = scrseed(max,max,max,inseed,max);
fbm [ max][ max][ max] = gauss(0.0,std,&seed);
  /* Compute all others. */
for (clevel=1;clevel<=level;clevel++) {
   std = std * ratio;
   dist = dist / 2;
   for (type=0;type<TYPES;type++) {
       for (i=start[type][0]*dist;i<=max-start[type][0]*dist;i+=2*dist) {
           for (j=start[type][1]*dist;j<=max-start[type][1]*dist;j+=2*dist) {
               for (k=start[type][2]*dist;k<=max-start[type][2]*dist;k+=2*dist) {
                   /* Compute value. */
                   seed = scrseed(i,j,k,inseed,max);
                   fbm [i][j][k]=gauss(expect(type,i,j,k,dist,max),std,&seed);
                   };
               };
           };
       };
   };
/* Write results out to file. */
for (k=0; k<max; k++) {
   /* Open new file. */
   sprintf(cbuf, "%s.%d", filename, k);
   if((fpframe = fopen(cbuf, "w")) == NULL) {
       printf("Cannot create frame file  %s ", cbuf);
       exit();
       };
   for (i=0; i<max; i++) {
       for (j=0; j<max; j++) {
               sum=  fbm[i][j][k];
       /*      printf (" %d %d %d %f ",i,j,k,fbm[i][j][k]);      */
               putc(sum, fpframe);
               };
       };
   fclose(fpframe);
   };
```

```
}
double expect (type,i,j,k,dist,max)
/* Compute expected value. */
int type, i, j, k, dist, max;
{
double exp;
int in, jn, kn, neighbour;
double w, sumw;
exp =0.0;
sumw = 0.0;
for (neighbour=0;neighbour< neigh[type]; neighbour++) {

    /* If an index is out of range, take the mirror image with negative weight. */
    w = weight[type][neighbour];
    in = i + dist * offset[type][neighbour][0];
    if (in>max || in <0) {
        w = -w;
        in = i - dist * offset[type][neighbour][0];
        };
    jn = j + dist * offset[type][neighbour][1];
    if (jn>max || jn <0) {
        w = -w;
        jn = j - dist * offset[type][neighbour][1];
        };
    kn = k + dist * offset[type][neighbour][2];
    if (kn>max || kn <0) {
        w = -w;
        kn = k - dist * offset[type][neighbour][2];
        };
/* Above, only one of the three indices can be out of range (Check!). */
    exp = exp + fbm[in][jn][kn]*w;
    sumw = sumw + w;
    };
  return exp/sumw;
}

double gauss ( mean, std, seed )
    /* Note that std is standard deviation, not variance. */
    /* Also seed is pointer, since it returns a new value. */
    double mean, std;
    int *seed;
    {
    /* Add your favourite Gaussian distribution generator here. */
    }
double my_ran (seed)
    int *seed;
    {
    /* Put a function you trust here. */
    double drand48();
    return( drand48());
    }
int scrseed(i,j,k,inseed,max)
int i,j,k,inseed,max;
{
return ( i * fudge[0] + j* fudge[1] + ( k%max )* fudge[2] + inseed );
}
```

Generalized Stochastic Subdivision

Some of the problems of stochastic subdivision (creases, 'bubbling' in animation) were addressed and largely solved by John Lewis [Lewi86, Lewi87]. In Lewis' generalized stochastic subdivision, each new interpolated value is computed by adding noise of known variance to the weighted sum of the current values in a neighbourhood of size $2S$

$$\hat{V}_{t+1/2} = \sum_{k=1-S}^{S} a_k V_{t+k}$$

Note the difference between this and the method used by Fournier et al. [Four82], where the value used is just the average of V_t and V_{t+1}. In other words, $S = 1$ and $a_0 = a_1 = 1/2$. The correct coefficients, a_k, are those which make $\hat{V}_{t+1/2}$ the best estimation of the interpolated value. It can be shown that if the autocorrelation function

$$R(\tau) = \mathbf{E}[V(t)V(t + \tau)]$$

is known, then the a_k can be computed from the relation

$$R\left(m - \frac{1}{2}\right) = \sum_{k=1-S}^{S} a_k R(m - k) \qquad \forall \quad -S \leq m \leq S$$

The computation of the a_k requires a matrix inversion (the above formula is, of course, a shorthand for $2S$ equations with $2S$ unknowns) but only has to be done once for a stationary process. The method permits the approximation of a wide range of processes, Markovian as well as non-Markovian, and even oscillatory. The choice of the correct size of neighbourhood is related to the process to be approximated.

    J.P. Lewis [Lewi89] extended the method to the generation of 'solid noises'. He also introduced a clever *sparse convolution* algorithm to generate approximations to noise of a required spectrum with the addition of relatively few elements. The elements are samples of several uncorrelated Poisson processes at uncorrelated locations. The result of their convolution with a filter is a noise with essentially the spectrum of the filter.

Spectral Synthesis

In some applications it is advantageous to generate the required distribution directly from the Fourier spectrum, and then to apply an inverse Fourier transform to obtain the spatial or temporal signal. This is how, as mentioned above, Voss generated samples of fBm.

    Mastin et al. [Mast87] used this approach to generate models of deep waves on fully developed wind seas. The spectrum is due to Pierson and Moskowitz and is an empirical model based on actual wave records. The starting point is white noise, and forward and inverse FFT were used. The resulting model is quite realistic and pleasing, but inherent to this method is the difficulty in animating the waves obtained. The animation techniques used and suggested in this paper consist in shifting different frequencies at different speeds, either arbitrarily or depending on a physical model for the speed of different frequencies. The problem here is that the frequency components in the Fourier domain do not correspond directly to individual waves, since the waves are far from being narrow-band signals. Therefore, in time the motion actually destroys the characteristic shape of the wave, assuming it was even there from the beginning.

Shinya [Shin90] used a similar method to generate wind fields. Even though at first glance the wind field has to be in four dimensions (3 space plus time), some observations help reduce it to two for most purposes. One is the so-called Taylor hypothesis, whereby the turbulence travels in the mean direction of the wind. This means that effectively one space dimension (say X) is also the time dimension. The other factor is that in most applications altitude can be ignored (note that there are formulas giving the wind speed as a function of the altitude and the ground speed). Applying this, Shinya obtained convincing animations of rice fields, grass, and trees under the influence of wind.

Stochastic Methods for Intensity Fluctuations

Wolfgang Krueger presented an interesting and useful method to simulate the intensity fluctuations caused by light scattering on specular surfaces [Krue88]. The goal is to extract from scattering theory the main moments of the distribution of the reflected light, that is the mean value, the variance, and the autocorrelation function, and use these values within a standard illumination model to generate realistic images of speckles and glints.

In most models of local illumination (see the book by Hall [Hall88] for more details) the specular term for the reflected intensity is of the form

$$I_{\text{spec}} = DSF$$

where D is the probability density function of the local slope (different laws have been used by Phong, Blinn, etc.), $S \leq 1$ is the term accounting for the self-shadowing of the surface irregularities, and F is the Fresnel coefficient (expressing the fraction of light reflected as a function of the geometry of illumination and the wavelength of the incident light; the latter is often ignored).

The important point is that this expression only gives the mean value of the reflected intensity. The variance of the scattered intensity, σ_I^2, is computed from the number N_{eff} of effectively contributing facets in a macrofacet model and is given by

$$\sigma_I^2 = \frac{1}{N_{\text{eff}}}$$

In turn, N_{eff} is computed as

$$N_{\text{eff}} = NDS$$

N is the number of facets covering the visible part of the surface. In practice, N is assigned arbitrarily for a qualitative evaluation of the model. Knowing σ_I^2, the task is to determine I_{fluc}, the specular intensity with the required variance. Krueger shows that one reasonable model gives

$$\Gamma\left(\alpha, \frac{\alpha I_{\text{fluc}}}{I_{\text{spec}}}\right) = RN$$

where $\alpha = 1/\sigma_I^2$, $\Gamma(\alpha, \beta)$ is the incomplete gamma function, and RN is a uniformly distributed random variable in $(0,1)$. The problem is then to invert this distribution, that is, to compute an I_{fluc} given a sample RN. There are three cases when this is straightforward:

when $\sigma_I^2 << 1$, which corresponds to glints on water or snow, then

$$I_{\text{fluc}} = I_{\text{spec}}\left(1 + 2\pi\sigma_I^2\right)^{0.5}(RN - 0.5)$$

when $\sigma_I^2 = 1$, which corresponds to a very noisy appearance, then

$$I_{\text{fluc}} = -I_{\text{spec}}\ln(RN)$$

when $\sigma_I^2 >> 1$, which corresponds to rather smooth fluctuations in specular reflection, then

$$I_{\text{fluc}} = I_{\text{spec}}\, \sigma_I^2\, RN^{\sigma_I^2}$$

For a correct model the autocorrelation should also be known. The autocorrelation of the scattered intensity at a given point P_i and a given time $t_i I_s(P_i, t_i)$ is written $C_s(P_1, t_1; P_2, t_2)$. Using the *random phase screen* (RPS) model of light scattering, and ignoring interference and diffraction, one approximates the autocorrelation of the scattered intensity by

$$C_s(P_1, t_1; P_2, t_2) = \text{perspective projection of } \left(\frac{C_{\text{facet}}(P_1, t_1; P_2, t_2)}{\sigma_H^2}\right)$$

where σ_H^2 is the mean height deviation of the surface, and $C_{\text{facet}}(P_1, t_1; P_2, t_2)$ is the autocorrelation of the height deviation. This latter function depends on the phenomenon to be modeled. In general, it can be expressed as a product of the spatial correlation and the time correlation

$$C_{\text{facet}}(P_1, t_1; P_2, t_2) = C_{\text{space}}(P_1, P_2) \times C_{\text{time}}(t_1, t_2)$$

Krueger gives as an example for a rippled water surface

$$C_{\text{space}}(P_1, P_2) = \sigma_H^2 \times \left(1 - \frac{|P_1, P_2|^2}{\tau_{space}^2}\right)$$

when $|P_1, P_2|^2 \leq \tau_{space}$ and 0 otherwise. τ_{space} is a correlation length and is related to σ_H and the mean slope m by

$$m = \sqrt{2}\, \frac{\sigma_H}{\tau_{space}}$$

The important difference between this model and the classic Phong/Blinn/Cook/Torrance models is the necessity to take autocorrelation into account, which prevents the shading computation from being strictly local. Techniques derived from Perlin's and Lewis' 3D noise synthesis methods must be used to incorporate this model into traditional rendering systems.

Conclusions and Challenges

In this short survey we have limited ourselves to modeling issues, and we did not touch upon the use of stochastic methods for rendering, such as stochastic sampling and filtering. It should be obvious that stochastic modeling methods are very useful and practical in computer graphics. It is also clear that we have not always paid proper attention to the integration of these models within classic modeling/rendering systems. The important issues of level of details, internal and external consistency have often been neglected in developing algorithms.

Several important specific issues which need further exploration are:

Many techniques require an extensive precomputation of stochastic objects. As scenes and the amount of detail become larger, it is more advantageous to compute objects 'on demand' and at a specified (varying) scale.

Stochastic textures, especially 3D ones, are very useful. The filtering of these textures, however, is difficult but necessary. Better and more efficient techniques must be developed.

To reach the previous goal of more efficient filtering techniques, one possible tool is the use of random processes that can be preintegrated, or can be expressed as the linear combination of elementary terms (basis functions). This allows the use of techniques similar to summed-area tables or NIL maps.

Many stochastic techniques, and indeed many modeling/rendering techniques, have not been tested in animation. It is one thing to generate an acceptable still picture; it is quite another to generate a consistent series of frames in an animation. If internal and external consistency is missing, the animation is fatally flawed. More testing will weed out many heretofore reputable algorithms.

As shown in the previous section, it is easier to compute the distribution of the reflected light than to compute the distribution of surface normals and then compute the reflected light. The general idea is to push the appearance of the stochastic elements as high in the display pipeline as possible, to lower the number of items flowing through the display pipeline. There is a tradeoff, however, between that goal and making the pipeline itself uniform. The parameters of that tradeoff must be explored.

REFERENCES

[Four80]
Fournier, A., Stochastic modelling in computer graphics, Ph.D. Dissertation, University of Texas at Dallas, 1980.

[Four82]
Fournier, A., Fussell, D. and Carpenter, L., Computer rendering of stochastic models, *CACM*, Vol. 25, No. 6, pp. 371–384, 1982.

[Four85]
Fournier, A. and Milligan, T., Frame buffer algorithms for stochastic models, *IEEE Comput. Graph. and Appl.*, Vol. 5, No. 10, pp. 40–46, October 1985.

[Four86a]
Fournier, A., and Grindal, D.A., The stochastic modelling of trees, in *Proc. Graphics Interface '86*, Vancouver, B.C., Canada, pp. 164–172, May 1986.

[Four86b]
Fournier, A., and Reeves, W.T., A simple model of ocean waves, *Comput. Graph.*, Vol. 20, pp. 75–84, August 1986 (SIGGRAPH 86).

[Fras76]
Fraser, D.A.S., *Probability and statistics: Theory and applications*, Boston, MA: Duxbury Press, 1976.

[Gard85]
Gardner, G.Y., Visual simulation of clouds, *Comput. Graph.*, Vol. 19, pp. 297–303, July 1985 (SIGGRAPH 85).

[Hall88]
Hall, R., *Illumination and Color in Computer Generated Imagery*, New York: Springer-Verlag, 1988.

[Heck86]
Heckbert, P.S., Survey of texture mapping, *IEEE Comput. Graph. and Appl.*, Vol. 6, No. 11, pp. 56–67, November 1986.

[Heck91]
Heckbert, P.S., *this volume*, pp. 101—111, 1991.

[Jule62]
Julesz, B., Visual pattern discrimination, *IEEE Trans. Inf. Theory*, Vol. 8, No. 2, pp. 84–92, February 1962.

[Kaji84]
Kajiya, J.T., and Von Herzen, B.P., Ray tracing volume densities, *Comput. Graph.*, Vol. 18, pp. 165–174, July 1984 (SIGGRAPH 84).

[Kaji89]
Kajiya, J.T., and Kay, T.L., Rendering fur with three dimensional textures, *Comput. Graph.*, Vol. 23, pp. 271–280, July 1989 (SIGGRAPH 89).

[Knut81]
Knuth, D.E., *The Art of Computer Programming: Volume 2, Seminumerical Algorithms* (2nd Ed.), Reading, MA: Addison-Wesley Co., 1981.

[Krue88]
Krueger, W., Intensity fluctuations and natural texturing, *Comput. Graph.*, Vol. 22, pp. 213–220, August 1988 (SIGGRAPH 88).

[Lewi86]

Lewis, J. P., Methods for stochastic spectral synthesis, in *Proc. Graphics Interface 86*, Vancouver, pp. 173–179, May 1986.

[Lewi87]

Lewis, J.P., Generalized stochastic subdivision, *ACM TOG*, Vol. 6, pp. 167–190, 1987.

[Lewi89]

Lewis, J.P., Algorithms for solid noise synthesis, *Comput. Graph.*, Vol. 23, pp. 263–270, July 1989 (SIGGRAPH 89).

[Ma85]

Ma, S.D., and Gagalowicz, A., Model driven synthesis of natural textures for 3-D scenes, *Proc. Eurographics 85*, pp. 91–108, Nice, October 1985.

[Mand68]

Mandelbrot, B.B., and Van Ness, J.W., Fractional Brownian motion, fractional noises and applications, *SIAM Rev.*, Vol. 10, No. 4, pp. 422–437, October 1968.

[Mand82a]

Mandelbrot, B.B., *The Fractal Geometry of Nature*, New York: W.H.Freeman, 1982.

[Mand82b]

Mandelbrot, B.B., Comments on computer rendering of fractal stochastic models, *CACM*, Vol. 25, No. 8, pp. 581–583, 1982.

[Mast87]

Mastin, G.A., Watterberg, P.A., and Mareda, J.F., Fourier synthesis of ocean scenes, *IEEE Comput. Graph. and Appl.*, Vol. 7, No. 3, pp. 16–23, March 1987.

[Mill86]

Miller, G.S.P., The definition and rendering of terrain maps, *Comput. Graph.*, Vol. 20, pp. 39–48, August 1986 (SIGGRAPH 86).

[Musg89]

Musgrave, F. K., Kolb, C.E., and Mace, R.S., The synthesis and rendering of eroded fractal terrains, *Comput. Graph.*, Vol. 23, pp. 41–50, July 1989 (SIGGRAPH 89).

[Nort82]

Norton, A., Rockwood, A.P., and Skolmoski, P.T., Clamping: A method of antialiasing textured surfaces by bandwidth limiting in object space, *Comput. Graph.*, Vol. 16, pp. 1–8, July 1982 (SIGGRAPH 82).

[Peac85]

Peachey, D.R., Solid texturing of complex surfaces, *Comput. Graph.*, Vol. 19, pp. 279–286, July 1985 (SIGGRAPH 85).

[Peit86]

Peitgen, H.O., and Richter, P.H., Eds., *The Beauty of Fractals*, Berlin: Springer-Verlag, 1986.

[Peit88]

Peitgen, H.O., and Saupe, D., (Eds), *The Science of Fractal Images*, Berlin: Springer-Verlag, 1988.

[Perl85]
Perlin, K., An image synthetizer, *Comput. Graph.*, Vol. 19, pp. 287–296, July 1985 (SIGGRAPH 85).

[Perl89]
Perlin, K., and Hoffert, E.M., Hypertexture, *Comput. Graph.*, Vol. 23, pp. 253–262, July 1989 (SIGGRAPH 89).

[Pipe84]
Piper, T.S., and Fournier, A., A hardware stochastic interpolator for raster displays, *Comput. Graph.*, Vol. 18, pp. 83–92, July 1984 (SIGGRAPH 84).

[Prat81]
Pratt, W., Faugeras, O., and Gagalowicz, A., Applications of stochastic texture filed models to image processing, *Proc. IEEE 69*, Vol. 5, pp. 542–551, May 1981.

[Shin90]
Shinya, M., Stochastic motion: Motion under the influence of wind, NTT Technical Report, January 1990.

[Smit84]
Smith, A.R., Plants, fractals and formal languages, *Comput. Graph.*, Vol. 18, pp. 1–10, July 1984 (SIGGRAPH 84).

[Szel89]
Szeliski, R., and Terzopoulos, D., From splines to fractals, *Comput. Graph.*, Vol. 23, pp. 51–60, July 1989 (SIGGRAPH 89).

[Voss85]
Voss, R.P., Fractal forgeries, in *Fundamental Algorithms for Computer Graphics*, Earnshaw, R.A., Ed., Heidelberg: Springer-Verlag, 1985.

3 Modeling

Supporting Complexity and Conceptual Design in Modeling Tools

Roy Hall

Abstract

Computer manipulation of complex designs poses problems of: establishing constraints; managing relationships; display intelligibility; movement through large databases to areas of interest; viewing information at a scale and/or level of detail appropriate to the current task; and for any database manipulation, extracting the appropriate display abstraction and providing a natural design abstraction for the manipulation. An approach for addressing these issues is presented. Central to this approach is the notion that geometry or any other presentational abstraction is an artifact generated from a nongeometric representation reflecting decisions made during the design process. A short tutorial is presented, followed by a review of work in progress in the construction of a software architecture to support long-term research with regard to computers in design. Quantifying and managing relationships and constraints are examined in detail.

Introduction

"What remains hard is modeling. The structure inherent in three-dimensional models is difficult for people to grasp and difficult too for user interfaces to reveal and manipulate. Only the determined model three-dimensional objects, and they rarely invent a shape at the computer, but only record a shape so that analysis or manufacturing can proceed. The grand challenges in three-dimensional graphics are to make simple modeling easy and to make complex modeling accessible to far more people."—Robert Sproull (1990)

The birth of computer technology was accompanied by visionary predictions of the future usefulness of this technology in aiding the design process; unfortunately, most of the predictions have not yet come to pass. Early experiments such as Sutherland's sketchpad [Suth63] foretold of the possibilities for CAD. The electronics industry has created tools that aid greatly in circuit design, PC board layout and fabrication, VLSI design, and a variety of other tasks. However, these techniques have not permeated into large scale design problems with significant success.

Computer-aided design tools become useful to the designer only when they offer demonstrable improvement over traditional (current) design methods. Simple design tasks are easily managed with traditional methods. However, the effectiveness of traditional methods has been overwhelmed by the complexity of modern technology. Management, manipulation, and presentation of complex databases are areas most promising in the application of computers to large complex design problems.

Typical properties of large scale design in fields such as architectural, automotive, aircraft, and machine design are:

> The performance requirements for the solution are ill-defined at the start of the process; i.e., the problem is ill-stated.
>
> The database of useful components is huge. Typically, designs make use of many standard parts which are selected from a monumentally large world of manufactured goods.
>
> The final solution is complex in terms of the size of the database; i.e, the number of individual elements in an assembled object may easily reach into millions.
>
> The final solution is complex in terms of the range of scale and detail; i.e., the size of the smallest element compared to the assembled object may easily reach 1:10,000, and 1:100,000 is not uncommon.
>
> The process follows iteration steps between treating relationships at a large scale and details at a very small scale, each providing vital information to the other; i.e., it is both a bottom up and top down process, during which there is often a high degree of ambiguity.
>
> There are a variety of different systems, each with its own symbology, conventions, and performance requirements, that must be integrated into the final design; e.g., structural, electrical, hydraulic, control, human interface.
>
> The final manifestation of the design is a three-dimensional geometric entity; however, it does not follow that the appropriate representation is a three-dimensional geometric database.

These properties of design lead to speculation that the geometry of the final design is a manifestation of nongeometric relationships and decisions, and therefore the underlying representation need not be geometric. In order to address these properties of large scale design, the representation must support:

> 'natural' rapid manipulation and editing, using appropriate display and design abstractions [East85] to create new solution schema;
>
> multiple concurrent solution schema;
>
> display at various levels of detail by filtering the representation through appropriate presentational abstractions;
>
> quick traversal through the representation to specific details and areas of interest;
>
> methods for annotating design decisions through textual notations, constraint specification, parametric construction, etc., which remain accessible and are maintained throughout the design process.

What is Design?

The process of design is little understood; consequently, it is difficult to advance an unambiguous definition.

It is unclear whether there is something universal about the design process that transcends discipline boundaries. Specifically, can a good designer design just about anything, or are design skills specific to a discipline? If the skills and the process are discipline specific, then efforts to treat design generically and to create design tools of a general nature cannot be successful.

THE DESIGN PROCESS

Consider descriptions of design given by Eastman [East85] and Mitchell [Mitc77]. Eastman describes design as: *"the specification of an artifact in sufficient detail so as to guarantee that it is both constructible and can realize pre-defined performance criteria."* In addressing architectural design Mitchell says: *"... it is useful to regard architectural design as a special kind of problem-solving process, and to discuss design within the general theory of problem solving. The view of problem-solving that will be introduced is one which has gained wide currency in recent years. It assumes that we can construct some kind of a* **representation** *of the system that interests us, and that problem-solving can be characterized as a process of* **searching** *through alternative* **states** *of the representation in order to discover a state that meets certain specified* **criteria.***"*

Both of these definitions suffer from the implicit assumptions that the problem is sufficiently well-defined that performance criteria are clearly stated and that the design can be evaluated with respect to the performance criteria. Instead, we often find that the largest part of the design exercise is establishing a complete definition of the problem. This aspect of designing is expressed by Gross et al. [Gros86] as: *"Designing is understood as a process of incrementally defining an initially ill-defined question, and concurrently proposing and testing possible answers. That is, not finding* **the** *solution to* **a** *problem, but finding* **a** *solution to* **the** *problem. ... Design problems are atypical problems in that they have many solutions. We do not find* **the** *solution to a set of design specifications; we find one solution out of many alternatives."*

In defending and clarifying this view, they state: *"Designing is looking for something whose characteristics are unfolded by the looking ... Designing has been described at various times, in various places, as optimizing or satisfying an objective function subject to a set of constraints. The description fails on two grounds. Objectives are almost always multiple. Two are too many. Any programming procedure would fail even were the constraints known and consistent. The constraints are not likely to be consistent because the objectives are multiple. Constraints and objectives can often be interchanged. Moreover, the constraints are not completely known. They are not just part of the problem. They are all of the problem."*

Solutions and Schema

Progressing from an ill-defined to a well-defined problem is generally the result of an iterative process of proposing a range of options (possible solutions), receiving and interpreting feedback, and restating the problem for the next iteration (see Figure 1). Hopefully, the feedback clarifies previously ill-defined elements of the problem, allowing for the generation of new solutions that are closer to *the design* than those of the previous iteration.

It is often the case that several schema are concurrently developed. Within the model, these must all be embodied to allow the flexibility required to change and iterate while mixing, matching, and comparing features from different schemes.

Designers typically explore ideas through an iterative process of visualizing the idea by sketching or physical modeling. The insertion of computers into the design iteration process creates additional layers of representation and interpretation. Unfortunately, these additional layers can impede the design process. In the words of McKim [McKi72]: "... *not all visualization materials are well-suited to exploring and recording ideas. Materials that involve the visualizer in difficult techniques, for instance, will absorb energy and divert attention away from thinking. Time-consuming techniques also impede rapid ideation, since ideas frequently come more quickly than they can be recorded. Frustration with an unwieldy material can block a train of thought or be reflected directly in diminished quality of thinking.*"

Scale and Complexity

The wide range of scale and the vast complexity of design poses an array of challenges in creating CAD tools. It is necessary to work at a variety of different

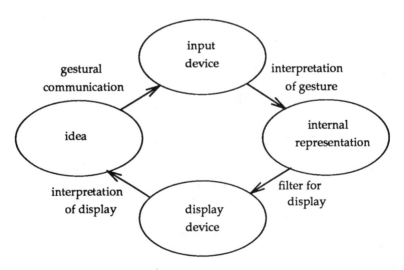

Figure 1. The design exploration loop, including the computer.

scales with unimportant information suppressed (not presented) or abstracted (presented in a simplified form) for clarity, but immediately accessible in full detail when required.

Display or presentational abstractions are one method of accomplishing this. As used by Feldman [Feld89], *"an abstraction is defined as a representation of an object in a way which emphasizes some particular aspect or quality of the total information which the object contains."*

Design Abstractions

The initial stages of design generally work with schematic representations of abstract notions and relationships. These are relationships between spaces, volumes, functions, support systems, site, circulation, etc. At a later time, geometric constructs are linked to the abstract notions. Eastman [East85] ennumerates the requirements for design abstractions as consisting of:

design data;

a set of operations or other tools to manipulate the data;

a set of relations that is always maintained in the data;

a set of tests and performance requirements that can be evaluated from the data.

Relationships

Managing the volume of data and the interactions and relationships is probably the most difficult task for the designer(s). Typically, design decisions late in the design process may violate decisions made early in the process. These violations continue unnoticed until very much later. Procedures and processes such as alignment, clearance, mating, infill, connection, etc., must be represented as an intent which can be reevaluated in response to context change. Maintaining only the result of such a process or procedure at a particular instant in time does not preserve and/or document the intent of the decisions that lead to the application of that procedure and/or process.

Ambiguity

Ambiguity is inherent in any ill-defined problem. Since the problem is ambiguous, solutions tend to progress from ambiguous abstractions to more defined forms. The progression from ambiguity to clear expression parallels the refinement of the problem statement. The representation must support placeholders and relationships that are not well defined.

THE RESULT: A DESIGN

We take the result of the design activity, *the design*, to be, as Eastman suggests, the specification of an artifact. It might be argued that *the design* is the artifact itself, in that the design process continues through the construction and/or manufacture of the artifact, and thus the design is not complete until the artifact is completed. However, if we assume *the design* should be fully specified before construction or manufacture begins, then post-specification design activities really indicate that the design process was not successful.

The specification of the artifact takes the form of written description, drawings, directions for manufacture, etc. We consider the design to be the database from which drawings and other presentation documentation are extracted. Note that this does not necessitate that the database represent the design in a manner analogous to the construction or manufacturing documentation.

A Review of Modeling Techniques

There are two main considerations in modeling, first the geometric representation of components, and second, the representation of the relationships between the components. In addressing problems of design, we believe that relationships between components are currently most problematic, and that identifying and managing relationships can be considered independently of the geometric representation. It should be possible to use any geometric representation within a framework of relationships. Thus, the discussion of geometric representation is but a brief overview. Instead, this section focuses on methods for specifying and maintaining relationships.

GEOMETRIC REPRESENTATION

There is a vast body of literature addressing the problem of geometric representation. The summary provided in this section is taken from Wyvill [Wyvi90] (see Figure 2). Other summary sources are Mortenson [Mort85] and Rossignac [Ross87].

Any function or procedure that provides 3D surface data, i.e., location and normal, can provide the basis for a modeling technique. The three main technique classifications are:

> surface modeling;
> solid modeling;
> generative processes.

Surface Modeling

Surface modeling techniques explicitly represent surfaces. Points are characterized as either on or off the surfaces. Surfaces are joined together to build solid objects, but it is not inherent in the nature of surface descriptions that constructable objects are represented.

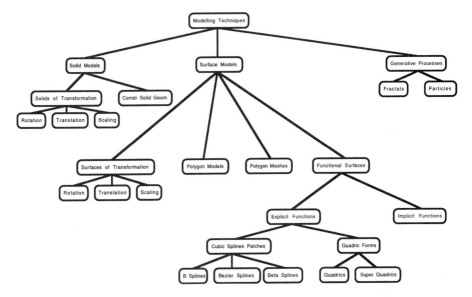

Figure 2. A taxonomy of modeling techiques (Courtesy of Brian Wyvill [Wyvi90]).

Solid Modeling

Solid models describe the volume of space occupied by the solid. Points are characterized as being either inside or outside the object.

Generative Processes

These are processes that generate a geometric description, either surface or solid, through some algorithmic process.

REPRESENTING RELATIONSHIPS

This section discusses methods for specifying relationships and the resulting impact on the design representation. The use of relationships relies on the identification of features (often geometric) and the specification of a process that relates them. In a general sense, relationships can be used to control and shape any of the geometric representations discussed in the previous section. Specifically, design should not be constrained by the geometric representation, and any appropriate representation should be available for any of the components in the design.

We can identify three general classes of relationships—those relating features within a part; those relating part positions within an assembly; and those relating features across different parts and/or assemblies. The remainder of this section provides a general overview of methods for relationship specification that are applied to these classes. Details and examples of the implementation of these methods are found in Appendices A and B.

Direct Manipulation

Direct manipulation techniques place features and/or objects in relationship to each other; however, no record of the relationships other than the resulting geometry and/or positioning transformation is maintained. Early direct manipulation accepted keyboard positioning commands. Later work used interactive dragging or positioning potentiometers. Methods that lock onto construction grids or to predefined angles mimicked drafting procedures [Robe80; Habe80; Feib81]. Manipulation methods for operating in a 3D perspective view instead of traditional orthographic projections were reported by Rogers [Roge80] and Nielson [Niel87]. The most recent work in this area is the snap-dragging technique of Bier [Bier90, 88, 87] and Bier and Stone [Bier86], which imposes temporary constraints to locate geometric entities but does not store information about these constraints as part of the model. This technique is applicable to both part geometry and assembly relationships in 2D and 3D.

Variational Geometry

Variational geometry is a constraint based approach to describing and resolving geometric relationships within a part [Fitz81; Lin81; Ligh82]. Light and Gossard note *"the central idea ... that dimensions, such as appear on a mechanical drawing, are a natural descriptor of geometry and provide the most appropriate means for altering the geometric model."* Variational geometry expresses relationships between locations of *characteristic points* describing the geometry, and constraints (dimensions, area, volume, etc.) as a set of error functions whose values converge to zero when all constraints are met. The error functions are differentiated to find a system Jacobian. Newton-Raphson iteration methods are used to adjust the positions of the *characteristic points* until the system converges. By examining the structure of the Jacobian, it is possible to identify conditions of under- or overdimensioning and where the inadequacies in the dimensioning scheme occur.

The basic notions of variational geometry were extended to the description of assemblies by Lee and Gossard [Lee85a] and Lee and Andrews [Lee85b]. Assembly alignment criteria are used to form a set of constraint equations that define the positioning transformations. The solution is similar to that of variational geometry; however, Lee and Andrews report a high likelihood of overconstrained systems and failure of the solution method to find a unique correct solution (see Appendix B).

While it has not appeared in the literature, the similarity in form of variational geometry and constrained assembly suggests that the technique generalizes for constraints across different parts and/or assemblies.

Constructive Specification

Constructive specification is similar to the snap-dragging technique of direct manipulation with the exception that the database consists of a record of the manipulations, not the resulting geometry and/or position transforms. The power in this technique is in the reevaluation of the manipulations in response to a query for display or to changes in context.

This is similar to generating a script of an interactive geometry creation and/or positioning session and replaying that script whenever the results of the session are required. Editing the script edits the resulting object [Nels85].

While the script of a geometry creation or assembly session is easy to generate, providing the facility for simple interactive graphic editing is not so simple. Simply adding the edit manipulations to the end of the script may result in extremely long cumbersome descriptions with many redundant and/or unnecessary operations. This necessitates some type of script optimization.

It should also be noted that the construction sequence may not necessarily reflect the important relationships in a way that makes them accessible as design decisions in later review. Specifically, they may not reflect the intent of the design but merely an expedient way to achieve an intermediate result.

An additional disadvantage is that the construction must be sequential. Cyclic construction or concurrent constraints cannot be maintained using constructive specification.

Parametric Specification

Parametric specification forces all relationships and constraints to be reduced to explicitly computable functions of parameters. Constraints are then explicitly maintained when parameters are altered. While this is the most direct method of maintaining concurrent constraints and assuring the correct solution is generated, it requires the user to program the relationships between parameters and geometry. Creating and editing this program for complex systems is a very difficult task. The resulting parameterization may be neither simple nor intuitive.

Energy Constraints

Energy constraints, as presented by Witkin et al. [Witk87], is a constraint based approach similar to variational geometry. Constraints are expressed through 'energy' functions.[†] Similar to the error functions of variational geometry, there is one energy function for each constraint. These functions, however, are expressed in terms of the parameters controlling the generation, assembly, and modification of parameterized models. The constraints may express dimensional, positional, area, volume, proximity, surface contact, or any number of other relationships.

An energy constraint function, similar to an error function, is a continuous function equal to zero only when the constraint is met and, unlike the error function, positive otherwise. Summing the energy constraint functions results in a system energy function. A solution is found by altering the system parameters to follow the gradient of the system energy function to a local minima.

[†]The reference to the constraint functions as 'energy' functions is misleading, since they generally do not model energy in a physical sense. Witkin et al. [Witk87] suggest that they might be thought of as modeling the magnitude of the force or energy attracting the parameters into a configuration where the constraint is met.

It should be noted that this method finds a solution in fully-, under-, and overconstrained problems. It allows priority weighting of constraints to cope with the typical design situation of overconstraint with conflicting goals. Witkin et al. also note the high probability of converging to incorrect local minima and suggest that user interaction is required to steer solutions through these incorrect solutions.

An Architecture for Research into Design

The previous sections examined the properties of design and the methods for saving and enforcing the relationships that are reflected in design decisions. The research effort directed towards modeling focused on creating an extensible architecture that supports any geometric and/or relationship representations.

REPRESENTING DESIGN

The representation of the design process refers to the machine internal database representation. There are three elements to the database. The first is a catalogue of *parts* and *processes* that may be used in a design; the second is a catalogue of data associated with each of the parts and processes. The third is the database *models* or assemblies of parts and processes resulting from a design process. A model is a special type of the generalized part/process, and as such, a model can contain other models.

A part/process is a class of object that must support the functions listed in Table 1. The object oriented nature of the approach allows simple extension of the part/process catalogue. Each instance of data created by a part/process is saved as a named entry in the data catalogue for that part/process.

A model is represented as a single level hierarchy of part/process and data pairs. A part/process may be represented as a hierarchy of other parts/processes. This allows the representation of a hierarchy of any depth, as is the case with recursive inclusions of models. Since a model is also a part, this provides a natural mechanism for building a complex design from simpler components.

A schematic representation of a model hierarchy is given in Figure 3. The object oriented nature of the software architecture requires each part/process type to be able to function as an independent entity with no explicit knowledge about any other part/process type. Any required information is transferred through specific inquiries to other part/process types.

We have taken the position that *natural* movement through and manipulation of complex databases is through selection processes using the visual abstractions that best represent design elements, and that the structure of the hierarchy may be completely hidden. The *current node* in the network implies a point of reference for editing and display. The current node function is able to display and edit itself, to display input function data and select input functions to become the current node, and to return control to the parent node. The display function is

Table 1. Part/process functionality.

Function	Description
initialize	initialize this part/process for use
terminate	terminate use of this part/process
create	interactively create data for a unique instance of the part/process
edit	interactively edit a previously created instance
delete	delete data for an instance of the part/process
list	list all data instances for this part/process
display	draw the part/process to the current display device
intersect	intersect a ray an instance of the part/process (used for interactive selection)

critical in that it provides the means to control detail, abstraction, and movement within the hierarchy.

Smithers [Smit89] argues that geometric databases cannot possibly support the design process because of the amount of nongeometric information in design. Eastman [East85] argues that the geometry that is displayed should be a result of a filtering operation that reviews the database, extracts information relevant to the current design activity, and generates geometric abstractions that facilitate the current design manipulations. The representation we use reflects these viewpoints.

While the current implementation provides great flexibility in model construction, display, and editing, it falls far short in preserving design intent as a recoverable and documented aspect of the design database. The following sections discuss our observations about our current implementation.

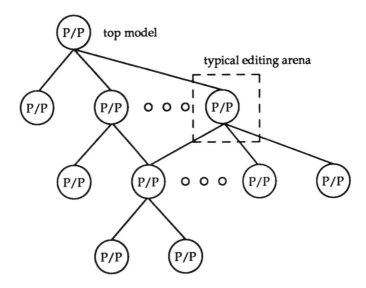

Figure 3. Representation of a model hierarchy.

PROCESS PRESENTATION

The presentation of the process is embodied in the geometric presentation of the artifact and the facilities for examining this artifact. While other presentations are possible (and will be implemented for study and evaluation), we initially assume that geometry is the most natural form of presentation and manipulation. The process is implicit in the construction of and movement through the model database.

Process Presentation Features

Interactive traversal through selection mechanisms using geometric display entities for picking is provided.

Automatic naming of generated part/process data instances is provided.

Process Presentation Problems

Context is missing at any point below the main model.

When a current part/process is identified, instances are not indicated. (This is particularly problematic for instances that are parts of submodels currently shown at levels of detail in which the instance does not appear.)

When the model starts to get large (complex) the data catalogues for the parts get too large to be useful. It is hard to name, hard to categorize, hard to remember, and hard to find part data. This is a particular problem in retrieving data that is not already part of the model.

The only presentation of the model is geometric. Other abstractions might make it easier to understand the organization of the data and to perform operations across levels of the hierarchy in a more natural way.

Currently there are no nongeometric part/process elements. In the future, we plan to implement constraints, alignment operators, etc. It is unclear that geometric abstractions will be appropriate for indicating and selecting these elements of the database.

OBSERVATIONS

The modeling software developed in this research is being used in a fourth-year design studio in the school of architecture at Cornell University. This provides an opportunity to test and observe users over 13-week periods of intensive use on design problems. This system was introduced into the studio during the spring semester of 1990.

One universal observation is that increased power and flexibility in the modeling system is manifest through a greater range of interaction options. Initially this was met with resistance and confusion. Several users continued to use an older, more primitive modeler until the problem became unmanageable and the new system was required.

Use statistics consisting of documentation of page and feature use for each user were gathered over the semester but have not yet been analyzed. We will use the analyzed statistics, observed response to the system, and user reviews and recommendations as input in the generation of experiments and exercises to attempt to verify and quantify the effectiveness of new modeling features and techniques.

FUTURE WORK

Future plans include the implementation of improved direct manipulation methods, addition of more powerful part/process operators, variational geometry, simultaneous constraints, constructive specification, and study of the usefulness of these techniques in addressing design problems.

Acknowledgements. The author acknowledges the work of Mimi Bussan, Leonard Wanger, Priamos Georghiades, Paul Wanuga, Mark Reichert, and Kathy Kershaw in implementing the Cornell modeling system. The author thanks Hewlett-Packard for the generous grants to the Program of Computer Graphics that provided the equipment that supported this work. The author also thanks the National Science Foundation for long term support of the research at the Program of Computer Graphics.

Appendix A

METHODS FOR SPECIFYING RELATIONSHIPS WITHIN A PART

In this appendix several methods for specifying and/or maintaining relationships within a part geometry are reviewed in detail. These methods are:

  direct specification;
  variational geometry;
  constructive specification;
  parametric specification;
  energy constraints.

The simple figure shown in Figure A1 is used for demonstration. Each method requires the user to make some decisions as to what is important about the geometry. Simply entering four ordered points defines the topology of the figure. The geometry is established by noting things like relationships to the axis system, lengths, etc. The following features are considered important in this figure:

  edge 4 is of length a and is along the x-axis;
  edge 1 is of length b and is along the y-axis;
  edge 2 is of length c.

Note that these requirements do not uniquely define the figure. The implications of this nonuniqueness are discussed in each example.

Every effort is made to present each method as described in the original reference, with the exception of terminology alterations for consistency. It is assumed

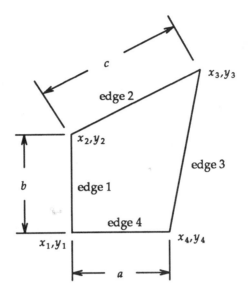

Figure A1. Simple part.

the reader is familiar with representations of lines and arcs, and with methods to compute intersections [Bowy83].

DIRECT SPECIFICATION

Direct specification takes two forms. The first is the construction of the rough topology, followed by moving the locations of the four vertices to achieve the desired results. The second is construction in the desired form. In both cases, the use of methods analogous to drafting are used to *construct* the locations of the vertices. Thus, it is the construction method that is of importance. The first case is considered here as it also demonstrates the techniques that are later used for editing.

The first step is to roughly sketch the figure. The construction sequence that follows is one of several possible sequences. First request a construction grid, locking to the grid, and locking to standard angles. Move (x_1, y_1) to the origin. Assuming the grid spacing is such that (x_2, y_2) falls on a grid intersection, snap the vertex to that intersection. Assume (x_4, y_4) does not fall on a grid intersection. Create a construction circle of radius a and snap the vertex onto that circle, using the angle lock to assure edge 4 is horizontal (see Figure A2a). Create a construction circle of radius c centered at (x_2, y_2). Snap the vertex (x_3, y_3) onto this circle and drag it to the desired place on the circle, as shown in Figure A2b. Obviously, there is some ambiguity at this step. The user must make a decision about the placement of the vertex, which can be placed anywhere on the construction circle. The stored data is the topology and the locations of the vertices.

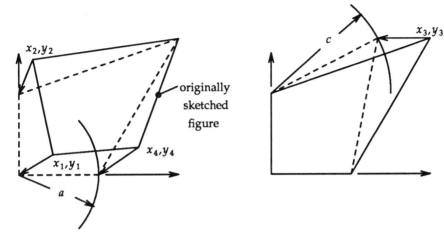

Figure A2. Construction technique.

Advantages in Direct Specification

It is very fast for simple construction.

It works well when you know what the geometry should be.

Editing is very simple.

Programming the interaction is very simple.

Disadvantages in Direct Specification

There is no record of important features in the figure.

There is no way to describe dependencies between features (for example, one edge being twice the length of another).

There is no record of dependencies between features of the figure and other features within the design.

VARIATIONAL GEOMETRY

As presented by Lin et al. [Lin81] and Light and Gossard [Ligh82], variational geometry describes the important features of the figure through a series of constraint functions relating geometry and dimensional parameters. These are continuous functions of the form

$$F_j(\vec{x}, \vec{d}) = r_j \qquad j = 1, 2, 3, \ldots, m \qquad (A1)$$

where
$\vec{d}$ = the vector of dimensional values;
$\vec{x}$ = the geometry vector;
r_j = the residual error;
m = the number of constraints.

The residual error of the constraint function is zero when the constraint is met. Generally, the constraint functions are nonlinear relationships between dimensions, $\vec{d}$, and positions of vertices, $\vec{x}$. Each component of a vertex that is unknown is considered a degree of freedom and appears in the $\vec{x}$ vector. The number of degrees of freedom is n.

A Newton-Raphson iteration method is used for solution. The $\vec{x}$ vector is adjusted iteratively until there is no residual error in any of the constraint functions. The method is to use the current residual error vector, $\vec{r}$, and the derivative of the system (the Jacobian, J) to determine a displacement, $\Delta \vec{x}$, to be added to the geometry vector

$$J \Delta \vec{x} = \vec{r} \tag{A2}$$

or

$$\begin{bmatrix} f_{1,1} & f_{1,2} & \cdots & f_{1,n} \\ f_{2,1} & f_{2,2} & \cdots & f_{2,n} \\ \vdots & \vdots & \ddots & \vdots \\ f_{m,1} & f_{m,2} & \cdots & f_{m,n} \end{bmatrix} \begin{bmatrix} \Delta x_1 \\ \Delta x_2 \\ \vdots \\ \Delta x_m \end{bmatrix} = \begin{bmatrix} r_1 \\ r_2 \\ \vdots \\ r_m \end{bmatrix}$$

The terms of the Jacobian matrix are the partial derivatives of the constraint functions with respect to the degree of freedom, $f_{i,j} = \partial F_i / \partial x_j$. At each solution step, the displacement is added to the geometry vector and the residuals and Jacobian are recomputed.

Consider again Figure A1. The first step is to sketch the figure; then dimensions are added, resulting in the generation of the following constraint equations

$$F_1 = x_1 \tag{A3}$$

$$F_2 = y_1 \tag{A4}$$

$$F_3 = x_2 - x_1 \tag{A5}$$

$$F_4 = y_2 - y_1 - b \tag{A6}$$

$$F_5 = x_4 - x_1 - a \tag{A7}$$

$$F_6 = y_4 - y_1 \tag{A8}$$

$$F_7 = c^2 - (x_3 - x_2)^2 - (y_3 - y_2)^2 \tag{A9}$$

The meanings of these are

F_1 : fixes vertex 1 to the origin in x;
F_2 : fixes vertex 1 to the origin in y;
F_3 : fixes edge 1 to be on the y-axis;
F_4 : fixes edge 1 to length b;
F_5 : fixes edge 4 to be on the x-axis;
F_6 : fixes edge 4 to length a;
F_7 : fixes edge 2 to length c.

If $m \neq n$, the Jacobian matrix is structurally nonsingular, indicating the figure is either under- or overconstrained. If $m = n$ and the Jacobian is singular, there is redundant dimensioning of the figure. Note that there are eight degrees of freedom and only seven constraint equations. The system is underconstrained, and an additional constraint is required. Several choices are available for an eighth constraint that produces a valid constraint scheme:

specifying length d of edge 3

$$F_8 = d^2 - (x_4 - x_3)^2 - (y_4 - y_3)^2 \qquad (A10)$$

specifying angle e of edge 2

$$F_8 = \frac{x_3 - x_2}{y_3 - y_2} - \tan e \qquad (A11)$$

specifying angle f of edge 3

$$F_8 = \frac{x_3 - x_4}{y_3 - y_4} - \tan f \qquad (A12)$$

Suppose we select angle specification of edge 3, Eq. (A12), as the final constraint. The Jacobian is then

$$
\begin{bmatrix}
1 & 0 & 0 & 0 & 0 & 0 & 0 & 0 \\
0 & 1 & 0 & 0 & 0 & 0 & 0 & 0 \\
-1 & 0 & 1 & 0 & 0 & 0 & 0 & 0 \\
0 & -1 & 0 & 1 & 0 & 0 & 0 & 0 \\
-1 & 0 & 0 & 0 & 0 & 0 & 1 & 1 \\
0 & -1 & 0 & 0 & 0 & 0 & 0 & 0 \\
0 & 0 & 2(x_3 - x_2) & 2(y_3 - y_2) & 2(x_2 - x_3) & 2(y_2 - y_3) & 0 & 0 \\
0 & 0 & 0 & 0 & 1 & -\tan f & -1 & \tan f
\end{bmatrix}
$$

Solving Eq. (A2) moves the vertices from the sketched position into the position meeting the constraints. Additionally, if any dimensions are changed, repeating the solution moves the vertex positions to meet the constraints.

Advantages in Variational Geometry

Important features are indicated by dimensions.

Dependencies between features are described in the dimensioning.

Dimensions can be derived from other design features, thus establishing relationships between components of the design.

Editing the topology and the constraints is conceptually simple for users familiar with standard drafting practices for machined parts.

Constraints are addressed simultaneously.

Disadvantages in Variational Geometry

Programming the interaction is not simple.

Solution after a dimension change may be slow, thus limiting the interactivity when making changes.

Redundant, and therefore overconstrained, dimensioning schemes are typical in some disciplines such as architecture.

Specifying a valid dimensioning scheme, while conceptually simple, may, in practice, be difficult for the user.

Dimension values can be selected for which the solution does not converge, or for which there may be several solutions and the incorrect one is selected. The user must be able to interact with the solution to steer ambiguous systems towards the correct solution.

CONSTRUCTIVE SPECIFICATION

Constructive specification is similar to direct manipulation except that the sequence of constructive functions required to build the figure is saved in unevaluated form. The geometry is generated by evaluating the functions.

Assume a system that lets a user create construction datums such as lines, planes, circles, spheres, etc. Locations are specified in relation to the datums. The example figure is drawn in the same fashion as in direct manipulation; however, the data representing the figure is the topology and the unevaluated construction steps, as opposed to the vertex locations.

Consider the datum references in Figure A3. The construction sequence for the figure is

point 1 at the intersection of A' and B';

point 2 at the intersection of B' and C';

point 3 at the intersection of E' and D' with the greatest y;

point 4 at the intersection of D' and A'.

The locations of the vertices are evaluated whenever required, such as for display or during datum editing. Moving datums to positions for which evaluation of the sequence fails can be detected and disallowed.

Advantages in Constructive Specification

It is easy for the user to initially specify objects.

Programming is simple except for compressing (eliminating) unnecessary construction steps from the description (which is critical after editing).

Disadvantages in Constructive Specification

Editing an existing topology of objects tacks more operations onto the end of the sequence. Compression schemes are required.

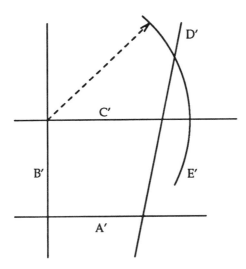

Figure A3. Construction datum for the simple part.

Easily specifying relationships after construction of the object is difficult.
The construction must be sequential. Cyclic constructions or concurrent
constraints cannot be handled by this technique.

PARAMETRIC SPECIFICATION

Parametric construction specifies each geometric location as a directly computable function of some parameters. For example, the sample figure can be
explicitly computed from a, b, c, and f as

$$x_1 = 0 \tag{A13}$$

$$y_1 = 0 \tag{A14}$$

$$x_2 = 0 \tag{A15}$$

$$y_2 = b \tag{A16}$$

$$temp_1 = b \cos f - a \sin f \tag{A17}$$

$$temp_2 = \sqrt{c^2 - (b \sin f + a \cos f)^2} \tag{A18}$$

$$x_3 = a + (temp_1 + temp_2) \sin f \tag{A19}$$

$$y_3 = (temp_1 + temp_2) \cos f \tag{A20}$$

$$x_4 = a \tag{A21}$$

$$y_4 = 0 \tag{A22}$$

Along with this description, a set of limits for a, b, c, and f are specified which assure the figure can be constructed, i.e.,

$$a > 0 \qquad (A23)$$

$$b > 0 \qquad (A24)$$

$$c > 0 \qquad (A25)$$

$$\left(b \sin f + a \cos f \right)^2 < c^2 \qquad (A26)$$

The validity is checked and, if valid, the figure is constructed for any choices of a, b, c, and f.

Advantages in Parametric Specification

It is easy to program a framework that accepts object definitions of this nature.

It is similar to variational geometry in that many constraints are handled simultaneously; however, parametric variation accounts for constraints implicitly through the functions which compute geometry.

The model can be quickly altered through parameter changes. It is dissimilar to variational geometry in that the geometry is determined by direct computation instead of through directed alteration.

Disadvantages in Parametric Specification

This method of thinking about a problem may not be 'natural' for a user.

Complex object specification is difficult for the user. Computation of each degree of freedom is through a function that accounts for the constraints.

While constraints are implicit in the geometry functions, they may not be apparent to the user in subsequent editing.

ENERGY CONSTRAINTS

As presented by Witkin et al. [Witk87], the relationships between features of a model are described through 'energy' constraint functions of the parameters controlling object definition, modification, and position. The energy constraint functions are continuous functions of the form

$$E_j(\vec{p}) \geq 0 \qquad j = 1, 2, 3, \ldots, m \qquad (A27)$$

where
$$\vec{p} = \text{the vector of parameters;}$$
$$m = \text{the number of constriants.}$$

Note that the parameter vector, $\vec{p}$, is different from the dimension and geometry vectors. In the case of the simple figure, we consider the parameter vector to be the geometry of the points. In a more general sense, the parameters are the height and radius of a cylinder, or the translation and rotation values used to generate a transformation matrix.

The value of an energy constraint function is zero when the constraint is met and positive otherwise. The total energy of the system is the sum of the individual energy constraint functions

$$E(\vec{p}) = \sum_{j=0}^{m} E_j(\vec{p}) \tag{A28}$$

Beginning with some initial configuration, $\vec{p}_0$, there is an initial system energy, $E(\vec{p}_0)$. A local minima or maxima in system energy is reached when $\nabla E(\vec{p}) = 0$. Witkin et al. suggest a steepest descent method to reach the local minima and note that Euler's method is the simplest to use

$$E(\vec{p}_{t+1}) = E(\vec{p}_t) + h\nabla E(\vec{p}_t) \tag{A29}$$

They suggest that a variety of other numerical methods be used for faster accurate convergence. Note that convergence to the correct solution (all constraints satisfied) is not guaranteed. All constraints are met if $E(\vec{p}) = 0$ when $\nabla E(\vec{p})$ converges to zero. User interaction is required to push incorrect solutions through local minima.

In cases of underconstraint the constraints are satisfied, and the appearance of the resulting model indicates to the user whether additional constraints are required to achieve the desired results. In cases of overconstraint, the system converges to some 'best fit' of the constraints. This suggests that importance weighting be included in the energy constraint functions.

In considering the simple figure, the geometry vector, $\vec{x}$, constitutes the parameters that define the object. The error functions of the earlier section on Variational Geometry, Eqs. (A3)–(A9), are made energy constraint functions simply by squaring them so they are nonnegative

$$E_1 = x_1^2 \tag{A30}$$

$$E_2 = y_1^2 \tag{A31}$$

$$E_3 = (x_2 - x_1)^2 \tag{A32}$$

$$E_4 = (y_2 - y_1 - b)^2 \tag{A33}$$

$$E_5 = (x_4 - x_1 - a)^2 \tag{A34}$$

$$E_6 = (y_4 - y_1)^2 \tag{A35}$$

$$E_7 = \left\{ c^2 - (x_3 - x_2)^2 - (y_3 - y_2)^2 \right\}^2 \tag{A36}$$

The system energy is the sum of these functions. The previously described solution technique is applied to find a configuration that minimizes the system energy.

Given an initial configuration for the geometry, this system converges to a solution that satisfies the constraints. Note, however, that the system is underconstrained and an additional constraint is required to assure that a unique configuration is defined.

While this example demonstrates energy constraints using a dimensioned part, the normal usage is with more traditional parameterized models. Thus, parameterized primitive creation, modification, and assembly are easily related through the energy constraints. The example in Appendix B clarifies implementation in the context of parameterized models.

Advantages in Energy Constraints

When used in the context of dimensioned parts, the advantages are the same as those of variational geometry.

Object specification constraints and assembly constraints are addressed simultaneously.

Solutions are generated for over- and underconstrained systems.

Disadvantages in Energy Constraints

When used in the context of dimensioned parts, the disadvantages are the same as those of variational geometry.

Over- and underconstrained problems may produce unexpected and confusing solutions.

Appendix B

Methods for Specifying Relationships Within an Assembly

In this appendix several methods for specifying and/or maintaining relationships within an assembly are reviewed in detail. These methods are:

direct specification;

simultaneous constraints (variational geometry);

constructive specification;

energy constraints.

The simple assembly in Figure B1 is used for demonstration. Assume the position of the base is fixed. The assembly is specified by positioning transforms for the cap and two bolts. A typical hierarchical representation for this assembly is shown in Figure B2, where T_{base} is an identity transformation. Note that the bolt is instanced in the assembly.

Direct Specification

Direct manipulation consists of specifying a series of steps that position the parts. The most rudimentary system for this might be interactively dragging the parts

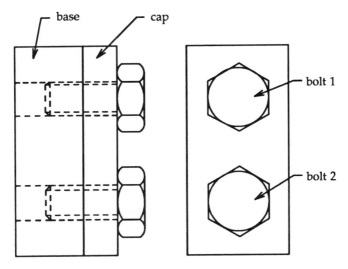

Figure B1. Simple bolt and plate assembly.

until they are visually positioned correctly. However, this is accompanied by large errors. Alignment operators as described by Bier [Bier88; Bier90] can be used for quick precise positioning. The sequence of operations is:

Match the face of the cap to the face of the base.

Match the center of one of the cap mounting holes to the center of one of the base mounting holes. Anchor this point on the cap.

Match the center of the other mounting hole in the cap to the center of the other mounting hole in the base.

Match the centerline of a bolt to the centerline of a mounting hole in the base.

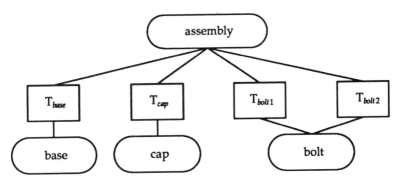

Figure B2. Hierarchical representation for the simple bolt and plate assembly of Figure B1.

Match the base of the head of the bolt to the face of the cap.

Repeat the procedure with the other bolt.

The resulting data structure looks like that of a typical hierarchical representation. Information describing the relationships used for positioning is completely lost.

Advantages in Direct Specification

It is very fast for simple construction.

Steps in positioning are analogous to physical assembly, thus are 'natural' to the user.

Editing is very simple.

Programming the interaction is very simple.

Disadvantages in Direct Specification

There is no record of the important relationships in the assembly.

There is no record of dependencies between features of the figure and other features within the design.

Only the resulting position transforms are saved. Editing any component in the assembly requires respecifying the positions of components in order for the assembly to remain correct.

SIMULTANEOUS CONSTRAINTS

Lee and Gossard [Lee85a] describe a data structure for storing the alignment constraints as part of the model. The essence is that each transformation in a typical hierarchy is replaced with a *virtual-link*, or perhaps more correctly, a virtual transformation. This virtual transformation is a list of alignments that are evaluated to compute the actual transformation. Each virtual link relates two assemblies/components; many of these assemblies/components have been omitted in Figure B3 for clarity.

Lee and Andrews [Lee85b] further develop the constrained assembly method by describing the construction of and solution to the equation sets that define the alignment constraints. The constraints are formulated into a single equation set, allowing the satisfaction of simultaneous constraints. A Newton-Raphson iteration method similar to that described by Light and Gossard [Ligh82] is used for solution.

Assuming the base position is fixed, there are three positioning transforms required, one to position each of the other components. The position transforms take the general form

$$\begin{bmatrix} t_{1,1} & t_{1,2} & t_{1,3} & 0 \\ t_{2,1} & t_{2,2} & t_{2,3} & 0 \\ t_{3,1} & t_{3,2} & t_{3,3} & 0 \\ t_{4,1} & t_{4,2} & t_{4,3} & 1 \end{bmatrix} \tag{B1}$$

Each position transform contains 12 unknowns. Thus, there must be at least 12 constraint equations in order to solve for the matrix. Since there are three matrices, this requires 36 constraint equations. These constraint equations take the same form as those for variational geometry. For each matrix there are six equations that must be satisfied to preserve scale and orthogonality. These are

$$F_1 = 1 - t_{1,1}^2 - t_{1,2}^2 - t_{1,3}^2 \tag{B2}$$

$$F_2 = 1 - t_{2,1}^2 - t_{2,2}^2 - t_{2,3}^2 \tag{B3}$$

$$F_3 = t_{1,1}\, t_{2,1} + t_{1,2}\, t_{2,2} + t_{1,3}\, t_{2,3} \tag{B4}$$

$$F_4 = t_{1,2}\, t_{2,3} - t_{1,3}\, t_{2,2} - t_{3,1} \tag{B5}$$

$$F_5 = t_{1,3}\, t_{2,1} - t_{1,1}\, t_{2,3} - t_{3,2} \tag{B6}$$

$$F_6 = t_{1,1}\, t_{2,2} - t_{1,2}\, t_{2,1} - t_{3,3} \tag{B7}$$

This provides 18 of the required 36 constraint equations. Suppose points and vector directions are identified as in Figure B4. The constraint equations for the system are

$$\begin{bmatrix} N_{2,x} & N_{2,y} & N_{2,z} & 0 \\ P_{5,x} & P_{5,y} & P_{5,z} & 1 \\ P_{6,x} & P_{6,y} & P_{6,z} & 1 \end{bmatrix} [T_{cap}] = \begin{bmatrix} N_{1,x} & N_{1,y} & N_{1,z} & 0 \\ P_{1,x} & P_{1,y} & P_{1,z} & 1 \\ P_{2,x} & P_{2,y} & P_{2,z} & 1 \end{bmatrix} \tag{B8}$$

$$\begin{bmatrix} N_{2,x} & N_{2,y} & N_{2,z} & 0 \\ P_{3,x} & P_{3,y} & P_{3,z} & 1 \end{bmatrix} [T_{cap}] = \begin{bmatrix} N_{4,x} & N_{4,y} & N_{4,z} & 0 \\ P_{7,x} & P_{7,y} & P_{7,z} & 1 \end{bmatrix} [T_{bolt1}] \tag{B9}$$

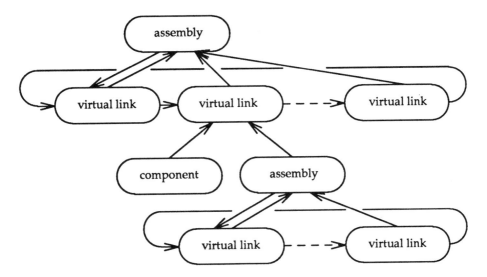

Figure B3. Hierarchical assembly described through vertual links.

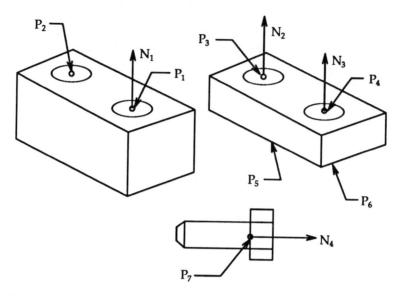

Figure B4. Part features referenced for assembly.

$$\begin{bmatrix} N_{3,x} & N_{3,y} & N_{3,z} & 0 \\ P_{4,x} & P_{4,y} & P_{4,z} & 1 \end{bmatrix} [T_{cap}] = \begin{bmatrix} N_{4,x} & N_{4,y} & N_{4,z} & 0 \\ P_{7,x} & P_{7,y} & P_{7,z} & 1 \end{bmatrix} [T_{bolt2}] \qquad (B10)$$

These constraints match hole centerlines and position faces against each other. This provides an additional 21 constraint equations.

Note that there are more constraint equations than unknowns. Lee and Andrews [Lee85b] observe this to be typically true and suggest that some of the equations are linearly dependent and can be removed, resulting in a match between the number of equations and the number of unknowns. Newton-Raphson iteration methods are then used to solve for the position transformation terms. They observe problems with convergence to incorrect solutions and problems in detecting linearly dependent equations. They suggest using a least squares technique on the entire equation set but do not report results from implementing this.

Advantages in Simultaneous Constraints

Important assembly features are indicated by the constraints.

Editing is conceptually simple.

Constraints are addressed simultaneously.

Disadvantages in Simultaneous Constraints

Solution after a dimension change may be slow, thus limiting the interactivity of making changes.

Constraints can be selected for which the solution does not converge, or for which there may be several solutions and the incorrect one is selected. The user must be able to interact with the solution to steer ambiguous systems towards the correct solution.

CONSTRUCTIVE SPECIFICATION

Constructive specification is similar to direct manipulation except that the sequence of positioning functions required to build the assembly is saved in unevaluated form. The position transforms are generated by evaluating these functions.

Advantages in Constructive Specification

Steps in positioning are analogous to physical assembly, thus are 'natural' to the user.

Editing is very simple.

Programming is simple except for compressing (eliminating) unnecessary positioning steps from the description (which is critical after editing).

Disadvantages in Constructive Specification

The construction must be sequential. Cyclic constructions or concurrent constraints are not handled by this technique.

ENERGY CONSTRAINTS

Refer to the previous section on energy constraints for a description of the energy constraint methodology. With respect to the assembly problem, imagine a representation of the assembly as shown in Figure B5. The transformation generation process might be the concatenation of rotation and translation matrices described by these parameters:

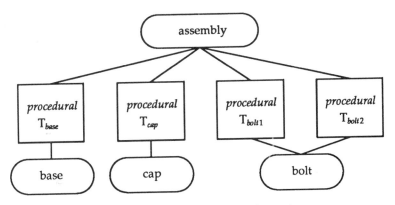

Figure B5. Assembly hierarchy using procedural transformations.

p_i :   rotation about the x-axis;

p_{i+1} :   rotation about the y-axis;

p_{i+2} :   rotation about the z-axis;

p_{i+3} :   translation in x;

p_{i+4} :   translation in y;

p_{i+5} :   translation in z.

Assuming the base position is fixed, the three remaining transformations expressed as transformation generation functions, $t()$, are

$$[T_{cap}] = t(p_1 \ldots p_6) \qquad (B11)$$

$$[T_{bolt1}] = t(p_7 \ldots p_{12}) \qquad (B12)$$

$$[T_{bolt2}] = t(p_{13} \ldots p_{18}) \qquad (B13)$$

The energy constraint functions[†] are then expressed as

$$E_1 = \left(\vec{N}_2 [T_{cap}] \cdot \vec{N}_1 \right) \qquad (B14)$$

$$E_2 = \left| P_5 [T_{cap}] - P_1 \right|^2 \qquad (B15)$$

$$E_3 = \left| P_6 [T_{cap}] - P_2 \right|^2 \qquad (B16)$$

$$E_4 = \left(\vec{N}_4 [T_{bolt1}] \cdot \vec{N}_2 \right) + 1 \qquad (B17)$$

$$E_5 = \left| P_7 [T_{bolt1}] - P_3 \right|^2 \qquad (B18)$$

$$E_6 = \left(\vec{N}_4 [T_{bolt2}] \cdot \vec{N}_3 \right) + 1 \qquad (B19)$$

$$E_7 = \left| P_7 [T_{bolt2}] - P_4 \right|^2 \qquad (B20)$$

Note that these energy functions are equivalent to the constraint functions of Eqs. (B8)–(B10). The system energy function is the sum of these energy constraint functions. The minimum energy solution meeting these constraints is found as previously described.

Advantages in Energy Constraints

When used in the context of assembly, the advantages are the same as those of variational geometry.

[†] Witkin et al. [Witk87] provide a comprehensive list of energy constraint function examples.

Object specification constraints and assembly constraints are addressed simultaneously.

Solutions are generated for over- and underconstrained systems.

Disadvantages in Energy Constraints

When used in the context of assembly, the disadvantages are the same as those of variational geometry.

Over- and underconstrained problems may produce unexpected and confusing solutions.

REFERENCES

[Bier86]
Bier, E.A., and Stone, M.C., Snap-dragging, *Comput. Graph.*, Vol. 20, 1986, pp. 233–240 (SIGGRAPH 86).

[Bier87]
Bier, E.A., Skitters and jacks: Interactive 3D positioning tools, in *Proc. of the 1986 Workshop on Interactive 3D Graphics* (Chapel Hill, NC, October 23–24, 1986), New York: ACM, 1987, pp. 183–196.

[Bier88]
Bier, E.A., Snap-dragging: Interactive geometric design in two and three dimensions, Ph.D. dissertation, Univ. California at Berkeley, Technical Report UCB/CSD 88/416, 1988.

[Bier90]
Bier, E.A., Snap-dragging in three dimensions, *Comput. Graph.*, Vol. 24, 1990, pp. 193–204.

[Bowy83]
Bowyer, A., and Woodwark, J., *A Programmer's Geometry*, London: Butterworth, 1983.

[East85]
Eastman, C., Abstraction: A conceptual approach for structuring interaction with integrated CAD systems, *Comput. and Graph.*, Vol. 9, No. 2, 1985, pp. 97–105.

[Feld89]
Feldman, S., An abstraction paradigm for modeling complex environments, Master's Thesis, Cornell Univ., 1989.

[Feib81]
Feibush, E., An interactive computer graphics geometric input and editing system for architectural design, Master's Thesis, Cornell Univ., 1981.

[Fitz81]
Fitzgerald, W.J., Using axial dimensions to determine the proportions of line drawings in computer graphics, *CAD*, Vol. 13, 1981, pp. 377–381.

[Gros86]
Gross, E., and Anderson, F., Designing with constraints, *The Computability of Design*, 1986 SUNY Buffalo Symposium on CAD, 1986, pp. 53–83.

[Habe80]
Haber, R., Computer-aided design of cable reinforced membrane structures, Master's Thesis, Cornell Univ., 1980.

[Lee85a]
Lee, K., and Gossard, D.C., A hierarchical data structure for representing assemblies: part 1, *CAD*, Vol. 17, 1985, pp. 15–19.

[Lee85b]
Lee, K., and Andrews, G., Inference of the positions of components in an assembly: part 2, *CAD*, Vol. 17, 1985, pp. 20–24.

[Ligh82]
Light, R., and Gossard, D., Modification of geometric models through variational geometry, *CAD*, Vol. 14, 1982, pp. 209–214.

[Lin81]
Lin, V. C., Gossard, D.C., and Light, R.A., Variational geometry in computer-aided design, *Comput. Graph.*, Vol. 15, 1981, pp. 171–177, (SIGGRAPH 81).

[McKi72]
McKim, R.H., *experiences in visual thinking*, Boston: PWS Publishers, 1972.

[Mitc77]
Mitchell, W., *Computer Aided Architectural Design*, New York: Petrocelli/Charter, 1977.

[Mort85]
Mortenson, M.E., *Geometric Modeling*, New York: John Wiley and Sons, 1985.

[Nels85]
Nelson, G., Juno, a constraint-based graphics system, *Comput. Graph.*, Vol. 19, 1985, pp. 235–243 (SIGGRAPH 85).

[Niel87]
Nielson, G.M., and Olsen, D.R. Jr., Direct manipulation techniques for 3D objects using 2D locator devices, in *Proc. of the 1986 Workshop on Interactive 3D Graphics* (Chapel Hill, NC, October 23–24, 1986), New York: ACM, 1987, pp. 175–182.

[Robe80]
Robertz, W., A graphical input system for computer-aided architectural design, Master's Thesis, Cornell Univ., 1980.

[Roge80]
Rogers, D. F., and Satterfield, S. G., B-spline surfaces for ship hull design, *Comput. Graph.*, Vol. 14, 1980, pp. 211–217 (SIGGRAPH 80).

[Ross87]
Rossignac, J.R., Constraints in constructive solid geometry, in *Proc. of the 1986 Workshop on Interactive 3D Graphics* (Chapel Hill, NC, October 23–24, 1986), New York: ACM, 1987, pp. 93–110.

[Smit89]
Smithers, T., AI-based design versus geometry based design, or, Why design cannot be supported by geometry alone, *CAD*, Vol. 21, 1989, pp. 141–150.

[Spro90]
Sproull, R.F., Parts of the frontier are hard to move, *Comput. Graph.*, Vol. 24, 1990, p. 9.

[Suth63]
Sutherland, I., Sketchpad, a man-machine graphical communication system, Ph.D. dissertation, Massachusetts Institute of Technology, 1963.

[Witk87]
Witkin, A., Fleisher, K., and Barr, A., Energy Constraints On Parameterized Models, *Comput. Graph.*, Vol. 21, 1987, pp. 225–232 (SIGGRAPH 87).

[Wyvi90]
Wyvill, B., A computer animation tutorial, in *Computer Graphics Techniques, Theory and Practice* (State of the Art in Computer Graphics, Exeter, UK, July 1988), Rogers, D.F., and Earnshaw, R.A., Eds., New York: Springer-Verlag, 1990, pp. 235–282.

Combinatorial Solid Geometry, Boundary Representations, and n-Manifold Geometry

Michael John Muuss and Lee A. Butler

Abstract

Combinatorial Solid Geometry (CSG) models are expressed as the Boolean combination of 'primitive' solids, rather than as an explicit representation of the final surfaces. However, many applications need an approximation of these complex CSG shapes expressed as a three-dimensional surface tessellation.

The intersection of two 3-manifolds can be a manifold of lower dimension. Because the winged-edge data structure can only represent 3-manifolds, these lower dimension results have produced serious added complexity to previous algorithms. This paper presents details of Weiler's radial-edge data structure and how it represents non-3-manifold conditions. With this more powerful representation, Boolean operations and other useful modeling operations are very easily implemented, using a three-part algorithm where elements are intersected, classified, and then evaluated.

At the systems design level, integrating n-manifold geometry into a hybrid CSG solid modeling system presents certain challenges. Of particular note are some of the design tradeoffs, the specification of tessellation tolerancing, the implementation of robust tessellation, and interfacing to facet-based analysis codes.

Motivation

Engineering drawings are suitable only for interpretation by human beings, not for automatic computerized analysis. A solid model is a computer description of closed, solid, three-dimensional shapes represented by an analytical framework, within which the three-dimensional material is completely and unambiguously defined [Deit83]. Completeness is assured because the representation contains a full description of a piece of solid matter; there is no view-specific information. These properties guarantee that all the spatial information necessary for any subsequent analysis is directly available from the model representation. Object structure and material properties can be computed at any point in the model at any time. Therefore, solid modeling is particularly suited to the automation of many manufacturing and analysis tasks [Muus87a]. Properly utilized, the solid model becomes the central element in the iterative process of taking a design from idea to prototype to working design to optimized design. This iterative process is termed the 'design loop' and is illustrated in Figure 1.

In a full scale solid modeling system there is no need for initial drawings: the designer expresses the initial structures directly into the modeling system's editor, just as a modern author creates his 'rough draft' directly into a word processor. At the completion of each version of the design, the model is subjected to a battery of analyses appropriate to the function of the object being designed. Strength, volume, weight, level of protection, and other similar evaluations can be reported, along with the production of a variety of images and/or drawings. These automated analyses help identify weaknesses or deficiencies *early in the design process*. In this way, the solid modeling system allows the designer to concentrate on the important, creative aspects of the design process. Freeing the designer of routine analysis permits designs to be finished in less time than previously required, or allows much more rigorously optimized designs to be delivered in comparable time frames and at the same cost as unoptimized designs created using older techniques [Deit85]. This makes it possible to produce highly detailed designs constructed with a philosophy of *system optimization* right from the start [Deit88].

For more than thirty years, solid geometric modeling methods have been used for engineering design and analyses [Magi67; Deit82; Deit84b]. Geometry and material information are passed to various application codes to derive certain measures of performance in structural analysis, thermal analysis, computational fluid dynamics (CFD), and vulnerability analysis. Building on the general paradigm, the same techniques support predictive signature models [Deit84a], including optical, millimeter wave (MMW), infrared (IR), magnetic, and X-ray signature generation tools. This type of predictive analysis must generally be supported by a solid geometric model.

Unfortunately, it is not often the case that building only *one* three-dimensional model of the design is enough. Each engineering analysis software package usually requires a different form of input, forcing the designer to construct more than one kind of geometric model. This can be very costly and time consuming. The time needed to create a single model ranges between one man-week and several man-years, depending on the complexity of the design. Having to spend the effort to manually create the same design in different formats to drive several analysis codes is an unfortunate and expensive necessity. The physical simulation techniques used in the application software are therefore constrained by the available techniques for extracting geometric information from the model.

Model Representations

Two major families of solid model representations exist. The first, developed in the late 1950s [Magi67], is the Combinatorial Solid Geometry representation (CSG-rep). CSG models are formed by Boolean combinations of 'primitive' solids

[Muus87a]. For example, a plate with a hole is most easily modeled as a plate primitive minus a cylinder primitive. Each primitive solid is a geometric entity described by some set of parameters that occupies a fixed volume in space. The simplest solid is the halfspace, defined as the infinite plane $ax + by + cz + d = 0$ and all points on one side of that plane [Requ82]. Most CSG systems offer quite a variety of primitive solids, ranging from various types of spheres, ellipsoids, boxes, and cones, to solids defined by swept or extruded curves.

The alternative to describing solids with primitives is to adopt a boundary representation (B-rep), of which there are two subtypes, *explicit* and *implicit*. In an explicit boundary representation, each solid is described by a specification of points on the surface of the solid, such as listing the vertices of all planar facets. Alternatively, there are implicit boundary representations, where the surface of the solid is described by an analytic function such as polynomials, Coons patches [Coon67], Bézier patches [Bezi74], splines [Roge90; deBo78], etc. Boundary representations are able to model objects with arbitrarily shaped surfaces but can require a large amount of information to achieve acceptable results.

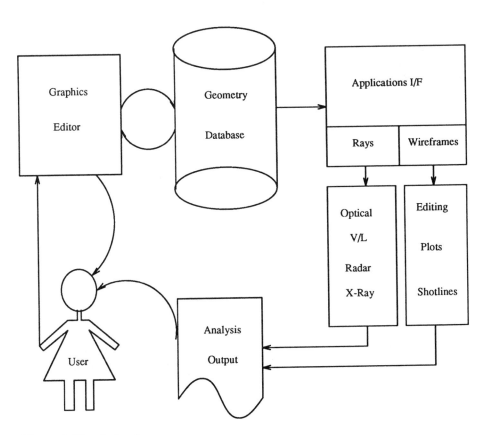

Figure 1. The design loop.

With traditional CSG primitives, it can be exceedingly difficult and nonintuitive to describe sculptured, free-form surfaces as a Boolean combination of primitives. But similarly, with pure boundary representations implementing Boolean operations *in the fundamental B-rep representation itself* can be difficult or impossible. Many current B-rep modelers implement Boolean operations as an external postprocessing operation, because current schemes to evaluate Boolean operations are not closed. As an example of this, B-spline ∩ B-spline might result in polygons rather than another B-spline [Thom84].

Many production CAD systems are actually hybrids of the two approaches, offering the designer the choice of primitive solids or boundary representations, as appropriate for each task. In practice, the implementation of the CSG- and B-rep portions of the software may be quite different; but at the highest level of abstraction each representation is just a different way of viewing the other. Faceted primitives such as boxes and wedges can be thought of as explicit B-reps, and smooth primitives such as spheres and cones can be thought of as implicit B-reps defined by analytic functions.

System-level Issues

The philosophy adopted in the BRL-CAD Package is to develop a broad set of analysis codes which access the same geometry database, to avoid the expense of remodeling designs in different ways to accommodate the input requirements of different analysis packages [Muus87b, Muus88]. A variety of procedural interfaces are provided so that the diverse collection of analysis codes is driven from a single, central geometric model [Muus90]. Support for many fundamentally different kinds of model interrogation was needed in order to meet this goal. An application program retrieves one or more objects from the model database, and via a natural object-oriented programming interface it requests those objects to either interrogate themselves or to convert themselves into the desired representation. This applications interface is depicted in Figure 2.

The BRL-CAD Package as it stood in 1989 is considered to be one of the very few production CAD systems based purely on the combinatorial solid geometry (CSG) technique. It is important to note that in CSG models there is no explicit representation of the surfaces of the solids stored; indeed, for complex Boolean combinations of complex primitives, some of the resultant shapes may have very convoluted topology and surfaces that may at best be high degree polynomials. However, there are many applications that benefit from being able to express an *approximation* of the final 'developed' shapes created using CSG modeling. The most obvious such application is to drive polygon-based rendering routines, for which there is direct hardware or firmware support on many workstations. In addition, there are many surface-based predictive infrared and radar signature programs. A technique for converting a CSG model to an approximate three-dimensional surface tessellation is the focus of this paper.

The technique for obtaining an explicit description of modeled objects must provide full support for Boolean operations, which places severe requirements on the design. Most importantly, it requires that the new representation used to hold the explicit description of the modeled objects must be *closed* under Boolean operations. That is, given the explicit description of objects A and B, then any Boolean combination of A and B must be representable as an explicit description expressed in terms of the same underlying representation.

A strictly polygonal representation could be selected. While performing Boolean operations on solids described as collections of polygons is not easy, the representation is (with certain special definitions) considered to be closed under Boolean operations; algorithms to accomplish the Boolean evaluation have been published for several years [Laid86].

A representation comprised exclusively of rectangular parametric surfaces, such as B-splines or similar tensor-product surface patches, could be used. However, research to date has shown that while B-spline surfaces can be combined using Boolean operations, the resulting object cannot be expressed strictly in terms of B-splines [Thom84]. Recent work has suggested that a representation comprised of trimmed B-splines and shared-edge polylines might be closed under Boolean operations [Cobb84], but a full implementation is not yet known to exist.

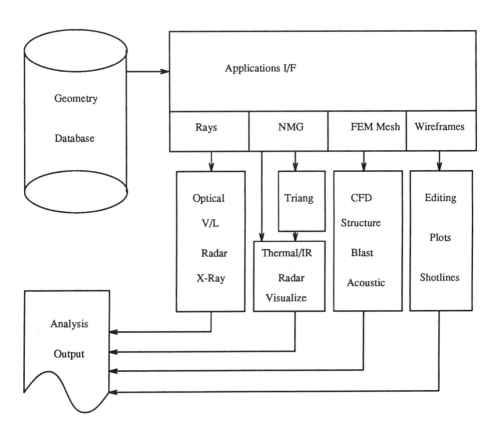

Figure 2. The applications interface.

Because the B-spline representation does not have closure under Boolean operations, it regrettably could not be used. Therefore, the explicit representation of modeled objects is expressed in terms of collections of polygons.

TOPOLOGY

The simplest strategy is to simply ignore topology and store solid objects as collections of polygons. However, it is quite difficult to verify that a given collection of polygons is in fact a valid solid, without any cracks, dangling faces, or missing faces. Implementing Boolean operations without any explicit topology is nearly impossible. Traditionally, solid modeling systems based on boundary representations have employed variations on the *winged-edge* data structure for storing topology [Weil85]. Within the winged-edge representation, an edge represents the boundary or intersection between exactly two faces. Unfortunately, this fails to handle other valid configurations, such as an edge being shared by four faces, or an edge being part of only a single 'dangling' face. These other configurations arise when the topology of an object is not that of a simple 3-manifold, i.e., when the topology of the object cannot be mapped to a sphere. These nonmanifold conditions arise in the construction of finite element meshes and from the use of the Boolean intersection ($\cap$) operation.

This limitation resulted in the development of a new data structure, dubbed alternately the 'radial-edge', 'Non-Manifold Topology' (NMT), 'Non-Manifold Geometry', or 'n-Manifold Geometry' (NMG) data structure [Weil87]. The radial-edge representation provides topological links between *all* faces which share an edge. This single representation has the ability to handle n-manifolds ($\mathbf{M}^n$) for $0 \leq n \leq 3$: 3-manifolds (solids), 2-manifolds (dangling faces), 1-manifolds (dangling edges), and 0-manifolds (lone points). It is regrettable that the name 'Non-Manifold' suggests that objects which are *not* n-manifolds can be represented; they cannot.

Consider the intersection of two solids that share only a single face, edge, or vertex. The result of the intersection is a manifold object of dimension less than three. The winged-edge data structure is unable to represent these Boolean results; thus, it is not closed under Boolean operations. To overcome this lack of closure, winged-edge systems substitute *regularized Boolean operators*, which are defined to produce only 3-manifold results; all lesser dimension results are discarded [Requ82]. In contrast, because all manifold objects of dimension less than three can be represented using the NMG data structures, NMG objects are closed under Boolean operations.

Implementing regularized Boolean operations on objects which are represented by winged-edge structures is quite tedious. In the algorithm it is quite advantageous to discover and retain shared topology, e.g., intersecting edges and vertices, yet the underlying representation is insufficiently powerful to store these relationships [Laid86]. By comparison, the radial-edge (NMG) data structures greatly aid this process, because all topological sharing is directly captured in the data structures, and any possible outcome of a Boolean operation is an object that is directly representable as an NMG object. This makes the Boolean algorithm easy to describe and implement.

Unwanted non-3-manifold results are easy to discard, but there is no way to retain them if the representation cannot express them. This is akin to the 'language limits thought' concept from cognitive psychology. Non-3-manifold results are useful in a variety of ways. One example is in interference or overlap checking. The intersection of two objects is computed. If the intersection is the null set, then the two objects are disjoint and there is space between them. If the intersection is a solid object, then the two objects overlap in the given volume, which generally signals a modeling error. If the intersection is a lone face, edge, or vertex, then the two objects exactly touch but do not overlap.

Generality comes at a significant price in increased memory use compared to the winged-edge data structure. Because of the anticipated frequency of occurrence of non-3-manifold conditions in CSG modeling, both intentionally and as part of various analysis operations, this implementation uses the NMG data structures to contain the approximate surface representation.

CONVERSION VERSUS POSTPROCESSING

Several primitive solids have very complex curved shapes, such as the torus, the truncated generalized cone, the hyperboloid of two sheets, the general polynomial solid, and the B-spline solid. These solids cannot be represented by a collection of polygons without losing essential information about the very nature of the solids. Yet the desire to have a homogeneous representation suggests that all existing solids be converted to a single new underlying representation, to take advantage of the Boolean closure property and to enable applications to access the explicit surface representation.

Two options to consider are either making a one-time conversion of all existing models to a polygonal form, and then performing all subsequent editing and processing on a polygonal database; or retaining the existing, implicit combinatorial solid geometry database, and providing some form of postprocessing capability to convert the implicit CSG shapes into an explicit, polygonal form.

Many existing application codes depend on being able to obtain very accurate surface normal and Gaussian curvature information at any point on an object. Polygonalization artifacts are entirely inappropriate in a CAD system used for high-resolution engineering analysis. Therefore, the existing CSG database must remain unchanged; any application that requires an explicit representation of the modeled shapes obtains it through some form of conversion. This can be thought of as a 'postprocessing' operation. With this strategy, the polygonal representation can be considered an *approximation* of a much more accurate underlying geometric model. It is impossible to choose a single resolution approximation that satisfies all applications. Using a coarse approximation quickly produces complaints about a lack of accuracy in the modeling system. For example, few engineering applications could tolerate square pipes being substituted for genuine round pipe. On the other hand, using a very fine approximation consumes gargantuan amounts of memory, which impedes simple operations such as model editing and display. In this implementation the approximation is created dynamically, so each application has the opportunity to control the resolution of the approximation being created, and to select exactly the required degree of resolution.

IMPLEMENTATION TACTICS

The selected strategy has several key points. Whenever an application requires an explicit description of the surface of an object, it accesses the *application interface* to obtain an approximation created to meet needed accuracy requirements. The application indicates what objects or object hierarchies are to be retrieved from the database and what the accuracy requirements are. In return it is given a collection of NMG data structures that contain the surface approximation of the indicated objects. Each retrieved solid is converted to an approximate faceted form by *tessellation*. As each Boolean operation is encountered, the tessellated solids are combined into a consistent set of solid tessellated objects. Until very recently it was this step that proved difficult [Laid86]. This architecture gives rise to the schematic diagram in Figure 3.

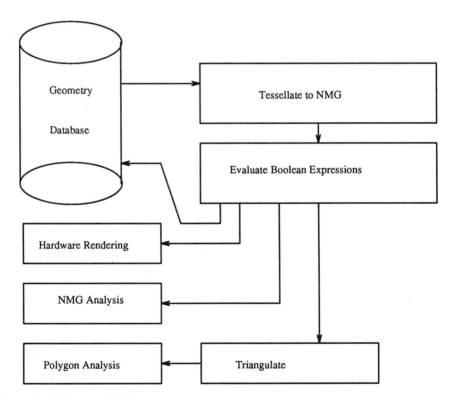

Figure 3. Schematic NMG wiring diagram.

The existing object-oriented programming interface already defined a standardized set of operations on geometric objects, including having a geometric object read itself into memory, describe itself, produce a wireframe representation of itself, and intersect a ray with itself. This interface is extended to define a new operation to require an object to tessellate itself into an NMG data structure. This has the highly desirable property that all the processing related to a given primitive solid remains centralized in a single solid-specific geometry module. Thus, adding a new primitive solid requires only the addition of a single module to the library; none of the analysis codes need to be modified when designers begin using a new kind of primitive.

From the schematic diagram it is clear that the final evaluated NMG solid object is employed in a variety of ways. The primary use is for input to visualization and analysis software that needs an approximate three-dimensional surface mesh of the solid model. However, a very powerful additional use is to create new faceted shapes, which are then stored back in the database as new geometric objects suitable for future editing or analysis. Each face of an NMG object is composed of one or more planar N-gons, each potentially nonconvex and with embedded internal loops. Applications that are prepared to deal with this topological richness may operate on the NMG representation directly. However, for those applications that require a simpler face topology, a simplification routine exists that reduces each face to a collection of planar N-gons. These simplified N-gons may be nonconvex but have no embedded internal loops. Finally, for applications that prefer faces to be collections of simple triangles, a *triangulator* routine is provided that converts the NMG faces into well-behaved triangles [Good89].

n-Manifold Topology and Geometry

The basic topological elements are the vertex, edge, loop, face, shell, region, and model. The relationship between these elements of the hierarchy is depicted in Figure 4. Note that for any element within the hierarchy, there is a direct path from that element to the element one level higher, and also to the element one level lower. The implementation described in this paper is heavily patterned after a description of the radial-edge data structures and operations written by Weiler [Weil87].

The *vertex* represents a unique topological point. The *edge* is a line or curve in space terminated by either one vertex or two distinct vertices. While the older winged-edge representation only allows for a pairwise topological connection between faces, the radial-edge representation topologically links all faces which share the edge as a line of intersection. The *loop* is either a single vertex or a circuit of one or more edges. A loop defines a circuit or a boundary of a space. The *face* consists of one or more loops and represents an actual surface area. The use of a loop within a face may define either an exterior loop or an interior loop. Exterior loops include an area in the face. Interior loops exclude an area from the face surface, thereby causing a hole in the face.

The *shell* is either a single vertex or a collection of faces, loops, and edges. The collection of faces in a shell may enclose a volume, thereby creating closed objects, or may represent arbitrary surfaces. Loops and edges of a shell are referred to as 'wire loops' and 'wire edges.' They may be used in creating wireframe aspects of the model. The *region* is a collection of shells, and the *model* is a collection of regions.

For the elements vertex, edge, loop, and face, there is a distinction between the existence of the element and instances of the use of the element. This allows multiple topological elements to share the same underlying form and geometry. The *vertexuse* is an instance or use of a vertex. The *edgeuse* is a directed instance of an edge. The *loopuse* is an instance of a loop. The *faceuse* is an instance or use of a face. Each side of the face is uniquely represented by a faceuse, i.e., every face is referenced by exactly two faceuses.

Finally, note that each topological element makes reference to a separate geometric element. As a result of this separation of topology and geometry, the kinds of geometric support in the modeling system may evolve into richer and richer forms while continuing to enjoy a common set of topological elements with a stable interface. For example, the system described in this paper is based upon planar faces. However, in the future, the geometry support of the system will be expanded to support curved faces while retaining the same interface to the topology.

The Data Structures in Detail

The first **long** (longword of memory) in any of the NMG structures is dedicated to a *magic number*. It is found either listed explicitly as the first entry in the structure definition, or it is hidden and obtained implicitly from the **struct nmg_list** substructure (described below) which is the first entry in the structure definition. Thus, it is always located at an offset of zero bytes from the start of the structure. This magic number serves a dual purpose. First, every subroutine that is passed a pointer as a parameter can dereference that pointer to obtain the magic number. If the magic number obtained does not match the magic number assigned for use with the expected kind of data structure, then either memory has become corrupted or a defective pointer has been provided as a parameter. Given that some NMG operations may have to dereference pointers through seven connected data structures, it is advantageous to detect invalid pointers as early in the process as possible. Second, some data structures employ *generic* pointers which may refer to one of several different kinds of structures. Rather than using an extra word of memory to store a type indicator, the generic pointer is dereferenced to obtain the magic number and thus the identity of the referred-to structure.

A count of the number of structures within a model is kept. Each structure type contains an integer 'index' member which uniquely identifies the instance of a structure type within the model. This assists algorithms which must temporarily associate some flag or bit of information with structures. In these instances, an array is allocated with the appropriate size so that there exists one array element for each structure in the model.

The NMG data structures make frequent use of doubly linked lists. With one exception, they are all implemented using the same list manipulation macros. (It is the radial-edge linked list which does not follow this form.) All linked lists are made up of **nmg_list** structures

```
struct nmg_list  {
  long             magic; /* magic number */
  struct nmg_list  *forw; /* 'forward', 'next' */
  struct nmg_list  *back; /* 'back', 'last' */
};
```

The magic number identifies the node as either a list head or as a structural element. The two pointers are to the successor and predecessor of the node in the list. Every list has one structure dedicated to functioning as the 'head' node. An empty list consists of a head node whose **forw** and **back** members are pointers to the head node. Defining the doubly linked list as having an explicit head means that the enqueue and dequeue operations operate on any member of the list, and they do not need to refer to the head. The names for linked list head nodes use the **_hd** suffix, and the first letters indicate the type of object in the list. For example, the head of a list of vertexuse structures would be called **vu_hd**. When a structure is to be a part of a linked list, the first element of the structure is an element '1', the list node which becomes a member of a linked

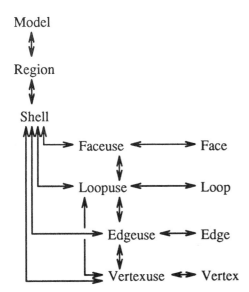

Figure 4. NMG structure hierarchy.

list. As described in the section on linked list implementation, by keeping this item as the first element in the list the list manipulation interface is made fully general for lists of all types of elements.

Consider the task of making a linked list of **edgeuse** structures. The first element of the **edgeuse** structure is an **nmg_list** structure named 1. Thus, the address of 1 is a *pun* (or homonym) for the address of the **edgeuse** structure. By adding 1 to a linked list, in reality the whole **edgeuse** structure is added to the linked list. This allows the list manipulation functions to be generalized to handle lists of any kind of structures. The manipulation routines merely operate on **nmg_list** objects and need not know details about what structure types are in the list. The only requirement is that the **nmg_list** structure must appear as the first element in the containing structure. A rich set of macros exists for insulating the programmer from all the details of inserting and deleting elements from a list, walking a linked list, and various initialization and clean-up operations.

When creating variable names and structure member names, the implementation makes heavy use of abbreviations. As a result, it is important to regularize the abbreviation strategy. The suffix _p is appended to the end of all pointer variables in the structures. The first characters of the variable indicate the type of object the pointer references. For example, a pointer to a vertex structure is v_p, and vu_p is a pointer to a vertexuse structure.

Some structure types have a variety of different structure types as 'parent' or 'child' structures. Since each structure maintains a pointer to its parent and children, a method for maintaining a syntactically correct handle for such objects is required. Such pointers are stored as unions of pointers to each possible type of structure required, plus a pointer to a magic number. For example, Figure 4 demonstrates that a **vertexuse** has either a **shell**, a **loopuse**, or an **edgeuse** for a parent. As a result, the **vertexuse** structure contains something similar to the following:

```
union {
    struct shell   *s_p;
    struct loopuse *lu_p;
    struct edgeuse *eu_p;
    long           *magic_p;
} parent;
```

This union provides a handle for each possible type of parent for the vertexuse structure. In addition, it contains a 'pointer to magic number' handle. This allows the type and validity of the parent to be identified as a particular structure type, before the parent structure is referenced. This union owes its existence to the Pascal origins of the implementation by Weiler. In the C language, a simple 'pointer to long integer' (or the ANSI C 'void *') and the language's ability to coerce one type of pointer into another using typecasting is sufficient. It is debatable whether typecasting or the union-name-handle approach produces more readable source code.

The simplest topological element is the *vertex*. A vertex represents a single point within the topological space of the object being modeled. It also serves as a linkage point for connecting the topological model with the geometrical data. The structures **vertex** and **vertexuse** can be conceptually viewed as in Figure 5. As seen in the structure declaration in Figure 6, the vertex contains a pointer to the geometry **vg_p**, and an **nmg_list** heading a doubly-linked list of all the uses of this vertex. The vertex structure is referenced through a vertexuse structure. The **l** element of the vertexuse structure is entered on the vertex structure's **vu_hd** list, a list of all uses of the vertex. A vertexuse may be referenced by any of the higher level objects: shell, loopuse, or edgeuse. The union **up** points to these three structure types, plus a pointer to a magic number, used as a handle for getting the magic number of the parent. **v_p** is a pointer to the actual vertex. The *vertex geometry* structure contains the coordinates in **point_t**, an array of three floating point numbers.

The next topological element is the *edge*. The edge represents a line or curve between a pair of vertices (Figure 7). As seen in Figure 8, the unique members of this structure are **eu_p**, which points to any one of the uses of the edge, and **eg_p**, which is a pointer to the edge geometry, for future curved-edge support. Note that the edge structure itself does not reference the endpoints of the edge. The endpoints are accessed through the edgeuse structure because almost all references to the edge endpoints occur while processing the edgeuse structures. Within the edgeuse structure, **e_p** ties the edgeuse to the edge.

Each edgeuse references one vertex via the vertexuse structure pointer **vu_p**. The other end of the edge/edgeuse is referenced through the first edgeuse's *mate* edgeuse, via pointer **eumate_p**. Conceptually, the eumate_p edgeuse is the use of the edge on the opposite side (interior/exterior wise) of the face from the

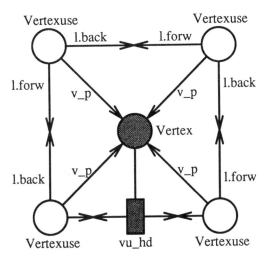

Figure 5. Vertex and vertexuse.

```
struct vertex {
    long              magic;
    struct nmg_list vu_hd;
    struct vertex_g *vg_p;
};
struct vertexuse {
    struct nmg_list    l;
    union {
        struct shell    *s_p;
        struct loopuse  *lu_p;
        struct edgeuse  *eu_p;
        long            *magic_p;
    } up;
    struct vertex       *v_p;
    struct vertexuse_a  *vua_p;
};
typedef double point_t[3];
struct vertex_g {
    long    magic;
    point_t coord;
};
```

Figure 6. Vertex and vertexuse structure.

existing edgeuse. The **eumate_p** and **radial_p** pointers form a linked list of the 'radial uses' of an edge. The edgeuse referenced by **eumate_p** is on the opposite loopuse/faceuse of the same loop/face (Figure 9). The edgeuse l list node is used to form loops of edges or to keep lists of all the 'wire edges' which are a part of a shell. Like the vertexuse, the edgeuse can be referenced by one of two

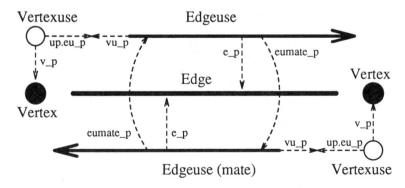

Figure 7. Edge and edgeuse.

```
struct edge {
    long              magic;
    struct edgeuse    *eu_p;
    struct edge_g     *eg_p;
};
struct edgeuse {
    struct nmg_list    l;
    union {
        struct loopuse    *lu_p;
        struct shell      *s_p;
        long              *magic_p;
    } up;
    struct edgeuse    *eumate_p;
    struct edgeuse    *radial_p;
    struct edge       *e_p;
    struct vertexuse  *vu_p;
};
```

Figure 8. Edge and edgeuse structure.

different types of structures higher in the hierarchy, and the same technique is used for providing handles for these parent structures.

A loop defines a boundary or circuit. Conceptually, a loop consists of either a series of one or more edges in a circuit or a single vertex (Figure 10). Like the edge, most of the information is stored in the loopuse structure (Figure 11). lu_p connects the loop to any one of the loopuses of the loop, from where the other use of the loop can be reached via lumate_p. The loop geometry (via lu_g) contains a bounding box.

The loopuse structure is where most of the loop details are handled. The linked list node allows faces and shells to keep lists of loopuses. The union up provides a handle for loopuse parents. lumate_p points to the other use of the same loop as this loopuse, often on the opposite surface of a face. The orientation defines whether this loopuse encloses space or excludes space within a face, i.e., whether this is an interior or exterior loop (Figure 12). The loopuse references the loop via lu_p. down_hd heads a list of the component elements which form the loop. When the loop is made up of edges, this list consists of a series of edgeuses. When the loop is formed on a single vertex, the first and only item in the list is the vertexuse.

Figure 10a depicts a use of a loop (a loopuse) where the boundary formed by the loop consists of a single vertex. Figure 10b depicts a loop which is formed of one edge, and Figure 10c depicts a loop which is formed of four edges. When the loopuse is made up of edgeuses, they are arranged to form a circuit. The mates to these edges also form a circuit for the loopuse mate. If the loopuses are a part of a faceuse, the edgeuses are arranged in a special orientation. When the

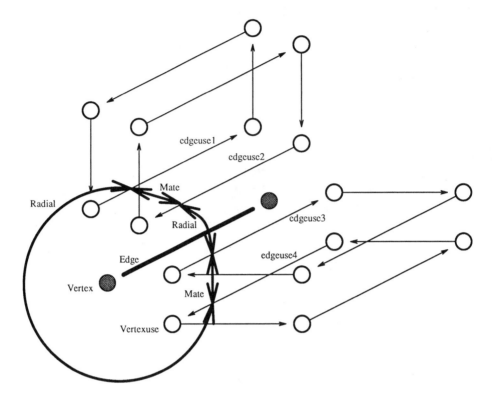

Figure 9. Radial-edge structure.

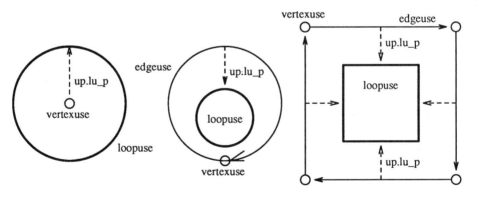

Figure 10. Variations of the loop.

```
struct loop {
    long                magic;
    struct loopuse  *lu_p;  /* Ptr to one use of this loop */
    struct loop_g *lg_p;  /* Geometry */
    long                index;
};
struct loopuse {
    struct nmg_list    l;
    union {
        struct faceuse  *fu_p;
        struct shell    *s_p;
        long            *magic_p;
    } up;
    struct loopuse      *lumate_p;
    char                orientation;
    struct loop         *l_p;
    struct nmg_list     down_hd;
    long                index;
};
```

Figure 11. Loop and loopuse structure.

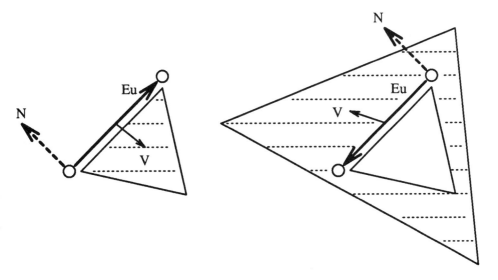

Figure 12. Orientation of edgeuses within a loopuse.

cross product of the vector of the edgeuse and the normal vector for the faceuse is taken, the resultant vector should point into and along the surface of the face (see Figure 11).

The face represents a planar or curvilinear surface with two-dimensional topology. fu_p points to one of the two faceuses of the face, the other being reached through that faceuse's fumate_p pointer. fg_p references the face geometry, which holds a bounding box and the plane equation. The plane equation $N[4]$ is such that a point A which lies on the plane satisfies

$$N_x A_x + N_y A_y + N_z A_z - N_3 = 0$$

Faceuses represent a *side* of the surface of a face, so each face has exactly two faceuses associated with it. The faceuse linked list node exists so that the shell can keep a list of faceuses in the shell. s_p points to the parent shell of the faceuse. The other use of the same face is indicated by fumate_p. orientation indicates which side of the face is represented, i.e., whether the surface normal of the faceuse is the same as in the face geometry structure, or whether the normal is reversed. f_p indicates the actual face. lu_hd is a list of all loops in the face.

```
struct faceuse {
    struct nmg_list   l;
    struct shell      *s_p;
    struct faceuse    *fumate_p;
    char              orientation;
    struct face       *f_p;
    struct nmg_list   lu_hd;
    long              index;
};
```

The shell represents a set of collected, interrelated, and sometimes connected items. l allows shells to be grouped in the parent region, which is pointed to by r_r. fu_hd, lu_hd, eu_hd are used to keep lists of the faceuses, wire loopuses, and wire edgeuses which make up the shell. When the shell consists of a single vertex, vu_p points to a single vertexuse. The shell attribute structure sa_p stores a bounding box for the entire shell.

```
struct shell {
    struct nmg_list     l;
    struct nmgregion    *r_p;
    struct shell_a      *sa_p;
    struct nmg_list     fu_hd;
    struct nmg_list     lu_hd;
    struct nmg_list     eu_hd;
    struct vertexuse    *vu_p;
    long                index;
};
```

Regions group associated shells within the model. The **nmgregion** is included in the model's list of regions through the linked list node at the head of the region structure. The **nmgregion** structure consists of a linked list node **l**, a pointer to the parent model **m_p**, and a list of shells which make up the region **s_hd**. The region attributes structure is used to store a bounding box for the entire region.

The model represents the top of the hierarchy for the NMG structures. The list **r_hd** keeps track of all regions or **nmgregions** in the model space. The integer **maxindex** contains the number of structures allocated in the model. It exists so that temporary arrays are allocated with one element for each structure in the model.

The Tessellators

The job of a tessellator is to convert a given solid into a faceted approximation stored in NMG data structures. There are two aspects to this conversion: establishing the topology of the approximation, and then generating the geometry to associate with the topology. Conversion of a faceted solid is exact, with each face, edge, and vertex of the NMG representation one-to-one with a topological element in the original representation.

Conversion of curved or implicitly defined solids to a faceted representation is necessarily inexact. To provide control over the nature and magnitude of the errors that are introduced by the faceted approximation used in the tessellation, three types of tolerances are passed to the tessellator. The *absolute* tolerance, which limits the maximum permissible difference between any point on the tessellation and the corresponding point on the original solid, is expressed as an absolute distance. This permits users to make absolute statements about the maximum distance error contained in any tessellation. For example, by using this mechanism it is possible to ensure that no face deviates from the true surface by more than two millimeters. The *relative* tolerance also limits the maximum error of any point; but it is expressed as a fraction between 0.0 and 1.0 of the diameter of the bounding sphere which encloses the original solid. This permits users to make statements about the relative error contained in any tessellation. For example, this could ensure that no face deviates from the true surface by more than five percent of the size of the solid. The *normal* tolerance limits the maximum angular error of the surface normal, permitting users to make statements about the accuracy of the surface normals. For example, this could ensure that the surface normals of all faces do not deviate from the exact surface normals of the corresponding points on the original solid by more than five degrees.

Tolerances can be set singly or in any combination. If no tolerances are set, each tessellator module establishes a default minimum tessellation; for example, most tessellators will not approximate a circle with fewer than six line segments. If more than one tolerance is specified, then on a solid by solid basis the most restrictive tolerance is applied. If both an absolute and a relative tolerance are given, then large solids would most likely be tessellated to satisfy the absolute tolerance, while small solids would most likely be tessellated to satisfy the relative tolerance. For example, if an abs=10mm and rel=1%, a large sphere of diameter 1000 mm would be subjected to the absolute tolerance, while a small sphere of diameter 10 mm would be subjected to the relative tolerance.

TESSELLATING THE TORUS

The topology of the torus is a rectangular mesh where the 'edges' of the mesh are connected together, side to side and top to bottom. This can be visualized as follows: if the torus is cut once and straightened, it becomes a right circular cylinder. If the cylinder is cut longitudinally and uncurled, it becomes a rectangle. The 'length' of this rectangle is the distance around the rim of the torus and is traversed as the angle α varies from 0 to 2π. The 'width' is the distance around one cross-section of the torus and is traversed as the angle β varies from 0 to 2π. The torus can also be constructed by constructing a circle in α with radius r_2 and then sweeping that circle out through β with radius r_1. The torus tessellator must determine the minimum number of facets that can be used to represent the torus while still satisfying the given error tolerances. Fortunately, the two axes of the torus are separable and both parts are circles, so this problem reduces to determining the fewest number of line segments that can be used to approximate a circle while still meeting the error tolerances.

Consider a triangle inscribed inside a circle of radius r. One vertex of the triangle is at the center of the circle O; the other two vertices touch the circle at points A and B, as shown in Figure 13. The line segment AB subtends an angle

$$\angle AOB = \theta$$

The point of maximum face distance error is C, the midpoint of AB

$$C = \frac{A + B}{2} \qquad \angle AOC = \frac{\theta}{2} = \gamma$$

Satisfying the surface normal tolerance is the easiest. If the circle is divided into line segments, the surface normal is exact at the midpoint C and has the largest error at the endpoints (A and B) of the line segment. The surface normal error at the endpoints is $\theta/2$. The relationship between the number of line segments n and the angle θ that each line segment subtends is

$$n = \frac{2\pi}{\theta}$$

Thus, to satisfy a surface normal error tolerance of $ntol$, the error at the endpoints is

$$\frac{\theta}{2} \leq ntol$$

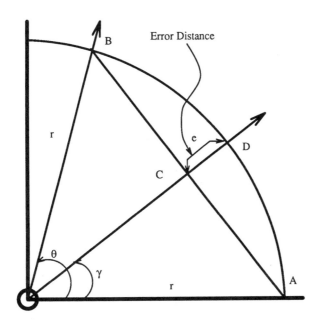

Figure 13. Calculating arc/chord error.

Therefore the minimum number of line segments that can be used is

$$nseg = \frac{2\pi}{2ntol} = \frac{\pi}{ntol}$$

Extend the line OC until it hits the circle, resulting in the point D. The face distance error inherent in the linear approximation of the circle is

$$e = |D - C| = r\left(1 - \cos\frac{\theta}{2}\right)$$

Thus, to meet the face distance error tolerance, a choice of θ is made so that e satisfies the relation

$$e \leq dtol$$

The maximum value of θ is

$$\theta = 2\cos^{-1}\left(1 - \frac{dtol}{r}\right)$$

and the minimum number of line segments that must be used is

$$nseg = \frac{2\pi}{\theta} = \frac{\pi}{\cos^{-1}\left(1 - \frac{dtol}{r}\right)}$$

To efficiently satisfy the maximum surface error tolerance, it is necessary to find the minimum number of line segments that must be used in each of the 'length' and 'width' directions. The appropriate radius is substituted into the formula for *nseg* to determine *nlen* (the number of segments needed in the length direction) and to determine *nw* (the number of segments needed in the width direction). The largest of *nlen* or *nw* or the number of segments required to satisfy the surface normal tolerance is used for the approximation.

All the vertices on the surface of the torus are generated by varying *len* from 0 to *nlen* while also varying *w* from 0 to *nw* and computing

$$\alpha = w\frac{2\pi}{nw} \qquad \beta = len\frac{2\pi}{nlen}$$

$$R = A\cos\beta + B\sin\beta$$

$$P = V + R + r_2\frac{R}{|R|}\cos\alpha + H\sin\alpha$$

where

V	vertex point at the center of the torus
A, B	perpendicular vectors, lie in the plane of the torus, defines 'length'
G, H	perpendicular vectors, defines 'width' direction
H	normal to plane of the torus
P	surface point
r_2	radius of torus around the rim

Tessellating the Ellipsoid

An ellipsoid is defined by a vertex point V at the center and three mutually perpendicular vectors A, B, and C which define the eccentricities. Through an affine transformation the ellipsoid is mapped to a unit sphere located at the origin. The algorithm begins by approximating the sphere by an octahedron, with the six vertices at $V \pm A$, $V \pm B$, and $V \pm C$. The four vertices $V \pm A$ and $V \pm B$ can be thought to lie on the 'equator' of the sphere, and $V \pm C$ are the 'poles'. Each hemisphere starts with four triangular faces. Each face of the octahedron is a triangle, $\triangle DEF$, as shown in Figure 14.

Points D, E, F lie on the surface of the unit sphere. Pick the points G, H, I as the midpoints of the three edges of ABC. Points G, H, I lie inside the unit

Figure 14. Initial octahedron face.

sphere. If each of these points G, H, I is viewed as a vector from the origin in the direction of the surface of the unit sphere, then renormalizing the vectors to unit length causes the points to lie on the surface of the unit sphere. To project point G onto the surface of the sphere, extend the vector from the origin through G to have unit length

$$G := \frac{G - O}{|G - O|}$$

This forces the point to lie on the surface of the unit sphere. Consider each of the four new triangles—$\triangle DGI$, $\triangle GHI$, $\triangle IHF$, and $\triangle GEH$—recursively until the tolerance is satisfied.

It is tempting to consider an adaptive subdivision algorithm, so that when the magnitudes of A, B, and C are not equal the areas of higher curvature are tessellated more finely. Unfortunately, it is not possible to use different levels of subdivision without introducing 'cracks' into the tessellation. Consider the case where triangle $\triangle GEH$ needs further subdivision but triangles $\triangle DGI$, $\triangle GHI$, and $\triangle IHF$ do not, as in Figure 15. The problem here arises because the edge GH in $\triangle GHI$ will no longer match up with edge GL in $\triangle GJL$ and edge LH in $\triangle LKH$, because point L has been normalized to meet the unit sphere. While cracks can be prevented by splitting $\triangle GHI$ into $\triangle GLI$ and $\triangle LHI$, this produces an irregularity in the topology of the tessellation that makes a nonrecursive formulation significantly more difficult.

Let

$$r = \max\left(|A|, |B|, |C|\right)$$

Then the distance tolerance $dtol$ can be expressed as a maximum angular (normal) tolerance as before

$$\theta = 2\cos^{-1}\left(1 - \frac{dtol}{r}\right)$$

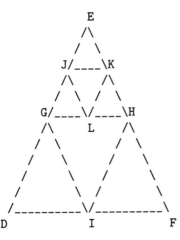

Figure 15. Partially subdivided octahedron face.

The final tolerance to use is the more strict of the surface normal tolerance *ntol* and the distance tolerance

$$tol = \min(ntol, \theta)$$

Thus, the number of triangles used around any one circumference of the ellipsoid is

$$nseg = \frac{\pi}{ntol}$$

Because the initial approximation to the ellipsoid is an octahedron, the number of segments is a multiple of four.

The coordinates of all the vertices of the tessellation of a unit sphere with *nseg* triangles are computed. Each of these coordinates is then transformed back into the coordinate system of the ellipsoid.

Evaluating Booleans

Assume that two objects A and B have been represented using NMG data structures. These objects may originally have been created in their NMG form, or they may have been converted by tessellation from some other form, such as a Combinatorial Solid Geometry (CSG) primitive. A critical aspect of both the tessellation and low-level intersection operations is establishing and using error bounds. Three error tolerances are provided to the tessellation routines. The geometry comparison and intersection routines consider any difference smaller than 1/50th of the smallest tessellation error to be insignificant.

Before the Boolean algorithm begins, the two objects are searched for geometric equivalences. If vertices or edges are discovered to have identical geometry in both objects, they become topologically shared. As sharing occurs, the topology of the two objects is combined: all the element *use* structures in the second object are rehomed to point at the element structure in the first object, and the duplicated element is eliminated.

The process of performing a Boolean operation on two objects is broken down into three steps:

All of the elements in both of the two objects are intersected with each other. The geometry of any points and edges of intersection are computed and are shared by adding topological references to both objects.

Each element of each object is classified with respect to the other object. The three classifications are inside (**in**), on the surface (**on**), or outside (**out**).

Which portions of the model are to be retained and which portions are to be discarded is decided. The exact choices made depend on the Boolean operation selected.

Because the operation is defined as

$$A = A \; bool\_op \; B$$

any elements from B that are retained are moved into the object A, and any remaining elements in B are destroyed.

INTERSECTION OPERATIONS

The first step in the Boolean process is the intersection and cutting of all the elements in the two objects with respect to each other. Each object is represented as an NMG *region*, which is a collection of *shells*. Every element of every shell in region A is intersected with every element of every shell in region B. The algorithm described includes optimizations for planar faces. The current implementation is restricted to dealing with planar faces, although the strategy employed encompasses curved faces by providing additional edge/face and face/face intersection subroutines. The flow of the intersection procedure is summarized in Figure 16.

When the bounding boxes of two faces overlap the two faces are intersected with each other, using the face/face intersection subroutine. In the case of planar face intersection, the plane equations of the two faces are compared. If the two faces are coplanar, their loops are intersected using a two-dimensional polygon clipping approach. All areas common to both faces wind up being defined by loops referenced by both faces.

If the two faces are not coplanar and the bounding boxes of the two faces overlap, then the line of intersection between the two faces is computed. If the line of intersection does not lie within *both* of the face bounding boxes, then the loops in the faces do not intersect each other and this face pair is skipped. This simple check significantly reduces the number of face intersections performed.

```
if bounding boxes of shell A and shell B overlap
  for each face in shell A,
    if bounding box of face A overlaps bound box of shell B
      for each face in shell B
        if bounding boxes of face A and face B overlap
          intersect edges of face A with plane of face B
          intersect edges of face B with plane of face A
          insert new topology & perform meshing
  for each wire edge in shell A,
    if wire edge A overlaps bounding box of shell B
      for each face in shell B
        if edge A intersects face B
          if necessary split edge at plane,
            insert vertex at plane intersection into face
      for each wire edge in shell B
        if wire edges intersect
          create any needed vertices in both wire edges
```

Figure 16. Shell intersection procedure.

Given that the two faces intersect, each edge of face A is intersected with face B, and each edge of face B is intersected with face A.

For planar faces, this edge/face intersection process takes the following form: If an endpoint of the edge is either topologically or geometrically in the plane of the other face, that vertexuse is registered in the list of points on the line of intersection. If the span of the edge crosses the plane of the other face, then a vertex is added at the point of intersection and the original edge is split into two edges. The new vertex which divides the edge lies on the line of intersection. The new vertexuse (for the edge) is added to the list of points along the line of intersection.

After each face/face intersection, the resulting list of points of intersection is sorted geometrically along the line of intersection. As the list of all points (and existing vertexuses) on the line of intersection is generated, the two faces are modified to share topological elements along the intersection. The list is then used to determine which segments of the line of intersection are shared between both faces. Such segments must be added to each face. Segments fall into one of three categories:

> Both endpoints are in the face. A check is made to be certain that an edge does not already exist between these two vertices. If it does not, then each of the two endpoints are examined. If they are part of the same loop of the face, then that loop is divided into two separate loops which share a common (new) edge (Figure 17, left). If the vertices belong to different loops, then an edge which connects the two loops is created and the two loops are joined into a single loop (Figure 17, right).

> When only one of the endpoints exists in the face, the loop which contains the existing vertex is extended to include the new point (Figure 18).

> When neither of the segment endpoints exist in the face, a new interior loop is created in the face (Figure 19).

When all the appropriate topology is inserted into the faces, the topology of the two faces is connected so that edges and vertices which are common to both faces are indeed shared. This process consists mainly of combining vertexuses onto a common vertex and arranging the radial-edge orientation of edgeuses about a shared edge.

All wire edges in each shell must be intersected with everything in the other shell. This involves calling the edge/face and edge/edge intersection routines, as before. If there is an intersection, the edge is split if necessary and the point of intersection is topologically linked to the other face or wire.

OBJECT CLASSIFICATION

When all intersections have been performed, every element in each shell is classified with respect to the other shell. Each face, loop, edge, and vertex is classified as being inside (**in**), on the surface of (**on**), or outside of (**out**) the other shell. Each shell is classified in turn against the other shell. First all elements of shell A are classified with respect to shell B, and then all elements of shell B are classified with respect to shell A.

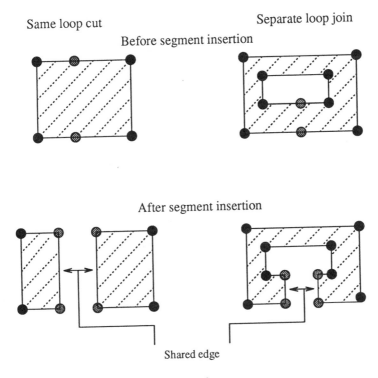

Figure 17. Segment insertion: Both points in face.

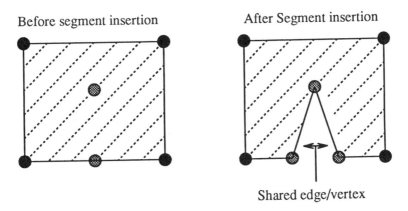

Figure 18. Segment insertion: One point in face.

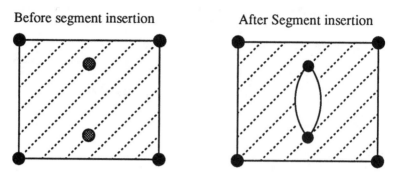

Figure 19. Segment insertion: No points in face.

In order to explain the classification algorithm, it is necessary to define the three kinds of faces. A *boundary face* serves (either alone or in conjunction with other faces) to define the surface of a three-dimensional solid, i.e., the set of boundary faces in a shell enclose a volume. The compliment of the boundary, i.e., all space that is not part of the boundary, has two parts, the *exterior* and the *interior*, where the interior is compact and the exterior is unbounded. With respect to a given solid, every face is either an *interior face*, a *boundary face*, or an *exterior face*. Interior and exterior faces are either *connected*, where all edges of the face lie on a boundary face, or *dangling*, where some edges of the face do not lie on a boundary face. An edge used only once and by a single face of a given shell is a *dangling edge* with respect to that shell. With the radial-edge data structure, this check is performed by a simple traversal of a linked list. When there are no boundary faces in a shell no topological element is inside the shell, so everything is classified as **out**. Ordinarily, solid objects are comprised of only boundary faces.

Vertex Classification

If a vertex in shell A has been previously classified against shell B, then any vertexuse of that vertex which is in shell A shares the same classification. In cases of elements found earlier to be **on** both objects, the classification is immediately evident from the topology (**onAonB**). By looking at the other vertexuses of a vertex, if there is a vertexuse in the topology of shell B then both the vertex and the current vertexuse are classified as being **onB**. All vertices which lie outside of the bounding box of shell B are easily classified as **outB**. Should this fail to classify the vertex, a raycasting approach is employed, applying the Jordan Curve theorem [Mort85].

A single ray is 'fired' from the vertex along an arbitrary line and is intersected with all the faces in shell B. Typically, this line is along one of the major axis directions, although it may be useful to send the ray in some other, nonaligned direction to reduce the probability of hitting the edge of a face or hitting the plane of a face edge-on. The number of *boundary faces* which the ray encounters are counted. If the number of crossings is odd, then the vertex is classified as **inB**. There are three difficult aspects: identifying boundary and nonboundary faces; determining if a hit on a face is inside or outside a face loop; handling the case where a ray exactly intersects an edge or a vertex.

A boundary face is recognized by the absence of conditions which make the face nonboundary. If a face has any dangling edges it is a nonboundary face. If for each edge of the face there exists an odd number of other face-loops of boundary faces of the same shell adjacent to the same edge, then the face is a boundary face. This requires an exhaustive analysis of all faces of the shell to determine if one face is a boundary face. Therefore, this information is calculated once for all faces of the shell; the results are tabulated.

Intersecting a Ray and a Face

Since faces consist of both interior loops (holes in the face) and exterior loops, it is important to be sure that a ray which hits the plane of a face actually hits inside the surface area of the face as well. The in/out status for the hit point is determined by examining the loop which has the subelement (edge or vertex) closest to the hit point. If the hit point is closest to an exterior loop of the face, then the ray hits the face if the point is inside the loop, as in hit point 1 in Figure 20a, or the ray misses the face if the point is outside the loop. Likewise, if the hit point is closest to an interior loop the ray misses the face if the hit point is inside the loop, as in hit point 3 in Figure 20a, or the ray hits the face if the point is outside the loop, as in hit point 2 in Figure 20a.

Intersecting a Ray and an Edge or Vertex

When the hit point of the ray lies on an edge or vertex of a face, further logic must be used to determine whether or not a hit actually occurs. If the ray hits an edge of a loop in a face and there is another loop belonging to the same face with the same type (interior/exterior) adjacent on the edge, then the hit is registered as if the ray had intersected the interior of the loop. For example, in Figure 20a hit point 4 is not a hit on the face because the edge is shared between two interior loops of the same face. On the other hand, in Figure 20a hit point 5 is a hit on the face because the edge is shared between two exterior loops of the face.

If the edge is an external boundary of several faces, then the ray direction is compared to the surface normals of the faces. For example, in Figure 20b ray V1 scores a single hit as it encounters the edge between the two faces, while ray V2 does not score a hit. It is important to note that the ray/edge test is done only once for all the faces which share that edge. When there are more than two faces of the shell sharing the edge, the hit/miss status for each pair of faces is determined at the time the edge is first encountered, and all faces are marked as having been processed.

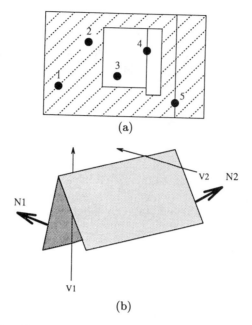

Figure 20. Raytracing hit points.

Edge Classification

Once all the vertex structures in shell A are classified against shell B, the edges are classified according to the rules in Table 1. If one or more of the endpoints is not **onB**, the edge takes its classification from that vertex. If both endpoints are classified as **onB**, the geometric midpoint of the line segment is computed. The midpoint is classified using the ray tracing technique, and the edge inherits that classification. An edge with one endpoint **inB** and one **outB** should not happen; this indicates a fatal error in the intersection process.

Loop Classification

A loop of a single vertex inherits the vertex's classification. A loop of edges containing an edge which is not **onB** inherits that classification. For example,

Table 1. Edge classification rules.

Endpoint classifications	Edge classification
both out	out
out/on	out
both on	use midpoint ray
in/on	in
both in	in
in/out	intersection error

if a loop contains an edge classified **inB**, then the loop is classified **inB**. A loop with edges both inside and outside shell B indicates an error in the intersection process. If all edges of a wire loop are classified as **onB** the loop is classified as **onB**, provided that there exists a loop in the topology of shell B which has exactly the same set of edges. Furthermore, an **on** loop is given the additional classification of **shared** or **antishared**. A shared face loop not only has a counterpart in the other shell, but the normals of the faces of which the loops are a part point in the same direction. A loop is antishared when the surface normals of the parent faces point in opposite directions.

BOOLEAN EVALUATION

After all the topological elements in objects A and B are classified, Boolean evaluation requires deciding which elements to retain and which to destroy. Every element is assigned one of eight combined classifications. The object from which the element originally came is always given an **on** classification. Elements from A are classified as one of **onAinB, onAonBshared, onAonBantishared, onAoutB**, while elements from B are classified as one of **inAonB, onAonB-shared, onAonBantishared**, or **outAonB**. All of these possibilities occur in the two example object pairs (four blocks viewed end-on) in Figure 21; the important face-loop classifications are appropriately labeled.

For the two blocks on the left of Figure 21, the bottom center face-loop exists in both objects A and B, and the orientation (outward surface normal) of the face-loop in both objects is the same (pointing towards the bottom of the page), so the face-loop is classified **onAonBshared**. For the two blocks on the right of Figure 21, the middle face-loop also exists in both objects A and B, but

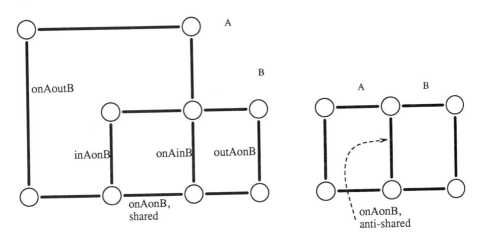

Figure 21. Classification of example objects.

the orientation of the two face-loops are opposite; this face-loop is classified **onAonBantishared**.

Because there are only eight possible classifications, the appropriate action for the Boolean evaluation algorithm is easily tabulated. These actions are found in Table 2. This same table exists in the source code for the Boolean evaluator. Placing these actions into a table permits a separation of *policy* and *mechanism* in the implementation. The policy is encoded in the entries of the table, and the mechanism is embodied in the code of the subroutine. This has two main benefits. First, code to perform any one action exists in only one place, ensuring consistent treatment of all cases. Second, this offers the potential for adding more Boolean operations at a later date by supplementing the table with another column.

Consider first the case of the subtraction operation, A minus B. The intent is to retain every part of A that is **in** only A, to kill every part of A that is also **in** B, and to kill every part of B. This policy is implemented by the tabulated rules. The entry for an element classified as **on** A and **out** B has a table entry of 'retain' (denoted more succinctly as **onAoutB** = `retain`) which preserves the main body of A. **onAinB** = `kill` and **onAonBshared** = `kill`, because these elements are **in** B and represent a portion to be subtracted. **outAonB** = `kill` to eliminate unused parts of B. **onAonBantishared** elements are retained because they are on the surface of A and on the surface of B, where the two surfaces touch. For subtraction, the antishared case is defined as either (a) shaving an infinitesimally thin layer off the surface of A, or (b) a null operation, where the A surface is retained unmodified and the B surface is killed. Because choice (a) would modify the volume of the resulting solid, it is not used; instead, choice (b) is selected. This policy is implemented in these three table entries: **onAonBantishared** = `retain`, **onBonAshared** = `kill`, and **onBonAantishared** = `kill`. Finally, elements classified as **inAonB** are listed in the table as `retain+flip` (retain and flip normal). The surface is retained because it becomes part of the new boundary between A and the outside world. However, the existing surface normal points *into* solid A, reflecting the fact that this surface was originally part of the exterior of solid B, so the surface normal is flipped. The results of subtracting sample objects B from A are illustrated in Figure 22.

Table 2. Boolean evaluation decision table.

A	B	$A - B$	$A \cup B$	$A \cap B$
on	in	kill	kill	retain
on	on shared	kill	retain	retain
on	on antishared	retain	kill	retain
on	out	retain	retain	kill
in	on	retain+flip	kill	retain
on shared	on	kill	kill	kill
on antishared	on	kill	kill	kill
out	on	kill	retain	kill

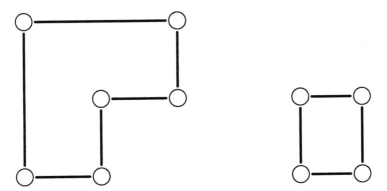

Figure 22. Subtraction performed on example objects.

While the discussion of the table entries is made in terms of surfaces defined by face-loops, the same reasoning and actions apply to the interior topological elements: wire-loops, loop-edges, wire-edges, edge-vertices, and lone vertices. The overall strategy is to process all the topological elements of object A and then all the elements of object B. The meat of the algorithm exists in an internal subroutine which starts by processing the loops in each face. Any loopuse which has a classification that maps to an action of `kill` is demoted into a collection of wire edges. The loop is 'demoted' rather than 'killed', so that edges and vertices that are shared in common with both objects are properly considered later in the subroutine. If none of the loops in the face are retained, then the faceuse is killed. If some loops in the face are retained, then the faceuse is retained; if the faceuse came from object B, then it is moved to object A. The faceuse's mate is also moved to object A, and the face normal is flipped. The algorithm then proceeds down from faces to processing wire-loops. If the loopuse has a classification that maps to an action of `kill` it is demoted into a collection of wire edges; otherwise it is retained and moved into object A if necessary. Next, wire-edges are processed. If the edge is marked `kill` it is demoted into vertices; otherwise, it is retained and moved into object A if necessary. Finally, lone vertices are processed. Because a vertex is a 0-manifold there is no lower dimension topological element to which it can be demoted, so vertices marked `kill` are deleted from the object.

Consider next the case of the union operation, $A \cup B$. The intent here is to retain all elements that are on the exterior of either A or B while eliminating any interior structure or redundant elements. More precisely, for solid modeling the formula for union is interpreted as

$$A \cup B := (A - B) + (B - A)$$

where the $+$ operation is a simple combination or sum operation. The elements that are on the exterior of exactly one of either A or B are classified as

onAoutB and **outAonB** and are retained. Elements that are on the exterior of both A and B appear twice, first as **onAonBshared** which is retained, and again as **onBonAshared**, which is killed (to avoid having the element become duplicated in the result). Interior structure is found in all elements classified as **onAinB**, **inAonB**, plus any antishared faces **onAonBantishared** and **onBonAantishared**. All elements with these classifications are killed. The result of performing the union operation on two example objects is shown in Figure 23.

Finally, consider the case of the intersection operation, $A \cap B$, as shown in Figure 24. The intersection operation retains all elements that are simultaneously part of both A and B, while discarding the excess. Clearly, elements classified **onAonBshared** and **onAonBantishared** are elements common to the two objects and are retained; elements classified **onBonAshared** and **onBonAantishared** are killed to prevent duplication. The elements exterior to one of the objects are classified **onAoutB** and **outAonB** and are also killed. Previously interior structure **onAinB** and **inAonB** is retained, as these elements form the new boundary when the noncommon elements are removed.

The technique just described for evaluating a Boolean formula works reliably and is simple to program and debug. Storing all the policy decisions in a table makes the algorithm very straightforward and simple to alter or augment.

Applications

Any application program that links to the application interface library **librt** can make use of the capability to produce an explicit approximate representation of the surface of any object at any time in the analysis process. This can be simultaneously intermixed with other forms of interrogation, so that an application might perform some operations using the approximate surface description, and other operations using ray tracing. The application need have no knowledge of the underlying primitives used to describe the objects in the database.

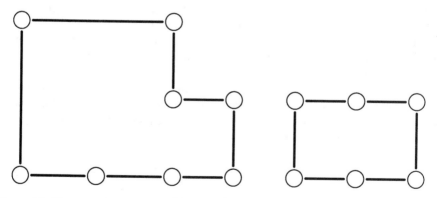

Figure 23. Union performed on example objects.

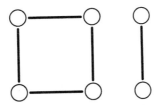

Figure 24. Intersection performed on example objects.

Previously, all renderings of the geometry databases were performed using an optical simulation program based on ray tracing. While ray tracing produces some very beautiful images, it requires a nontrivial amount of processing time. For visualizing the shape of an object a lower quality image produced in significantly less time is acceptable. If the display is fast enough, this also provides an improved interface for geometry editing operations. Being able to edit a seemingly solid object in a rendered form greatly assists in this task.

In the design of vehicles, it is very useful to be able to make predictions about the thermal behavior of the vehicle before the prototype is constructed. If simulation of the thermal behavior of the vehicle reveals heat distribution that is not consistent with the design criteria, it is a simple matter to modify the vehicle geometry or substitute different construction materials in an attempt to improve the situation. Rerunning the thermal simulation allows assessing the effect of these changes. To simulate the thermal behavior of the vehicle it is necessary to calculate a complete heat balance for the entire vehicle, in addition to obtaining the geometry and material property information. The heat balance must account for all the internal sources and radiators of heat, plus external thermal loading due to solar radiation and contact with the earth.

In many cases it is possible to compute a reasonable approximation to the thermal behavior of a vehicle using a description of the surfaces of the vehicle and some 'lump parameters' for the thermal mass of the various components and the primary heat sources. This is the approach taken by PRISM, the Physically Reasonable Infrared Simulation Model [Reyn89]. For predicting a thermal signature, such as might be seen on an imaging infrared sensor, it is necessary to take the simulated patterns of thermal energy radiation and convolve them with the transfer function of the atmosphere that lies between the vehicle and the sensor to determine the patterns of energy presented to the sensor. That pattern in turn must be convolved with the transfer function of the sensor itself in order to predict the signal measured by the sensor. In the design of sensor systems, it is important to know the nature of vehicle signatures over a range of detection bands and for a variety of signal processing schemes [Rapp76, Rapp83]. This provides opportunities for vehicle designers to retain control over the thermal signatures of their vehicles, as well as giving sensor designers an environment for testing and refining improved sensors.

When a metallic vehicle is illuminated with radar energy, that energy is partly absorbed and partly dispersed back into the surroundings. Some of the illumination energy returns to the transmission position, and it does so carrying an electronic 'signature' of the vehicle [Toom82]. Depending on the applications envisioned, a vehicle designer is usually interested in either maximizing the strength of the radar signature (for example, to make boats and commercial aircraft easier to locate in foul weather), or minimizing the strength and recognizability of the radar signature, such as in the design of low-observable ('stealth') aircraft. The most promising technique is the method of moments [Harr82; Moor84], which requires a polygonalization of the surface of the vehicle as input. In order to achieve high accuracy, each surface polygon must be no wider than one-fifth of one wavelength of the radar signal. The relationship between frequency f and wavelength λ is given by

$$\lambda = \frac{c}{f} = \frac{3 \times 10^8 \ m/s}{f \ Hz}$$

Radar frequencies begin in the UHF range, with P-band radars transmitting from 225 MHz to 390 MHz at a wavelength of about one meter [IEEE76]. A millimeter wave (W-band) radar transmitting at 94 GHz emits a signal with a wavelength of 3.2 millimeters. A radar transmitting at a higher frequency has a very short wavelength indeed. Table 3 gives the relationship between frequency f, wavelength λ, and the maximum facet size. Thus, the method of moments technique requires exceptionally fine surface tessellations. Tessellating full size vehicles this finely produces a gargantuan number of facets. Computing a solution to problems of such size is barely within the reach of present-day supercomputers.

Summary

A detailed look was taken at how different analysis applications can interrogate a solid model to extract relevant information. For a CSG solid modeling system, the lack of an explicit representation for the final, developed shapes was identified as critical. With a goal of not impairing the fidelity of existing geometry databases, the systems engineering issues associated with creating an explicit representation for CSG solid models were considered. A strategy using n-Manifold Geometry data structures was adopted. The implementation of the NMG data structures was presented in significant detail. To convert existing primitive shapes into NMG objects the details of several tessellation algorithms were examined, with particular attention being paid to the topic of rigorous user-controlled error bounds on the algorithms.

Evaluating Boolean combinations of tessellated objects has only recently become tractable. The use of the NMG data structures makes these operations quite straightforward. The details of a three-stage algorithm for Boolean evaluation were presented in sufficient detail to permit the reader to implement this technique. A whole gamut of new applications is now able to process existing

Table 3. Relationship between frequency and facet size.

Band	Frequency	Wavelength	Facet Size
P	300 MHz	1000 mm	600mm
L	1 GHz	300 mm	60mm
X	10 GHz	30 mm	6mm
W	94 GHz	3.2 mm	0.64mm

CSG geometry databases. This represents a major and important capability, the true significance of which will only become apparent over the next few years.

Acknowledgements. The authors would like to thank Dr. Paul Deitz for providing unflagging support and encouragement for this effort. He has established a research atmosphere that breeds good work and in which it is fun to work. The authors would also like to thank Prof. David F. Rogers for once again persuading us to take the time to write all this down. Finally, the clarity of the paper was greatly improved thanks to numerous suggestions by Susanne Muuss and Christopher Johnson.

REFERENCES

[Bezi74]
 Bézier, P.E., *Mathematical and Practical Possibilities of UNISURF*, New York: Academic Press, 1974.

[Cobb84]
 Cobb, E.S., Design of sculptured surfaces using the B-spline representation, Ph.D. dissertation, University of Utah, June 1984.

[Coon67]
 Coons, S.A., Surfaces for computer-aided design of space forms, Tech. report MAC-TR-41, Project MAC, MIT, NTIS AD No. 663-504, Cambridge, MA, June 1967.

[deBo78]
 deBoor, C., A practical guide to splines, *Applied Mathematical Sciences*, Vol. 27, New York: Springer-Verlag, 1978.

[Deit82]
 Deitz, P.H., Solid modeling at the US Army Ballistic Research Laboratory, Proc. 3rd NCGA Conf., Vol. 2, pp. 949–960, 13–16 June 1982.

[Deit83]
 Deitz, P.H., Solid geometric modeling—The key to improved materiel acquisition from concept to deployment, presented at Defense Computer Graphics 83, Washington DC, 10–14 October 1983.

[Deit84a]
 Deitz, P.H., Predictive signature modeling via solid geometry at the BRL, Sixth KRC Symposium on Ground Vehicle Signatures, Houghton, MI, 21–22 August 1984.

[Deit84b]
Deitz, P.H., Modern computer-aided tools for high-resolution weapons system engineering, DOD Manufacturing Technology Advisory Group MTAG-84 Conf., Seattle, WA, 25–29 November 1984.

[Deit85]
Deitz, P.H., The future of Army item-level modeling, Army Operations Research Symposium XXIV, Fort Lee, VA, 8–10 October 1985.

[Deit88]
Deitz, P.H., Mermagen, W., Jr., and Stay, P., An integrated environment for Army, Navy, and Air Force target description support, Proc. Tenth Annual Symposium on Survivability and Vulnerability, April 1988.

[Good89]
Goodrich, M.T., Triangulating a polygon in parallel, *Jour. Algorithms*, Vol. 10, 1989.

[Harr82]
Harrington, R.F., *Field Computation by Moment Methods*, Malabar, FL: Krieger, 1982.

[IEEE76]
IEEE, IEEE Standard 521, Institute of Electrical and Electronic Engineers, Piscataway, NJ, 30 November 1976.

[Laid86]
Laidlaw, D.H., Trumbore, W.B., and Hughes, J.F., Constructive solid geometry for polyhedral objects, *Comput. Graph.*, Vol. 20, pp. 161–170, 1986 (SIGGRAPH 86).

[Magi67]
MAGI, A geometric description technique suitable for computer analysis of both nuclear and conventional vulnerability of armored military vehicles, MAGI Report 6701, AD847576, August 1967.

[Moor84]
Moore, J., and Pizer, R., Eds., *Moment Methods in Electromagnetics*, New York: Wiley, 1984.

[Mort85]
Mortenson, M., *Geometric Modeling*, p. 377, New York: Wiley, 1985.

[Muus87a]
Muuss, M.J., Understanding the preparation and analysis of solid models, in *Techniques for Computer Graphics* (State of the Art in Computer Graphics, Stirling, UK, July 1986), Rogers, D.F., and Earnshaw, R.A., Eds., New York: Springer-Verlag, 1987.

[Muus87b]
Muuss, M.J., et al., Ballistic Research Laboratory CAD package, Release 1.21, BRL Internal Publication, June 1987.

[Muus88]
Muuss, M.J., et al., Ballistic Research Laboratory CAD Package, Release 3.0— A solid modeling system and ray-tracing benchmark, BRL Internal Publication, October 1988.

[Muus90]
Muuss, M.J., Multiple families of engineering analyses interrogating a single geometric model, Proc. 8th Army Math. Conf., Ithaca, NY, 19–22 June 1990.

[Rapp76]
Rapp, J.R., A computer model for predicting infrared emission signatures of an M60A1 tank, BRL Report No. 1916, NTIS AD No. B013411L, August 1976.

[Rapp83]
Rapp, J.R., A computer model for estimating infrared sensor response to target and background thermal emission signatures, BRL Memorandum Report ARBRL-MR-03292, August 1983.

[Requ82]
Requicha, A.A.G., and Voelcker, H.B., Solid modeling: A historical summary and contemporary assessment, *IEEE Comput. Graph. and Appl.*, Vol. 2, No. 2, pp. 9–24, March 1982.

[Reyn89]
Reynolds, W.R., PRISM User's Manual Version 2.0, Keweenaw Research Center, Michigan Technological University, Houghton, MI 49931, October 1989.

[Roge90]
Rogers, D.F., and Adams, A.J., *Mathematical Elements for Computer Graphics*, 2nd ed., New York: McGraw-Hill, 1990.

[Thom84]
Thomas, S.W., Modelling volumes bounded by B-spline surfaces, Ph.D. dissertation, University of Utah, June 1984.

[Toom82]
Toomay, J.C., *Radar Principles for the Non-Specialist*, London: Lifetime Learning Publications, 1982.

[Weil85]
Weiler, K.J., Edge-based data structures for solid modeling in curved-surface environments, *IEEE Comput. Graph. and Appl.*, Vol. 5, No. 1, pp. 21–40, January 1985.

[Weil87]
Weiler, K.J., The radial edge structure: A topological representation for non-manifold geometric modeling, in *Geometric Modeling for CAD Applications*, Wozny, M., McLaughlin, H., and Encarnacao, J., Eds., pp. 37–66, Amsterdam: North Holland, December 1987.

Rational B-spline Curves and Surfaces for CAD and Graphics

Les A. Piegl

Abstract

Rational B-splines, commonly referred to as NURBs, have become standard tools for representing and designing free-form as well as standard analytic shapes for Computer-Aided Design and Computer Graphics. This paper surveys important properties of NURBs and provides a set of tools that help the reader develop fundamental algorithms necessary to design and visualize geometric entities defined by NURBs.

Introduction

Nonuniform rational B-splines, commonly referred to as NURBs, have become *de facto* industry standards for the representation and design of geometry. The reasons for the popularity and widespread use of NURBs are that they

    offer one canonical form for the representation of both analytic and free-form shapes;

    provide the flexibility to design a large variety of shapes;

    can be evaluated by numerically stable and accurate algorithms;

    offer nice geometric interpretations and powerful geometric tools;

    are invariant under affine and perspective transformations;

    are generalizations of nonrational B-splines, and rational and nonrational Bézier curves and surfaces.

In this paper we give a summary of all the important tools with which one must be familiar when designing and visualizing geometry defined by NURBs.

Definitions and Elementary Properties

B-SPLINES DEFINED

The simplest way of defining B-splines is by recurrence. The following recurrence equation is due to deBoor, Cox, and Mansfield [deBo72, deBo78; Cox72]. Assume that we are given a *nondecreasing* knot sequence $U = \{\ldots, u_i \leq u_{i+1}, \ldots\}$. Then the *ith* B-spline of degree p is defined as

$$N_{i,p}(u) = \frac{u - u_i}{u_{i+p} - u_i} N_{i,p-1}(u) + \frac{u_{i+p+1} - u}{u_{i+p+1} - u_{i+1}} N_{i+1,p-1}(u) \qquad (1)$$

where
$$N_{i,0}(u) = \begin{cases} 1 & \text{if } u \in [u_i, u_{i+1}) \\ 0 & \text{otherwise} \end{cases}$$

Using $N_{i,0}(u)$ and the recurrence equation (Eq. 1), we see that

$N_{i,p}(u)$ is a polynomial of degree $\leq p$;

$N_{i,p}(u)$ is nonnegative;

$N_{i,p}(u) = 0$ if $u \notin [u_i, u_{i+p+1})$, that is, $N_{i,p}(u)$ has a local support of $(p+1)$ spans;

if $u \in [u_i, u_{i+1})$, then the nonvanishing B-splines are $N_{i-p,p}(u)$, $N_{i-p+1,p}(u), \ldots, N_{i,p}(u)$;

$\sum_{j=i-p}^{i} N_{j,p}(u) = 1$, which is called the partition of unity property.

The derivative of Eq. (1) is computed recursively as

$$N'_{i,p}(u) = \frac{p}{u_{i+p} - u_i} N_{i,p-1}(u) - \frac{p}{u_{i+p+1} - u_{i+1}} N_{i+1,p-1}(u) \qquad (2)$$

The easiest way to verify this is by using the divided difference formulation of B-splines [deBo78; Lee83], which are not discussed in this paper.

An important identity is obtained by refining a given knot sequence. Suppose that the knot u^* is inserted into $[u_i, u_{i+p+1})$ so that the new knot sequence is

$$\bar{u}_i = u_i, \ldots, \bar{u}_l = u^*, \ldots, \bar{u}_{i+p+2} = u_{i+p+1}$$

This new sequence defines two new B-splines, $\overline{N}_{i,p}(u)$ and $\overline{N}_{i+1,p}(u)$. They are related to $N_{i,p}(u)$ [Lee83; Boeh80] by

$$N_{i,p}(u) = \frac{u^* - \bar{u}_i}{\bar{u}_{i+p+1} - \bar{u}_i} \overline{N}_{i,p}(u) + \frac{\bar{u}_{i+p+2} - u^*}{\bar{u}_{i+p+2} - \bar{u}_{i+1}} \overline{N}_{i+1,p}(u) \qquad (3)$$

The easiest verification of this identity is by using divided differences [Boeh80]. A different but more involved proof is given by Lee [Lee83].

It is clear from Eq. (1) that the knot vector uniquely determines the B-splines. Based on the distribution of the knots, we distinguish two kinds of B-splines:

periodic, defined by the knot vector

$$U = \{0, 1, \ldots, n\} \qquad (4)$$

nonperiodic, defined by

$$U = \{\underbrace{0,0,\ldots,0}_{p+1}, u_{p+1}, \ldots, u_{m-p-1}, \underbrace{\alpha, \alpha, \ldots, \alpha}_{p+1}\} \tag{5}$$

In this paper we use nonperiodic B-splines, i.e., we always assume that the end knots are repeated with multiplicity $p + 1$. Periodic B-splines are everywhere $(p - 1)$-times continuously differentiable, whereas nonperiodic B-splines are infinitely continuously differentiable in the interior of a knot span, and $(p - k)$-times continuously differentiable at a knot where k is the multiplicity of the knot [deBo78; Lee83].

Finally, let us look at the set of B-splines defined by the special knot vector

$$U = \{\underbrace{0,0,\ldots,0}_{p+1}, \underbrace{1,1,\ldots,1}_{p+1}\}$$

It can be shown that the B-splines defined over this knot vector degenerate to the Bernstein polynomials

$$B_{i,p}(u) = \binom{p}{i} u^i (1-u)^{p-i}$$

Specifically, $B_{i,p}(u) = N_{i,p}(u)$ $u \in U = \{\underbrace{0,0,\ldots,0}_{p-i+1}, \underbrace{1,1,\ldots,1}_{i+1}\}$

NURBs CURVES DEFINED

A NURBs curve of degree p is a vector-valued piecewise rational polynomial function of the form [Vers75; Till83; Pieg87a; Pieg91]

$$C(u) = \frac{\displaystyle\sum_{i=0}^{n} w_i P_i N_{i,p}(u)}{\displaystyle\sum_{i=0}^{n} w_i N_{i,p}(u)} \tag{6}$$

where the vectors P_i form a so-called *control polygon*, the w_i are called *weights*, and $N_{i,p}(u)$ are the degree p nonperiodic B-splines defined over the knot vector (Eq. 5) (see Figure 1). In this paper we choose $\alpha = 1$ for simplicity. For ease of computation, we introduce the following *rational basis functions*

$$R_{i,p}(u) = \frac{w_i N_{i,p}(u)}{\displaystyle\sum_{j=0}^{n} w_j N_{j,p}(u)} \tag{7}$$

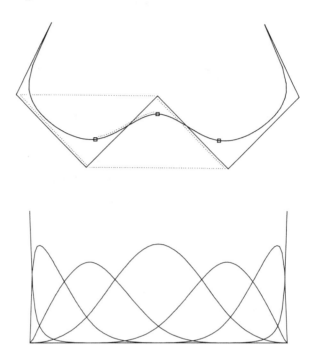

Figure 1. Cubic NURBs curve with associated basis functions. The dotted curve segment is contained in the convex hull (dotted area) of four control points.

The curve defined by Eq. (6) is then written as

$$C(u) = \sum_{i=0}^{n} P_i R_{i,p}(u) \tag{8}$$

If we assume that $w_i \geq 0$, then the $R_{i,p}(u)$, which are rational polynomials
of degree p, have the same properties as the $N_{i,p}(u)$, i.e., nonnegativity, local
support, and partition of unity.

Based on the knot vector (Eq. 5) and on the properties of rational basis functions, we deduce the following geometric properties of rational B-spline curves:

endpoint interpolation: Using the recurrence equation (Eq. 1), you can con-
vince yourself that $N_{0,p}(u) = [(u_{p+1} - u)/u_{p+1}]^p$. Since the B-splines sum
to 1 at a particular u value, $N_{0,p}(u)$ must be the only B-spline that is nonzero
at $u = 0$. Therefore, $R_{0,p}(0) = 1$ and so $C(0) = P_0$. Similarly, $C(1) = P_n$.

strong convex hull property: If $u \in [u_i, u_{i+1})$, then the nonvanishing B-splines
are $N_{i-p,p}(u), \ldots, N_{i,p}(u)$, which are nonnegative and sum to 1. This means
that $R_{i-p,p}(u), \ldots, R_{i,p}(u)$ are nonnegative and sum to 1. That is, $C(u)$
must be in the convex hull of $P_{i-p}, \ldots, P_i$.

local approximation: Since $R_{i,p}(u)$ vanishes outside the interval $[u_i, u_{i+p+1})$,
if the control point P_i is moved *or* the weight w_i is changed, only the portion
of the curve defined over this interval is modified.

transformation invariance: A NURBs curve is invariant under the most commonly used graphical transformations, e.g., rotation, scaling, translation, parallel and perspective projections.

In many graphical interrogation techniques, e.g., shading, the computation of derivatives is needed. The derivatives of rational functions look rather complicated, especially in the case of higher order derivatives that contain a denominator with an expression taken to a high power. To avoid this, we use

$$C(u) = \frac{w(u)\,C(u)}{w(u)} = \frac{q(u)}{w(u)}$$

where $w(u)$ denotes the denominator of Eq. (6). The derivative of this form is simply

$$\dot{C}(u) = \frac{\dot{q}(u) - \dot{w}(u)\,C(u)}{w(u)} \tag{9}$$

where $\dot{q}(u)$ is the derivative of the numerator of Eq. (6). The nice property of this form is that the denominator is not taken to the power of two. This equation can be generalized to obtain higher order derivatives by taking the derivatives of $q(u)$

$$q^r(u) = [\,w(u)\,C(u)\,]^r = \sum_{i=0}^{r} \binom{r}{i} w^i(u)\,C^{(r-i)}(u)$$

$$= w(u)\,C^r(u) + \sum_{i=1}^{r} \binom{r}{i} w^i(u)\,C^{(r-i)}(u)$$

from which we obtain

$$C^r(u) = \frac{q^r(u) - \sum_{i=1}^{r}\binom{r}{i} w^i(u)\,C^{(r-i)}(u)}{w(u)} \tag{10}$$

The only computation that needs to be detailed is the evaluation of the rth derivative of a nonrational curve. Denoting $w_i P_i$ by A_i, $q(u)$ has the form

$$q(u) = \sum_{i=0}^{n} A_i N_{i,p}(u)$$

From Eq. (2) we have

$$q'(u) = \sum_{i=0}^{n} A_i\,\frac{p}{u_{i+p} - u_i}\,N_{i,p-1}(u) + \sum_{i=0}^{n} A_i\,\frac{p}{u_{i+p+1} - u_{i+1}}\,N_{i+1,p-1}(u)$$

Changing the summation variable in the second sum from i to $i+1$, and noting that $N_{0,p-1}(u)$ vanishes, we have

$$q'(u) = \sum_{i=1}^{n} p\,\frac{A_i - A_{i-1}}{u_{i+p} - u_i}\,N_{i,p-1}(u) = \sum_{i=1}^{n} A_i^1\,N_{i,p-1}(u) \tag{11}$$

This equation generalizes to the rth derivative as

$$q^r(u) = \sum_{i=r}^{n} A_i^r \, N_{i,p-i}(u) \tag{12}$$

where

$$A_i^r = (p - r + 1) \frac{A_i^{(r-1)} - A_{i-1}^{(r-1)}}{u_{i+p+1-r} - u_i} \tag{13}$$

The assignment or computation of weights has always been a problem. In the *Design algorithms* sections techniques for interactive adjustment of curves and surfaces are given. In this section a geometric meaning is associated with each weight, that helps to develop algorithms for interactive shape modification. Assume that the geometric meaning of w_i is sought. Since it affects the curve only in $[u_i, u_{i+p+1})$, we restrict our investigations to this interval and define the points (see Figure 2 and Piegl [Pieg89a])

$$B = C(u; w_i = 0)$$
$$N = C(u; w_i = 1)$$
$$B_i = C(u; w_i \neq \{0, 1\}) \tag{14}$$

N and B_i are expressed as

$$N = (1 - \alpha) \, B + \alpha P_i$$
$$B_i = (1 - \beta) \, B + \beta P_i \tag{15}$$

where

$$\alpha = R_{i,p}(u; w_i = 1)$$
$$\beta = R_{i,p}(u) \tag{16}$$

From the expressions for α and β we obtain the identity

$$\frac{1 - \alpha}{\alpha} : \frac{1 - \beta}{\beta} = \frac{P_i N}{BN} : \frac{P_i B_i}{BB_i} = w_i \tag{17}$$

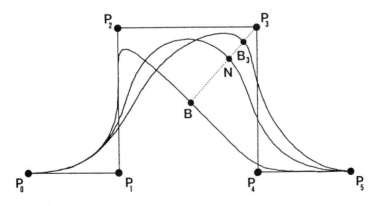

Figure 2. Geometric meaning of weights.

This is called the *cross ratio* or *double ratio* of the four points P_i, B, N, and B_i (in that order) and is *the* fundamental quantity of projective geometry. From Eqs. (15) and (17) we have

as w_i changes, the point $C(u)$ sweeps out the straight line segment P_iB;

if w_i increases/decreases, the position of B_i moves closer/farther to/from P_i; therefore, the curve is pulled/pushed toward/away from P_i.

NURBs Surfaces Defined

A NURBs surface of degree p in the u direction, and degree q in the v direction, is a bivariate, vector-valued piecewise rational polynomial function of the form

$$S(u,v) = \frac{\sum\limits_{i=0}^{n}\sum\limits_{j=0}^{m} w_{i,j}P_{i,j}N_{i,p}(u)N_{j,q}(v)}{\sum\limits_{i=0}^{n}\sum\limits_{j=0}^{m} w_{i,j}N_{i,p}(u)N_{j,q}(v)} \tag{18}$$

where the $P_{i,j}$ form a control net, $w_{i,j}$ are the weights as in the case of curves, and $N_{i,p}(u)$ and $N_{j,q}(v)$ are the degree p and q nonperiodic B-splines defined over the knot vectors

$$U = \{\underbrace{0,0,\ldots,0}_{p+1}, u_{p+1},\ldots, u_{r-p-1}, \underbrace{1,1,\ldots,1}_{p+1}\} \tag{19}$$

$$V = \{\underbrace{0,0,\ldots,0}_{q+1}, v_{q+1},\ldots, v_{s-q-1}, \underbrace{1,1,\ldots,1}_{q+1}\} \tag{20}$$

where $r = n+p+1$ and $s = m+q+1$ (Figure 3). Introducing the *rational basis functions*

$$R_{i,j}(u,v) = \frac{w_{i,j}N_{i,p}(u)N_{j,q}(v)}{\sum\limits_{k=0}^{n}\sum\limits_{l=0}^{m} w_{k,l}N_{k,p}(u)(u)N_{l,q}(v)} \tag{21}$$

the surface (Eq. 18) is written as

$$S(u,v) = \sum_{i=0}^{n}\sum_{j=0}^{m} P_{i,j}R_{i,j}(u,v) \tag{22}$$

Assuming that $w_{i,j} \geq 0$, the rational basis functions (Eq. 21) are nonnegative, have support rectangle $[u_i, u_{i+p+1}) \times [v_j, v_{j+q+1})$, and sum to 1. The analysis of surfaces is quite similar to those of curves; therefore, we only summarize the most important properties, i.e.,

endpoint interpolation: $S(0,0) = P_{0,0},\ldots, S(1,1) = P_{n,m}$;

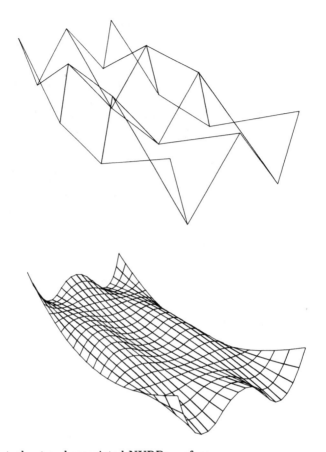

Figure 3. Control net and associated NURBs surface.

strong convex hull: if $u \in [u_i, u_{i+1})$ and $v \in [v_j, v_{j+1})$, then $S(u,v)$ is in the convex hull of $P_{i-p,j-q}, \ldots, P_{i,j}$;

local approximation: if the control point $P_{i,j}$ is moved, or if the weight $w_{i,j}$ is changed, then only those points of the surface are modified which are defined over the rectangle $[u_i, u_{i+p+1}) \times [v_j, v_{j+q+1})$;

transformation invariance: a NURBs surface is invariant under the commonly used graphical transformations.

To obtain partial derivatives we use

$$S(u,v) = \frac{w(u,v)S(u,v)}{w(u,v)} = \frac{q(u,v)}{w(u,v)}$$

the partial derivative of which is

$$S_\alpha(u,v) = \frac{q_\alpha(u,v) - w_\alpha(u,v)\, S(u,v)}{w(u,v)} \tag{23}$$

where α denotes either u or v. The mixed partial derivatives are obtained by differentiating $q(u,v)$, that is

$$q_{uv}(u,v) = \frac{\partial^2}{\partial u \partial v} \left[w(u,v) S(u,v) \right]$$

$$= w_{uv}S + w_u S_v + w_v S_u + w S_{uv}$$

from which we get

$$S_{uv} = \frac{q_{uv} - w_{uv}S - w_u S_v - w_v S_u}{w} \tag{24}$$

where, for simplicity, we drop the arguments.

To evaluate this form, we need partial derivatives of nonrational surfaces. Using the results obtained for curves, we have

$$q_u(u,v) = p \sum_{i=1}^{n} \sum_{j=0}^{n} A_{i,j}^{(1,0)} N_{i,p-1}(u) N_{j,q}(v) \tag{25}$$

where $A_{i,j} = w_{i,j} P_{i,j}$, and $A_{i,j}^{(1,0)} = \frac{A_{i,j} - A_{i-1,j}}{u_{i+p} - u_i}$. The v-directional partial derivative is obtained similarly. The mixed partial derivative is simply the v-directional derivative of Eq. (25), that is

$$q_{uv}(u,v) = p q \sum_{i=1}^{n} \sum_{j=1}^{m} A_{i,j}^{(1,1)} N_{i,p-1}(u) N_{j,q-1}(u) \tag{26}$$

where

$$A_{i,j}^{(1,1)} = \frac{A_{i,j}^{(1,0)} - A_{i,j-1}^{(1,0)}}{v_{j+q} - v_j}$$

The weight $w_{i,j}$ carries the same geometric meaning as in the case of curves, i.e., it is the cross ratio of four points: $P_{i,j}$, $S(u,v; w_{i,j} = 0)$, $S(u,v; w_{i,j} = 1)$, and $S(u,v; w_{i,j} \neq \{0,1\})$ [Pieg89b].

Computational Algorithms

GEOMETRIC INTERPRETATION

In this section we provide an elegant geometric interpretation of NURBs that results in efficient evaluation routines and in a compact data base. The idea is to use *homogeneous coordinates*, that is, to represent the point $P = [x \quad y \quad z]$ in the form of $P^w = [wx \quad wy \quad wz \quad w]$ in 4D. Notice that P is obtained from P^w by dividing by the fourth component, that is, by mapping P^w from the origin to the hyperplane $w = 1$. Now the geometric construction of NURBs curves is as follows [Vers75; Till83; Pieg87a, Pieg91] (see Figure 4):

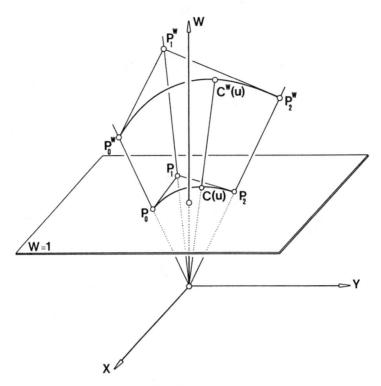

Figure 4. Geometric construction of NURBs curves.

for a given set of control points and weights, construct the weighted vertices
$P_i^w = [\,w_i x_i \quad w_i y_i \quad w_i z_i \quad w_i\,]$;

define a nonrational curve in 4D

$$C^w(u) = \sum_{i=0}^{n} P_i^w N_{i,p}(u)$$

map the curve from the origin onto the plane

$$C(u) = \text{MAP}\,(C^w(u)) = \frac{\displaystyle\sum_{i=0}^{n} w_i P_i N_{i,p}(u)}{\displaystyle\sum_{i=0}^{n} w_i N_{i,p}(u)}$$

where MAP denotes the perspective projection from the origin onto the
hyperplane $w = 1$.

We use this interpretation in the algorithms that follow, that is, nonrational forms are evaluated in 4D, and the results are located in 3D by using the projection MAP. It is defined explicitly as

$$\text{MAP}\,(x_1, x_2, \ldots, x_n) = \begin{cases} \left(\dfrac{x_1}{x_n}, \ldots, \dfrac{x_{n-1}}{x_n} \right) & \text{if } x_n \neq 0 \\ \text{direction}(x_1, \ldots, x_{n-1}) & \text{if } x_n = 0 \end{cases}$$

DIRECT EVALUATION

Assume that a NURBs curve is to be evaluated at the parameter value $u \in [u_i, u_{i+1})$. Since the nonvanishing B-splines are $N_{i-p,p}(u), \ldots, N_{i,p}(u)$, the program fragment looks like

```
ALGORITHM A1:
  Cw=0.0;
  for(k=i-p; k<=i; k++) {
    Cw=Cw+Pw[k]*Np[k];
  }
  C=MAP(Cw);
```

In the case of surfaces where $u \in [u_i, u_{i+1})$ and $v \in [v_j, v_{j+1})$, a similar algorithm is obtained.

```
ALGORITHM A2:
  Sw=0.0;
  for(k=i-p; k<=i; k++) {
    for(l=j-q; l<=j; l++) {
      Sw=Sw+Pw[k][l]*Np[k]*Nq[l];
    }
  }
  S=MAP(Sw);
```

The only unknowns in algorithms A1 and A2 are the B-splines. An efficient algorithm for the computation of all the nonvanishing B-splines is found in deBoor [deBo78, pp. 132–135].

CORNER CUTTING

Suppose again that $u \in [u_i, u_{i+1})$. Then by Eq. (1) we have

$$C^w(u) = \sum_{j=i-p}^{i} P_j^w N_{j,p}(u)$$

$$= \sum_{j=i-p}^{i} P_j^w \frac{u - u_j}{u_{j+p} - u_j} N_{j,p-1}(u) + \sum_{j=i-p}^{i} P_j^w \frac{u_{j+p+1} - u}{u_{j+p+1} - u_{j+1}} N_{j+1,p-1}(u)$$

Using the index transformation $j \to j+1$ in the second sum, and noting that $N_{i-p,p-1}(u) = N_{i+1,p-1}(u) = 0$, we have

$$C^w(u) = \sum_{j=i-p+1}^{i} P_{j,1}^w N_{i,p-1}(u) \tag{27}$$

where
$$P_{j,1}^w = \frac{(u-u_j)P_j^w + (u_{j+p}-u)P_{j-1}^w}{u_{j+p}-u_j} \tag{28}$$

Applying the idea recursively yields (Figure 5)

$$C^w(u) = \sum_{j=i-p+k}^{i} P_{j,k}^w N_{i,p-k}(u) \tag{29}$$

where
$$P_{j,k}^w = \frac{(u-u_j)P_{j,k-1}^w + (u_{j+p-k+1}-u)P_{j-1,k-1}^w}{u_{j+p-k+1}-u_j} \tag{30}$$

Now, if $k = p$ we have

$$C^w(u) = \sum_{j=i}^{i} P_{j,p}^w N_{i,0}(u) = P_{j,p}^w$$

This results in the following algorithm:

```
ALGORITHM A3:
  for(j=0; j<=p; j++) Qw[j]=Pw[i-p+j];
  for(k=1; k<=p; k++) {
    for(j=0; j<=p-k; j++) {
      a=u-U[i-p+k+j];
      b=U[i+1+j]-u;
      Qw[j]=(a*Qw[j+1]+b*Qw[j])/(a+b);
    }
  }
C=MAP(Qw[0]);
```

The idea of curve corner cutting is extended to surfaces by using the 4D representation, that is

$$S^w(u,v) = \sum_{i=0}^{n} \sum_{j=0}^{m} P_{i,j}^w N_{i,p}(u) N_{j,q}(v) \tag{31}$$

This tensor product form is written as

$$S^w(u,v) = \sum_{i=0}^{n} \left[\sum_{j=0}^{m} P_{i,j}^w N_{j,q}(v) \right] N_{i,p}(u)$$

$$= \sum_{i=0}^{n} P_{i,j}^w(v) N_{i,p}(u) \tag{32}$$

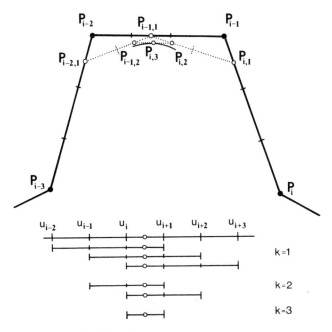

Figure 5. Corner cutting algorithm for curves.

Since $P_{i,j}^w(v), i = 0, \ldots, m$ are B-spline curves, the surface is evaluated by using curve evaluation. Suppose that $u \in [u_i, u_{i+1})$ and $v \in [v_j, v_{j+1})$. The control net to be cut is $P_{i-p,j-q}^w, \ldots, P_{i,j}^w$. The algorithm first cuts each row (column) of control points in the $u(v)$ direction, and then cuts the resulting polygon in the $v(u)$ direction.

Geometry Tools

KNOT INSERTION

Assume that $u \in [u_i, u_{i+1})$ and that a new knot u is to be inserted into the knot vector U. The new knot vector is

$$\overline{U} = \{\bar{u}_0 = u_0, \ldots, \bar{u}_i = u_i, \bar{u}_{i+1} = u, \bar{u}_{i+2} = u_{i+1}, \ldots, \bar{u}_{m+1} = u_m\}$$

Using Eq. (3) we obtain

$$C^w(u) = \sum_{j=i-p}^{i} P_i^w N_{i,p}(u)$$

$$= \sum_{j=i-p}^{i} P_i^w \frac{u - \bar{u}_j}{\bar{u}_{j+p+1} - \bar{u}_j} \overline{N}_{j,p} + \sum_{j=i-p+1}^{i+1} P_{i-1}^w \frac{\bar{u}_{j+p+1} - u}{\bar{u}_{j+p+1} - \bar{u}_j} \overline{N}_{j,p}$$

$$= \sum_{j=i-p}^{i+1} Q_{j,1}^w N_{i,p}(u) \tag{33}$$

where

$$Q_{i-p,1}^w = \frac{u - \bar{u}_{i-p}}{\bar{u}_{i+1} - \bar{u}_{i-p}} \, P_{i-p}^w = P_{i-p}^w$$

$$Q_{i+1,1}^w = \frac{\bar{u}_{i+p+2} - u}{\bar{u}_{i+p+2} - \bar{u}_{i+1}} \, P_i^w = P_i^w \qquad (\bar{u}_{i+1} = u)$$

and

$$Q_{j,1}^w = \frac{(u - \bar{u}_j)P_j^w + (\bar{u}_{j+p+1} - u)P_{j-1}^w}{\bar{u}_{j+p+1} - \bar{u}_j}$$

$$= \frac{(u - u_j)P_j^w + (u_{j+p} - u)P_{j-1}^w}{u_{j+p} - u_j} \tag{34}$$

for $i - p + 1 \leq j \leq i$ (Figure 6). The new control points of the curve are

$$P_0^w, \ldots, P_{i-p}^w, Q_{i-p+1,1}^w, \ldots, Q_{i,1}^w, P_i^w, \ldots, P_n^w$$

Inserting the same knot one more time (insert u at the left endpoint) yields

$$Q_{j,2}^w = \frac{(u - u_j)Q_{j,1}^w + (u_{j+p-1} - u)Q_{j-1,1}^w}{u_{j+p-1} - u_j} \tag{35}$$

for $i - p + 2 \leq j \leq i$. The new control polygon is

$$P_0^w, \ldots, P_{i-p}^w, Q_{i-p+1,1}^w, Q_{i-p+2,2}^w, \ldots, Q_{i,2}^w, Q_{i,1}^w, P_i^w, \ldots, P_n^w$$

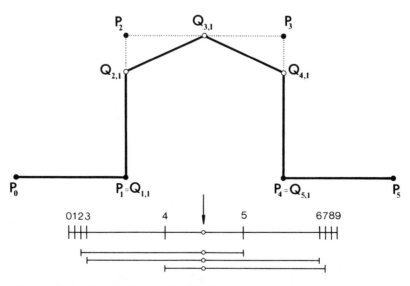

Figure 6. Inserting a knot into a cubic NURBs curve.

Set $k = 2$ in Eq. (30). Now, if we compare Eqs. (28) and (30) with Eqs. (34) and (35) we see that knot insertion gives exactly the control points of the intermediate stages of the corner cutting algorithm. From this it follows that adding knots with multiplicity p results in the point on the curve $C^w(u)$. The above knot insertion equations can be put into a more concise form. Assume that $u \in [u_i, u_{i+1})$ and u is to be inserted with multiplicity $r \leq p$; then the new control points are obtained as follows [Boeh80]

$$Q_{j,r}^w = \alpha_{j,r} Q_{j,r-1}^w + (1 - \alpha_{j,r}) Q_{j-1,r-1}^w \tag{36}$$

where

$$\alpha_{j,r} = \begin{cases} 1 & j \leq i - p + r - 1 \\ \dfrac{u - u_j}{u_{j+p-r+1} - u_j} & i - p + r \leq j \leq i \\ 0 & j \geq i + 1 \end{cases}$$

with $Q_{j,0}^w = P_j^w$. If $r = p$, then $C^w(u) = Q_{j,p}^w$.

CURVE SPLITTING

It is shown in this section that Eq. (36) can be used to split the curve at $u \in [u_i, u_{i+1})$. First, an important characteristic of B-splines is established. According to the recursive definition of Eq. (1), $N_{i,p}(u)$ is defined in terms of $N_{i,p-1}(u)$ and $N_{i+1,p-1}(u)$. These B-splines are defined over the intervals $[u_i, u_{i+p})$ and $[u_{i+1}, u_{i+p+1})$, respectively. Now, if we look at the shape of $N_{i,p}(u)$ in the interval $[u_i, u_{i+1})$, we see that it is independent of the location of the knot u_{i+p+1}, since $N_{i,p-1}(u)$ is independent of this knot and $N_{i+1,p-1}(u)$ vanishes over $[u_i, u_{i+1})$. Similarly, the shape of $N_{i,p}(u)$ in the interval $[u_{i+p}, u_{i+p+1})$ is independent of the position of the knot u_i.

Now let us insert a knot $u \in [u_i, u_{i+1})$ p-times, so that the knot vector is

$$U = \{\ldots, u_i, \underbrace{u, \ldots, u}_{p}, u_{i+1}, \ldots\}$$

It follows from the previous discussion that p multiple knots are essentially the same as $(p + 1)$ multiple knots, since the shapes of the B-splines in the intervals $[u_i, u)$ and $[u, u_{i+1})$ are independent of the last and of the first occurrences of the u's, respectively. That means that insertion of the knot u with multiplicity p *splits* the curve into two parts defined by the control polygons

$$P_L = \{Q_0^w, \ldots, Q_i^w\}$$
$$P_R = \{Q_i^w, \ldots, Q_{n+p}^w\}$$

and by the knot vectors

$$U_L = \{\underbrace{0, \ldots, 0}_{p+1}, u_{p+1}, \ldots, u_i, \underbrace{u, \ldots, u}_{p+1}\}$$

$$U_R = \{\underbrace{u, \ldots, u}_{p+1}, u_{i+1}, \ldots, u_{m-p-1}, \underbrace{1, \ldots, 1}_{p+1}\}$$

Decomposition into Piecewise Bézier Form

The knot insertion algorithm is more powerful than it seems at first glance. It is shown here that the algorithm can be used to obtain the piecewise Bézier representation of a NURBs curve or surface (Figure 7). Let us consider the knot span $[u_i, u_{i+1})$ and insert these knots with multiplicity $p - 1$ (so that the total multiplicity is p). The new knot vector is then

$$U = \{\ldots, v_l = u_i, v_{l+1} = u_i, \ldots, v_{l+p-1} = u_i,$$

$$v_{l+p} = u_{i+1}, \ldots, v_{l+2p-1} = u_{i+1}, \ldots\} \tag{37}$$

Now let us look at $N_{l-1,p}(u)$. Since its shape in the interval $[u_i, u_{i+1}) = [v_l, v_{l+p})$ is independent of v_{l-1}, we can increase the multiplicity of v_l. A Bernstein polynomial defined over the interval $[u_i, u_{i+1}) : [(u_{i+1} - u)/(u_{i+1} - u_i)]^p$ results. Similar results can be obtained for the B-splines $N_{l,p}(u), \ldots, N_{l+p-1,p}(u)$, which means that after inserting each intermediate knot with multiplicity $p - 1$ we obtain the piecewise Bézier representation of a NURBs curve. One piece of a Bézier curve, defined over $[u_i, u_{i+1}]$, has the analytic form

$$C^w(u) = \sum_{j=0}^{p} Q_{l+j}^w \binom{p}{j} \frac{(u - u_i)^j (u_{i+1} - u)^{p-j}}{(u_{i+1} - u_i)^p} \tag{38}$$

where $l = p(i - p)$.

Knot Refinement

In many practical applications, the insertion of several knots with different multiplicities is required (Figure 8). The refinement of a knot vector can be done by inserting each knot in turn, using Eq. (36). While this is a feasible solution, a more efficient method can be devised. Assume that the elements of the vector $X = \{x_0, x_1, \ldots, x_r\}$, $x_i \le x_{i+1}$ are to be inserted into the knot vector $U = \{u_0, u_1, \ldots, u_m\}$, where $m = n + p + 1$. Furthermore, assume that X 'fits' into the knot vector U, that is, there exist indices a and b such that $X \in [u_a, u_b)$. Knots with multiplicities are treated as different; e.g., if one wants to insert two knots x and y with multiplicities 2 and 3, respectively, then $X = \{x, x, y, y, y\}$. The algorithm is

```
ALGORITHM A4:
    for(j=0; j<=a-p; j++) Qw[j]=Pw[j];
    for(j=b-1; j<=n; j++) Qw[j+r+1]=Pw[j];
    for(j=0; j<=a; j++) V[j]=U[j];
    for(j=b+p; j<=m; j++) V[j+r+1]=U[j];
    i=b+p-1; k=b+p+r;
    for(j=r; j>=0; j--) {
        while(x[j]<=U[i] && i>a) {
            Qw[k-p-1]=Pw[i-p-1];
```

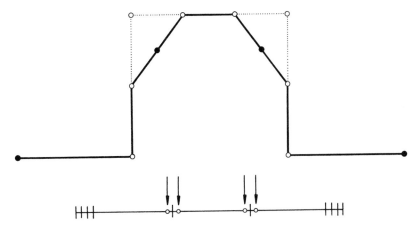

Figure 7. Decomposing a cubic NURBs curve into piecewise Bézier curves.

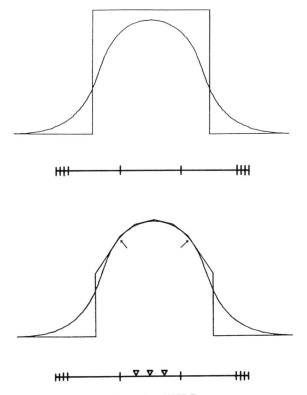

Figure 8. Refining the knot vector of a cubic NURBs curve.

```
      V[k]=U[i]; k--; i--;
   }
   Qw[k-p-1]=Qw[k-p];
   for(l=1; l<=p; l++) {
      ind=k-p+1;
      alfa=V[k+1]-x[j];
      if(abs(alfa)<TOL) Qw[ind-1]=Qw[ind]; else {
         alfa /= (V[k+1]-U[i-p+1]);
         Qw[ind-1]=alfa*Qw[ind-1]+(1.-alfa)*Qw[ind];
      }
   }
   V[k]=x[j]; k--;
}
```

The algorithm takes as input the weighted vertices $P_0^w, \ldots, P_n^w$, the knot vector U, and the vector X, and outputs the new control vertices $Q_0^w, \ldots, Q_{n+r+1}^w$ and the new knot vector $V = \{v_0, \ldots, v_{m+r+1}\}$. The algorithm works backwards and overwrites intermediate control points while inserting a knot [Boeh85].

DEGREE ELEVATION

Another useful tool in NURBs-based geometric design is degree elevation. Degree elevation and knot insertion are the two most important tools used to make different NURBs curves and surfaces compatible, i.e., they are of the same degree and are defined over the same knot vector(s).

Assume that we are given a NURBs curve

$$C_p^w = \sum_{i=0}^{n} P_i^w N_{i,p}(u) \tag{39}$$

defined over the knot vector

$$U = \{u_0, \ldots, u_m\} = \{\underbrace{0, \ldots, 0}_{p+1}, \underbrace{u_1, \ldots, u_1}_{m_1}, \ldots, \underbrace{u_s, \ldots, u_s}_{m_s}, \underbrace{1, \ldots, 1}_{p+1}\}$$

where $m_1, \ldots, m_s$ denote the multiplicities of the inner knots. The degree elevated curve has the form

$$C_{p+1}^w = \sum_{i=0}^{ne} Q_i^w N_{i,p+1}(u) \tag{40}$$

where $ne = n + s + 1$, $N_{i,p+1}(u)$ is defined over the knot vector

$$V = \{v_0, \ldots, v_{me}\} = \{\underbrace{0, \ldots, 0}_{p+2}, \underbrace{u_1, \ldots, u_1}_{m_1+1}, \ldots, \underbrace{u_s, \ldots, u_s}_{m_s+1}, \underbrace{1, \ldots, 1}_{p+2}\}$$

$me = m + s + 2$, and the Q_i^w are computed as follows [Cohe85, Cohe86]

$$P_{i,p-k+1}^w = \frac{(v_{j+k+1} - u_i)P_{i,p-k}^w + (u_{i+k+1} - v_{j+k+1})P_{i-1,p-k}^w}{u_{i+k+1} - u_i} \tag{41}$$

$$Q_{i,p-k+1}^w = \frac{(v_{j+k} - u_i)Q_{i,p-k}^w + (u_{i+k+1} - v_{j+k})Q_{i-1,p-k}^w}{u_{i+k+1} - u_i} + P_{i,p-k+1}^w \tag{42}$$

for $k = p, p-1, \ldots, 1$ and $i = r-k+1, \ldots, r$, where r is such that $u_r \leq v_j < u_{r+1}$, and $P_{i,0}^w = Q_{i,0}^w = P_i^w$. If $k = 1$, then $i = r$ and $Q_j = Q_{r,p}^w/(p+1)$.

Constructional Techniques

CONIC SECTIONS

One of the greatest advantages of NURBs is their capability of representing conic sections *precisely*. Since conic sections are important in many graphics and CAD applications, a reasonably detailed discussion is given here. Let us start with one segment whose end tangents are not parallel (Figure 9). Because only one segment is given no interior knots are present, that is, the NURBs representation degenerates to the rational Bézier form

$$C(u) = P_0 R_{0,2}(u) + P_1 R_{1,2}(u) + P_2 R_{2,2}(u) \tag{43}$$

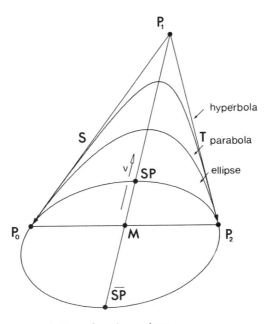

Figure 9. NURBs representation of conic sections.

where
$$R_{i,2}(u) = \frac{w_i B_{i,2}(u)}{\displaystyle\sum_{j=0}^{2} w_j B_{j,2}(u)}$$

where $B_{i,2}(u) = \binom{2}{i} u^i (1-u)^{2-i}$ are the Bernstein polynomials of degree two and $U = \{0, 0, 0, 1, 1, 1\}$. We show that the curve (Eq. 43) is indeed a conic section. To do so, local coordinates $S = P_0 - P_1$ and $T = P_2 - P_1$ are introduced. A general point lying inside the control triangle $P_0 P_1 P_2$ is expressed as

$$C(u) = P_1 + \alpha(u)\,S + \beta(u)\,T = \alpha(u)P_0 + (1 - \alpha(u) - \beta(u))P_1 + \beta(u)P_2$$

Comparing with Eq. (43) yields

$$\alpha(u) = R_{0,2}(u)$$

$$\beta(u) = R_{2,2}(u)$$

Using the identity $B_{0,2}(u) \cdot B_{2,2}(u) = [\,B_{1,2}(u)/2\,]^2$, we get

$$\alpha(u)\beta(u) = k\left[\frac{R_{1,2}(u)}{2}\right]^2 \qquad k = \frac{w_0 w_2}{4 w_1^2}$$

yielding
$$\alpha(u)\beta(u) = k[1 - \alpha(u) - \beta(u)]^2 \tag{44}$$

which is the *implicit* equation of a conic in the P_1, S, T *oblique* coordinate system. The constant k is called the *conic shape invariance* [Vers75; Forr68; Lee86]. Various values of $w_0 : w_1 : w_2$ lead to different parameterizations; however, the expression $w_0 w_2 / 4 w_1^2$ *must* remain the same. The importance of shape invariance is that we can change the weights for a particular curve segment without altering the shape of the curve.

The type of the conic is determined by looking at the denominator of Eq. (43). The denominator can be written as

$$w(u) = (1-u)^2 w_0 + 2u(1-u)w_1 + u^2 w_2$$

$$= (w_0 - 2w_1 + w_2)u^2 + 2(w_1 - w_0)u + w_0$$

The roots are given by

$$u_{1,2} = \frac{w_0 - w_1 \pm \sqrt{1 - 4k}}{w_0 - 2w_1 + w_2}$$

This leads to the following classification:

$4k < 1 \Longrightarrow$ ellipse (no infinite points);
$4k = 1 \Longrightarrow$ parabola (one infinite point);
$4k > 1 \Longrightarrow$ hyperbola (two infinite points).

Assuming that $w_0 = w_2 = 1$ (call this parameterization the *normal* parameterization), the above conditions are expressed in terms of w_1 as

$w_1^2 < 1 \to w_1 < 1$ and $w_1 > -1 \Longrightarrow$ ellipse;
$w_1^2 = 1 \to w_1 = 1$ or $w_1 = -1 \Longrightarrow$ parabola;
$w_1^2 > 1 \to w_1 > 1$ or $w_1 < -1 \Longrightarrow$ hyperbola.

Is it possible to have a negative weight? Look at the curve

$$\overline{C}(u) = \frac{w_0 P_0 B_{0,2}(u) - w_1 P_1 B_{1,2}(u) + w_2 P_2 B_{2,2}(u)}{\overline{w}(u)} \tag{45}$$

with $\overline{w}(u) = w_0 B_{0,2}(u) - w_1 B_{1,2}(u) + w_2 B_{2,2}(u)$, that is, set the middle weight to a negative value. The coordinates $\overline{\alpha}$ and $\overline{\beta}$ of $\overline{C}(u)$ are

$$\overline{\alpha}(u) = R_{0,2}(u; -w_1) = \frac{w_0 B_{0,2}(u)}{\overline{w}(u)}$$

$$\overline{\beta}(u) = R_{2,2}(u; -w_1) = \frac{w_2 B_{2,2}(u)}{\overline{w}(u)}$$

and

$$1 - \overline{\alpha}(u) - \overline{\beta}(u) = \frac{-w_1 B_{1,2}}{\overline{w}(u)}$$

It can be proven that $\overline{\alpha}$ and $\overline{\beta}$ satisfy the same implicit equation (Eq. 44) as α and β. That is, $\overline{C}(u)$ describes the *same* conic. Furthermore, since

$$\overline{C}(u) - P_1 = \frac{w(u)}{\overline{w}(u)}[C(u) - P_1] \qquad (\overline{w}(u) \neq 0)$$

points P_1, $C(u)$, and $\overline{C}(u)$ are collinear. In other words, changing the sign of the middle weight results in the complementary arc (traversed in the reversed order).

Suppose now that we use the normal parameterization, that is, $w_0 = w_2 = 1$. An important point, called the *shoulder point*, is introduced as the point obtained at the parameter value $u = 1/2$

$$SP = \frac{1}{1 + w_1} M + \frac{w_1}{1 + w_1} P_1$$

where $M = (P_0 + P_2)/2$. Because of the normal parameterization, it can be seen that the tangent at SP is parallel to $P_0 P_2$, i.e., the conic attains its maximum distance from $P_0 P_2$ at the shoulder point. Introducing another parameter v along the line MP_1, SP can be expressed as

$$SP = (1 - v)M + vP_1$$

from which we get $w_1 = v/(1 - v)$. The parameter v is a good shape design tool; the designer places his shoulder point directly, instead of guessing a pure number. Another useful application of this parameterization is to obtain the representation of the circular arc (Figure 10). Since the circular arc is symmetric with respect to the perpendicular bisector of P_0P_2, the control triangle must be isosceles [Vers75; Pieg87a; Forr68; Lee86; Pieg89c]. Furthermore, from elementary geometry it follows that $\angle(SP, P_0, P_2) = \angle(SP, P_0, P_1)$. Since SPP_0 bisects the angle $\angle(P_2, P_0, P_1)$, it divides the line segment P_1M in the ratio $MP_0 : P_0P_1$. That is

$$w_1 = \frac{v}{1-v} = \frac{MP_0}{P_0P_1} = \frac{P_0P_2}{2P_0P_1}$$

To obtain a full circle we piece together n arcs sweeping $360/n$ degrees. A practical choice is $n = 4$. Piecing Bézier segments is achieved by using double knots; in particular, to obtain a square-based representation of the full circle we need the knot vector $U = \{0, 0, 0, 1/4, 1/4, 1/2, 1/2, 3/4, 3/4, 1, 1, 1\}$. The control points lie at the corners of a square as well as at the midpoints of the sides. Due to the symmetry of this configuration, the curve is, in fact, C^1 and curvature continuous. On examining the construction closely, it turns out that two control points and consequently two knots can be removed to yield the following construction [Pieg89c] (Figure 11)

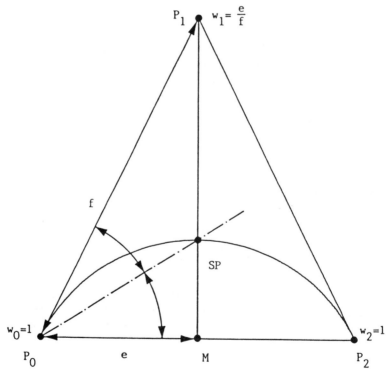

Figure 10. Construction of a circular arc.

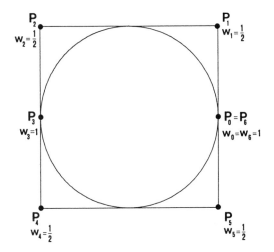

Figure 11. The seven-control-point square-based NURBs circle.

$$U = \{0, 0, 0, \frac{1}{4}, \frac{1}{2}, \frac{1}{2}, \frac{3}{4}, 1, 1, 1\}$$

$$W = \{1, \frac{1}{2}, \frac{1}{2}, 1, \frac{1}{2}, \frac{1}{2}, 1\}$$

$$P = \{P_0, \ldots, P_6\}$$

There are two special cases regarding circular arc constructions—semicircles, and arcs sweeping an angle greater than 180 degrees. Semicircles can be represented by 'halving' the representation above, that is

$$U = \{0, 0, 0, \frac{1}{2}, 1, 1, 1\}$$

$$W = \{1, \frac{1}{2}, \frac{1}{2}, 1\}$$

$$P = \{P_0, \ldots, P_3\}$$

where $P_0, \ldots, P_3$ form half of the square. Arcs sweeping an angle between 180 and 360 degrees can be (temporarily) described by using a negative weight for w_1 [Pieg90]. To remove the negative weight and obtain a new set of control points that includes the curve in its convex hull, only the knot $u = 1/2$ needs to be inserted. As a useful exercise, we leave the detail calculations to the reader.

EXTRUDED SURFACES

A very common operation in geometric design is linear extrusion. Given a NURBs curve

$$C(u) = \sum_{i=0}^{n} P_i R_{i,p}(u) \tag{46}$$

a unit vector W, and an extrusion distance d, the objective is to obtain a NURBs surface by extruding the curve (Eq. 46) in the direction W a distance d. Since the surface is linear in the direction of the extrusion, the desired form is

$$S(u,v) = \sum_{i=0}^{n} \sum_{j=0}^{1} P_{i,j} R_{i,j}(u,v) \tag{47}$$

where $R_{i,j}(u,v)$ are degree $(p,1)$ rational basis functions, $P_{i,0} = P_i$, $P_{i,1} = P_i + d \cdot W$, and the knot vectors are $U = \{u_0, \ldots, u_m\}$, the knot vector of Eq. (46), and $V = \{0,0,1,1\}$.

RULED SURFACES

Given two *arbitrary* NURBs curves

$$C_k(u) = \sum_{i=0}^{n_k} P_{i,k} R_{i,p_k}(u) \qquad k = 0,1 \tag{48}$$

defined over the knot vectors $U_0 = \{u_0^0, \ldots, u_{m_0}^0\}$ and $U_1 = \{u_0^1, \ldots, u_{m_1}^1\}$. A surface is sought that is 'ruled' in the v direction, i.e., it is linear in the v direction and has the properties $S(u,k) = C_k(u), k = 0,1$ (Figure 12). The required surface form is the same as Eq. (47); however, because the u-directional boundary curves are arbitrary, and because all the isoparametric curves in one direction must be of the same degree and must be defined over the same knot vector, we need to do the following:

If $p_0 \neq p_1$, then raise the degree of the lower order curve. Create a new set of control points and a new knot vector.

If the two knot vectors are not the same, then merge them by using the knot refinement technique discussed above.

With C_0 and C_1 made compatible, and with the common knot vector, define a NURBs surface of the form in Eq. (47), with degree in the u direction equaling $\max(p_0, p_1)$.

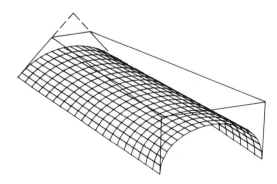

Figure 12. Ruled surface between a circular arc and a cubic curve.

SURFACES OF REVOLUTION

Let $C(v) = \sum_{j=0}^{m} P_j R_{j,p}(v)$ be a NURBs curve defined in the xz plane (call it a *profile* curve). Obtain a surface of revolution by revolving the curve about the z-axis (Figure 13). Since the direction of the revolution is the u direction, and since each u-directional isoparametric curve must be a circle, the surface form is obtained by combining the profile curve's form with one of the circle representations. Choosing the square-based circle form, we have

$$S(u,v) = \sum_{i=0}^{6} \sum_{j=0}^{m} P_{i,j} R_{i,j}(u,v) \qquad (49)$$

where $R_{i,j}(u,v)$ are degree 2 in the u direction, and $P_{i,j}$ are obtained as follows: $P_{0,j} = P_j$, and for a fixed j, $P_{i,j}$ $(i = 0, \ldots, 6)$ lie on a plane perpendicular to the

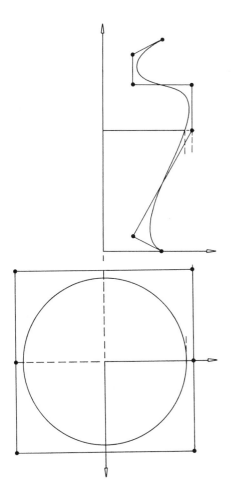

Figure 13. Construction of surface of revolution.

z-axis and form a square of half-width equal to the distance between $P_{0,j}$ and the z-axis, with center on the z-axis. The weights are computed as

$$w_{i,j} = \{w_j, \frac{1}{2}w_j, \frac{1}{2}w_j, w_j, \frac{1}{2}w_j, \frac{1}{2}w_j, w_j\} \qquad i = 0, \ldots, 6$$

See the control net and the corresponding surface of revolution in Figure 14.

QUADRIC AND OTHER COMMONLY USED SURFACES

Most of the commonly used surfaces are obtained by either extrusion or by revolution. For example, a right circular cylinder of height H is obtained by extruding the bottom circle in the direction of the axis a distance H. The right circular cone is a special case of the cylinder, obtained by degenerating either the top or

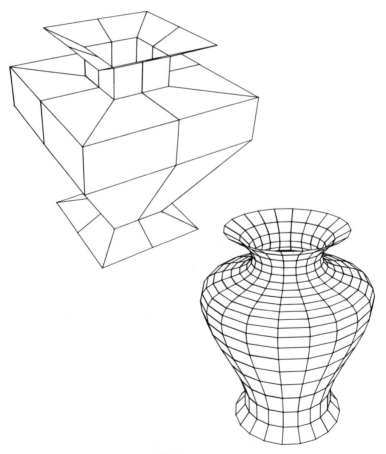

Figure 14. Control net and corresponding surface revolution.

the bottom circle. The sphere is obtained by revolving a semicircle about the z-axis. Other rotational symmetric quadrics, such as paraboloids or hyperboloids of one or two sheets, are obtained by revolving parabolic or hyperbolic arcs about the z-axis. Nonrotational symmetric quadrics are obtained from rotational symmetric ones via affine transformations. For example, a paraboloid whose cross section with a plane perpendicular to the z-axis is an ellipse (instead of a circle) is obtained by applying the affine transformation $x' = x$, $y' = by/a (b < a)$, $z' = z$ to the control points and leaving the weights unchanged (remember the transformation invariance property of NURBs). The ratio of the minor and the major axes of the cross-sectional ellipse is b/a.

Other commonly used surfaces are the torus, toroidal patches (used for rounding edges), and conoids (ruled surfaces between circles/circular arcs and straight line segments). The full torus is obtained by revolving a full circle about the z-axis, whereas the toroidal patch is the result of revolving a circular arc about the z-axis with 360 degrees or less. Conoids are ruled surfaces, and so the process discussed above is used. If one or both of the boundary curves are Bézier curves, then the degree elevation process is simplified by using the formula for Bézier curves: $Q_i^w = (1 - \alpha) P_i^w + \alpha P_{i-1}^w$, $\alpha = i/(n+1)$, $i = 0, \ldots, n+1$.

Design Algorithms

CURVE INTERPOLATION

In a typical design situation we are given two types of data: pure 3D data points, through which a curve has to be passed, and weighted data points, e.g., control points of a curve as a result of another process. In the first case nonrational interpolation is recommended, whereas in the second case a 'true' rational interpolant must be computed.

Assume first that we are given 3D data points $Q_k = (x_k, y_k, z_k)$, $k = 0, \ldots, n$. A nonrational B-spline curve (special case of NURBs) is sought that, for certain parameter values, agrees with Q_k, that is,

$$Q_k = \sum_{i=0}^{n} P_i N_{i,p}(u_k) \qquad k = 0, \ldots, n \qquad (50)$$

In order to solve this set of equations, we need the degree, the knot vector, and the parameter values at which the Q_k are assumed. In practice low-degree curves are preferred, e.g., second- or third-degree; however, the method we are about to present works with any degree which is less than or equal to n. The parameter values are obtained by the well-known chord length method, or by the *centripetal* method [Lee89], which is less well-known

$$u_0 = 0 \qquad u_i = u_{i-1} + \frac{\sqrt{|Q_i - Q_{i-1}|}}{\sum\limits_{j=1}^{n} \sqrt{|Q_j - Q_{j-1}|}} \qquad u_n = 1 \qquad (51)$$

The knot vector should reflect the distribution of these parameters. Therefore, the following technique is recommended [Till86]

$$U = \{\underbrace{0,\ldots,0}_{p+1}, v_1,\ldots,v_{n-p}, \underbrace{1,\ldots,1}_{p+1}\}$$

where
$$v_j = \frac{1}{p}\sum_{i=j}^{j+p-1} u_i \qquad j = 1,\ldots,n-p$$

With this data, the linear system (Eq. 50) can be solved by simple Gauss elimination without pivoting [deBo78]. If in addition to the data points derivatives are also given (or computed), then we need $2(n+1)$ control points to find an interpolatory spline. The systems to be solved are

$$Q_k = C(u_k) = \sum_{i=0}^{2n+1} P_i N_{i,p}(u_k)$$

$$D_k = p\sum_{i=1}^{2n+1} \frac{P_i - P_{i-1}}{v_{i+p} - v_i} N_{i,p-1}(u_k) \tag{52}$$

where D_k denote the derivatives at each data point. Since we have $2(n+1)$ control points, we need $2(n+1)+p+1$ knots. To obtain such knot vectors for $p = \{2,3\}$

$$p = 2 \;:\; U = \{0,0,0, \frac{u_1}{2}, u_1, \frac{u_1+u_2}{2}, u_2, \ldots, \frac{u_{n-1}+1}{2}, 1,1,1\}$$

$$p = 3 \;:\; U = \{0,0,0,0, \frac{u_1}{2}, \frac{2u_1+u_2}{3}, \frac{u_1+2u_2}{3}, \ldots, \frac{u_{n-1}+1}{2}, 1,1,1,1\}$$

Although these averaging techniques are rather heuristic, they work quite well in practice [Till86].

The following version of the above algorithm has gained widespread acceptance in the CAD industry: Given data points Q_k, $k = 0,\ldots,n$, and end tangents t_0 and t_n, obtain a cubic NURBs curve that interpolates the data points *at the knot values* and is tangential to t_0 and t_n at the endpoints (Figure 15). Since the data points are assumed at the knot values, the knot vector is

$$U = \{0,0,0,0, u_1, u_2, \ldots, u_{n-1}, 1,1,1,1\}$$

where the $u_k, k = 1,\ldots,n-1$, is computed as detailed above. Evaluating the curve at u_k yields

$$Q_k = C(u_k) = P_k N_{k,3}(u_k) + P_{k+1} N_{k+1,3}(u_k) + P_{k+2} N_{k+2,3}(u_k)$$

since $N_{k+3,3}(u)$ vanishes at u_k. For the first and the last control points we have $P_0 = Q_0$ and $P_{n+2} = Q_n$. Furthermore, since t_0 and t_n are the end tangent vectors

$$P_1 = Q_0 + \alpha u_1 t_0$$

$$P_{n+1} = Q_n - \beta(1 - u_{n-1})t_n$$

must hold (if t_0 and t_n are tangent directions, then use unit tangent vectors). For most practical applications, the choice $\alpha = \beta = 1/3$ is quite satisfactory. The remaining control points are computed by

$$Q_1 = a_1 P_1 + b_1 P_2 + c_1 P_3$$

$$Q_2 = a_2 P_2 + b_2 P_3 + c_2 P_4$$

$$\vdots = \vdots$$

$$Q_{n-2} = a_{n-2}P_{n-2} + b_{n-2}P_{n-1} + c_{n-2}P_n$$

$$Q_{n-1} = a_{n-1}P_{n-1} + b_{n-1}P_n + c_{n-1}P_{n+1}$$

where
$$a_k = N_{k,3}(u_k)$$

$$b_k = N_{k+1,3}(u_k)$$

$$c_k = N_{k+2,3}(u_k)$$

The above system can be put into the following matrix form

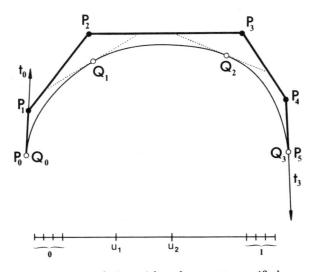

Figure 15. Cubic NURBs interpolation with end tangents specified.

$$
\begin{pmatrix}
Q_1 - a_1 P_1 \\
Q_2 \\
\vdots \\
Q_{n-2} \\
Q_{n-1} - c_{n-1} P_{n+1}
\end{pmatrix}
=
$$

$$
\begin{pmatrix}
b_1 & c_1 & 0 & \cdots & 0 & 0 & 0 \\
a_2 & b_2 & c_2 & \cdots & 0 & 0 & 0 \\
\vdots & \vdots & \vdots & \ddots & \vdots & \vdots & \vdots \\
0 & 0 & 0 & \cdots & a_{n-2} & b_{n-2} & c_{n-2} \\
0 & 0 & 0 & \cdots & 0 & a_{n-1} & b_{n-1}
\end{pmatrix}
\begin{pmatrix}
P_2 \\
P_3 \\
\vdots \\
P_{n-1} \\
P_n
\end{pmatrix}
\tag{53}
$$

which is a tridiagonal system easily solvable by standard algorithms.

Now we turn our attention to rational interpolation. If only the weighted vertices are given, i.e., $(w_k x_k, w_k y_k, w_k z_k, w_k)$, $k = 0, \ldots, n$, then simply interpolate in 4D space. However, if in addition to the data points 3D derivatives $(\dot{x}, \dot{y}, \dot{z})$ are also given, then we need to find 4D derivatives for 4D interpolation. Denoting the weighted data points by (X_k, Y_k, Z_k, W_k), we have

$$
\dot{X}_k = \dot{w}_k x_k + w_k \dot{x}_k
$$

$$
\vdots
$$

$$
\dot{W}_k = \dot{w}_k
$$

Thus, we need to compute $\dot{w}_k$. There are a number of ways to compute derivatives from positional data. Perhaps the easiest method is to take the vector difference $\dot{w}_k = w_{k+1} - w_{k-1}$. A more sophisticated one is to fit a spline 'curve' through the w_k so that $w(u_k) = w_k$. Then $\dot{w}_k = \dot{w}(u)|_{u=u_k}$. With $\dot{w}_k$ just computed, $(\dot{X}_k, \dot{Y}_k, \dot{Z}_k, \dot{W}_k)$ can be obtained, and we proceed in exactly the same way as detailed above. Note that the interpolation method above is independent of the dimension.

The above methods were global in the sense that the interpolant was generated by using *all* the data points. There are a number of local methods based on heuristic choices of tangents at data points. We outline here one method that has gained considerable interest in industry [Akim70]. It is based on a clever choice of the tangents computed at each data point by using five neighboring points, the point in question Q_k, and two points on each side of it, i.e., Q_{k-2}, Q_{k-1} and Q_{k+1}, Q_{k+2}. More precisely

$$
\begin{aligned}
T_k &= (1 - \alpha)s_k + \alpha s_{k+1} \\
s_k &= Q_k - Q_{k-1}
\end{aligned}
\qquad k = 1, \ldots, n
$$

The choice of α is crucial to avoiding unwanted oscillations. If we impose the condition that collinear data points be interpolated by line segments, then one possible choice is

$$\alpha = \frac{|s_{k-1} \times s_k|}{|s_{k-1} \times s_k| + |s_{k+1} \times s_{k+2}|}$$

where $\times$ denotes the cross product. This definition of α fails to provide the tangents T_0, T_1, T_{n-1}, and T_n unless we initialize the vector differences s_{-1}, s_{-2}, s_{n+1}, and s_{n+2}. For closed curves we choose

$$s_0 = s_n \qquad s_{-1} = s_{n-1} \qquad s_{n+1} = s_1 \qquad s_{n+2} = s_2$$

For open curves the following is recommended [Pieg87b]

$$s_0 = 2s_1 - s_2 \qquad s_{-1} = 2s_0 - s_1 \qquad s_{n+1} = 2s_n - s_{n-1} \qquad s_{n+2} = 2s_{n+1} - s_n$$

Using these tangents, the interpolant is obtained in three steps:

Obtain a piecewise cubic Hermite interpolant, using *unit* tangent vectors at each data point, i.e., $T_i^u = T_i/|T_i|$. If the segment between Q_i and Q_{i+1} is parameterized between u_i and u_{i+1}, then adjust u_{i+1} with respect to u_i, such that

$$\left|\dot{H}(u_i)\right| = \left|\dot{H}\left(\frac{u_i + u_{i+1}}{2}\right)\right| = \left|\dot{H}(u_{i+1})\right| = \left|T_i^u\right|$$

where $H(u)$ denotes the Hermite interpolant. The above choice of the parameterization provides a relatively uniform velocity for the point that sweeps out the segment.

Convert the piecewise Hermite curve into piecewise Bézier form. A Bézier segment defined over $[u_i, u_{i+1}]$ is given by

$$C(u) = \sum_{j=0}^{3} P_{i,j} \binom{3}{j} \frac{(u - u_i)^j (u_{i+1} - u)^{3-j}}{(u_{i+1} - u_i)^3}$$

where $P_{i,0} = Q_i$, $P_{i,3} = Q_{i+1}$, and the inner Bézier control points are obtained as

$$P_{i,1} = P_{i,0} + \gamma T_i^u \qquad \gamma = \frac{u_{i+1} - u_i}{3}$$
$$P_{i,2} = P_{i,3} - \gamma T_{i+1}^u$$

Obtain the NURBs representation of the C^1 piecewise Bézier curve. The control points are

$$P_{0,0}, P_{0,1}, P_{0,2}, P_{1,1}, \ldots, P_{n-1,1}, P_{n-1,2}, P_{n-1,3}$$

and the knot vector is

$$U = \{0, 0, 0, 0, u_1, u_1, \ldots, u_{n-1}, u_{n-1}, u_n, u_n, u_n, u_n\}$$

An example is shown in Figure 16.

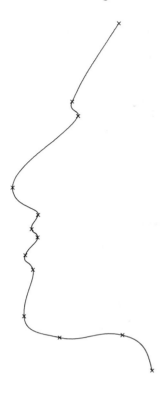

Figure 16. Cubic NURBs interpolant using a local method.

SURFACE INTERPOLATION

Both the global and the local curve interpolation techniques can be extended to surfaces. Assume that we are given a rectangularly arranged set of $(n+1)\times(m+1)$ data points $Q_{r,s}$, $r = 0,\ldots,n$; $s = 0,\ldots,m$. We are seeking a degree (p,q) surface that interpolates $Q_{r,s}$, that is

$$Q_{r,s} = S(u_r, v_s) = \sum_{i=0}^{n}\sum_{j=0}^{m} P_{i,j}N_{i,p}(u_r)N_{j,q}(v_s) \qquad (54)$$

To be able to solve Eq. (54), we need the parameter values u_r and v_s and the two knot vectors. Algorithm A5 computes reasonable parameter values in the u direction [Till86]. It uses the centripetal method to obtain u values in the u direction for each row of data points, and then computes the average of the u values in the v direction for each column of data points.

```
ALGORITHM A5:
  for(s=0; s<=m; s++) {
    uu[0][s]=0.0; uu[n][s]=1.0; chl=0.0;
    for(t=1; t<=n; t++) chl += sqrt(Q[t][s]-Q[t-1][s]);
    for(r=1; r<n; r++) {
      uu[r][s]=uu[r-1][s]+sqrt(Q[r][s]-Q[r-1][s])/chl;
```

```
      }
    }
    u[0]=0.0; u[n]=1.0;
    for(r=1; r<n; r++) {
      sum=0.0;
      for(s=0; s<=m; s++) sum += u[r][s];
      u[r]=sum/(m+1);
    }
```

The computation of v parameters is similar, and the knot vectors are computed as before. From these parameter values the knot vectors can be obtained as detailed above. There are two basic ways to solve for the unknown control points in Eq. (54). The first is to solve the matrix equation directly

$$[Q] = [A][P][B]$$

where $\quad [Q] = [Q_{r,s}] \qquad [A] = [N_{i,p}(u_r)] \qquad [P] = [P_{i,j}] \qquad [B] = [N_{j,q}(v_s)]$

It can be proven [deBo78] that $[A]$ and $[B]$ are positive definite (and banded) and thus are invertible, to yield

$$[P] = [A]^{-1}[Q][B]^{-1}$$

The second method is to interpolate each row (column) of data points and to fit a surface through the interpolatory curves. This method is essentially a surface lofting, which is dealt with in the next section.

The method for local curve interpolation is extended to surfaces as follows: Fit a bicubic Hermite surface to each rectangle $Q_{i,j}$, $Q_{i+1,j}$, $Q_{i,j+1}$, and $Q_{i+1,j+1}$. The bicubic Hermite surface needs the following input data: corner points, u- and v-directional tangents, and twist vectors (mixed partial derivatives) at each corner. The tangents in the u and v directions are obtained by using the curve technique for each row and column of data points. The mixed partial derivatives are obtained as follows [Pieg88]

$$mp_{i,j} = (1-\alpha)(1-\beta)(s_{i,j} - s_{i-1,j}) + (1-\alpha)\beta(s_{i+1,j} - s_{i,j})$$
$$+ \alpha(1-\beta)(s_{i,j+1} - s_{i-1,j+1}) + \alpha\beta(s_{i+1,j+1} - s_{i,j+1})$$

where $\quad \alpha = \dfrac{|s_{i,j-1} \times s_{i,j}|}{|s_{i,j-1} \times s_{i,j}| + |s_{i,j+1} \times s_{i,j+2}|} \qquad s_{i,j} = Q_{i,j} - Q_{i-1,j}$

$\qquad \beta = \dfrac{|r_{i-1,j} \times r_{i,j}|}{|r_{i-1,j} \times r_{i,j}| + |r_{i+1,j} \times r_{i+2,j}|} \qquad r_{i,j} = Q_{i,j} - Q_{i,j-1}$

Using this data, the bicubic Bézier surface that interpolates $Q_{i,j}, \ldots, Q_{i+1,j+1}$ can be obtained. Thus, the control points along the boundaries are obtained in exactly the same way as in the case of curves. The four inner control points are computed as

$$P^i_{1,1} = \quad \gamma m p_{i,j} + P^i_{0,1} + P^i_{1,0} - P^i_{0,0}$$

$$P^i_{2,1} = -\gamma m p_{i+1,j} + P^i_{3,1} - P^i_{3,0} + P^i_{2,0}$$

$$P^i_{1,2} = -\gamma m p_{i,j+1} + P^i_{1,3} - P^i_{0,3} + P^i_{0,2}$$

$$P^i_{2,2} = \quad \gamma m p_{i+1,j+1} + P^i_{2,3} + P^i_{3,2} - P^i_{3,3}$$

where $\gamma = (u_{i+1} - u_i)(v_{j+1} - v_j)/9$, $P^i_{r,s}$, $r,s = 0,1,2,3$, denote the control points of the ith patch, and u_i and v_j are obtained by algorithm A5. This Bézier patch network is $C^{1,1}$ continuous, i.e., derivative continuous, in both u and v directions. Thus, it can be converted into NURBs form using double knots. The control net of the NURBs surface is obtained from the Bézier net by discarding control points along the common boundaries of the joining patches; the knot vectors are

$$U = \{0,0,0,0,u_1,u_1,\ldots,u_{n-1},u_{n-1},1,1,1,1\}$$
$$V = \{0,0,0,0,v_1,v_1,\ldots,v_{n-1},v_{n-1},1,1,1,1\}$$

Note that in the case of surfaces we cannot adjust the parameterization the way we did in the case of curves, since each row (column) of data points uses the same parameter values. A local interpolant is illustrated in Figure 17.

CROSS-SECTIONAL DESIGN

Cross-sectional design is concerned with surface definition based on a set of curves. One of the most common surface construction techniques is *lofting*, where a set of (cross-sectional) curves are given, and a surface is sought that passes through these curves. In the case of NURBs, the cross-sectional curves become the isoparametric lines of the NURBs surface that interpolates them. The surface, called a lofted or *skinned* surface, is obtained in three steps (Figure 18):

(1) Make all cross-sectional curves compatible, i.e., all curves should have the same degree and number of control points, and should be defined over the same knot vector. If we assume that all cross-sectional curves are parameterized between 0 and 1, say, then knot insertion/refinement and degree elevation can be used to make them compatible. If this is not the case, then reparameterizations are also necessary. Assuming that compatibility has been achieved, the cross-sectional curves have the form

$$C^w_k(u) = \sum_{i=0}^{n} Q^w_{i,k} N_{i,p}(u) \qquad k = 0,\ldots,K \qquad (55)$$

defined over the knot vector U.

(2) Since the curves of Eq. (55) are isoparametric curves in the u direction, v values $v_k(k = 0,\ldots,K)$, for which $S^w(u,v_k) = C^w_k(u)$, need to be

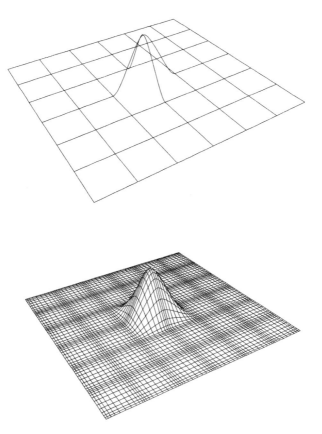

Figure 17. Local surface interpolation.

computed. These values can be computed by algorithm A5, using the control points in place of the data points.

(3) With the v values computed in step 2, interpolate through the control points of Eq. (55). More precisely, for each i, $i = 0, \ldots, n$, interpolate through $Q_{i,k}^w$ $(k = 0, \ldots, K)$ to obtain

$$C_i^w(v) = \sum_{j=0}^{m} P_{i,j}^w N_{j,q}(v) \tag{56}$$

Since each curve is assumed at a certain parameter value v_k, we have $C_i^w(v_k) = Q_{i,k}^w$. Each interpolation uses the same knot vector V, which is computed as detailed above. The points $P_{i,j}^w$ are the control points of the lofted surface

$$S^w(u,v) = \sum_{i=0}^{n} \sum_{j=0}^{m} P_{i,j}^w N_{i,p}(u) N_{j,q}(v) \tag{57}$$

defined over the knot vectors U and V.

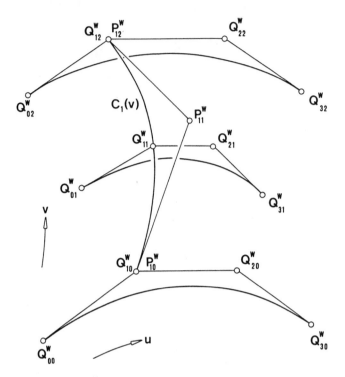

Figure 18. Lofting with NURBs surfaces.

Although the surface (Eq. 57) interpolates through the curves (Eq. 55), its shape depends on

> the position of the cross-sectional curves. If they are very unevenly spaced (which is unlikely in most practical applications), then the surface can behave very badly;
>
> the choice of the v values and the V knot vector used for interpolation in step 3;
>
> the continuity of the cross-sectional NURBs curves. Notice that the algorithm works in 4D space, i.e., it uses the weighted control vertices. Even if a curve is C^1 in 3D space, its 4D correspondent may be only C^0 if we use multiple knots. An example is the circle which is C^1 in 3D but C^0 in 4D because of the double knots. That is, if we use the lofting technique with the circle as one of the cross-sectional curves, then the resulting surface is C^0 continuous only. However, if we refrain from using multiple knots, then the lofting algorithm generates C^{p-1} continuous surfaces in 4D, whose 3D map preserves this continuity.

In practical implementations, several tricks are applied to improve the quality of the lofting surface. For example, in step 3 tangent information is also used to improve the interpolation. If all of the cross-sectional curves are planar, and in most practical applications they are, then at each $Q_{i,k}$ (in 3D space!) we use the normal to the plane of $C_k(u)$ as the tangent. To help in placing the cross-sectional curves one can use a so-called *spine* curve, which becomes part of the surface. Reference points are chosen on each cross-sectional curve and on the spine, which are then matched; the section curves are rotated perpendicular to the spine at the reference point or placed parallel to one another (Figure 19).

A special case of the lofting operation, called *sweeping*, is obtained by using the same curve as the cross-sectional curve. If, in the very special case, the constant shape curve is positioned along the spine curve so that the reference points lie actually on the section curves, then the swept surface also has the spine curve interpolated.

If the spine curve happens to be a circle, then the sweep operation generates a rotationally swept surface. This can be extended to obtain the so-called *swinging* operation (Figure 20). Swinging is defined by two curves; one curve lies in the xz plane and is called the *profile* curve

$$P(v) = \sum_{j=0}^{m} P_j R_{j,q}(v) \tag{58}$$

The other curve lies in the xy plane and is called the *trajectory* curve, i.e.

$$T(u) = \sum_{i=0}^{n} T_i R_{i,p}(u) \tag{59}$$

The swung surface is then defined as

$$S(u,v) = [\,\alpha P_x(v)T_x(u) \quad \alpha P_x(v)T_y(u) \quad P_z(v)\,] \tag{60}$$

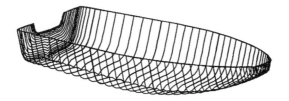

Figure 19. Lofted surface. (Courtesy of Charles Woodward.)

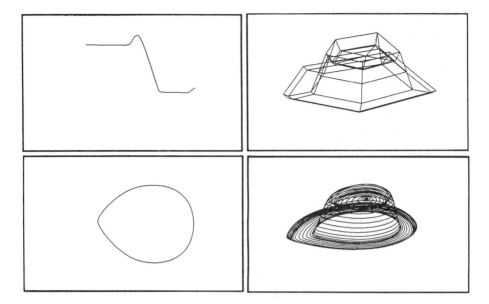

Figure 20. NURBs swinging. (Courtesy of Charles Woodward.)

where α is an arbitrary scaling factor for the xy dimensions. Multiplying the x and y components of Eqs. (58) and (59) yields the control points and weights of the surface of Eq. (60)

$$Q_{i,j} = [\,\alpha P_{j,x} T_{i,x} \quad \alpha P_{j,x} T_{i,y} \quad P_{j,z}\,] \qquad w_{i,j} = w_i \cdot w_j$$

INTERACTIVE SHAPE MODIFICATIONS

NURBs are excellent candidates for interactive shape design. There are two basic ways to alter the shape of a NURBs curve or surface: repositioning control points, and changing the weights. Although the repositioning of knot values alters the shape as well, it is not recommended because of unpredictability and lack of geometric insight.

Assume that the shape of a NURBs curve is to be updated by interactively repositioning the control point P_i. Let us denote the current position of P_i by P_{iold} and its new position by P_{inew}. Then, since $P_{inew} = P_{iold} + (P_{inew} - P_{iold})$, we have

$$C_{new}(u) = C_{old}(u) + (P_{inew} - P_{iold})R_{i,p}(u) \qquad (61)$$

This interactive update generalizes to surfaces in a straightforward manner (see [Roge82])

$$S_{new}(u,v) = S_{old}(u,v) + (P_{inew,jnew} - P_{iold,jold})R_{i,j}(u,v) \qquad (62)$$

The movement of a control point induces a change in the surface shape. Although interactive control point repositioning can be mastered to a level where it becomes a useful design tool, it is preferable to work directly with the curve or with the surface. The shape modification eventually is achieved by repositioning a control point; however, this repositioning is *computed* rather than *guessed*. Assume that a point on the curve at a parameter value u is to be pulled a distance d in the direction W. This pull is accomplished by repositioning *any* control point P_i for which $u \in [u_i, u_{i+p+1})$. The new position of P_i is obtained as

$$P_i^{new} = P_i + \alpha W$$

where
$$\alpha = \frac{d}{|W| R_{i,p}(u)}$$

Any control point is generally not very useful for practical purposes. Intuitively, the best choice seems to be the control point which is the closest to the curve point to be pulled. Such a control point can be picked as follows:

For each control point, compute the average of p consecutive knots, that is

$$x_i = \frac{1}{p}(u_{i+1} + u_{i+2} + \cdots + u_{i+p})$$

In the B-spline literature the x_i are called *nodes*.

Select the control point whose node is the closest to the parameter value of the curve point.

For more sophisticated shape modifications, the simultaneous repositioning of several control points is required. Such shape modifications are warping, flattening, bending, stretching, twisting, etc. Here, we discuss warping in some detail. The idea of warping is to introduce a bump into a curve or a surface. Warping NURBs is obtained by applying to the control points conventional techniques used for polygonal/polyhedral objects [Cobb84] (Plate 4). Warping is a local operation that repositions a set of control points around a user-chosen warp center. Assume that such a center (a control point) has been chosen, along with the direction toward which the surface is to be warped. The control points that lie within the distance D from the warp center are repositioned in the chosen direction a distance αd, where

$$\alpha = \begin{cases} \left(1 - \dfrac{e}{D}\right)^{2^{(-w)}} & w < 0 \\[2mm] \left(1 - \dfrac{e}{D}\right) & w = 0 \\[2mm] \left(1 - \dfrac{e}{D}\right)^{2^{w}} & w > 0 \end{cases}$$

where w is the warp factor and e is the distance between the control point to be repositioned and the warp center. α varies between 0 and 1, that is, the warp center is moved a distance d, the control points that lie farther than D are not moved, and those that lie in between are moved a distance less than d. The computation of e is crucial to obtaining proper warp effects. For topological reasons, we recommend the following distance measure: *accumulated Euclidean distance that is the sum of the lengths of the line segments traversed on the path from a control point to the warp center*.

Now we turn our attention to interactive weight modification [Roge90]. Suppose that the shape of the NURBs curve is to be modified by changing the weight w_i. More specifically, let us increment its value by Δw_i. The new weighted control point has coordinates $P_i^w = x_i(w_i + \Delta w_i),\ y_i(w_i + \Delta w_i),\ z_i(w_i + \Delta w_i),\ w_i + \Delta w_i)$; therefore, the updated curve has the form

$$C_{new}^w(u) = \sum_{i=0}^{n} P_i^w N_{i,p}(u) + P_i^{\Delta w} N_{i,p}(u) = C_{old}^w(u) + P_i^{\Delta w} N_{i,p}(u) \quad (63)$$

where $P_i^{\Delta w} = (\Delta w_i x_i, \Delta w_i y_i, \Delta w_i z_i, \Delta w_i)$

Surfaces can be updated similarly, using the formula

$$S_{new}^w(u,v) = S_{old}^w(u,v) + P_{r,s}^{\Delta w} N_{r,p}(u) N_{s,q}(v) \quad (64)$$

Changing a pure number to achieve predictable shape modifications is not as easy as moving a control point. From Eqs. (15) and (17) it follows that as the curve point moves toward P_i, the value of the corresponding weight w_i changes from a finite value to $+\infty$, that is, there is a nonlinear correspondence between changing a weight and placing a curve point to achieve the desired shaping effect. Therefore, Eqs. (63) and (64) must be modified to make them useful for practical purposes. Of the many possible ways a weight can be adjusted, we discuss the following three [Pieg89a]:

direct push/pull. The user is prompted to pick a point B_i on the curve (or choose a parameter value), a control point P_i toward which the curve is to be pulled/pushed, and a distance d or the new position of B_i along the line $P_i B_i$ (Figure 21). Based on Eq. (17), the new value of w_i is computed as

$$w_i^{new} = \frac{P_i N}{BN} : \frac{P_i B_i^{new}}{BB_i^{new}} = \frac{P_i N}{BN} : \frac{P_i B_i \pm d}{BB_i \pm d}$$

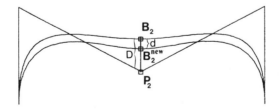

Figure 21. Direct push/pull with specified distance.

which, after rearrangements and substitutions, yields

$$w_i^{new} = w_i^{old} \left[1 \pm \frac{d}{R_{i,p}(u)(D-d)} \right] \qquad D = |P_i - B_i| \qquad (65)$$

where, in the case of pull the $+$, and in the case of push the $-$, is to be applied; and $d = |B_i^{new} - B_i^{old}|$.

automatic push/pull. Instead of entering a distance or a new position of the curve point B_i, we set a default increment and move B_i along the line $P_i B_i$ with equal increments. This is implemented as follows: the designer picks either a point on the curve or a control point. If a curve point B_i is picked, then the corresponding parameter value and the closest node are computed. The node determines the control point P_i and the distance $D = |P_i - B_i|$. Now, if a key is hit, then d is updated as $d = d + \Delta d$ (d is set initially to zero) and the new weight w_i^{new} is computed. If the designer keeps hitting the key, the curve is modified incrementally until the desired shape is reached. If a control point is picked instead of a curve point, then the system automatically computes the node and sets $B_i = C(x_i)$, and the process continues as in the previous case.

segmented modifications. Because of the locality property of B-splines, w_i affects the curve only in the interval $[u_i, u_{i+p+1})$. However, this locality can be insufficient, i.e., w_i can affect a larger portion of the curve than is desired. To localize a portion of the curve, we do the following: assume that the parameter values corresponding to the segment endpoints are u_l and u_r. If u_l and/or u_r are not part of the knot vector, then they are inserted. Now let $S = \{u_l, \ldots, u_r\}$ be a subset of the knot vector. If S contains exactly p inner knots, then w_l is the weight that affects the curve in the interval $[u_l, u_r)$. If S contains more than p inner knots, then the weights $w_l, \ldots, w_{r-p-1}$ are all local to $[u_l, u_r)$ (although they do not affect the curve over the entire interval). If, however, S contains less than p inner knots, then additional knots need to be inserted until p inner knots are obtained; thus, the scope of w_l's effect is restricted to $[u_l, u_r)$. In order to preserve continuity, knot refinement should be done in such a way as to avoid multiple knots in $[u_l, u_r)$.

The above ideas can be extended to surfaces [Pieg89b] by generalizing Eq. (65) as

$$w_{i,j}^{new} = w_{i,j}^{old} \left[1 \pm \frac{d}{R_{i,j}(u,v)(D-d)} \right] \qquad \begin{array}{l} D = |P_{i,j} - B_{i,j}| \\ d = |B_{i,j}^{new} - B_{i,j}^{old}| \end{array} \qquad (66)$$

While interactive weight adjustment results in a large variety of shapes, in many practical applications the adjustment of more than one weight is required. In this paper we discuss how to adjust two weights simultaneously. One might think that this is unnecessary, as two weights can always be adjusted independently of one another using the technique discussed above. However, from the properties of rational basis functions it follows that if w_i is increased, then the curve is pulled toward P_i, and at the same time it is *pushed away* from P_j, $j \neq i$. That is, if the curve is to be pulled towards P_i and P_j simultaneously, then increasing w_i pushes the curve away from P_j. This makes the independent adjustment of w_i and w_j very difficult. Therefore, we attack the problem in a different way. Let $M = C(u; w_i = w_j = 0.0)$ (Figure 22). Then it is relatively easy to check that

$$C(u) = (1 - \alpha_i - \alpha_j) M + \alpha_i P_i + \alpha_j P_j \tag{67}$$

with $\alpha_i = R_{i,p}(u)$ and $\alpha_j = R_{j,p}(u)$. That is, the curve point lies within the triangle MP_iP_j, and α_i and α_j are the barycentric coordinates with respect to the vertices of the triangle. Now, if the curve point moves to a different position, then it can be expressed as

$$C^{new}(u) = (1 - \alpha_i^{new} - \alpha_j^{new}) M + \alpha_i^{new} P_i + \alpha_j^{new} P_j \tag{68}$$

where $\quad \alpha_k^{new} = \dfrac{w_k^{new} N_{k,p}(u)}{\displaystyle\sum_{l \neq i,j} w_l N_{l,p}(u) + w_i^{new} N_{i,p}(u) + w_j^{new} N_{j,p}(u)} \quad k = i, j \tag{69}$

If we express w_i^{new} and w_j^{new} as $\beta_i w_i$ and $\beta_j w_j$, then after simple manipulations we have

$$\beta_i = \frac{1 - \alpha_i - \alpha_j}{\alpha_i} : \frac{1 - \alpha_i^{new} - \alpha_j^{new}}{\alpha_i^{new}}$$

$$\beta_j = \frac{1 - \alpha_i - \alpha_j}{\alpha_j} : \frac{1 - \alpha_i^{new} - \alpha_j^{new}}{\alpha_j^{new}} \tag{70}$$

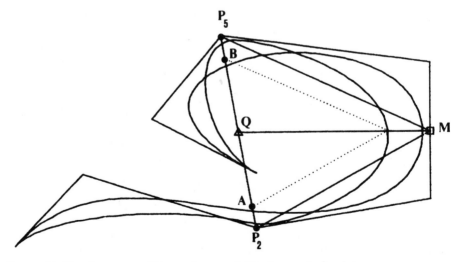

Figure 22. Simultaneous pull towards nonneighboring control points.

The barycentric coordinates can either be computed by evaluating rational basis functions or, and this is what is recommended, by utilizing their geometric interpretations: α_i and α_j divide the line segment P_iP_j into three subsegments in the ratio

$$P_iA : AB : BP_j = \alpha_j : (1 - \alpha_i - \alpha_j) : \alpha_i$$

From this, the computations of α_i and α_j are straightforward.

The derivation above gives a nice insight into the geometric properties of simultaneous pull:

As $C(u)$ changes its position, w_i and w_j change their values simultaneously. If $C^{new}(u)$ is inside the triangle MP_iP_j, then w_i^{new} and w_j^{new} remain positive. However, if it leaves the triangle, then either α_i^{new} or α_j^{new} or $(1 - \alpha_i^{new} - \alpha_j^{new})$ becomes negative; hence, either w_i^{new} or w_j^{new} or both are negative.

In order for α_i and α_j to be nonvanishing, the knot spans $[u_i, u_{i+p+1})$ and $[u_j, u_{j+p+1})$ should overlap and u should belong to the intersection of these spans. That is, as long as $j - i \leq p, j > i$, and u is in the intersection of these spans, the curve can be simultaneously pulled/pushed toward/away from P_i and P_j by repositioning the curve point inside the triangle MP_iP_j.

To make life easier, an automated version of the above algorithm can be created:

Choose P_i and P_j such that $j - i \leq p, (j > i)$.

Get M and $C(u)$ for $u = (u_j + u_{i+p+1})/2$.

Get the intersection of P_iP_j with $MC(u)$; call it Q.

Set default increments along $MC(u)$ and $C(u)Q$.

When a key is hit, a new position of $C(u)$ is computed by placing it with a default increment away from its original position toward M or Q. This computes w_i^{new} and w_j^{new} and hence achieves simultaneous pulls towards P_i and P_j.

Simultaneous pulls for surfaces can be handled similarly. Because of space restrictions, the detailed discussion is omitted here with a reference to the author's paper [Pieg89b].

REFERENCES

[Akim70]
 Akima, H., A new method of interpolation and smooth curve fitting based on local procedures, *Jour. ACM*, Vol. 17, pp. 589–602, 1970.

[Boeh80]
 Boehm, W., Inserting new knots into B-spline curves, *CAD*, Vol. 12, pp. 199–201, 1980.

[Boeh85]
 Boehm, W., and Prautzsch, H., The insertion algorithm, *CAD*, Vol. 17, pp. 58–69, 1985.

[Cobb84]
Cobb, E.S., Design of sculptured surfaces using the B-spline representation, Ph.D. dissertation, University of Utah, 1984.

[Cohe85]
Cohen, E., Lyche, T., and Schumaker, L.L., Algorithms for degree-raising of splines, *ACM TOG*, Vol.4, pp. 171–181, 1985.

[Cohe86]
Cohen, E., Lyche, T., and Schumaker, L.L., Degree-raising of splines, *Jour. Approximation Theory*, Vol. 46, pp. 170–181, 1986.

[Cox72]
Cox, M.G., The numerical evaluation of B-splines, *J. Inst. Maths. Applics.*, Vol. 10, pp. 134–149, 1972.

[deBo72]
deBoor, C., On calculating with B-splines, *Jour. Approximation Theory*, Vol. 6, pp. 50–62, 1972.

[deBo78]
deBoor, C., *A Practical Guide to Splines*, New York: Springer-Verlag, 1978.

[Forr68]
Forrest, A.R., Curves and surfaces for computer-aided design, Ph.D. dissertation, University of Cambridge, Cambridge, UK, 1968.

[Lee83]
Lee, E.T.Y., A B-spline primer, Boeing document, 1983.

[Lee86]
Lee, E.T.Y., Rational Bézier representation for conics, in *Geometric Modeling*, Farin, G., Ed., Philadelphia, PA: SIAM, 1986.

[Lee89]
Lee, E.T.Y., Choosing nodes in parametric curve interpolation, *CAD*, Vol. 21, pp. 363–370, 1989.

[Pieg87a]
Piegl, L., and Tiller, W., Curve and surface constructions using rational B-splines, *CAD*, Vol. 19, pp. 485–498, 1987.

[Pieg87b]
Piegl, L., Interactive data interpolation by rational Bézier curves, *IEEE Comput. Graph. and Appl.*, Vol. 7, No. 4, pp. 45–58, April 1987.

[Pieg88]
Piegl, L., Hermite- and Coons-like interpolants using rational Bézier approximation form with infinite control points, *CAD*, Vol. 20, pp. 2–10, 1988.

[Pieg89a]
Piegl, L., Modifying the shape of rational B-splines. Part 1: Curves, *CAD*, Vol. 21, pp. 509–518, 1989.

[Pieg89b]
Piegl, L., Modifying the shape of rational B-splines. Part 2: Surfaces, *CAD*, Vol. 21, pp. 537–546, 1989.

[Pieg89c]
Piegl, L., and Tiller, W., A menagerie of rational B-spline circles, *IEEE Comput. Graph. and Appl.*, Vol. 9, No. 5, pp. 48–56, September 1989.

[Pieg90]
Piegl, L., Algorithms for computing conic splines, *ASCE Jour. Comput. Civil Engineering*, Vol. 4, No. 3, pp. 180–198, 1990.

[Pieg91]
Piegl, L., On NURBS: A survey, *IEEE Comput. Graph. and Appl.*, Vol. 11, No. 1, pp. 55–71, January 1991.

[Roge82]
Rogers, D.F., and Satterfield, S.G., Dynamic B-spline surfaces, in *Proc. 4th Int. Conf. Comput. Applics. in the Automat. of Shipyard Operations and Ship Design*, pp. 190–196, Amsterdam: North Holland, 1982.

[Roge90]
Rogers, D.F., and Adlum, L.A., Dynamic rational B-spline surfaces, *CAD*, Vol. 22, No. 9, pp. 609–616, 1990.

[Till83]
Tiller, W., Rational B-splines for curve and surface representation, *IEEE Comput. Graph. and Appl.*, Vol. 3, No. 6, pp. 61–69, September 1983.

[Till86]
Tiller, W., Geometric modeling using non-uniform rational B-splines: Mathematical techniques, *SIGGRAPH 86 Tutorial Notes*, Dallas, TX, 1986.

[Vers75]
Versprille, K.J., Computer-aided design applications of the rational B-spline approximation form, Ph.D. dissertation, Syracuse University, Syracuse, NY, 1975.

4 Graphical User-Computer Interfaces

Software Tools for Designing and Implementing User–Computer Interfaces

James Foley

Abstract

Software tools for use in implementing the user interface component of an inter-active application program are described. The tools include interaction technique toolkits and user interface management systems (UIMSs). Interactive design tools for creating dialogue boxes and menus are discussed. The development of UIMSs is traced, and contemporary themes in UIMS research are explored. A specific UIMS, the User Interface Design Environment (UIDE), is discussed as an example of the importamce of providing both data models and control models in a UIMS.

Introduction

Developing high-quality user interfaces is becoming the critical step in bringing many different computer applications to end users. Ease of learning and speed of use typically must be combined in an attractively-designed interface which appeals to application (not computer) oriented end users. This is a complex undertaking, requiring the skills of the computer scientist, application specialist, graphic designer, human factors expert, and psychologist.

User interface software is the foundation upon which the interface is built. The quality of the building blocks provided by the software establishes the framework within which the designer works. The tools should allow the designer to experiment quickly with different design approaches, and should be accessible to the nonprogramming designer.

In this paper we examine the software components, beyond the basic graphics subroutine packages and window managers, that are used in implementing interfaces. Figure 1 shows the various levels of user-interface software, and suggests the roles for each. The figure shows that the application program has access to all software levels; programmers can exploit the services provided by each level, albeit with care, because calls made to one level may affect the behavior of another level. In this paper we discuss just the interaction technique toolkit and user-interface management system layers. See Foley et al. [Fole90] and other texts for discussions of the window manager and graphics subroutine package layers.

Interaction-technique Toolkits

Interaction techniques are the means by which users interactively input information to a computer system. A typical set of interaction techniques includes a dialogue box, file-selection box, alert box, help box, list box, message box, radio-button bank, radio buttons, choice-button bank, choice buttons, toggle-button bank, toggle button, fixed menu, pop-up menu, text input, and scroll bar. Interaction-technique toolkits are subroutine libraries of interaction techniques which are made available for use by application programmers. Widely used toolkits include the Andrew window-management system's toolkit [Pala88], the Macintosh toolkit [Appl85], OSF/Motif [Open89] and InterViews [Lint89] for use with X Windows [Sche86], several toolkits that implement OPEN LOOK [Sun89] on both X Windows and NeWS, Presentation Manager [Micr89], and the SunView window-management system's toolkit [Sun86].

The look and feel of a user–computer interface is determined largely by the collection of interaction techniques provided for it. Designing and implementing a good set of interaction techniques is time consuming, requiring experimentation with users to ensure ease of learning and speed of use. This toolkit approach, which helps to ensure a consistent look and feel among application programs, is clearly a sound and well-accepted software engineering practice. Considerable programmer productivity is gained by using an existing toolkit.

Interaction-technique toolkits can be used not only by application programs, but also by the window manager. A common toolkit is an important and commonly-used ingredient in providing a look and feel that unifies both multiple applications and the windowing environment itself. This makes the menu style used to select window operations the same style used within applications.

As shown in Figure 1, the application program has access to the operating system, window-manager system and graphics package, toolkit, and user-interface management system (UIMS). The interactive design tools allow nonprogrammers to design windows, menus, dialogue boxes, and dialogue sequences. The toolkit can be implemented on top of the window-management system. In the absence of a window system, toolkits can be implemented directly on top of a graphics subroutine package. However, because elements of a toolkit include menus, dialogue boxes, scroll bars, and the like, all of which are conveniently implemented in windows, the window system substrata is normally used.

In the X Window system, interaction techniques are called *widgets*. We adopt this name for use here. Each widget is normally implemented as a window. In

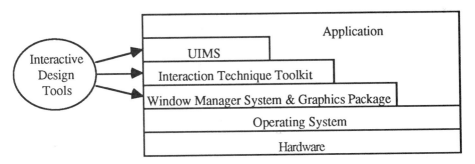

Figure 1. Levels of user-interface software.

X Windows, subwindows may also be used. For instance, a radio-button bank is a window containing a subwindow for each radio button. Complex dialogue boxes can have dozens of subwindows.

Interaction-technique toolkits typically report user actions to the application program by means of calls back to procedures which carry out the functions implied by the user actions; hence, the procedures are often called *callback procedures*. The procedures are in some cases part of the toolkit: for instance, procedures to highlight the current menu item, to select and deselect radio buttons, and to scroll a list or file-selection box. Callbacks can also be provided by the application: for instance, procedures to carry out a command selected from a menu, to check the validity of each character as it is typed into a text input area, or simply to record the fact that a button has been selected. Figure 2 shows part of a dialogue box and some of the callback procedures that might be associated with the box. CopyProc checks each character entered to ensure that it is numeric and that the total number entered does not exceed some upper bound. PaperSourceProc manages the radio-button bank for the paper source to ensure that one and only one button is on and to maintain the current selection. CoverPageProc performs a similar function for the cover-page radio-button bank.

Notice that the previous list of widgets includes both high- and low-level items, some of which are composites of others. For example, a dialogue box might contain several radio-button banks, toggle-button banks, and text input areas. Hence, toolkits include a means of composing widgets together, typically via subroutine calls. Figure 3 shows just some of the code needed to specify the SunView [Sun86] dialogue box of Figure 4. Some toolkits are built using object-oriented programming concepts: Each widget is an instantiation of the widget's definition, possibly with overrides of some of the methods and attributes associated with the definition. A composite consists of multiple instances.

Creating composites by programming, no matter what the mechanism, is tedious. Interactive editors allow composites to be created and modified quickly, facilitating easy changes to user-interface details based on user feedback to the design team. Cardelli has developed a sophisticated interactive editor that allows spatial constraints between widgets to be specified [Card88]. At run time,

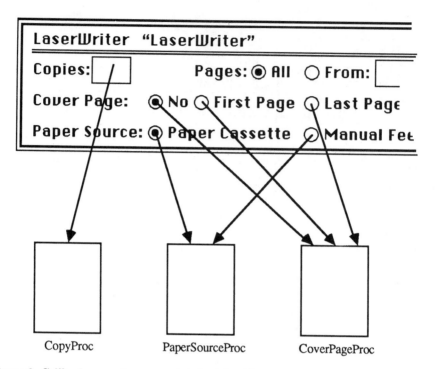

Figure 2. Callback procedures associated with widgets in a dialogue box.

when the dialogue box's size can be changed by the user, the constraints are used to keep the widgets neatly spaced. In the interactive editor shown in Figure 5 a scrolling-list box is being dragged into position. The menu to the left shows the widgets that can be created; from top to bottom, they are buttons, icons, pictures, static text, text input, check boxes, radio buttons, scrolling lists, rectangles (for visual grouping, as with the radio-button banks), lines (for visual separation), pop-up menus, and scroll bars. Several commercially available dialogue box editors include Guide from Sun Microsystems [Sun90] and UIMX from Visual Edge [Visu90].

The output of these editors is a representation of the composite, either as data structures that are translated into code, or as code, or as compiled code. In any case, mechanisms are provided for linking the composite into the application program. Programming skills are not needed to use the editors, so the editors are available to user-interface designers and even to sophisticated end users. These editors are typical of the interactive design tools shown in Figure 1.

Another approach to creating menus and dialogue boxes is to use a higher-level programming-language description. In MICKY [Olse89], an extended Pascal for the Macintosh, a dialogue box is defined by a record declaration. The data type of each record item is used to determine the type of widget used in the dialogue

```
print_frame =
    window_create(
        frame,   FRAME,           {Surrounding box.}
        WIN_SHOW,                        TRUE,
        FRAME_NO_CONFIRM,          TRUE,
        FRAME_SHOW_LABEL,          TRUE,
        FRAME_LABEL,        "Print", {Header at top of window.}
        0);                        {Zero means end of list.}

    print_panel =                   {Panel inside the window.}
        window_create(print_frame,  PANEL,
            WIN_ROWS,               PRINT_WIN_ROWS,
            WIN_COLUMNS,            PRINT_WIN_COLS,
            0);

    print_uickb_name =              {Header at top of panel}
        panel_create_item(print_panel, PANEL_MESSAGE,
            PANEL_LABEL_STRING,     "UICKB: Untitled",
            PANEL_ITEM_X,           ATTR_COL(PRINT_NAME_COL),
            PANEL_ITEM_Y,           ATTR_ROW(PRINT_NAME_ROW),
            0);

    print_report_choice_item =
        panel_create_item(print_panel,  PANEL_CHOICE,
            {List of mutually exclusive options.}
            PANEL_ITEM_X,           ATTR_COL(PRINT_REPORT_COL),
            PANEL_ITEM_Y,           ATTR_ROW(PRINT_REPORT_ROW),
            PANEL_LABEL_STRING,     "Report",
            PANEL_LAYOUT,           PANEL_VERTICAL,{Or horizontal}
            PANEL_CHOICE_STRINGS,
                "Completeness", "Consistency", "Schema", 0,
            PANEL_NOTIFY_PROC,      print_report_choice_proc,
            {Name of callback procedure.}
            0);
```

Figure 3. Some of the SunView code needed to specify the dialogue box of Figure 4. (Courtesy of Kevin Murray, The George Washington University.)

box: enumerated types become radio-button banks, character strings become text inputs, Booleans become checkboxes, and so on. Figure 6 shows a dialogue box and the code that creates it. An interactive dialogue-box editor is used to change the placement of widgets. Figure 7 shows a menu and the code from which it is generated.

Peridot [Myer86, 88] takes a radically different approach to toolkits. The interface designer creates widgets and composite widgets interactively, by example. Rather than starting with a base set of widgets, the designer works with an interactive editor to create a certain look and feel. Examples of the desired

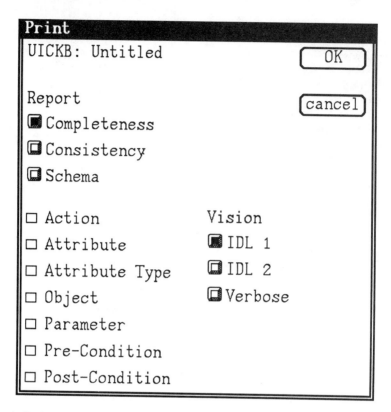

Figure 4. Dialogue box created using the SunView window-manager system's toolkit. The code specifying this box is shown in Figure 3. (Courtesy of Kevin Murray, The George Washington University.)

widgets are drawn, and Peridot infers relationships that allow instances of the widget to adapt to a specific situation. For instance, a menu widget infers that its size is to be proportional to the number of items in the menu choice set. To specify the behavior of a widget, such as the type of feedback given in response to a user action, the designer selects the type of feedback from a Peridot menu, and Peridot generalizes the example to all menu items.

User-interface Management Systems

A user-interface management system (UIMS) is built on top of an interaction technique toolkit and provides additional functionality in implementing the user interface. All UIMSs provide some means of defining admissible user-action sequences and may in addition support overall screen design, help and error messages, macro definition, undo, and user profiles. Some recent UIMSs also manage the data associated with the application.

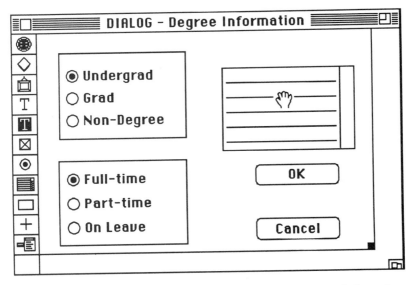

Figure 5. The Now Software (formerly SmethersBarnes) Prototyper dialogue-box editor for the Macintosh. (Courtesy Now Software, Portland, OR.)

UIMSs, like toolkits, can increase programmer productivity (in one study, up to 50 percent of the code in interactive programs was user-interface code [Sutt78]), speed up the development process, and facilitate iterative refinement of a user interface as experience is gained in its use. The more powerful the UIMS, the less the need for the application program to interact directly with the operating system, window system, and toolkit.

```
type
    Str40     = string[40]
    textStyle = record
                    font : Str40;
                    points (*Name = 'Point Size'): integer
                end
```

Figure 6. A dialogue box created automatically by MICKY from the extended Pascal record declaration. (Courtesy Dan Olsen, Jr., Brigham Young University.)

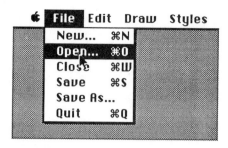

```
procedure NewDrawing (
  (* Menu=File Name='New...' Key=N *)
  DrawFile : OutFileDesc);                {Name of dialogue box to be shown.}
procedure OpenDrawing (
  (* Menu=File Name='Open...' Key=O *)
  DrawFile : InFileDesc);                 {Name of dialogue box to be shown.}
procedure CloseDrawing;
  (* Menu=File Name=Close Key=W *)
procedure SaveDrawing;
  (* Menu=File Name=Save Key=S *)
procedure SaveDrawingAs (
  (* Menu=File Name='Save As...' *)
  DrawFile : OutFileDesc);                {Name of dialogue box to be shown.}
```

Figure 7. A menu created automatically by MICKY from the extended Pascal record declaration. (Courtesy Dan Olsen, Jr., Brigham Young University.)

In some UIMSs, user-interface elements are specified in a programming language that has specialized operators and data types. In others, the specification is done via interactive graphical editors, thus making the UIMS accessible to nonprogrammer interface designers. The former approach tends to be more powerful, the latter more accessible.

Applications developed on top of a UIMS are typically written as a set of subroutines, often called *action routines* or *semantic action routines*. The UIMS is responsible for calling appropriate action routines in response to user inputs. In turn, the action routines influence the dialogue—for instance, by modifying what the user can do next on the basis of the outcome of a computation. Thus, the UIMS and the application share control of the dialogue—this is called the *shared-control* model. A UIMS in which the action routines have no influence over the dialogue is said to follow an external-control model; control resides solely in the UIMS. External control is not as powerful a model as is shared control.

UIMSs vary greatly in the specific capabilities they provide to user-interface designers, but the one essential ingredient is a dialogue-sequence specification, to control the order in which interaction techniques are made available to the end user. For this reason, in the next section we turn our attention to dialogue sequencing; then, in that same section we discuss more advanced UIMS concepts. Further background on UIMSs is found in [Hart89; Myer89; Olse87].

Permissible sequences of user actions are defined in a variety of ways: via transition networks (also called state diagrams), recursive transition networks, event languages, or by example, where the designer demonstrates the allowable action sequences to the system, and the system 'learns' what sequences are possible. Common to all these methods is the concept of a user-interface *state* and associated user actions that can be performed from that state. Each of the specification methods encodes the user-interface state in a slightly different way, each of which generalizes to the use of one or more *state variables*.

If a context-sensitive user interface is to be created, the system response to user actions must depend on the current state of the interface. System responses to user actions include invocation of one or several action routines, changes in one or more of the state variables, and enabling, disabling, or modifying interaction techniques or menu items in preparation for the next user action. Help should also be dependent on the current state. Since the outcome of computations performed by the action routines should affect user-interface behavior, the action routines must be able to modify the state variables. Thus, state is at the heart of context-sensitivity, a concept central to contemporary user interfaces.

The simplest and least powerful, but nevertheless useful, sequence specification method is the *transition network* or *state diagram*. Transition networks have a single state variable, an integer indicating the current state. User actions cause transitions from one state to another; each transition has associated with it zero or more action routines that are called when the transition occurs. In addition, states have associated action routines executed whenever the state is entered. This shorthand is convenient for actions that are common to all transitions entering a state.

Action routines affect the current state of the transition network in one of two ways. First, they place events in the event queue, which in turn drives the interaction handling. This approach implicitly modifies the state, although to ensure that the state change is immediate the event must be put at the front of the queue, not at the back. Alternatively, action routines modify the state more directly by simply setting the state variable to a new value. The first approach is cleaner from a software-engineering view, whereas the second is more flexible but more error-prone.

Transition networks are used with several UIMSs [Jaco83, 85; Schu85; Rube83; Wass85]. Figure 8 shows a transition network for a simple application having the following commands:

select an object (establishes a CSO, i.e., a currently-selected object);

deselect the CSO (so there is no CSO);

create an object (establishes a CSO);

delete the CSO (so there is no CSO);

copy the CSO to the clipboard (requires a CSO, makes the clipboard full);

paste from the clipboard (requires that the clipboard be full, creates a CSO);

clear the clipboard (requires the clipboard be full, empties the clipboard).

Not all commands are available in all states. In general, as seen in Figure 8, action routines associated with transitions should appear on diagrams of this sort, with the names of the user actions (user commands in this case); we omit them here because the actions are obvious.

Some of these UIMSs provide interactive transition-network editors, which makes the networks simple to specify. The first UIMS, developed by Newman and called The Reaction Handler, included such an editor [Newm68].

Transition networks are especially useful for finding sequencing inconsistencies and are easily used to determine the number of steps required to complete a task sequence. Thus, they also serve as a means of predicting how good a particular design will be, even before the complete interface is implemented.

Transition networks, however, have drawbacks. Specifically, the user-interface state is typically based on a number of state variables. Mapping all possible

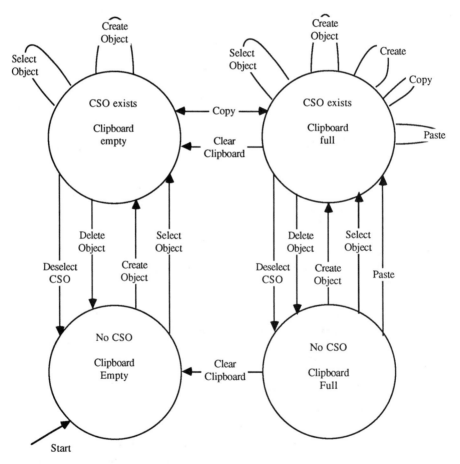

Figure 8. A transition network with four states.

combinations of values of these variables onto a single state is awkward and nonintuitive for the user-interface designer. For example, in Figure 8, four states are needed to encode the two conditions

CSO exists/does not exist;

clipboard full/clipboard empty.

Notice also that whether or not any objects exist should also be encoded, since objects must exist for the command SelectObject to be available in the starting state. Four more states would be needed to encode whether any objects do or do not exist.

Concurrency creates a similar state-space growth problem. Consider two user-interface elements—say, two concurrently active dialogue boxes—each with its own 'state' encoding the selections currently allowable or currently made. If each dialogue-box state can be encoded in 10 states, their combination requires 100 states; for three dialogue boxes, 1000 states are needed; and so on. This exponential growth in state space is unacceptable. Jacob [Jaco86] combines transition networks with object-oriented programming concepts to specify complete user interfaces while limiting the state-space explosion. Objects are self-contained entities within the interface, and each object has its own transition network to specify its behavior, which is independent of that of other objects. The UIMS portion of HUTWindows, the Helsinki University of Technology Window Manager and UIMS, uses a similar strategy [Koiv88].

Globally available commands similarly enlarge the transition network. If help is to be globally available, each state must have an associated help state, a transition to the help state, and a reverse transition back to the originating state. This is also needed for the help to be context-sensitive. Undo must be done similarly, except that the transition from an undo state returns to a state different from the one from which it was entered. As the number of transitions relative to the number of states increases, we end up with complex 'spaghetti' transition networks.

Various specialized constructs have been developed to simplify transition networks. For instance, we alleviate the help problem by using subnetworks, in a fashion analogous to subroutines, to hide localized repetitive detail. Transition networks with subnetworks are called *recursive transition networks*. The state variables in this case are the entire stack of saved states, plus the state of the currently active transition network. Several other powerful diagramming techniques, all derived from transition networks, are described in Wellner [Well89].

Backus-Naur Form (BNF) is also used to define sequencing, and is equivalent in representational power to recursive transition networks (both are equivalent to push-down automata). BNF, illustrated in Figure 9, can also be shown diagrammatically as in Figure 10. It is difficult to read BNF and to obtain a good overview of the sequencing rules, but BNF form can be processed to provide an evaluation of certain aspects of user-interface quality [Bles82; Reis82], or to generate command-language parsers [John78]. Several older UIMSs are based on BNF specifications [Hana80; Olse83; Olse84].

```
<command> ::= <create> | <polyline> | <delete> | <move> | STOP
<create> ::= CREATE + <type> + <position>
<type> ::= SQUARE | TRIANGLE
<position> ::= NUMBER + NUMBER
<polyline> ::= POLYLINE + <vertex list> + END_POLY
<vertex_list> ::= <position> | <vertex_list> + <position>
<delete> ::= DELETE + OBJECT_ID
<move> ::= MOVEA + OBJECT_ID + <position>
```

Figure 9. Backus-Naur Form representation of the sequencing rules for a simple user interface.

Transition networks, whether recursive or not, encode user-interface state in a small number of state variables. *Augmented transition networks* (ATNs), a more flexible derivative of transition networks, encode user interface state by which node of the ATN is active and with the values of explicit state variables. Responses can be the calling of action routines, the setting of these explicit state variables, and a change in which node of the ATN is active. Of course, the state variables can also be set by action routines. Figure 11 shows an ATN in which the Boolean state variable CB, set by several of the transitions, is used to affect flow of control from one state to another. The variable CB is **true** if

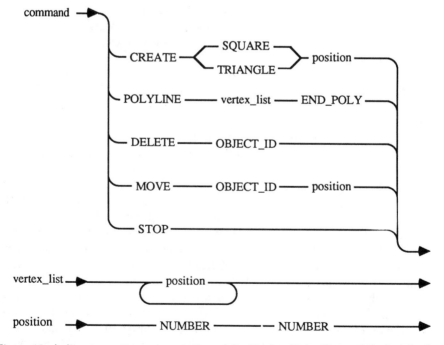

Figure 10. A diagrammatic representation of the Backus-Naur Form equivalent to that in Figure 9.

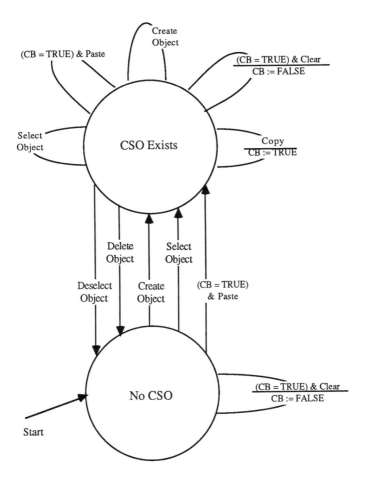

Figure 11. An augmented transition network (ATN) representing the same user interface as that in Figure 8.

the clipboard is full. Transitions can be conditionally dependent on the value of explicit state variables (the Boolean CB in this case), and can also set state variables. In general, the application program also sets state variables.

Just as transition networks are made more general with subnetworks, so too ATNs can call lower-level ATNs. ATNs that call other ATNs are called *augmented recursive transition networks* [Wood70]; researchers have used these networks to model user interfaces [Kier85].

As transition networks become more complicated, with logical expressions on transition and subroutine calls, we are led toward more program-like specifications. After all, programming languages are the most powerful way yet developed of specifying sequencing and the multiple conditions often associated with transitions. Several *event languages* have been developed specifically for user-interface specification [Card85; Flec87; Garr82; Gree85a; Hill86; Sioc89]. The user interface depicted in Figures 8 and 11 can be described in a typical event language, as shown in Figure 12. Event languages, unlike traditional programming languages, have no explicit flow of control. Instead, whenever an **if** condition becomes true, the associated actions are executed. Thus, the event language is a production-rule system.

Green [Gree87] surveys event languages and all other sequence-specification methods mentioned, and shows that general event languages are more powerful than are transition networks, recursive transition networks, and grammars. He

```
if Event = SelectObject then
  begin
    cso := true
    perform action routine name
  end
if Event = DeselectCSO and cso = true then
  begin
    cso := false
    perform action routine name
  end
if Event = CreateObject then
  begin
    cso := true
    perform action routine name
  end
if Event = DeleteCSO and cso = true then
  begin
    cso := false
    perform action routine name
  end
if Event = CopyCSO and cso = true then
  begin
    cb := true
    perform action routine name
  end
if Event = PasteClipboard and cb = true then
  begin
    cso := true
    perform action routine name
  end
if Event = ClearClipboard and cb = true then
  begin
    cb := false
    perform action routine name
  end
```

Figure 12. A typical event language, with a Pascal-like syntax.

also provides algorithms for converting these forms into an event language. ATNs that have general computations associated with their arcs are also equivalent to event languages.

If event languages are so powerful, why do we bother with the various types of transition networks? Because, for simple cases, it is easier to work with diagrammatic representations. One of the goals of UIMSs is to allow nonprogrammers who specialize in user-interface design to be directly involved in creating an interface. This goal is probably best met with transition network-oriented tools that are easier to use, although somewhat less powerful. Networks provide a useful, time-proven tool for laying out a dialogue, and they appear to help the designer to document and understand the design. The diagrammatic representations are especially compelling if user actions are performed on interaction objects such as menus, dialogue boxes, and other visible objects. Then diagrams of the type shown in Figure 13 can be created interactively to define dialogue sequences. If needed, conditions (such as the CB = true in Figure 11) are associated with the arcs.

A quite different way to define syntax is by example. Here, the user interface designer places the UIMS into a 'learning' mode, and then steps through all acceptable sequences of actions (a tedious process in complex applications, unless the UIMS infers general rules from the examples). The designer might start with

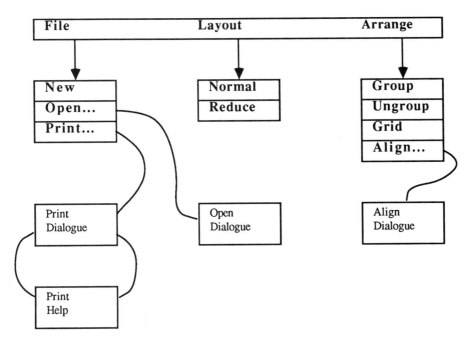

Figure 13. Several menus and dialogue boxes linked together. The return paths from dialogue boxes to the main menu are not shown.

a main menu, select an item from it, and then go through a directory to locate the submenu, dialogue box, or application-specific object to be presented to the user in response to the main menu selection. The object appears on the screen, and the designer indicates the position, size, or other attributes that the object should have when the application is actually executed. The designer goes on to perform some operation on the displayed object and again shows what object should appear next, or how the displayed object is to respond to the operation; the designer repeats this process until all actions on all objects are defined. This technique works for sequencing through items that have already been defined by the interface designer, but it is not sufficiently general to handle arbitrary application functionality. User-interface software tools with some degree of by-example sequencing specification include Menulay [Buxt83], TAE Plus [Mill88], and the SmethersBarnes Prototyper [Coss89]. Peridot, mentioned earlier, builds interaction techniques (i.e., hardware bindings) by example.

UIMSs are finding their way into regular use. Early UIMSs suffered from rigid interaction styles that did not allow custom-tailoring to suit users' needs and were overly dependent on transition networks. Commercial UIMSs are now used on a large scale, and are becoming as essential to developing interactive graphics application programs as are graphics subroutine packages, window managers, and interaction-technique toolkits.

Next-generation UIMS Concepts

UIMSs have tended to focus on sequence control and visual design. Transition networks provide a good basis for sequencing, and interactive editors are just right for visual design. However, as discussed in Foley et al. [Fole90], a user-interface design includes conceptual, functional, sequencing, and hardware-binding levels. Much recent UIMS development addresses the functional and conceptual designs as well. Thus, there is more focus on combining sequencing control with a higher-level model of objects and commands, and also on integrating intelligent help systems into the UIMS.

Representations at a higher level than that of transition networks are clearly needed. Consider how difficult it is to add to the transition network of Figure 8 additional states to record whether any objects have yet been created. It is also difficult to modify the dialogue to include a currently-selected object (CSO) concept, a command mode, or global attribute values. And the sequencing specifications provide no information about what operations can be performed on what objects, and certainly give no glimmer of what parameters are needed to perform an operation.

The first step away from a sequencing orientation and toward higher levels of abstraction was taken by COUSIN [Haye83, 84, 85], which automatically generates menus and dialogue boxes from a specification of commands, parameters, and parameter data types. The innovation of COUSIN is in defining all the parameters needed by a command as an integral unit. COUSIN has enough information that a prefix or postfix syntax could also be generated. Green took a similar approach, adding preconditions and postconditions to specify the semantics of user commands [Gree85b]. Olsen's MIKE system declares commands and parameters, also generating a user interface in a fashion similar to COUSIN [Olse86]. In addition, MIKE supports direct manipulation of objects to specify positions, and causes commands to be executed when a button-down event occurs in a window or subwindow.

All these significant advances are focused on commands. If a UIMS is to mediate between the user and the application in direct-manipulation interfaces, however, it must have some knowledge of the objects to be manipulated. HIGGINS was the first UIMS to incorporate a data model [Huds86, 87, 88], one that is based on objects and relations between objects. The UIMS and action routines share the data model, so that changes made to data objects are immediately reflected in the display. *Active values* are used to propagate changes among interdependent objects and from objects to their visual representations. The George Washington University User Interface Management System (GWUIMS) uses active values and object-oriented programming concepts to achieve a similar objective [Sibe86]. GWUIMS II also uses a data model [Hurl89], as does the Serpent UIMS [Bass88]. Although the details vary, all the data models make use of object-oriented programming concepts and active values, and are closely related to developments in database-management systems in the area of semantic data models [Hull87].

Another way to define user interfaces consisting of interconnected processing modules is with data-flow diagrams. For instance, the NeXT Interface Builder [Next90] allows objects to be interconnected so that output messages from one object are input to another object. Type checking is used to ensure that only compatible messages are sent and received.

Data-flow diagrams are also used to specify the detailed behavior of some or all of a user interface, although doing so takes on considerable programming flavor and suffers the same problems of scale seen with flowcharts and transition networks. Work in this area is surveyed in Borning and Duisberg [Born86]; a more recent project is described in Smith [Smit88].

The rest of this chapter considers in detail one particular next-generation UIMS.

The User Interface Design Environment

The User Interface Design Environment (UIDE) project at The George Washington University and at Georgia Institute of Technology developed a new user-interface specification method, which includes a single-inheritance data model, the commands that can be applied to each type of object in the data model, the parameters needed by the commands, the parameter data types, the conditions under which commands are available for use (that is, command preconditions), and the changes that occur to state variables when a command is executed (that is, command postconditions) [Fole87, 88, 89].

To illustrate the method, we start with the sample application developed in the section on user-interface management systems. We add a data model, which here is a single class of objects with two subclasses, square and triangle. In addition, there are two distinguished instances of objects, the CSO and the clipboard object, both of which may or may not exist at any given time. The specification is shown in Figure 14. The preconditions are the conditions on state variables that must be satisfied for a command to be invoked, whereas postconditions are changes in state variables.

Not only is this specification sufficient to automatically create an operational interface to the application's action routines, but it is also represented such that

> menu items are enabled and disabled, using preconditions;
>
> users are told why a command is disabled, again using preconditions;
>
> users are told or shown what to do to enable a command, by back chaining to determine what commands must be invoked to satisfy the preconditions of the command in question;
>
> users are given a partial explanation of what a command does, using the postconditions;
>
> some user-interface design-consistency rules are checked;
>
> different interaction techniques can be assigned for use in specifying commands and command parameters;
>
> speed of use of the interface is predictable for various task sequences and for various interaction techniques;
>
> the specification is transformed into a functionally-equivalent but slightly different interface.

UIDE goes several steps beyond the capabilities of the typical User Interface Management System (UIMS), with which the designer works at the syntactic and lexical levels of design, focusing on command names, screen and icon design, menu organization, sequencing rules, and interaction techniques. The UIDE designer is able to work at a higher level of abstraction. This approach is possible because the operations on objects specify all the units of information and the context needed to carry out the operation. This contrasts with lower-level Backus-Naur Form and Augmented Transition Network specifications, where this knowledge is not explicitly represented and therefore cannot be used to assist in designing or implementing the interface.

UIDE is implemented with the Automated Reasoning Tool (ART) from Inference Corporation, on a Sun 3/60 and HP 370. All components shown in Figure 15 are implemented and are operational. As is typical of a research project, the modules are continuously being enhanced to provide more capabilities.

The user-interface design is represented internally as instances of seven ART schemata, or frames. The most important slots and the relationships between the seven schemata are shown in Figure 16. A detailed discussion of the schemata slots is found in Foley et al. [Fole88]. Externally, the design is represented in IDL (Interface Definition Language), which was developed to present the conceptual design of the user interface in a structured and readable presentation. This

```
class object                                    {First the data model}
  subclasses triangle, square;
  actions CreateObject, SelectObject;
  attributes position range [0..10] x [0..10]  {Attribute name and data type}
class triangle, square;
  superclass object;
  inherits   actions
  inherits   attributes
instance CSO
  of object
  actions DeselectCSO, DeleteCSO, CopyCSO
  inherits   attributes
instance CB
  of object
  actions ClearClipboard, Paste
  inherits   attributes
```

```
{Initial values for state variables}
initial Number (object) := 0; csoExists := false; cbFull := false;
```

```
{Actions on objects, with preconditions, postconditions, and parameters}
precondition Number (object) ≠ 0;
SelectObject (object);
postcondition csoExists := true;
```

```
precondition csoExists := true;
DeselectCSO (CSO implicit);
postcondition csoExists := false;
```

```
precondition;
CreateObject (position, object);
postcondition Number (object) := Number (object) +1; csoExists := true;
```

```
precondition csoExists := true;
DeleteCSO (CSO implicit);
postcondition Number (object) = Number (object) - 1; csoExists := false;
```

```
precondition csoExists := true;
CopyCSO (CSO implicit);
postcondition cbFull := true;
```

```
precondition cbFull := true;
Paste (CB implicit);
postcondition csoExists := true;
```

```
precondition cbFull := true;
ClearClipboard (CB implicit);
postcondition cbFull := false;
```

Figure 14. A high-level specification of a user interface incorporating a data model, sequencing information, and command parameters.

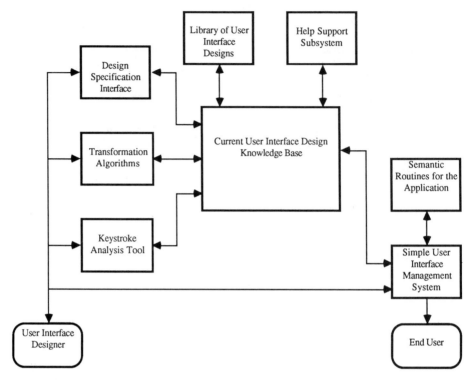

Figure 15. The overall organization of the User Interface Design Environment (UIDE).

paper presents user-interface design examples using IDL. Figure 17 shows the
IDL representation of the knowledge base for a simple 'squares and triangles'
application that is used in examples throughout the balance of this paper. There
are two types of objects, squares and triangles, that are subclasses of shape.
The attributes of each object are color, angle, and position. The objects can
be created, deleted, and rotated. As seen from the example, IDL is a fairly
high-level specification, akin to Problem Definition Languages. In the following
sections, each of the major components of UIDE is discussed.

Design Specification Interface

The design definition interface allows a designer to specify the user interface. The
major stages for this are building the design knowledge base, checking the knowledge base for completeness, and analyzing the knowledge base for consistency.
Completeness checks verify that all schemata in the knowledge base contain
enough information for the transformation system to operate and for SUIMS,
the Simple UIMS, to implement the interface. Consistency checks examine the
overall design knowledge base, advising the designer of potential inconsistencies.

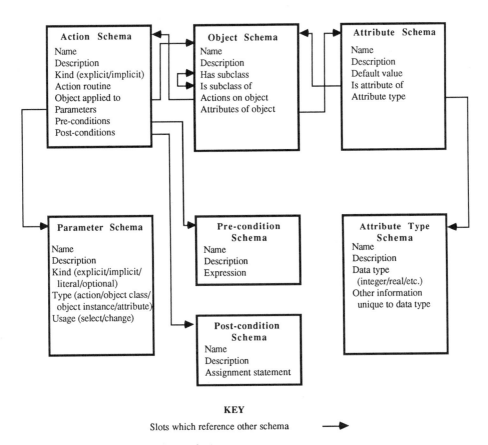

KEY

Slots which reference other schema   ⟶

Figure 16. Schemata and their relations.

The designer inputs information by selecting options from menus and replying to prompts. This type of interface is used to avoid forcing the designer to learn IDL syntax rules. Any element of the design can be specified at any time, allowing the designer to move freely from one part of a design specification to another. However, this also increases the possibility of an incomplete design. Feedback is provided concerning the design element currently being specified. At any point the designer can display the entire knowledge base in IDL. Figure 18 shows the design specification interface midway through specifying the squares and triangles application. This interface, shown here with a partially-completed design, has multiple windows which are used to view and specify the design knowledge base.

In the upper left window is the main menu, used for system actions, window selection, consistency and completeness checks, help, transformations, find and quit.

The Global Lists window, in the upper right, contains eight lists and a panel. The panel buttons apply to any of the eight lists. The lists give the names

```
class object                                    {First the data model}
   subclasses triangle, square;
   actions CreateObject, SelectObject;
   attributes position range [0..10] x [0..10] {Attribute name and data type}
class triangle, square;
   superclass object;
   inherits  actions;
   inherits  attributes;

{Initial values for state variables}
initial Number (object) := 0;

{Actions on objects, with preconditions, postconditions, and parameters}
precondition true;
CreateObject (position, object);
postcondition Number (object) := Number (object) +1;

precondition Number(object) > 0;
RotateObject(object, angle);
postcondition null;

precondition Number(object) > 0;
DeleteObject(object);
postcondition Number(object) = Number(object) - 1;
```

Figure 17. IDL representation of design for the squares and triangles example.

of all the schema in the design. The objects level list gives the names of the subobjects of the object highlighted in the objects list.

The lower right window shows one of the seven schemata types: the parameter view. On the left side is a list of all the actions that use the parameter 'position'. In the middle right are fields, buttons, and cycles for specifying the parameter's attributes. On the lower right is a text editing area for providing a description of the parameter (schema). Parameters are associated with the 'Add Action' button.

The lower left window shows the object class hierarchy. This is a direct manipulation view. Objects can be repositioned, renamed, cut, pasted, and copied. The object can be repositioned in the hierarchy, thereby changing large amounts of inherited data quickly.

There is an important difference between completeness and consistency checks. An incomplete design cannot be used by the transformation algorithms (see the next section), so the completeness of a design must be checked before a transformation algorithm is applied. If a transformation algorithm is applied to an incomplete knowledge base, it fails in a manner similar to compilation of a Pascal program with incomplete declarations. However, an inconsistent design can be transformed, and may be exactly what the designer intends. Consider as an example a design with two subclasses of shape, square and circle. It is inconsistent

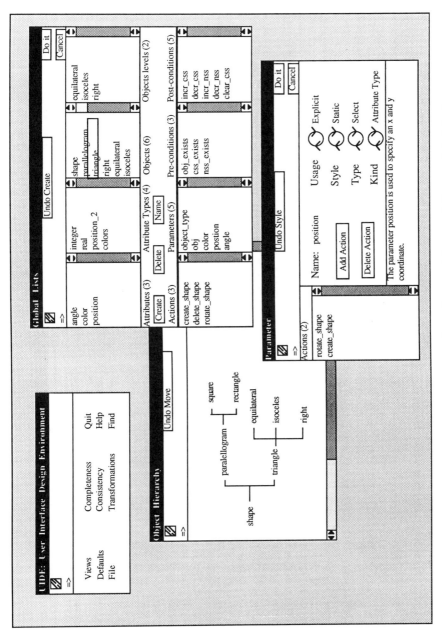

Figure 18. The design specification interface, shown with a partially-completed design.

to have a RotateSquare action without having a comparable RotateCircle action, but this is not incomplete. Of course, a design that is complete and hence can be transformed may not work as intended, just as a program which successfully compiles may not run as expected.

We have developed a small rule base for analyzing a design's completeness and consistency. Additional rules can be added to the rule base with minimal effort, providing the opportunity to expand the rule base as our experience grows. Some of the completeness and consistency rules with which we are working are shown in Figure 19. The designer is informed of inconsistency rule violations but is not forced to correct the violation(s). The designer often has a reason, not known to UIDE, for the design choice. The designer must, however, attend to violated completeness rules.

Completeness Rules:

- Proper class hierarchy - The class hierarchy graph must be a tree, starting at the root class. There can be neither cycles nor nodes with indegree greater than one (assuming our current single inheritance model).
- Complete information - Required information for each schema must be present. The "free-style" form of definition, in which the designer can work in whatever sequence seems most natural, can readily lead to missing information.
- Pre-condition variable never set - A variable which is used in a pre-condition is never given a value.

Consistency Rules:

- Unused post-condition variable - A variable which is set in a post-condition is not used in any pre-condition. The variable is redundant.
- Class hierarchy fragments - subclasses without a designated superclass are not part of the class hierarchy. The designer may want to have some class hierarchy subtrees which are not connected to the class hierarchy.
- Single subclass - a class will normally have more than one subclass.
- Comparable actions - Subclasses of the same class will normally have the same actions. If triangles can be rotated, it is likely that squares should also be able to be rotated.
- Comparable attributes - Subclasses of the same class will normally have the same attributes. If triangles have attributes, then squares would likely have the same attributes.
- Comparable domains - Given a class with two subclasses, then two comparable actions, one applied to the class, the other applied to one of the two subclasses, would be better organized by moving the action from the class down to the subclass which does not currently have an action directly associated with it. A similar argument pertains to attributes.
- Inverse Actions - Actions typically have inverse actions (Delete is the inverse of both create and duplicate). The inverse can often be identified by examining post-conditions: if none can be identified, the designer is notified.

Figure 19. Some completeness and consistency rules.

User-interface Transformations

A user-interface designer typically develops and evaluates a number of alternative conceptual designs. Some of the alternatives are slight variations on one another, while other designs are quite different. UIDE automatically generates alternative conceptual designs which are slight variations on one another. This is done via transformations which are applied to the user-interface knowledge base and are in the spirit of correctness-preserving program transformations. Each transformation automatically creates a new user-interface design with the same functionality as the original, but with a slightly different user view of the functionality. This automatic generation of alternatives saves considerable designer effort by allowing the designer to quickly apply and test different design paradigms.

First, the basic interface design is entered into the knowledge base—objects, attributes, actions, pre- and postconditions. Several generic design paradigms have been implemented as transformation algorithms. The transformations include factoring (sometimes also called orthogonalization), special cases of which are the creation of a currently-selected object (CSO), a currently-selected command, and a currently-selected attribute value; establishing a currently-selected set (CSS) as a generalization of the CSO concept; establishing initial default values; specializing and generalizing commands based on object and command hierarchies; modifying the scope of certain types of commands; and consolidating commands based on precondition and postcondition equivalence. The transformations are discussed in depth in Foley et al. [Fole87].

In this section, the Currently-Selected Set transformation is discussed in some detail to illustrate the general concept of transformations. The transformations are implemented with ART rules which instantiate, modify, or delete the seven types of schema shown in Figure 16. Here, NSS is the set of nonselected objects, and CSS is the set of selected objects. CSS and NSS are disjoint, and together include all objects. The effect of a transformation on the knowledge base is illustrated on the set of actions from the example of Figure 17, in which pre- and postconditions based on the number of instances of object class 'shape' control when the RotateShape and DeleteShape actions are available.

The Currently-Selected Set (CSS) transformation factors a specified class of objects out of the actions which operate on that object class. This means, in general, that the object is no longer selected by the user when the action is invoked, but instead is given in advance of the action, and might be used by several actions. More specifically, a CSS is a set of selected objects which can be operated on by a succession of actions. The user selects the set of objects, and each subsequent action requested by the user is applied to each member of the CSS. The CSS transformation adds actions to add an object to the CSS, remove an object from the CSS, and clear the CSS. The action to add an object to the CSS has a postcondition which increases by one the size of the CSS, and decreases by one the size of the remaining, nonselected set of objects (called the NSS). A precondition, requiring that the CSS be nonempty, is added to actions which operate on instances of the object class which has been factored. In Figure 20, these actions are RemoveFromCSS, ClearCSS, RotateShape, and DeleteShape.

Also, the keyword implicit is added to the factored object instance parameter in each of these actions. Our definition of CSS is that a newly-created object becomes the CSS, and that any other objects which were in the CSS are now deselected. Hence, a postcondition is added to all actions which create a new instance of the class, asserting that the CSS has size one. Actions which delete an object of the class being factored have an additional postcondition asserting that the CSS is empty, because the deletion applies to the CSS, leaving it empty. Figure 20 shows the set of actions that results when the previous example of Figure 17 is transformed to have a CSS.

There are several alternative definitions of the CSS concept. For instance, a newly created object might not be placed in the CSS. Similarly, deletion might

{Initial values for state variables}
initial Number(*object*) = 0;
initial Number(CSS_Object) = 0;   {CSS (Currently Selected Set) initially empty.}
initial Number(NSS_Object) = 0;   {NSS (Non-Selected Set) initially empty.}

precondition Number(NSS_Object) > 0;   {To add to the CSS, there must be some non selected objects.}
addToCSS(*object*, *CSS* **implicit**);
postcondition Number(*CSS_Object*) = Number(*CSS_Object*) + 1;
postcondition Number(*NSS_Object*) = Number(*NSS_Object*) - 1;

precondition Number(*CSS_Object*) > 0;
RemoveFromCSS(*object*, *CSS* **implicit**);
postcondition Number(*CSS_Object*) = Number(*CSS_Object*) - 1;
postcondition Number(*NSS_Object*) = Number(*NSS_Object*) + 1;

precondition Number(*CSS_Object*) > 0;
ClearCSS(*CSS* **implicit**);
postcondition Number(*NSS_Object*) = Number(*NSS_Object*) + Number(*CSS_Object*);
postcondition Number(*CSS_Object*) = 0;   {All currently selected objects become non selected objects.}

precondition true;
CreateObject(*object*, *position*, *color*, *angle*);
postcondition Number(*object*) = Number(*object*) + 1;   {Creation increases the Number of objects.}
postcondition Number(*NSS_Object*) = Number(*NSS_Object*) + Number(*CSS_Object*);
    {When object is created, the existing CSS, if any, is deselected, thus adding to the NSS.}
postcondition Number(*CSS_Object*) = 1;
    {Size of the CSS after creation action is 1: the newly-created object.}

precondition Number(*CSS_Object*) > 0;   {In order to rotate a object, it must first be selected.}
RotateObject(*object* **implicit**, *angle*);   {Shape to rotate is implicit in the CSS.}
postcondition null;

precondition Number(*CSS_Object*) > 0;
DeleteObject(*object* **implicit**);   {Shape to delete is implicit in the CSS.}
    {Deletion decreases the total Number of objects.}
postcondition Number(*object*) = Number(*object*) - Number(*CSS_Object*);
postcondition Number(*CSS_Object*) = 0;   {Deleting CSS empties it.}

Figure 20. The squares and triangles application after being transformed to have a CSS (Currently-Selected Set).

not empty the CSS, but rather could replace the CSS with the existing object(s) which were most recently in the CSS. The set of actions for operating on the CSS (add, remove, clear) might include an AddMultipleObjects action, or might not have one of the remove or clear actions. There are extant examples of these and other alternative definitions of CSS. Our knowledge representation provides a useful way to precisely specify the alternatives: future versions of UIDE will give the designer a choice of these various alternatives.

Other transformations work similarly, and are not described here in as much detail. In each case, schemata for actions, parameters, preconditions, and post-conditions are added, removed, or modified. The class hierarchy specialization transformation adds specialized actions in place of a general action. For instance, CreateTriangle and CreateSquare actions replace the CreateShape action seen in the previous examples. Class hierarchy generalization does the opposite. Attribute value specialization adds specialized actions for each value of an enumerated attribute. If color in the above example is red, green, or blue, then CreateShape is replaced with CreateShapeRed, CreateShapeGreen, etc. Attribute value generalization does the opposite.

The Currently-Selected Command transformation adds a SetCommand action with a postcondition asserting that the command is selected. The actual action has a precondition added requiring that the command be selected. The object naming transformation adds a name parameter to the parameter list of actions which creates an object, and adds an action to change an object's name.

All interfaces which are created by applying arbitrary sequences of transformations form an equivalence class of interfaces. Each such equivalence class is represented by its canonical form, which is a unique member of the equivalence class. While we have no proof, we believe that the canonical form is one in which all actions are generalized (pushed up) to the highest possible level of abstraction; all parameters are explicit; no defaults exist; and all modes, both action and object, are removed. Proof of this conjecture, and developing an algorithm which finds a sequence (which is nonunique) of transformations to take any member of the equivalence class into the canonical form are open research problems. The canonical form is the most compact representation of the various alternatives and is useful for defining a standard interface between a UIMS and the semantic modules which implement the functionality of an interface.

Simple User Interface Management System (SUIMS)

The transformation algorithms allow the designer to create a variety of functionally equivalent user-interface designs for an application. However, none of these designs prescribes a presentation style, dialogue syntax, or set of interaction techniques. SUIMS allows these aspects of the interface to be determined, and to be saved for re-use if an interface is further transformed. SUIMS uses both the basic knowledge base (see the previous section on the User Interface Design Environment) and an additional knowledge base which describes the runtime context for both SUIMS and the application. SUIMS also has a set of rules which operate on the knowledge base. Salient parts of this additional knowledge base and rule base are described in this section.

The SUIMS window schemata control the screen layout using both initial and updated settings. Initial settings, window sizes and positions, and the way new windows are added are provided when a window is first created. Once the window is created, SUIMS maintains all of the changes (size and position), even if the window is temporarily deleted or made invisible. This allows the designer to interactively rearrange screen layouts to modify an existing or initial layout. Such changes become a permanent part of the user-interface design.

A set of Interaction Techniques is defined in the knowledge base for carrying out the different interaction tasks: CommandSelection, ClassSelection, Instance-Selection, AttributeSelection, PositionSelection, TextInput, and IntegerInput. There is a set of available interaction techniques that can be used for each task, and an indication of whether the technique is enabled or disabled. The designer can change these settings at run-time, depending on the interaction style desired and the interaction devices that are supported and made available. For instance, we have implemented pointing, type-in, and menu selection for the InstanceSe-lection interaction task. There are no restrictions on the number of interaction techniques enabled for each interaction task. However, if none are enabled, the interaction task cannot be carried out. If more than one technique is enabled, the user chooses which one to use.

SUIMS application objects are instantiated by SUIMS whenever an action which creates an object is invoked by the user. SUIMS maintains the attribute values for each object, and also makes them available to the application's seman-tic action procedures. Thus, these objects are the data shared between SUIMS and the application. SUIMS links to the semantic action routines using active value slots in the object schema; the action routines are encapsulated as meth-ods, and invoked automatically by ART whenever a slot value changes. The action routines can be written as ART rules, LISP, C, or any other language which can be linked with LISP.

Interaction objects handle interactions between the user and SUIMS, and de-termine what messages are exchanged. This is similar to the approach used by Sibert et al. [Sibe86]. SUIMS actions are standard actions, defined in a man-ner similar to the designer-defined actions, and are not specified in the design description. Examples of such actions are quit, exit, undo, and help.

In addition to the built-in actions, SUIMS implements all actions whose se-mantics are completely specified via postconditions. Semantic action routines are not required, for example actions not present in the canonical design but introduced by transformations, like those for handling the currently-selected set (CSS): AddToCSS, RemoveFromCSS, ClearCSS. This is possible because SUIMS is in charge of application objects. This is an important aspect of the usage of postconditions.

SUIMS is a shared control UIMS: it is in charge and invokes the application's semantic action routines. The action routines in turn modify the knowledge base which controls SUIMS, hence creating the shared control. Action routines are optional, and SUIMS can prototype the application without them.

In the above discussion of the knowledge bases, syntax is not explicitly mentioned. Syntax definition plays an important role in the specification of a dialogue between the user and the system, depending on the level of abstraction in the I/O sequencing definition or the ordering of I/O events. SUIMS is nearly syntax free, putting minimal constraints on the sequence of user actions. The only ordering imposed is that a command must be selected before its parameters, except for parameters which have been factored out by a transformation algorithm and hence set globally. The user can change parameter values, as long as the command has not been performed or canceled. When all necessary parameters have been provided, SUIMS either performs the command, or, if confirmation mode is on, waits for the user to explicitly confirm that all parameters have their desired values. The confirmation provides more equality in the treatment of parameters, by giving the user the opportunity to modify the last parameter value entered as well as the ones previously entered. It also allows proper handling of parameter defaults and a variable number of parameters. The designer chooses whether to require confirmation.

SUIMS cycles through a set of steps:

Establish and update the screen layout.

Check all preconditions and recognize enabled actions.

Accept the action that the user has selected.

Process each parameter according to its kind (explicit, implicit, etc.).

Accept parameter values in arbitrary order, using any of the enabled interaction techniques.

Confirm implicitly (if all missing information is provided), explicitly (if required), or cancel an action.

Execute an action.

Evaluate postconditions.

SUIMS does not perform each step in each cycle. Postconditions are evaluated only if the selected action is not canceled; the screen layout is updated only when required by changes made to the knowledge base. Only preconditions which have changed because of postcondition changes are actually evaluated.

User-interface Evaluation

One way to assess a user-interface design is to evaluate its speed of use. This is usually done in the current user–computer interface design methodologies by implementing the interface, giving a human subject a series of tasks to perform, and measuring the time to complete the tasks. We have implemented a keystroke analysis tool that automates the speed of use-evaluation process, using the Card, Moran, and Newell Key Stroke Level Model [Card80]. The implementation was straightforward, because the conceptual design and SUIMS run-time knowledge base hold much of the information needed for performing the analysis.

The Keystroke Model predicts how much time a skilled user who makes no mistakes takes to perform a short task using a given design and set of interaction techniques, ignoring perceptual acquisition times. The time to carry out a task is the sum of the times needed to carry out primitive operators:

$$T(\texttt{Execute}) = K(\texttt{Keystrokes}) + P(\texttt{Pointing at screen objects})$$
$$+ H(\texttt{Homing on devices}) + D(\texttt{Drawing})$$
$$+ M(\texttt{Mental preparations}) + R(\texttt{System response time})$$

User tasks are represented as scripts, which are sequences of application actions. Figure 21 shows a script based on the squares and triangles example. The major components of the keystroke analysis tool are script definition, script transformation, and script translation. The task scripts can be created interactively, by example. The designer simply carries out a task, and the sequence of actions is recorded. It is also possible for the designer to define scripts using a text editor. When transformations are applied, scripts themselves are transformed automatically to conform to the set of actions in the current design knowledge base. Figure 22 shows the scenario script from Figure 21 after the Currently-Selected Set transformation has been applied to the design. The scripts are translated into sequences of operators (K, P, H, D, M) using rules provided by the Keystroke Model.

The interaction techniques and transformations have a major effect on the keystroke analysis results. For example, the predicted times for the script of Figure 21 vary from 64 seconds with mouse-based interaction techniques to 114 seconds with keyboard-based interaction techniques. When the transformed script of Figure 22 is used, these times become 46 and 89 seconds, respectively.

Help

The help system uses the conceptual design and SUIMS run-time knowledge bases to generate context-sensitive help messages. Two kinds of help are provided: explanations of why a command is disabled, and explanations of the semantics of a command.

Although help messages can be generated by the designer, especially the description of the semantics, doing so slows down the iterative design process. Action parameters and action postconditions may be affected by design transformations, and new commands can be created by transformations. Automatic generation of help messages frees the designer from the need to create or modify help messages whenever a new design is produced. The messages generated by the help system can, if desired, be modified once the final design is developed.

Explanations of why a command is disabled are based on the unsatisfied preconditions for that command. For example, assume the design of Figure 17, with no object instances yet created. If the user selects the RotateShape command, SUIMS responds with "RotateShape—Sorry, but this command is now

```
script-name = script1
create_shape(obj1=triangle, color1=white, position1=(50,140), angle1=5)
create_shape(obj1=square, position1=(200,100), angle1=145, color1=black)
rotate_shape(obj2=triangle, angle2=60)
rotate_shape(obj2=square, angle2=60)
delete_shape(obj3=triangle)
delete_shape(obj3=square)
```

Figure 21. A simple task script based on the squares and triangles application.

disabled". If the user then requests an explanation, SUIMS responds "Command RotateShape is disabled because there is no shape". If the angle attribute is factored out, and a value for angle has not been provided yet, the explanation is "Command RotateShape is disabled because there is no shape, and angle of shape is not set."

Explanations of what a command does are based on the command semantics as represented by the command's postconditions. Because our postconditions do not completely encode a command's semantics, in general only partial semantics are provided. Typical explanations, given in a natural-language-like form, indicate whether the command creates, deletes, or modifies an object, what object class and/or attribute are affected, and other consequences such as deselecting all previously selected objects.

Rules which generate command descriptions make use of actions, action parameters, action postconditions, application objects, object attributes, and their relationships. The reasoning involves four main steps, each associated with specific units of information from the knowledge base.

> Is the action type Create, Delete or Modify, and what is created, deleted, or modified? This is an action's primary effect, and is inferred from the action postconditions and the action parameters.

> Are there other consequences that affect the current context and the state of the knowledge base? This is a secondary effect, and is inferred from postconditions. An example is selecting or deselecting one or more object instances.

```
script-name = script1-transformed

create_shape(obj1=triangle, color1=white, position1=(50,140), angle1=5)
create_shape(obj1=square, position1=(200,100), angle1=145, color1=black)
    {Square is selected, now select triangle too.}
add_to_CSS_shape(obj5=triangle)
    {Now both object are selected, one rotate command is enough, object does not have to be
specified.}
rotate_shape(obj, angle2=60)
    {Both object are still selected, one delete command is enough, object does not have to be
specified.}
delete_shape(obj3)
```

Figure 22. A simple task script based on the squares and triangles application after the script has been transformed using the Currently-Selected Set (CSS) transformation.

How do command parameters affect object attributes? This is inferred from the description of the action parameters, objects on which the action operates, and attributes of these objects. Each command parameter is distinguished according to its usage: whether its value serves as a selection criterion, or is used to change the corresponding object attribute.

Assemble the appropriate message for each action, based on all relevant information.

Consider the reasoning process involved in determining an action's type (its primary effect). Whether an action creates or deletes an object or just modifies an existing object is deduced by keeping track of the object counts, with the number of objects in each class (e.g. square, triangle, shape) and the number in the two sets (CSS, NSS) which partition these classes. If postconditions explicitly state a change in the number of objects, then it is easy to deduce the action type. The rules are

```
number(square) = number(square) +1 ⇒ creates square
number(square) = number(square) −1 ⇒ deletes square
[not delete] AND [not create] AND [some attribute modified]
    ⇒ modifies attribute ...
```

If direct counts are not used indirect reasoning is used, based on cumulative changes in all subsets which partition the object class. In the following example, CSS_shape and NSS_shape partition the shape class, and the number of instances in the shape class is equal to the sum of the number of instances in CSS_shape and NSS_shape.

```
number(NSS_shape) = number(NSS_shape) + number(CSS_shape)
{ deselect previously selected objects }
number(CSS_shape) = 1
⇒ creates new instance

number(CSS_shape) = 0
number(NSS_shape) does not change
⇒ deletes number(CSS_shape) instances
```

Figure 23 shows the help description assuming a design with object 'shape' factored out to form a Currently-Selected Set (CSS).

The help system is useful to the designer as well as to the user, because the help messages represent the system's understanding of the designer's intent. The system can be thought of as being a 'cautious assistant' who, when asked to do something, paraphrases the task as it has been understood. If something is not understood, a warning is given.

The help support system can be augmented in several possible ways. The first is to add descriptions for other kinds of meta-objects (i.e., types of schemata in the knowledge base), as well as application actions. Another is to link all meta-object descriptions, building a help network through which the user navigates. Links in the network correspond to meta-object relationships. Another natural

HELP for the create_shape command:

The create_shape command has 4 parameters: (angle, position, color, object class).

The create_shape command will:
- Create an instance of the subclass of shape, determined by parameter object class, which is one of: ("square" "triangle").

In addition:
- Previously selected objects from class shape are deselected.
- The new instance becomes the currently selected object.
- angle becomes the angle attribute of the newly created instance of shape.
- position becomes the position attribute of the newly created instance of shape.
- color becomes the color attribute of the newly created instance of shape.

Figure 23. Description generated by the UIDE help system for the CreateShape command after object 'shape' has been factored out to create a Currently-Selected Set.

extension is to provide an explanation of how to enable a disabled command. In order to provide an answer to this kind of question, the help support system needs the capability to solve the specific 'navigation' problem of going from the current state to the state where the given action is enabled. The schemata provide a task-specific model of some of the concepts of concern to the user, i.e., the actions, objects, attributes, etc. Also, the help system could mark each schema instance to record how frequently the user successfully used the concept, in order to provide customized help messages.

We have extended the basic UIDE help to provide context-sensitve, animated help [Suka90]. The pre- and postconditions are used to back-chain from the state implied by the user's help request to the current state. The sequence of actions to reach the implied state are shown to the user on the screen: a mouse icon moves around to make menu selections, object selections, and to drag objects on the screen. Similarly, a keyboard icon indicates text which must be entered. The first prototype of the system [Suka88] works with UNIX file manipulations and a Macintosh-style direct manipulation interface. For instance, if the user asks for help on copying files and there is an open directory, the system animates the process of opening a second directory, selecting a file from the first directory, and dragging the file to the second directory. If two directories are open but one nearly obscures the other on the screen, the system animates moving the nearly obscured directory, selecting a file from one, and dragging it to the other.

Summary

UIDE is an evolving system whose capabilities are continually being developed. The largest application for which an interface has been generated so far is a subset of a Macintosh MacDraw-like application, with actions to create, delete, cut, copy, and paste objects. Objects handled are shapes (squares, triangles), lines (simple and polylines), and text, with attributes of position, angle, color, size, line thickness, and text font. Actions that modify these attributes are also provided: move, rotate, scale, change thickness, and change font.

We are persuaded that UIDE represents a step forward in user-interface development tools. The key to UIDE's utility is its use of a higher-level representation of a user-interface design than in traditional UIMSs. On the other hand, the current representation is not sufficiently robust. It is itself being further refined to represent relationships other than the class hierarchy and various dependencies between objects.

Acknowledgements. The Graphics and User Interface Research Group at GWU provided the intellectual environment supporting this work. Direct contributors to UIDE include C. Gibbs, D. Gieskens, W. Kim, S. Kovacevic, L. Moran, K. Murray, H. Senay, and J. Sibert. Financial support has been provided by the National Science Foundation, Sun Corporation, Inference Corporation, Software Productivity Consortium, Siemens Corporation, and the Department of EE & CS Industrial Liaison Program.

REFERENCES

[Appl85]
Apple Computer, *Inside Macintosh*, Reading, MA: Addison-Wesley, 1985.

[Bass88]
Bass, L., Hardy, E., Hoyt, K., Little, M., and Seacord, R., Introduction to the serpent user interface management system, Software Engineering Institute, Carnegie-Mellon University, Pittsburgh, PA, March 1988.

[Bles82]
Bleser, T., and Foley, J., Towards specifying and evaluating the human factors of user-computer interfaces, *Proc. Human Factors in Computer Systems Conference*, New York: ACM, 1982, pp. 309–314.

[Born86]
Borning, A., and Duisberg, R., Constraint-based tools for building user interfaces, *ACM TOG*, Vol. 5, No. 4, Oct. 1986, pp. 345–374.

[Buxt83]
Buxton, W., et al., Towards a comprehensive user interface management system, *Comput. Graph.*, Vol. 17, 1983, pp. 35–42 (SIGGRAPH 83).

[Card80]
Card, S., Moran, T., and Newell, A., The keystroke-level model for user performance time with interactive systems, *CACM*, Vol. 23, July 1980, pp. 398–410.

[Card85]
Cardelli, L., and Pike, R., Squeak: A Language for Communicating with Mice, *Comput. Graph.*, Vol. 19, 1985, pp. 199–204 (SIGGRAPH 85).

[Card88]
Cardelli, L., Building user interfaces by direct manipulation, *Proc. ACM SIGGRAPH Symposium on User Interface Software*, New York: ACM, 1988, pp. 152–166.

[Coss89]
Cossey, G., *Prototyper*, Portland, OR: Now Software, 1989.

[Flec87]
Flecchia, M., and Bergeron, R., Specifying complex dialogs in algae, *Proc. CHI + GI '87*, New York: ACM, 1987, pp. 229–234.

[Fole87]
Foley, J., Kim, W., and Gibbs, C., Algorithms to transform the formal specification of a user-computer interface, *Proc. INTERACT '87*, 2nd IFIP Conference on Human-Computer Interaction, Amsterdam: Elsivier Science Publishers, 1987, pp. 1001–1006.

[Fole88]
Foley, J., Gibbs, C., Kim, W., and Kovacevic, S., A knowledge base for user interface management system, *Proc. CHI '88—1988 SIGCHI Computer-Human Interaction Conference*, New York: ACM, 1988, pp. 67–72.

[Fole89]
Foley, J., Kim, W., Kovacevic, S., and Murray, K., Designing interfaces at a high level of abstraction, *IEEE Software*, Vol. 6, No. 1, Jan. 1989, pp. 25–32.

[Fole90]
Foley, J., A., van Dam, S. Feiner, and J. Hughes, *Computer Graphics: Principles and Practice*, Reading, MA: Addison-Wesley, 1990.

[Gree85a]
Green, M., The University of Alberta user interface management system, *Comput. Graph.*, Vol. 19, 1985, pp. 205–213 (SIGGRAPH 85).

[Gree85b]
Green, M., The design of graphical user interfaces, Technical Report CSRI-170, Computer Systems Research Institute, Univ. Toronto, 1985.

[Gree87]
Green, M., A survey of three dialog models, *ACM TOG*, Vol. 5, 1987, pp. 244–275.

[Hana80]
Hanau, P.. and Lenorovitz, D., Prototyping and simulation tools for user/computer dialogue design, *Comput. Graph.*, Vol. 14, 1980, pp. 271–278 (SIGGRAPH 80).

[Hart89]
Hartson, R., and Hix, D., Human-computer interface development: Concepts and software, *ACM Computing Surveys*, Vol. 21, March 1989, pp. 5–92.

[Haye83]
Hayes, P., and Szekely, P., Graceful interaction through the COUSIN command interface, *Int. Jour. Man-machine Studies*, Vol. 19, September 1983, pp. 285–305.

[Haye84]
Hayes, P., Executable interface definitions using form-based interface abstractions, in *Advances in Computer-Human Interaction*, Hartson, H.R., Ed., Norwood, NJ: Ablex, 1984.

[Haye85]
Hayes, P., Szekely, P., and Lerner R., Design alternatives for user interface management systems based on experience with COUSIN, *Human Factors in Computer systems, Proc. CHI '85*, New York: ACM, 1985, pp. 169–175.

[Hill86]

Hill, R., Supporting concurrency, communication, and synchronization in human-computer interaction—The sassafras UIMS, *ACM TOG*, Vol. 5, 1986, pp. 179–210.

[Huds86]

Hudson, S. and King, R., A generator of direct manipulation office systems, *ACM Trans. on Office Info. Systems*, Vol. 4, April 1986, pp. 132–163.

[Huds87]

Hudson, S., UIMS support for direct manipulation interfaces, ACM SIGGRAPH Workshop on Software Tools for User Interface Management, *Comput. Graph.*, Vol. 21, April 1987, pp. 120–124.

[Huds88]

Hudson, S., and King, R., Semantic feedback in the Higgens UIMS, *IEEE Trans. Software Engineering*, Vol. 14, Aug. 1988, pp.1188–1206.

[Hull87]

Hull, R., and King, R., Semantic database modeling: Survey, applications, and research issues, *ACM Computing Surveys*, Vol. 19, Sept. 1987, pp. 201–260.

[Hurl89]

Hurley, D., and Sibert, J., Modeling user interface-application interactions, *IEEE Software*, Vol. 6, Jan. 1989, pp. 71–77.

[Jaco83]

Jacob, R., Using formal specifications in the design of the user-computer interface, *CACM*, Vol. 26, April 1983, pp. 259–264.

[Jaco85]

Jacob, R., A state transition diagram language for visual programming, *IEEE Comput.*, Vol. 18, August 1985, pp. 51–59.

[Jaco86]

Jacob, R., A specification language for direct-manipulation user interfaces, *ACM TOG*, Vol. 5, 1986, pp. 283–317.

[John78]

Johnson, S., and Lesk, M., Language development tools, *The Bell System Technical Jour.*, Vol. 57, July–August 1978, pp. 2155-2176.

[Kier85]

Kieras, D., and Polson, P., An Approach to the Formal Analysis of User Complexity, *Int. Jour. Man-machine Studies*, Vol. 22, No. 4, April 1985, pp. 365–394.

[Koiv88]

Koivunen, M., and Mäntylä, M., HutWindows: An improved architecture for a user interface management system, *IEEE Comput. Graph. and Appl.*, Vol. 8, January 1988, pp. 43–52. **au: note accents in name of second author; ok?**

[Lint89]

Linton, M., Vlissides, J.. and Calder, P., Composing user interfaces with Inter-Views, *IEEE Computer*, Vol. 22, February 1989, pp. 8–22.

[Micr89]

Microsoft Corporation, *Presentation Manager*, Bellevue, WA: Microsoft Corp., 1989.

[Mill88]
Miller, P., and Szczur, M., Transportable Application Environment (TAE) plus experiences in 'Object'ively modernizing a user interface environment, *Proc. OOP-SLA '88*, New York: ACM, 1988, pp. 58–70.

[Myer86]
Myers, B., Creating highly-interactive and graphical user interfaces by demonstration, *Comput. Graph.*, Vol. 20, 1986, pp. 249–257 (SIGGRAPH 86).

[Myer88]
Myers, B., Creating User Interfaces by Demonstration, New York: Academic Press, 1988.

[Myer89]
Myers, B., User-interface tools: Introduction and survey, *IEEE Software*, Vol. 6, Jan. 1989, pp. 15–23.

[Newm68]
Newman, W.M., A System for Interactive Graphical Programming, 1968 Spring Joint Computer Conference, Thompson Books, Washington, DC, pp. 47–54.

[Next90]
NeXT, *Interface Builder*, Sunnyvale, CA: NeXT Inc., 1990.

[Olse83]
Olsen, D., and Dempsey, E., SYNGRAPH: A graphical user interface generator, *Comput. Graph.*, Vol. 17, 1983, pp. 43–50 (SIGGRAPH 83).

[Olse84]
Olsen, D., Pushdown automata for user interface management, *ACM TOG*, Vol. 3, July 1984, pp. 177–203.

[Olse86]
Olsen, D., MIKE: The Menu Interaction Kontrol Environment, *ACM TOG*, Vol. 5, 1986, pp. 318–344.

[Olse87]
Olsen, D., Ed., ACM SIGGRAPH Workshop on Software Tools for User Interface Management, *Comput. Graph.*, Vol. 21, April 1987, pp. 71–147.

[Open89]
Open Software Foundation OSF/MOTIF manual, Cambridge, MA, 1989.

[Pala88]
Palay, A., et al., The Andrew toolkit: An overview, *Proc. 1988 Winter USENIX*, Feb. 1988, pp. 9–21.

[Reis82]
Reisner, P., Further developments toward using formal grammar as a design tool, *Proc. Human Factors in Computer Systems Conference*, New York: ACM, 1982, pp. 304–308.

[Sche86]
Scheifler, B., and Gettys, J., The X Window System, *ACM TOG*, Vol. 5, 1986, pp. 79–109.

[Schu85]
Schulert, A., Rogers, G., and Hamilton, J., ADM—A Dialog Manager, *Human Factors in Computer systems, Proc. CHI '85*, New York: ACM, 1985, pp. 177–183.

[Sibe86]

Sibert, J., Hurley, W., and Bleser, T., An object-oriented user interface manage-ment system, *Comput. Graph.*, Vol. 20, 1986, pp. 259–268 (SIGGRAPH 86).

[Sioc89]

Siochi, A., and Hartson, H.R., Task-oriented representation of asynchronous user interfaces, *Proc. CHI '89*, New York: ACM, 1989, pp. 183–188.

[Smit88]

Smith, D., Building interfaces interactively, *Proc. ACM SIGGRAPH Symposium on User Interface Software*, New York: ACM, 1988, pp. 144–151.

[Suka88]

Sukaviriya, P., Dynamic construction of animated help from application context, *Proc. ACM SIGGRAPH 1988 Symposium on User Interface Software and Tech-nology (UIST '88)*, New York: ACM, 1988 .

[Suka90]

Sukaviriya, P., and Foley, J., Coupling a UI framework with automatic genera-tion of context-sensitive animated help, *Proc. ACM SIGGRAPH 1990 Symposium on User Interface Software and Technology (UIST '90)*, New York: ACM, 1990, pp. 152–166.

[Sun86]

Sun, *SunView Programmer's Guide*, Mountain View, CA: Sun Microsystems, Inc., 1986.

[Sun89]

Sun, *OPEN LOOK Graphical User Interface*, Mountain View, CA: Sun Microsys-tems, Inc., 1989.

[Sun90]

Sun, *GUIDE User's Manual*, Mountain View, CA: Sun Microsystems, Inc., 1990.

[Sutt78]

Sutton, J., and Sprague, R., A survey of business applications, *Proc. American Institute for Decision Sciences 10th Annual Conference*, Part II, Atlanta, GA, 1978, p. 278.

[Visu90]

Visual Edge, *UIMX User's Manual*, Ville St. Laurent, Quebec, Canada, 1990.

[Wass85]

Wasserman, A., Extending Transition Diagrams for the Specification of Human-Computer Interaction, *IEEE Trans. Software Engineering*, SE-11, August 1985, pp. 699–713.

[Well89]

Wellner, P., Statemaster: A UIMS based on statecharts for prototyping and target implementation, *Proc. CHI '89*, New York: ACM, 1989, pp. 177–182.

[Wood70]

Woods,W., Transition network grammars for natural language analysis, *CACM*, Vol. 13, October 1970, pp. 591–606.

5 Visualization

Volumetric Visualization Techniques

Craig Upson

Abstract

Recently there has been a tremendous interest in visualization techniques which can effectively portray volumetric data. In this paper we present a classification of the most common techniques, as well as an introduction to the algorithms which govern their implementation.

Introduction: The Visualization Process

SIMULATING NATURE

Before we delve into a discussion about scientific visualization and how it is done, it is useful to back up a step and talk about where this technology fits into the overall process of numerical simulation (in as much as we cover them here, the steps are the same for the experimental sciences). In the computational sciences, the main goal is to understand the workings of nature. In order to accomplish this, the scientist proceeds through several steps, from observing natural events or phenomena to analyzing the results of a simulation of the phenomena.

The initial steps in this process are the domain of the experimentalist: observing nature, and condensing the relevant information into a physical model of the phenomena of interest. At this stage, the scientist makes judgments as to which variables are significant and which can be ignored. For example, a scientist observing a large scale meteorological event such as a tornado collects data on the wind speed, the relative humidity, the ground temperature, and many other factors before trying to predict the tornado's course. From these data (and much, much more) he derives basic relationships between the primary variables affecting the storm and the probability of a severe tornado. Eventually, as he acquires a sufficient number of data points, his predictive abilities sharpen and he formalizes the connections into hypotheses which, if they survive the test of time, become physical laws. From these laws, the physicist, mathematician, theoretical chemist, etc., derive mathematical equations that relate the observations and the driving conditions or parameters. In general, these equations are in the form of partial differential equations and as such are not capable of being solved numerically. In some limited cases the equations have an exact analytic solution, although this is rare.

The Computational Cycle

When 'exact' analytic methods fail, the scientist hands the problem to a computational scientist, to devise an algorithm which approximates the partial differential equations (PDEs). First the continuum in which the PDE is valid is discretized into cells or onto a grid. Then coupled ordinary differential equations are derived, and a further discretization in time yields the system of algebraic equations which are solved via computer. It is the job of the computational scientist to find schemes for this numerical approximation which are accurate and robust and which converge to the correct solution.

The discretization of space, or grid, represents a sampling of the real world at a small number of selected points. Thus, the interface between that which is not modeled (the rest of the world) and that which is (the computational domain) must be handled with care. To satisfy these constraints, the scientist establishes boundary conditions to handle the spatial approximation of the rest of the world, and initial conditions to approximate the temporal conditions leading up to the time the simulation begins. This information comprises the data necessary to start the simulation.

The solution is then computed, and the results are analyzed to determine their similarity with the observed phenomena. The size of the circles in Figure 1 between each of the steps mentioned above symbolizes the typical amount of data that is passed between each stage of the simulation process. The largest circle is very often that of the data produced by the numerical simulation. This is the fundamental problem currently plaguing large scale numerical simulations:

> the scientist can produce large volumes of output data from a relatively small amount of input data;
>
> in addition to this, the scientist produces this data faster than it can be stored onto a mechanical device, such as a disk;
>
> he also produces and stores this data faster than he can comprehend its significance.

Scientists and engineers formulate equations and compute their solutions faster than they can analyze their meaning. For this reason, more and more scientists and engineers are looking to visualization for help.

In reality, the steps described above are not organized into a linear set of processes but are more accurately viewed as a computational cycle (Figure 2), since a researcher typically iterates several times through each step, as well as through the cycle, before he is satisfied he has solved the problem he intended to solve. In this diagram, the experimentalist's and theorist's work is categorized as research, giving foundation to the computational scientist's simulation model. The results of the analysis step lead to either modification of the computer program should inaccuracies or instabilities be discovered, to a revised simulation

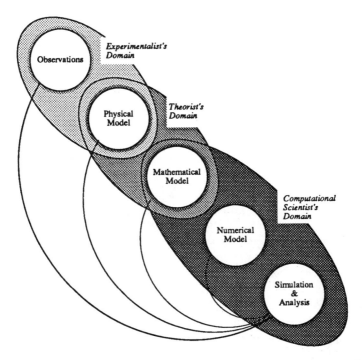

Figure 1.   Simulating natural phenomena: The boxes represent processes; the circles'
sizes indicate the relative volume of information passing between each pair of processes.

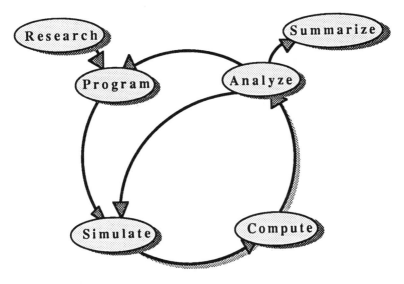

Figure 2. The computational cycle.

definition should it be insufficient to resolve the phenomena, or to a summary of the results if all went well.

The formulation of the simulation process in this manner is analogous to a design optimization process. Hence, visualization plays a role in the computational sciences which is similar to its role in the engineering sciences. As such, the scientist, or designer, needs to have as much interactive control as possible at each step.

THE ANALYSIS CYCLE

Deriving Interesting Data: Filtering

Just as the simulation process is best represented as a cycle, the analysis step is best decomposed into several subprocesses that themselves form a cycle (see Figure 3). The first three steps of this cycle each transform data from one form to another; the fourth step displays the product. The filtering step takes raw simulation data and transforms it into a more condensed, or perhaps more relevant, representation. In general, the data produced by the simulation leads the researcher down avenues that require either a more detailed view of the data or a different functional form. As an example, PLOT3D, a common computational fluid dynamics postprocessing program, derives 41 three-dimensional scalar fields from five produced by most aerodynamic simulation programs [Feld87]. Frequently these derived functions give the scientist the insight needed to understand the phenomena. However, it is usually not possible to predict what representation is needed before the analysis step begins. Thus, it is necessary to have maximum flexibility at this stage of the analysis. An example of the types of operations that occur at this stage are extracting an N–M-dimensional space from an N-dimensional domain, or scaling, interpolating, and averaging data.

Creating Geometric Primitives: Mapping

The product of this filtering process, a more condensed set of data, is then converted into a form which is rendered into images. Any set of data can be transformed into a broad array of geometric primitives, which is the topic of the next section. For example, a three-dimensional scalar field can be visualized using everything from point primitives (zero-dimensional) to volumetric cells (three-dimensional). Each representation form reveals different aspects of the information contained within the data set, and the scientist typically moves from one form to the next, or compares several representations to extract the required information. Each primitive type has a concomitant set of surface or volumetric properties assigned to it, which give it distinguishing visual characteristics.

Moreover, it takes dramatically different numbers of primitives to represent the same set of data; thus, there is a trade-off between an informative and an economical representation (both in terms of compute resources required to generate the primitives, and the amount of memory and disk required to store it). For three-dimensional data sets it is possible to generate up to an order of magnitude more data in the form of geometric primitives than the raw data they

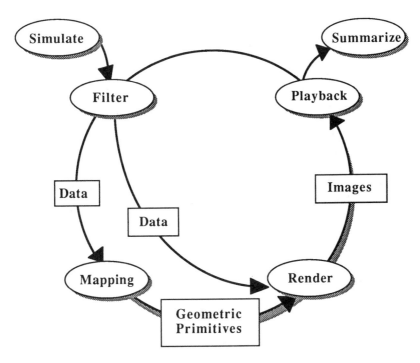

Figure 3. The analysis cycle.

represent [Upso89a]. The generation of a large number of primitives can also be very compute-intensive, as computationally demanding as the simulation itself.

Turning Primitives into Images: Rendering

Once the geometric representation of the data is chosen, the scientist or engineer assigns visual properties to each primitive or collection of primitives, and initiates the image creation or rendering process. It is at this time that frame composition, colors, transparency, texture, and shading methods are determined. This rendering step is the easiest of the entire visualization process to define. In general, the rendering techniques used in the computational sciences are a small subset of those used by the entertainment and television computer animation industry, since the scientists' goals are usually not visual realism but scientific insight. This property permits several of the commonly used algorithms to be implemented in hardware, such as z-buffering of points, lines, and polygons, sphere rendering for molecular modeling, and volumetric rendering for medical imaging. While a hardware implementation is more restrictive and currently of lower quality than that achievable in software, it is also much faster. In the computational sciences, interactive speed is more important than elaborate illumination models.

Once an image is created, the immediate questions are: what does it mean? and, is it correct? To answer these questions, the scientist or engineer returns to the theorist and/or experimentalist for correlative information. Frequently this means that the computational scientist or engineer needs to compare an image from the simulation with one derived from a physical experiment (see Figure 4 and Plate 5).

Image Display: Playback

The final step in the analysis cycle is displaying the images created. This is often accomplished by continuously replaying the current set of computed images as new ones are added to the list. This 'continuous movie loop' brings out the relevant characteristics of the simulation and thus brings out the driving mechanisms. Different types of information are obtained by playing the images at different speeds. Fast sequencing of images gives the scientist or engineer the gross features of the evolution (particularly in time) which are impossible to grasp at slow speeds, while slow playback allows the mind to focus on small scale phenomena that perhaps give rise to larger structures which grow to dominate the dynamics.

Looping Back: What is Wrong with This Picture?

The analysis cycle is an iterative process. Often the scientist or engineer does not know *a priori* which part of the data is the most important to analyze. He is not sure what is the best way to map that data into geometric primitives, and which assignment of rendering attributes is most effective. This is usually determined during the process of rendering images and seeing the effects. The whole process is one of exploration, and the exact path from simulation to images cannot be predicted before one embarks upon the journey.

Visual Representation Forms

GEOMETRIC PRIMITIVES—THE VISUALIZATION MAPPING SPACE

The topic of this section is the mapping from the scientific domain, whether it be numerical simulation data or a data set derived from a physical experiment,

Figure 4. Large scale structure in a turbulent shear layer. The fluid in the top half of the image is flowing faster than the bottom fluid, which causes the unstable interface. This image was created with spark shadow photography.

into a visual representation or image. A set of data can be visualized in a variety of ways, using a variety of geometric primitives. Figure 5 shows a selection of the options available for this mapping process. The horizontal axis is the dimensionality of the underlying data, whether it is the Dow Jones Industrial Average over the last 10 years (one-dimensional), the surface temperature of the world at a given instant (two-dimensional), the concentration of a marine pollutant (three-dimensional), or the motion of air in a room (N-dimensional data, actually six). The vertical axis is the dimensionality of the geometric primitive chosen to represent data, varying from points (zero-dimensional) to hyperpatches, voxels, and cells (three-dimensional).

To obtain more information we map other attributes from the data onto these primitives. An example of this might be creating a relief map of the topography of the United States (a set of polygons representing a height field) and coloring each pixel of each polygon by the temperature at that location. In this manner, we use a two-dimensional primitive (polygons) with some attribute mapping to portray two functions which vary in two-dimensional space. The whole trick in scientific visualization is to pick the best way to perform this mapping, the one that gives you insight into the problem you are trying to solve. There are multiple ways to represent any data. In the previous example we could have chosen to show the temperature as a height field and the topography with color, or temperature as bar-graph columns above a contour-based topographic

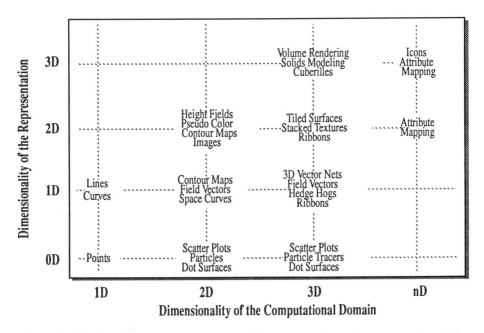

Figure 5. The visualization mapping space: The mapping from the computational domain into the visualization domain.

map. The choice is ours. We use this mapping space diagram to explore various visualization scenarios throughout the rest of this paper.

We will explore this two-dimensional space (it can be more than two-dimensional—a third axis might be image quality or interactivity) by marching through the suite of geometric primitives from points to volumetric elements, or hyperpatches.

ZERO-DIMENSIONAL PRIMITIVES

Points

Using points to represent complex phenomena is tedious work. It takes a tremendous number of points to give a feeling for the correct structure, form, or motion. One advantage of point-based representations is that they are very easy to render. They adapt very well to hardware implementations, and, in fact, some machines are optimized for this primitive. Another advantage is that a wide variety of data can be visualized using points. Examples range from depicting fire (as was done in the genesis sequence in the film Star Trek [Reev85]) to more scientific simulations of fluids. A common laboratory technique is to visualize fluids by injecting metal flecks into a tank and ascertaining the fluid's state by the motion of the metal tracers. The numerical analog of this technique is commonly used in computational fluid dynamics; by choosing the correct geometric properties it can generate surprisingly real images.

On the other hand, points can be used to show form rather than motion. When the Evans and Sutherland Picture System workstations were one of the only graphics devices around, several algorithms were developed by computational chemists to show electron density surfaces [Conn85]. As graphics workstations became more powerful and began rendering polygons in addition to lines and points, the chemists, for the most part, stayed with point representations because they were the most informative. The use of points to display surfaces, or dot surfaces as they are called, is again becoming more common as workstations have dramatically improved vertex transformation speeds. Since a surface can be decomposed into hundreds of thousands of points, this places a very heavy demand on the workstation if interactivity is required.

Markers

Markers are point primitives that have an associated stencil representation. This stencil is a two-dimensional bit pattern which is displayed at the point location perpendicular to the viewing direction. In other words, the plane of the stencil is always parallel to the screen. The pattern consists of a binary mask with an associated color triplet, so when it is rendered all locations within the bit mask which are 'on' are displayed, and all locations which are 'off' are invisible. The big payoff with markers is that they are very efficient to render with most graphics workstations, and the user has complete control of the stencil pattern. The pattern (which is typically 16 × 16 pixels in size) varies from a single 'on' pixel, or point, to crossbars, to mini-icons such as the sphere representation with a highlight in Figure 6.

One drawback to markers is that you really do not have much control over the size of the marker. In most hardware implementations you can scale the marker size up by integral factors, but not continuously. This means that you cannot really get a perspective effect. Another drawback with markers is that they are very hard to follow if the image, or animation sequence, contains moderate numbers of them. In general, it is easy to understand the motion of a few point primitives, say 50 or so, but as the number grows to the thousands you can no longer follow individual markers and can get quite confused. If the number becomes very large and each primitive projects into a single pixel in the image, then the representation begins to approximate a continuous distribution, or form. At this point the image again becomes understandable. Examples of this are commonly found in computational (and experimental) fluid dynamics.

Tracer Particles

As mentioned above, point primitives are used to depict motion as well as form. In the example shown in Figure 7 particles, represented as points, are used to trace the motion of a fluid much in the same manner as metallic flakes, smoke, or oil droplets are used by scientists to visualize laboratory experiments [Vand82; Kaka88].

An Algorithm

To numerically simulate this effect, the fluid velocity field, a vector field of two or three components, is used to move or advect the particles in space and time. Each particle has the following information associated with it:

current location (x, y, z);
color triplet (R, G, B);
transparency;
size;
lifespan.

The velocity field, current location, and time step are used to create the new

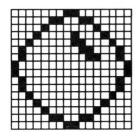

Figure 6. Sphere marker stencils. The actual size is only 16 pixels wide when used in an image. At this reduced size the marker is quite effective.

location at the new time by solving the equation of motion

$$V = \frac{dP}{dt}$$

where V is the vector velocity (u, v, w), P is the particle location (x, y, z), and dt is the step size in time. This equation is solved in its simplest form for the new particle location by the forward Euler approximation

$$x(t + dt) = x(t) + u\big(x(t), y(t), z(t)\big)\, dt$$
$$y(t + dt) = y(t) + v\big(x(t), y(t), z(t)\big)\, dt$$
$$z(t + dt) = z(t) + w\big(x(t), y(t), z(t)\big)\, dt$$

The velocity field must be interpolated in space (and perhaps in time, if the simulation is time varying) to coincide with the current location of the particle. This is usually accomplished with bilinear (2D) or trilinear (3D) interpolation within each cell. To determine the value of the point (x, y) in two dimensions, weights are assigned to the four vertex nodes which correspond to the subareas A_1 through A_4 in Figure 8, where

$$A_1 = \big(x - x(i)\big)\big(y - y(j)\big)$$
$$A_2 = \big(x(i+1) - x\big)\big(y - y(j)\big)$$
$$A_3 = \big(x(i+1) - x\big)\big(y(j+1) - y\big)$$
$$A_4 = \big(x - x(i)\big)\big(y(j+1) - y\big)$$

Thus, an interpolated velocity component is

$$u(x, y) = A_1 u\big(x(i+1), y(j+1)\big) + A_2 u\big(x(i), y(j+1)\big)$$
$$+ A_3 u\big(x(i), y(j)\big) + A_4 u\big(x(i+1), y(j)\big)$$

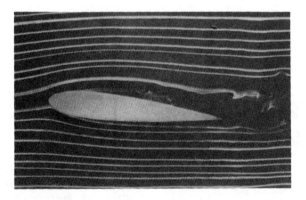

Figure 7. Experimental flow visualization: Smoke is used to visualize the flow of air over a wing.

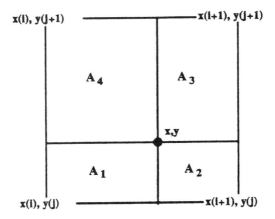

Figure 8. Bilinear interpolation within a cell by area weighting for the point (x, y). Each area (Ai) is summed with the scalar field value of the node opposite the point.

Thus, after one advection step each particle is moved from its previous location $p(x, y, t)$ to a new location $p(x, y, t + dt)$ (see Figure 9). The three-dimensional analog of this is straightforward. The critical parameter in this formulation is the step size. The forward Euler method is unconditionally unstable, which means that the step size must be very small to approximate the correct motion, especially if the equations are stiff. If there are hundreds of thousands of particles it becomes computationally intensive to advect each primitive with such a small time step. For this reason, other numerical methods with more stable characteristics are used [Pres86].

The particle motion, assuming that the numerical technique accurately reflects the underlying data, is tangent to the vector field. If a series of previous locations of a given particle are strung together to form a curve, then the resulting

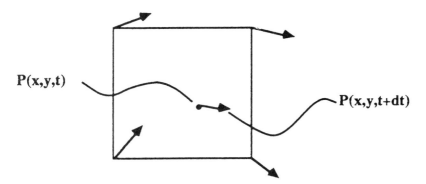

Figure 9. The vectors at each vertex represent the flow direction at that point. The vector in the center of the cell is the velocity that the particle experiences.

curve is a flow line [Buni85] . Again, as mentioned above, small numbers of particles give a microscopic view of the flow field; large numbers result in an overall distribution, giving the feeling of a tracer dye (Plate 6). In this image, a moderate number of particles are used to show the large vertical motion of air commonly observed in large scale thunderstorms [Wihl81]. Particle trails show the time history of a small number of particles. As the number of trails grows, the image rapidly begins to resemble spaghetti.

The image in Plate 7 is the result of a two-dimensional 'simulation' of the planet Jupiter's atmosphere for the MGM film 2010 [Yaeg86]. The fluid motion was created by solving the Navier-Stokes equations on the planet's surface. The visualization is based on advecting millions of particles (approximately 10 million). Each particle has an associated color based on its original location when the simulation started; in this manner, particles have a history of where they were first released or born. Each pixel color is the result of averaging the colors of all particles which project into it, since many particles are mapped into each pixel to minimize 'holes' in the resulting image.

POINT-BASED IMPLICIT SURFACES

An Algorithm

Points can also represent spatial forms [Clin88]. This is accomplished by either subdividing an existing surface representation, or by creating a surface from a scalar field and a threshold, thus solving the equation

$$F(x, y, z) = \text{Threshold}$$

This is commonly called an isosurface. The basic steps in creating an isosurface are:

March through the field, cell by cell, testing to see if the scalar field evaluated at the cell's vertices brackets the threshold value (Figure 10)

$$\text{Min}\left\{F(\text{vertices})\right\} \leq \text{Threshold} \leq \text{Max}\left\{F(\text{vertices})\right\}$$

If the cell passes this test, then it is bisected in each dimension. This results

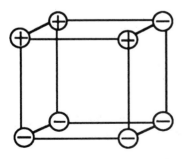

Figure 10. A data cell in 3D. The plus marks (+) at vertices indicate the field variable is higher than the threshold; minus marks (−) correspond to values lower than the threshold.

in eight new cells which are placed on an active cell stack.

Each new cell is again tested; if it passes it is bisected, and those cells are placed on the stack to be reevaluated.

This bisection process continues until the cell size meets the required criteria (usually almost pixel-sized).

The resulting list of active subcells is now used to create a point list, since each cell projects into a point.

This point list is z-buffered to create a surface.

To create more realistic surfaces, the points are illuminated. This is accomplished by calculating the surface gradient at each location in the point list

$$\text{Grad}(x, y, z) = \left[\begin{array}{ccc} \dfrac{dF(x,y,z)}{dx} & \dfrac{dF(x,y,z)}{dy} & \dfrac{dF(x,y,z)}{dz} \end{array} \right]$$

where this gradient is calculated analytically if the field has an analytic form, or numerically as

$$\frac{dF(x,y,z)}{dx} = \frac{F\big(x(i+1), y(j), z(k)\big) - F\big(x(i), y(j), z(k)\big)}{x(i+1) - x(i)}$$

$$\frac{dF(x,y,z)}{dy} = \frac{F\big(x(i), y(j+1), z(k)\big) - F\big(x(i), y(j), z(k)\big)}{y(j+1) - y(j)}$$

$$\frac{dF(x,y,z)}{dz} = \frac{F\big(x(i), y(j), z(k+1)\big) - F\big(x(i), y(j), z(k)\big)}{z(k+1) - z(k)}$$

This numerical differentiation occurs at the computational domain's nodes and must be interpolated to the point in the list. In actuality, the center differenced gradient is defined at the centroid of the cell. If complete accuracy is needed, this should be averaged back onto the vertices of the cell. The shading coefficient, assuming diffuse reflection only, is computed at this point by taking the dot product of the normalized light source and gradient vectors in the standard manner [Fole82]

$$\text{Shade} = \frac{\text{Grad}\,(x, y, z)}{|\text{Grad}\,(x, y, z)|} \cdot \text{Light}\,(x, y, z)$$

The point color is simply the product of this shade and the original color. For additional image clarity, depth cueing is used.

It takes a large number of points to represent a surface. In the subsequent sections we discuss other methods to depict surfaces using vectors and polygons. The decision as to which method to use depends upon the visual effect desired and the amount of time one is willing to wait while computing the image. In general, point representations are more economical to use, since they are so easy to render in hardware. However, several hardware platforms are more optimized to render polygons than points, so there is little advantage on these systems to using a point representation.

One advantage of a dot surface (see Plate 8) over a polygonal one is that it has no connectivity and that it is so easy to calculate. As we see in the next sections, the complexity to compute the geometric representation rises with the dimensionality of the primitives used. This is partially due to the more complicated data structures required for higher-dimensional geometric primitives. Rendering speeds are also a function of the number of primitives that must be traversed to create an image. When we map these geometric atoms into the image plane, their projected size (in pixels) partially controls the efficiency of the algorithm. If, on average, a primitive maps onto a single pixel, or just a few pixels, then a point representation is more economical than other techniques. Suppose we have a polygonal isosurface containing 500,000 polygons (as is the case in some medical images). If we are creating an image at video resolution $(640 \times 486 = 311040$ pixels) then we save time by using points. If, on the other hand, our image is 4000×3000, or 12 million pixels, then a polygonal form is perhaps more economical.

Contour Plots are perhaps the most common representation form for two-dimensional data. Perhaps this is because vector graphics terminals and workstations are, to date, more available than those that render shaded polygons and higher-dimensional primitives. Over the past five years this situation has changed, to the extent that now there are very few vector devices produced; almost all are raster-based. In any event, this visualization form is quite useful.

An Algorithm

Contouring, like constructing a dot surface, consists of finding all locations of the scalar field in which the value of that field is equal to a given constant

$$F(x, y, z) = \text{Threshold}$$

Unlike a point representation, linear contours are constructed by connecting the locations with line segments in the appropriate manner.

The way most contouring techniques work is:

Divide the computational domain into a mesh of cells. These cells are typically quadrilaterals or triangles.

Process the mesh cell by cell

Over each edge or line segment of each cell, test to see if the selected constant value is contained within the range of the endpoints

$$F(\text{endpoint1}) \leq \text{Threshold} \leq F(\text{endpoint2})$$

If it is, then calculate the intersection location.

Continue this test/intersect operation on all remaining edges.

Using line segments, connect this intersection point with others on the edges of this cell.

Process the next cell.

This process is sped up by noting that each edge is tested and intersected twice when it only needs to be done once, and that the algorithm can be parallelized and vectorized. In three dimensions it is tested four times.

Figure 11 is a simple example of a two-dimensional contour map of the scalar field $\sin(x)\cos(y+\pi)$, with eight contour levels. One of the traditional drawbacks with vector contouring is that you only see a small portion of the data—only those locations in which the field is equal to the chosen contour value(s). The rest of the data is hidden. If you choose the contour values incorrectly, then you get a biased view of the data. This drawback is also an advantage at times.

Techniques described in the next sections display more, and in some cases all, of the information contained within the data, but they fail to convey quantitative information. This is a traditional trade-off in scientific visualization: the compromise between quantity of information and qualitative information, the holistic vs. the specific. Thus, the goal of this paper is to convey the multiplicity of visualization methods available for any given set of data.

ONE-DIMENSIONAL PRIMITIVES

Contouring Extensions

There are several three-dimensional extensions of contouring. In fact, a number of methods used for scientific visualization are traced back to this simple technique (Figure 12). Each of the visualization techniques in this graph is discussed in the following sections. The vertical axis is a measure of the discretization of the representation. For example, in this dimension a continuous color image (i.e., a photograph) is more continuous than the vector-based edge enhancement of that image (contour map).

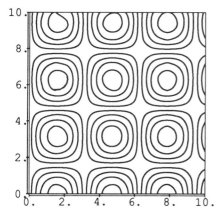

Figure 11. Two-dimensional contour map.

Three-dimensional Vector Nets

An Algorithm

While keeping with the use of vector primitives, the prime three-dimensional extension is that of a vector net. The most straightforward implementation of this technique is to simply compute three orthogonal sets of contour lines, one set in the xy plane, one in the yz plane, and one in the zx plane (Figure 13). These line segments are then displayed together. Each set consists of several parallel planar contours. Thus, if the domain consists of 10 nodes in the x dimension, 20 nodes in the y dimension, and 30 nodes in the z dimension, the resulting vector net has 10 parallel contours in x, 20 parallel contours in y, and 30 parallel contours in z [Fuch77]. This algorithm has the advantage that it is simple and can be computed in parallel. The disadvantages are that all lines are displayed, even the ones that should be occluded by others closer to the viewer. To remove these 'hidden lines' one has to use another algorithm [Wrig72, Wrig79].

While the representation of an isosurface of a scalar field using vectors has the advantage that little is hidden from view (Plate 9), allowing the full isosurface to be displayed, the amount presented can be overwhelming at times. For this reason, hidden line methods are more popular (but more compute-intensive). In addition to this, depth cueing is used to increase comprehensibility.

Techniques that are simplifications of polygonal isosurface methods are becoming increasingly common. A threshold surface is computed using polygons (as discussed in the next section) and instead of displaying the polygons, a vector representation is implemented by using only the edges of the polygons. The reason this is more popular is that the same geometric representation is used to display the data in two different ways, allowing the user to switch between the two. This permits the user to make the traditional trade-off between image quality and computational complexity.

Vectors, Hedgehogs, Ribbons

Visualization techniques for vector and tensor fields are few and far between. The representation alternatives are limited primarily to iconic forms, which are discussed in more detail in a later section. Within the category of iconic representations are arrows (also called vectors) and hedgehogs (which show displacements, or surface normals).

Ribbons composed of vectors or polygons are used by computational chemists to simplify a representation of a large molecule. By portraying only the backbone of the molecule by a flat ribbon that twists with the molecule, the scientist has a concise idea of the most important aspect of the compound under study. People studying fluids are beginning to pick up on this idea, to show the rotational effects in fluid dynamics simulations [Helm89a, Helm89b; Hult89]. Again, the major benefit lies in reducing the image complexity to the bare minimum needed to comprehend the science.

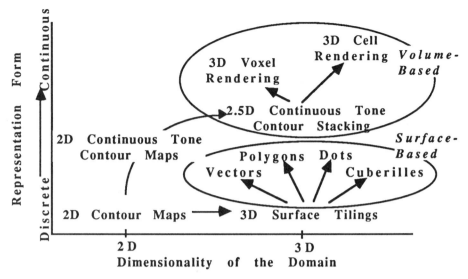

Figure 12. The origins of several visualization techniques are traced back to line-based two-dimensional contour maps. These extensions result in higher-dimensional and/or more continuous representations.

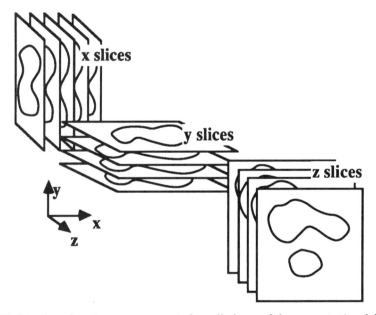

Figure 13. Line-based contours are computed on all planes of the computational domain.

Two-dimensional Primitives: Surfaces

The Two-dimensional Image as Primitive

Continuous Tone Contour Maps

Line-based contour maps in 2D can be generalized into continuous color contours. As the number of contour levels increases, the spacing between levels approaches zero. If we now assign a unique color to each contour level, the result is a continuous distribution of color over the domain, with the color directly related to the scalar field we are visualizing. Of course, the technique used to calculate these maps is not to use line primitives but to use polygons which conform to the computational cell with color interpolation over the vertices, assuming that the cell size from the domain is much larger than the image pixel size. If not, then a one-to-one mapping between computational cell and pixel is used.

The key to this technique lies in the judicious use of the color assignment. This mapping of the range of the scalar function in two space into a subset of three-dimensional color space is called pseudocoloring. A transfer function accomplishes the mapping

$$F(x,y) \rightarrow \big\{ \text{Red}\,\big(F(x,y)\big), \text{Green}\,\big(F(x,y)\big), \text{Blue}\,\big(F(x,y)\big) \big\}$$

The mapping shown in Figure 14 is used extensively in scientific and engineering simulations, resulting in the visible spectrum from blue to cyan, green, yellow, orange, and red.

Other cues can be added to increase the 'readability' of the image. Even though the data is two-dimensional, a fictitious light source can be added. This light source creates a shading variation over each cell by treating the scalar field

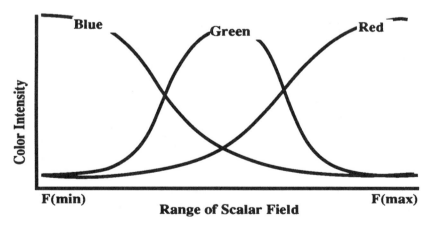

Figure 14. A typical color transfer function mapping the range of the scalar field into color space.

as a height function

$$Z(x,y) = F(x,y)$$

and calculating the diffuse illumination by taking the dot product of the 'surface normal' with the light source vector. The surface normal at each cell vertex is approximated by calculating the partial derivatives either by an analytic evaluation (if the function F is known analytically) or by finite differences and computing the vector product

$$\vec{N}(x,y,z) = \frac{d\vec{F}(x,y)}{dx} \times \frac{d\vec{F}(x,y)}{dy}$$

The normalized surface normal $\vec{N}(x,y,z)/|\vec{N}(x,y,z)|$ is then dotted with the light source (which is traditionally in the upper left corner) to give the shading factor for each vertex (Plate 10)

$$\text{Shading}(x,y) = \vec{N}(x,y,z) \cdot \overrightarrow{\text{Light}}(x,y,z)$$

This scalar is then multiplied by the vertex color to yield the illuminated vertex value.

While some of the ambiguity in continuous color contour maps is minimized by 'pseudoshading', additional cues result from the inclusion of self-shadowing. If we assume that the light source is in a convenient location (say in the upper left with an elevation of 45 degrees, as is typical in topographic maps) and that it is located at an infinite distance (so all the rays are parallel), then calculating the effects of shadowing is greatly simplified (Figure 15). A given vertex is shadowed if other vertices occlude its light. We determine this by maintaining a list of current maximum peaks along a column to the left of the current vertex as we march through vertices from top to bottom, left to right.

If the current vertex is within the shadow mask of one of its neighbors to the northwest, then the shading for that vertex is attenuated. Since the light source is at a 45 degree angle with respect to the domain, the shadow mask is trivial to calculate and maintain.

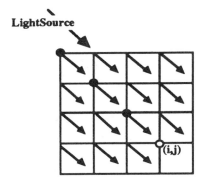

LightSource

Figure 15. The shadowing calculation for node (i,j) depends only upon those nodes between it and the light source, as indicated with black circles.

2.5-DIMENSIONAL RENDERING TECHNIQUES

An Algorithm

These two-dimensional methods are extended to 3D by stacking several of them in three space. If we now associate a fourth transfer function in addition to the previous three color functions, mapping the scalar field value into an opacity component (see Figure 16), we can see through portions of one 2D slice onto another farther away. The peaks of the opacity transfer function in this graph cause regions which are colored blue-green, green, and orange to be visible, while the valleys create transparent areas in the image.

The image is rendered by processing the 2D maps from farthest away to closest to the viewing plane. As we march through the pixels in the current map, a pixel in the image is computed by matting, or compositing, its previous value with the current map pixel (Figure 17). The amount of color contributed by the current map pixel is regulated by the opacity transfer function O as

$$\text{Pixel(red)} = \Big(1 - O\big(F(x,y,z)\big)\Big)\text{Pixel(red)}$$
$$+ O\big(F(x,y,z)\big)\text{Red}\big(F(x,y,z)\big)$$

$$\text{Pixel(green)} = \Big(1 - O\big(F(x,y,z)\big)\Big)\text{Pixel(green)}$$
$$+ O\big(F(x,y,z)\big)\text{Green}\big(F(x,y,z)\big)$$

$$\text{Pixel(blue)} = \Big(1 - O\big(F(x,y,z)\big)\Big)\text{Pixel(blue)}$$
$$+ O\big(F(x,y,z)\big)\text{Blue}\big(F(x,y,z)\big)$$

where $O = 1$ is completely opaque and $O = 0$ is completely transparent. As each layer is added, the image becomes more complete. We use all the other illumination techniques discussed in the previous section to add additional details. As in the two-dimensional case, the key to making meaningful images lies in the proper choice of the color and transparency transfer functions (see Plate 11).

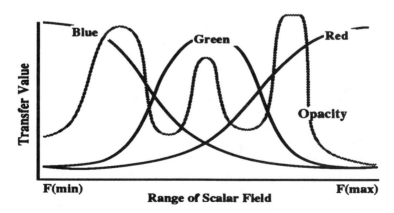

Figure 16. Typical Red, Green, Blue, Opacity transfer function graphs.

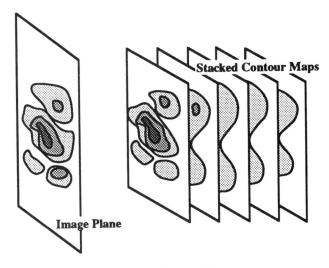

Figure 17. Continuous tone contour stacking in 3D.

Obviously, to be interactive this technique requires an efficient matting function as well as very high speed memory.

The drawback with compositing 2D images is that the technique is inherently two-dimensional. We cannot rotate the domain much before we see between the 2D image planes. While we could determine how we traverse the data set, i.e., in which dimension to perform the matting operation, depending on the viewpoint, there is always an angle for which artifacts are introduced.

Polygonal Surfaces

We have previously looked at representations of other surfaces by points and vectors. We now look at methods used to construct an isosurface using polygons as primitives.

When constructing the dot surface we determined whether or not to display a point by looking at the linear variation between two adjacent nodes. A two-dimensional cell is used to calculate line segments for a vector net in three dimensions. To construct a polygonal isosurface we need to consider the variation of the scalar field in three dimensions. For most recent algorithms, the three-dimensional cell is the basic building block for this technique.

However, earlier methods consisted of stacking parallel contour lines in three space and trying to build a polygonal mesh between the two by correlating adjacent points along the contours [Kepp75; Chri78]. This method works quite well unless a single closed contour on one plane splits into multiple closed loops on the next plane. In this case it is difficult to determine the connectivity. In fact, there are multiple permissible connectivities. Other techniques, relying on the topology of the data to make this determination, are being investigated [Artz81].

An Algorithm

Recently, several techniques were published that generate polygonal surfaces by processing computational cells [Lore87; Upso86; Yost87; Kerl89]. In a three-dimensional scalar field, cells consist of rectangular subregions bounded by eight vertices at the corners of the cell. If we assume that the variation of the field is linear in each direction within the cell, or trilinear over the entire cell, then the algorithms work as follows:

> March through the computational domain cell by cell.
>
> For each cell, determine whether or not the surface passes through it.
>
> If the range of the scalar field within the cell contains the threshold value, then the cell contains a portion of the surface
>
> $$\mathrm{Min}\big(F(x,y,z)\big) \leq \mathrm{Threshold} \leq \mathrm{Max}\big(F(x,y,z)\big)$$
>
> where $x = \{x(i), x(i+1)\}$ $y = \{y(j), y(j+1)\}$ $z = \{z(k), z(k+1)\}$ for the cell with indices (i, j, k).
>
> If the cell contributes to the surface, then we need to determine the polygons that compose the surface. This is accomplished by computing an index into a look-up table based on the status of the corner nodes.
>
> Build the index by characterizing each corner node as 1 (one) if the scalar field at that node is greater than the threshold, and 0 (zero) if it is less than the threshold. By combining these zeros and ones we build up an eight-bit index—one bit per corner node.
>
> This index is used in a look-up table which determines how many triangles are needed, where they are, and what their connectivity is.
>
> Each edge, or adjacent node pair, that brackets the threshold value is interpolated to get the exact intersection point of the threshold with the edge.
>
> These points, along with the connectivity, determine the surface variation within the cell.

An example within a single cell is shown in Figure 18. In general triangles are used to represent the surface, since these are planar, are the easiest to compute, and most graphics workstations are optimized to render them.

The calculation of the shading coefficients for each polygonal vertex is quite straightforward. The gradient of the scalar field is used to compute this shading coefficient in the same manner as dot surfaces. This results in a smooth surface normal for each vertex. The traditional method of computing normals for each polygon of which a given vertex is a member and then averaging these to determine the vertex normal is a much more compute-intensive process. This requires yet another connectivity list (in this case, a list of all the polygons for which each vertex is a member) which complicates the computation. While this newer shading calculation results in smoother illumination, it accomplishes this by first differentiating the field analytically or numerically and then interpolating this value. In some cases, the original data may be obscured. Again, this is the trade-off between visual aesthetics and preserving information.

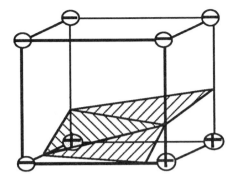

Figure 18. The polygons computed for a single cell. The corners marked with a '+' indicate the associated value at that node is greater than the threshold; those with a '−' are below the threshold.

Rendering Tricks

While a surface representation has advantages in that surfaces are in general easier to understand than vectors, the disadvantage is that only a small portion of the data is being displayed. In essence we take a scalar field in three dimensions and reduce the amount of information to only a surface within this volume. We attempt to squeeze more information out of the data by using several nested isosurfaces. Since an isosurface calculated at a higher threshold value is completely contained within those at lower thresholds, we need to make the outer surfaces semitransparent to see the inner ones. In general, this means that the opacity increases linearly from the outer (lowest threshold) surface to the inner (highest threshold) surface. This inner surface is usually opaque.

The effects of transparency help to get more information out of the image, but they also create problems. If we assign a unique color for each surface (which is the only way transparency makes sense), the final color for each pixel in the image is the accumulation of all the colors of all the surfaces that are mapped into that pixel. This means that if both a red and a green surface are mapped into a pixel, the resultant color is some combination of the two, ranging from yellow to orange. It is very difficult to get fully saturated colors (i.e., fully red, or blue, etc.) when such mixing occurs. The way to get around this is to subtract color components from a contour's color triplet. For example, if the outer surface is blue, or (0.0, 0.0, 1.0) in RGB space, and the inner contour is red (1.0, 0.0 0.0), we expect that in regions where they overlap the color will be some shade of violet to magenta. In those rendering packages which accept negative colors for objects, we can set the inner contour's color to (1.0, 0.0, -0.5). This subtracts out at least half the blue of the outer contour when the two overlap (which is everywhere there is red) and gives a more intense, more saturated red color. In this manner color bleeding is reduced.

Transparent objects are more computationally expensive to render than are opaque objects. This is due to the additional sorting that must be performed to correctly represent transparent objects. Instead of the typical z-buffering used for opaque objects, in which the final color of a pixel is the color and shade of the polygon which is closest to the viewer at that location, a transparency rendering algorithm must sort all those transparent polygons that project into each pixel. The final displayed color is a sum from front to back of the colors of all transparent polygons weighted by their transparency coefficient. Thus, the time to render an image with transparency is directly dependent on the depth complexity of the scene. In an effort to balance computational speed with image quality, a common compromise is to view the image without sorting transparent polygons. In this case, all transparent objects are displayed in the order in which they are encountered; however, they may or may not be displayed in the correct viewing order. While this technique at times leaves something to be desired, it is an excellent trade-off when interactivity is an issue.

In order to squeeze the most performance from graphics hardware, several imaging tricks are usually performed. Included in this category is that of quickly eliminating all polygons that are pointed away from the viewing direction or 'back face culling'. While this almost always works with opaque polygons, it is almost always a problem with transparent objects. When you look through an object you also expect to see the other side. So in order to minimize confusing artifacts when viewing transparent objects, back face culling is usually not performed. This slows down the already fairly expensive transparency operation.

Plate 12 illustrates polygonal isosurfaces and the effects of transparency. The data, from computational cosmology, is of the matter density of a simulated portion of the universe 13 billion years after a big bang [Cent83].

Attribute Mapping

Central to the work of scientists and engineers is the task of comparing and correlating information. In the computational sciences, this means trying to combine multiple sets of data into a single image which exposes regions that are either positively or negatively correlated. This is accomplished with polygonal isosurfaces by using one scalar field to determine the form of an object (by iso-surface generation) and another field mapped into the coloration of that object. This pseudocoloring of the polygonal isosurface is accomplished by interpolating the second field variable at each vertex of the isosurface, and then mapping the resulting value into a color triplet. The usual color transfer functions are used to accomplish this mapping. Linear interpolation of the vertex colors over the polygon results in smooth color transitions in the object. In this manner, we see the variation of the second field variable at all the locations where the first variable is equal to the threshold value.

The effects of pseudocoloring by way of color-per-vertex mapping is different than three-dimensional texture mapping [Peac85], as is seen in the next section on volume rendering. In the color-per-vertex case, only three color samples are made for each triangle in the isosurface. If the surface is texture-mapped, a second field is sampled (via interpolation) at each pixel of each polygon in the final image. If the resolution of both data sets is similar, then both of these techniques result in similar images. But if one field variable has a significantly different spatial resolution than the other, then the pseudocolor mapping yields inaccurate images.

Higher-order Surfaces: NURBs

Nonuniform Rational B-Splines, or NURBs, are representations for higher-order, i.e., higher than linear, surfaces [Bart87; Roge90]. This classification includes a suite of different order surfaces from bilinear to bicubic and beyond.

Little work has been published on isosurface tiling volumetric data using spline interpolants, due primarily to the fact that this representation form induces a tremendous amount of smoothing to the data. This smoothing is undesirable for numerical simulations, as it hides instabilities that could grow to corrupt the simulation later on. On the other hand, in the industrial design field a smooth representation is often the goal.

THREE-DIMENSIONAL PRIMITIVES: VOLUMES

Volumetric primitives, as currently used, differ from the other representations discussed so far, in that they are directly rendered without an intermediate geometric mapping step. Referring back to Figure 3, notice the diagonal arc that connects the data filtering process with the rendering step. In general, this is the path taken with volumetric primitives. This minimizes the amount of processing that must be accomplished prior to rendering, as the geometric mapping process is generally very compute-intensive for large data sets. This fact, as well as the ability of volumetric techniques to present a complete three-dimensional data set for viewing without reducing its dimensionality, contributes to the recent interest in volumetric rendering techniques [Upso89b].

Up to now we have been a bit careless about the way we described and accessed data from a computational domain. When we discussed pseudocolored contour maps, we mapped each point of the computational domain into pixels and essentially ignored the structure of the cells. When we constructed vector contour maps and polygonal isosurfaces, we defined a cell as a two- or three-dimensional region of space bounded by its four or eight corner nodes. In this section on three-dimensional primitives we divide the discussion into two techniques, with the sole differentiation between the two being the manner in which the data structure is accessed. Techniques for volume rendering typically restrict the types of data with which they deal to internally rectilinear meshes in three space. This means that the computational domain consists of rectangular box-shaped cells, with the mesh itself represented as a 3D matrix in logical space

$$F\big(x(i), y(j), z(k)\big) = F(i, j, k)$$

where
$$x = \{x(1), x(2), \ldots, x(ni)\}$$
$$y = \{y(1), y(2), \ldots, y(nj)\}$$
$$z = \{z(1), z(2), \ldots, z(nk)\}$$

Thus, there are $ni\,nj\,nk$ samples, or nodes, in the computational domain. These nodes have a volume element associated with them defined at the centroid of

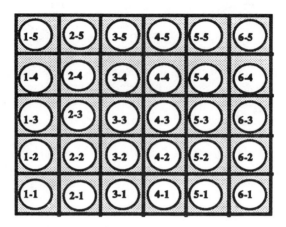

Figure 19. Two-dimensional schematic with nodes (in circles) defined at the center of each cell.

the volume, as shown in Figure 19. Data accessed in this manner lends itself to voxel techniques for volumetric rendering.

Alternatively, several nodes can be associated with a single volume element (see Figure 20 for a 2D representation). In this case they are located at the corners of the volumetric cell. When data is defined in this form, cell-based volumetric rendering is the logical choice. Associated with each cell are eight nodes defined at its corners.

Volume rendering is a direct three-dimensional extension of continuous tone, or pseudocolored, contour maps. If the domain is accessed as a series of samples in three space without any interpolation form imposed on the grid, then a voxel representation is most natural. Data from experimental collection devices such

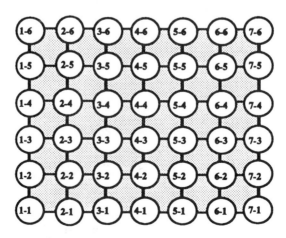

Figure 20. Two-dimensional domain with a cell-based representation.

as Computed Axial Tomography (CAT), Magnetic Resonance Imaging (MRI), and Positron Emission Tomography (PET) scans fall into this category. To date, the majority of the uses of volumetric rendering come from medical applications [Herm79; Cook83]. Each sample point in the three-dimensional domain represents an intensity averaged over a small sample volume. The variation between adjacent samples is either lost in the collection process or is beyond the resolution of the device to capture. In numerical simulations, the interpolation form between nodes is inherent in the numerical technique and is used during the visualization process if absolute accuracy is needed.

In a voxel representation, the data is accessed such that a sample volume or cell is defined by one value. This intensity value is constant over the cell, or voxel in this case. Thus, any other properties associated with a voxel are also constant over the spatial domain of the voxel, including such attributes as transparency, shading, and coloration.

An Algorithm

Since the data is assumed to be simply defined as a matrix in three space, the algorithms used to create images take full advantage of its simplistic data structure. For this algorithm let us first make the big assumption that the domain is aligned exactly in the optimal orientation: the x-axis is parallel to the image plane's x-axis, the y-axis is parallel to the image plane's y-axis, and the z-axis is perpendicular to the image, with z increasing towards the viewpoint. Further assume that there is no perspective in the image; an orthographic projection is used. With these assumptions, a typical algorithm is as follows (see also Figure 21):

Assign color transfer functions, as with pseudocolored contour maps, which map the range of the scalar field into color space

$$\text{Red}\left(F(x,y,z)\right)$$
$$\text{Green}\left(F(x,y,z)\right)$$
$$\text{Blue}\left(F(x,y,z)\right)$$

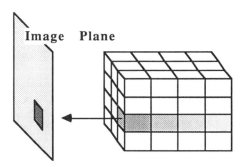

Figure 21. Voxel rendering technique. The pixel color results from the summation of the color opacity contributions of all voxels along the projection.

This transfer function is usually the result of a complicated material classification scheme. These algorithms are used to probablistically assign a material type for each voxel based upon the value of the scalar field at that voxel.

Assign an opacity (or transparency, which is a bit more complicated) transfer function

$$\text{Opacity}\left(F(x,y,z)\right)$$

The final color for each voxel is then the product of its color and opacity

$$\text{Color Opacity} = \text{Red}\left(F(x,y,z)\right)\,\text{Opacity}\left(f(x,y,z)\right)$$
$$\text{Green}\left(F(x,y,z)\right)\,\text{Opacity}\left(f(x,y,z)\right)$$
$$\text{Blue}\left(F(x,y,z)\right)\,\text{Opacity}\left(f(x,y,z)\right)$$

Since the data set is oriented in the optimal manner, no sorting is needed to create the view. Voxel values along an ($x = $ constant, $y = $ constant) line are summed in z to create a color (and opacity) for each pixel. Each voxel, starting from the farthest away, is overlaid on top of the voxels behind it, in a back-to-front manner (Figure 21) [Dreb88]. Either direction, back-to-front or front-to-back, can be used. In fact, the algorithms presented in the next section all process from front-to-back. This summation process can be highly vectorized and parallelized.

Since we want to see what the data looks like from all directions and in perspective, we transform the volume into this canonical orientation, using the normal translation, rotation, scaling, and perspective transformations. These are perhaps best performed on two-dimensional (image) slices of the volume [Catm80]. Care must be taken during this resampling process, since it is easy to introduce artifacts.

This method of image construction is very similar to that discussed for 2.5-dimensional rendering methods using image stacking, and in fact is derived from that method. Each voxel is a space-filling object, whereas each pixel in the image stacking method is an area-filling object. The difference occurs when you rotate the object. In the 2.5D method, the data disappears at some rotation angles; in the voxel method it is always visible, due to the resampling.

Voxel algorithms are appropriate when individual voxels project into a small number of pixels on the screen. Since the voxel representation is not continuous between adjacent cells (it is a step function), we see jumps between adjacent pixels in the image that map from different voxels in the data. Plate 13 is from a very small, simple data set consisting of an $8 \times 8 \times 8$ voxel grid modeling a sphere

$$F(x,y,z) = \text{Constant} - \sqrt{(x - x\text{center})^2 + (y - y\text{center})^2 + (z - z\text{center})^2}$$

This assigns low values to the corners of the domain and high values to the center.

In the voxel rendered image on the left in Plate 13 are the effects of assuming that the representation is constant over each voxel. As each voxel maps into several hundreds of pixels, the low resolution of the data set is prominent. The image on the right in Plate 13 is from a cell representation using volume rendering which assigns values to corner nodes and interpolates the field between them.

As the projected size of each voxel approaches one pixel in the final image the representation becomes more continuous, and the quality is limited by the resolution of the image, not the data set. In Plate 14, an image of benzene's electron density map, the data set resolution is $100 \times 100 \times 50$ voxels, and even though the image was computed at 1280×1024, the discrete representation is much less obvious. In this case, a voxel maps into about 10 pixels on a side (approximately 1,000,000 pixels vs. 10,000 voxels in the screen direction).

Cell-based Representations

If the database is defined at the corners of cells rather than at the centroids of voxels, then a different visual representation form is possible. Over each cell a functional form is assigned to the scalar field. This functional form, or interpolant, varies from algorithm to algorithm, but the most common is linear in each dimension or trilinear over the cell. Using this form, the scalar field is continuous and differentiable over the cell but continuous and not differentiable at the cell faces. Other forms, such as tricubic, maintain differentiability between cells but require much more sophisticated interpolation.

Techniques that use a cell-based representation fall into two categories, image-space and object-space oriented. Those that are image-space based typically use ray tracing, thus sampling the database at the image resolution [Kaji84; Sabe88; Levo88; Upso88]. Object-space methods sample the data at its resolution and project the result onto the image plane [Upso88].

An Algorithm: Image-space Cell Rendering

The basic algorithm underlying image-space methods is (see Figure 22):

> Assign color and opacity transfer functions as in voxel-based rendering methods.

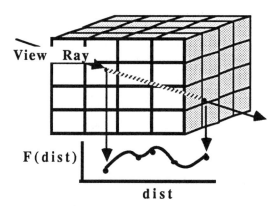

Figure 22. Ray tracing schematic.

Transform the data volume into the desired viewing orientation. This is not restricted to one perpendicular to the viewing direction.

For each pixel in the image, fire a ray from the viewpoint through the pixel into the database.

Each ray is tracked through the volume, accumulating color and opacity with every grid intersection it encounters. Since the data set is so nicely structured, it is easy to determine which cell the ray encounters next; thus, no searching or sorting is required.

At each intersection evaluations are made of the scalar field, shading functions, and other illumination keys such as depth cueing. Each new scalar field interpolation point is mapped, via the transfer functions, into color and opacity values. These are summed into the current pixel color and opacity. Additional evaluations are made at intermediate points along the ray if increased accuracy is required, or if the function is changing rapidly.

The ray is tracked until its accumulated opacity reaches unity, or until the end of the volume is reached, at which time the colors are stored for the pixel and the algorithm moves onto the next pixel.

The drawback to ray tracing volumes is the traditional one of aliasing, which is inherent in image-space algorithms. Figure 23 illustrates the problem in two dimensions. Cells which are close to the view point are sampled at acceptable rates. As the rays progress farther into the volume, the number of cells which are incorrectly sampled or even missed increases.

An Algorithm: Object-space Cell Rendering

To avoid this problem of sampling the database, we must reverse the direction of the mapping. In image-based methods, we start at the image plane and project

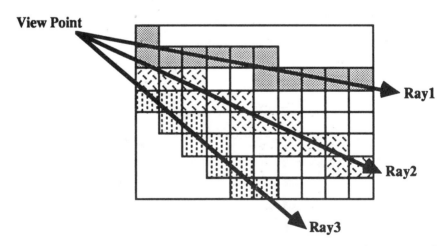

Figure 23. Ray tracing the volume leads to aliasing if the image resolution is too low. The white cells between rays, not visited by rays at this sampling rate, do not contribute to the final image.

through the volume. In object-based algorithms, information starts at the object cell and projects into the image plane. The basic algorithm is (see Figure 24):

Assign transfer functions for color and opacity.

Sweep through the computational domain, cell by cell. The ordering of the cells is determined by their distance from the image plane. Again, since the data structure is so simple it is easy to determine which cell should be processed first and which cells occlude or partially occlude others. In general, this results in a spiral processing order about the cell closest to the viewpoint.

For each cell compute the eight trilinear interpolation coefficients $\{f\}$ and $\{s\}$ for the scalar field F and the illumination function S (based on the gradient as with dot surfaces) as a function of the vertex values. This can be represented as a system of eight equations for each function, one per vertex

$$F(x, y, z) = f_1 + f_2 x + f_3 y + f_4 z + f_5 xy + f_6 xz + f_7 yz + f_8 xyz$$

$$S(x, y, z) = s_1 + s_2 x + s_3 y + s_4 z + s_5 xy + s_6 xz + s_7 yz + s_8 xyz$$

Compute the bounding box of the cell projected onto the image plane.

On each pixel within the bounding box, integrate from the nearest to the farthest edge of the cell (Figure 24). At each integration point interpolate the scalar field, the shading function, and other illumination keys such as

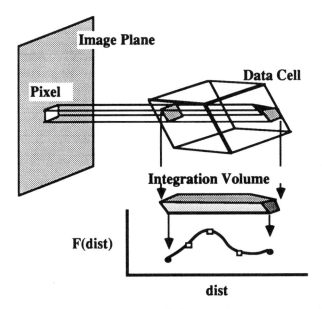

Figure 24. Colors and opacity are summed through the integration volume for each pixel into which the cell projects. The distribution curve on the bottom represents the variation in the scalar field over an integration path.

depth cueing. Sum the color opacity values into the pixel color and opacity. When each pixel in the cell has been calculated, move onto the next cell.

By these exhaustive calculations, sampling artifacts are minimized (see Plate 15). Since all cells and all nodes of all cells are processed, the entire database is traversed during the rendering step.

The drawback of an object-space method is the tremendous amount of calculation required to compute an image. Several cells can be processed independently, as can all the pixels into which each cell projects, thus making this algorithm a prime candidate for highly parallel architectures.

Properties of Volume Primitives

While we are all used to looking at volumetric phenomena in nature, e.g., clouds, water, and gases, we are quite unaccustomed to computing images using volumetric primitives. The basic kernel of volume rendering is that of accumulating color and opacity from structures near the viewpoint while modulating the color of more distant structures. This color accumulation results in color blending. Thus, if a green structure is behind a red object the resulting color is somewhere between the two, depending on the opacity transfer function of the field. This blending is much more pronounced than with nested contour surfaces, since in the volumetric case color is not only defined on surfaces but is continuous in space. Animation helps resolve this ambiguity and is more important with volumetric than with surface- and vector-based images. This is in part due to the tremendous amount of information included in the image.

Traditional methods of shading the data by calculating the surface normal and 'dotting' it with the light source vector are also used with volumetric methods; however, they take on new meaning. How does one shade a volume that has no surfaces? The answer lies in some nasty looking physics, which predicts how light scatters through matter [Kaji84]. In general, this is too expensive to calculate correctly so it is ignored; the gradient of the field is used by assuming that the evaluation point is on a level surface.

As in other methods, such as continuous tone contour maps, one of the most crucial aspects of volumetric techniques lies in the appropriate choice of transfer functions. These can be arbitrarily chosen or can be a function of an additional scalar field. For example, the color transfer function in Plate 15 (cell rendering) is a function of the pressure field, as is the opacity. However, we could have used another field variable, such as the scalar flow speed, to determine the color of each point in the space and used the pressure to determine the form (opacity) of the image. We could also have used the velocity vector field (u, v, w) to map into color space (RGB or HSV) using solid texture mapping [Peac85; Upso88; Good89]. This extra flexibility results in almost too many choices, and it becomes overwhelming to navigate through the parameter space. This trend is generalized as

The higher the dimensionality of the representation, the greater the dimensionality of the viewing parameter space.

Beyond Three Dimensions: Icons

Most of the representation forms presented up to now attempt to visualize the field variable in a continuous manner. Some techniques result in more continuous representations than others, i.e., volume rendering as compared to vector net surfaces. But for all, the goal is to link one primitive to the next to approach a continuum. Iconic representations, on the other hand, are inherently discrete. The advantage of icons lies in their great potential for conveying information concerning a high-dimensional domain [Cher73; Pick88].

Vectors

Recall that a vector field associates a magnitude and a direction with every point in space. There are several commonly used methods for visualizing vector fields. In two dimensions, a common visualization is to use markers shaped like arrows, whose direction is that of the local field, and whose length represents the magnitude of the field at that point. An overall length scale of the visualization is adjusted to bring out the variation which is of most interest. At present, this is often done by trial and error and is best performed interactively. If only directional information is needed, all the vectors are made the same length.

Also, care must be taken not to fill the visualization space with too many primitives. This is a common problem with iconic representations: they take up too much screen real estate and are best used on small regions of the domain where a microscopic view is desired. Icons are also assembled with polygons which are illuminated by a light source for additional directional information. While only a few polygons are needed to build a single solid arrow, the number grows extremely large for an entire vector field. Attribute mapping, using the normal color transfer functions, is also used to correlate another field variable with the vector field; however, the image becomes busy and difficult to interpret.

With the aid of an interpolant, a 1D 'rake' or 2D grid can be introduced into the visualization space to visualize all the vectors emanating from it. This provides a computed analogue of the tool used in experimental flow visualization, consisting of a wire mesh with a piece of yarn tied onto each mesh intersection.

Ellipsoids

There are a few methods available for visualizing rank two-tensor fields in three dimensions . At each point a tensor is represented as a 3×3 matrix. By a suitable change of basis vectors, we derive a frame of 3-vectors (called the principal axes) in which the tensor is diagonal, with zeros for all nondiagonal elements of the matrix. The values of the diagonal elements are called the principal values, or eigenvalues. Each of these values is associated with a geometric object. The easiest technique is to use a set of axes which mark the field at each point. A more complicated marker is the tangent quadric, an example of which is the Lame' ellipsoid for stress tensors in solid mechanics [Fung65; Fung77], where the principal axes of the ellipsoid are the principal stress directions, and the axis lengths are their magnitudes. Integrating along the directions defined by the principal axes forming a path in space [Dick89a, Dick89b] yields further information concerning the tensor field.

Another method using markers on surfaces was developed by Todd [Todd86a, Todd86b] to represent the Dupin indices (tangent conics) to the surface. In three dimensions, these are the tangent quadrics, and are either ellipsoids, paraboloids, or hyperboloids, depending on the signs of the principal values of the tensor.

Cuberilles

Cuberilles are a cross between voxel and iconic representations. In this technique, objects generally in the shape of cubes (hence the name) are used to visualize scalar fields by the use of isosurfaces. Each cell in the domain is tested to see if it is on or near the threshold of the isosurface. If it is, an object conforming spatially to that cell is placed in the image. In this manner, a blocky representation is used to visualize the surface [Chen85]. As a cube has only three visible faces, there are only three distinct shades in the image. Several improvements in the illumination model have recently been made to improve the visual realism of the display. The reason this is included under the heading of iconic representations is that the space-filling object need not be a cube, but could be any other iconic shape with additional attributes mapped onto its surface.

REFERENCES

[Artz81]
   Artzy, E., Frieder, G., and Herman, G., The theory, design, implementation and evaluation of a three-dimensional surface detection algorithm, *Comput. Graph. Image Process.*, Vol. 15, No. 1, pp. 1–24, January 1981.

[Bart87]
   Bartels, R., Beatty, J., and Barsky, B., *An Introduction to Splines for use in Computer Graphics and Geometric Modeling*, Los Altos, CA: Morgan Kaufmann, 1987.

[Buni85]
   Buning, P., and Steger, J., Graphics and flow visualization in computational fluid dynamics, *Proc. AIAA 7th Computational Fluid Dynamics Conference*, AIAA-85-1507-CP, 1985.

[Catm80]
   Catmull, E., and Smith, A.R., 3D transformations of images in scanline order, *Comput. Graph.*, Vol. 14, pp. 279–285, 1980 (SIGGRAPH 80).

[Cent83]
   Centrella, J., and Melott, A., Three dimensional simulation of large scale structure in the universe, *Nature*, Vol. 305, pp. 196–198, 1983.

[Chen85]
   Chen, L., Herman, G., Reynolds, R., and Udupa, J., Surface shading in the cuberille environment, *IEEE Comput. Graph. and Appl.*, Vol. 5, No. 12, pp. 33–43, December 1985.

[Cher73]
Chernoff, H., The use of faces to represent points in k-dimensional space graphically, *Jour. Amer. Stat. Assoc.* , Vol. 68, pp. 361–368, June 1973.

[Chri78]
Christiansen, H., and Sederberg, T., Conversion of complex contour line definitions into polygonal element mosaics, *Comput. Graph.*, Vol. 12, pp. 187–192, 1978 (SIGGRAPH 78).

[Clin88]
Cline, H., Lorensen, W., Ludke, S., Crawford, C., and Teeter, B., Two algorithms for the reconstruction of surfaces from tomograms, *Medical Phys.*, Vol. 15, No. 3, pp. 320–327, June 1988.

[Conn85]
Connolly, M.L., Depth buffer algorithms for molecular modeling, *Jour. Molecular Graph.*, Vol 3, pp. 19–24, 1985.

[Cook83]
Cook, L., Dwyer, S., Batnitzky, S., and Lee, K., A three-dimensional display system for diagnostic imaging applications, *IEEE Comput. Graph. and Appl.*, Vol. 3, No. 5, pp. 13–19, August 1983.

[Dick89a]
Dickinson, R.R., A unified approach to the design of visualization software for the analysis of field problems, *SPIE Proc.*, Vol. 1083, pp. 173–180, January 1989.

[Dick89b]
Dickinson, R.R., Interactive 4-D visualization of fields, Technical Report CS-89-15, Dept. Computer Science, University of Waterloo, Waterloo, Ontario, Canada N2L 3G1, 1989.

[Dreb88]
Drebin, R., Carpenter, L., and Hanrahan, P., Volume rendering, *Comput. Graph.*, Vol. 22, p. 65-74, August 1988 (SIGGRAPH 88).

[Feld87]
Feldman, L., and Rapagnani, N., Fast interactive graphics and the numerical electronic-wind tunnel, Air Force Weapons Laboratory Technical Report, AFWL-TN-87-33, 1987.

[Fole82]
Foley, J.D., and van Dam, A., *Fundamentals of Interactive Computer Graphics*, Reading, MA: Addison-Wesley, 1982.

[Fuch77]
Fuchs, H., Kedem, Z., and Uselton, S., Optimal surface reconstruction from planar contours, *CACM*, Vol. 20, pp. 693–712, 1977.

[Fung65]
Fung, Y., *Foundations of Solid Mechanics*, Englewood Cliffs, NJ: Prentice-Hall, p. 75, 1965.

[Fung77]
Fung, Y.C., *A First Course in Continuum Mechanics*, Englewood Cliffs, NJ: Prentice-Hall, 1977.

[Good89]

Goodsell, D., and Olsen, A., Molecular applications of volume rendering and 3D texture maps, Proc. Volume Visualization Workshop, Upson, C., Ed., Dept. Computer Science, University of North Carolina at Chapel Hill, NC, pp. 27–31, 1989.

[Helm89a]

Helman, J., and Hesselink, L., Surface representations of two- and three-dimensional fluid flow topology, in *Proc. Visualization 90*, pp. 6–13, Los Alamitos, CA: IEEE Computer Society Press, October 1990.

[Helm89b]

Helman , J. and Hesselink, L., Representation and display of vector field topology in fluid flow data sets, *IEEE Comput.*, Vol. 22, No. 8, pp. 27–36, August 1989.

[Herm79]

Herman, G., and Lui, H., Three-dimensional display of human organs from computed tomograms, *Comput. Graph. Image Process.*, Vol. 9, No. 1, pp. 1–21, January 1979.

[Hult89]

Hultquist, J.P.M., Numerical flow visualization in a functional style, NASA Applied Research Office Report RNR-89-008, April 1989.

[Kaji84]

Kajiya, J., and Von Herzen, B., Ray tracing volume densities, *Comput. Graph.*, Vol. 18, pp. 165–173, July 1984 (SIGGRAPH 84).

[Kepp75]

Keppel, E., Approximating complex surfaces by triangulation of contour lines, *IBM Jour. Res. Devel.*, Vol. 19, pp. 1–21, 1975.

[Kerl89]

Kerlick, G.D. ISOLEV: A level surface cutting plane program for CFD data, NAS Applied Research Office Report RNR-89-006, May 1989.

[Levo88]

Levoy, M., Display of surfaces from volume data, *IEEE Comput. Graph. and Appl.*, Vol. 8, No. 5, pp. 29-37, May 1988.

[Lore87]

Lorensen, W., and Cline, H., Marching cubes: A high resolution 3D surface construction algorithm, *Comput. Graph.*, Vol. 21, pp. 163–170, August 1987 (SIGGRAPH 87).

[Kaka88]

Kakayama, Y., Ed., *Visualized Flow: Fluid Motion in Basic and Engineering Situations Revealed by Flow Visualization*, Tokyo: Pergamon Press, 1988.

[Peac85]

Peachey, D., Solid texturing of complex surfaces, *Comput. Graph.*, Vol. 19, pp. 279–286, 1985 July (SIGGRAPH 85).

[Pick88]

Pickett, R., and Grinstein, G., Iconographic displays for visualizing multidimensional data, Proc. IEEE Internat. Conf. Syst. Man and Cybern., Beijing, Peoples Republic of China, 1988.

[Pres86]
Press, W., Flannery, B., Teukolsky, S., and Vetterling, W., *Numerical Recipes: The Art of Scientific Computing*, Cambridge, UK: Cambridge Univ. Press, 1986.

[Reev85]
Reeves, W., and Blau, R., Approximate and probabilistic algorithms for shading and rendering structured particle systems, *Comput. Graph.*, Vol. 19, pp. 313–322, July 1985 (SIGGRAPH 85).

[Roge90]
Rogers, D.F., and Adams, A.J., *Mathematical Elements for Computer Graphics*, 2nd ed., New York: McGraw-Hill, 1990.

[Sabe88]
Sabelli, P., A rendering algorithm for visualizing 3D scalar fields, *Comput. Graph.*, Vol. 22, pp. 51–58, August 1988 (SIGGRAPH 88).

[Todd86a]
Todd, P.H., *Intrinsic Geometry of Biological Surface Growth*, No. 67 in Lecture Notes in Biomathematics, Berlin; Springer-Verlag, 1986.

[Todd86b]
Todd, P.H., and McLeod, R.J.Y., Numerical estimation of the curvature of surfaces, *CAD*, Vol. 18, pp. 53–57, 1986.

[Upso86]
Upson, C., The visual simulation of amorphous phenomena, *Visual Comput.*, Vol. 2, No. 5, pp. 321–326, 1986.

[Upso88]
Upson, C., and Keeler, M., V-buffer: Visible volume rendering, *Comput. Graph.*, Vol. 22, pp. 59–64, August 1988 (SIGGRAPH 88).

[Upso89a]
Upson, C., and Fangmeier, S., The role of visualization and parallelism in a heterogeneous supercomputing environment, in *Proc. Parallel Processing for Computer Vision and Display*, Reading, MA: Addison-Wesley, 1989.

[Upso89b]
Upson, C., Ed., Proc. Volume Visualization Workshop, Dept. Computer Science, University of North Carolina at Chapel Hill, NC, 1989.

[Vand82]
Van Dyke, M., *An Album of Fluid Motion*, Stanford, CA: Parabolic Press, 1982.

[Wihl81]
Wilhelmson, R., and Klemp, J., A three-dimensional numerical simulation of splitting severe storms on 3 April 1964, *Jour. Atmospheric Sci.*, Vol. 38, pp. 1581–1600, 1981.

[Wrig72]
Wright, T., A one-pass hidden-line remover for computer drawn three-space objects, Proc. Summer Computer Simulation Conf., pp. 61–267, 1972.

[Wrig79]
Wright, T., and Humbrecht, J., ISOSURF—An algorithm for plotting iso-valued

surfaces of a function of three variables, *Comput. Graph.*, Vol. 13, pp. 182–189, August 1979 (SIGGRAPH 79).

[Yaeg86]

Yaeger, L., Upson, C., and Myers, R., Combining physical and visual simulation—Creation of the planet Jupiter for the film 2010, *Comput. Graph.*, Vol. 20, pp. 85–93, August 1986.

[Yost87]

Yost, J., Computational fluid dynamics for realistic image synthesis, Master's thesis, University of Utah, Dept. Computer Science, Salt Lake City, UT, August 1987.

Biographies

Biographies

State of the Art in Computer Graphics—
Visualization and Modeling

David F. Rogers

David F. Rogers is Professor of Aerospace Engineering at the United States Naval Academy. In 1959, he earned a Bachelor of Aeronautical Engineering degree from Rensselaer Polytechnic Institute and subsequently was awarded the M.S.AE and Ph.D. degrees from the same Institute.

Dr. Rogers is the author of three textbooks on computer graphics, including *Mathematical Elements for Computer Graphics* and *Procedural Elements for Computer Graphics*. He is a member of SIGGRAPH, ACM, the Society of Naval Architects and Marine Engineers, and an Associate Fellow of the American Institute of Aeronautics and Astronautics. Dr. Rogers is the founder and former Director of the Computer Aided Design/Interactive Graphics Group at the United States Naval Academy. He is editor for the Springer-Verlag Series *Monographs in Visual Communication* and is the editor of *Computers & Education*. He also is a member of the editorial boards of *The Visual Computer* and of the *Computer Aided Design Journal*.

Professor Rogers was Co-Chair of the BCS/ACM International Summer Institute on *State of the Art in Computer Graphics* held in Scotland in 1986 and in Exeter in 1988. He was also co-chairman of ICCAS '82, The International Conference on Computer Applications in the Automation of Shipyard Operation and Ship Design. He is a member of the International Program Committee for ICCAS. He was also co-chairman of the International Program Committee for Computer Graphics Tokyo '85.

Professor Rogers was Fujitsu Research Fellow at the Royal Melbourne Institute of Technology in Melbourne, Australia in 1987 and a Visiting Professor at the University of New South Wales, Sydney, Australia in 1982. He was an Honorary Research Fellow at University College London in England during 1977–78, where he studied Naval Architecture.

Professor Rogers was one of the original faculty who established the Aerospace Engineering Department at the United States Naval Academy in 1964. He has both an experimental and a theoretical research background. He has research interests in the areas of highly interactive graphics, computer aided design and manufacturing, numerical control, computer aided education, hypersonic viscous flow, boundary layer theory, and computational fluid mechanics.

Rae A. Earnshaw

Dr. Rae Earnshaw is Head of Computer Graphics at the University of Leeds, with interests in graphics algorithms, integrated graphics and text, display technology, CADCAM, and human-computer interface issues. He has been a Visiting Professor at IIT, Chicago, USA; Northwestern Polytechnical University, Xian, China; and George Washington University, Washington, DC, USA. He was a Director of the NATO ASI on *Fundamental Algorithms for Computer Graphics* held in England in 1985, and a Co-Chair of the BCS/ACM International Summer Institute on *State of the Art in Computer Graphics* held in Scotland in 1986 and in Exeter in 1988. He was also a Director of the NATO ASI on *Theoretical Foundations of Computer Graphics and CAD* held in Italy in 1987.

He is a member of SIGGRAPH, ACM, IEEE, IEEE Computer Society, an Associate Fellow of the Institute of Mathematics and its Applications, and a Fellow of the British Computer Society.

Michael F. Cohen

Michael Cohen is an adjunct Assistant Professor of computer science at the University of Utah. Until 1988 he was on the faculty of the Program of Computer Graphics at Cornell University, where he conducted research in the area of realistic image synthesis. He worked on the development of the radiosity method, and has also investigated uses of dynamic simulation within the context of computer animation. Professor Cohen has lectured widely in the area of image synthesis at SIGGRAPH, INRIS (France), LIENS (France), ZGDV (Germany), and at numerous Universities in the United States.

Frank C. Crow

Frank Crow is currently with Apple Computer. He was formally with the Imaging Area in the Computer Science Laboratory at Xerox Palo Alto Research Center (Xerox PARC) in Palo Alto, California and previously taught at Ohio State University and the University of Texas. He has spent considerable effort on developing algorithms for realistic image synthesis, and on systems and architectures for realizing them. He has a long standing interest in parallel algorithms and architectures for computer display.

James D. Foley

James Foley is currently Professor of Computer Science and Director of the Graphics, Visualization, and Usability Center, College of Computing, at Georgia Institute of Technology in Atlanta, GA. He was formally Professor and Chairman of Electrical Engineering and Computer Science at The George Washington University. He earned his Ph.D. at the University of Michigan. His general research interests are user interfaces and interactive computer graphics; his research currently focuses on building user interface management systems. He is co-author, with A. van Dam, S. Feiner and J. Hughes, of *Computer Graphics, Principles and Practice* (2nd ed.). Foley is a Fellow of the IEEE and serves on the editorial boards of *Computers and Graphics, ACM Transactions on Information Systems, IEEE Computer Graphics and Applications,* and *IJMMS*.

Alain Fournier

Alain Fournier is an Associate Professor and the Director of Imager, the computer graphics research group, in the Department of Computer Science at the University of British Columbia. For the past ten years he has been teaching computer science and has been active in research in computer graphics, especially in the areas of modeling and geometric algorithms. His more than 30 publications in computer graphics include papers on the stochastic modeling of terrain, on the realistic modeling of ocean waves, on various antialiasing schemes, and on theoretical models of computer graphics devices to better analyze the complexity of basic algorithms. With W. T. Reeves he was the guest editor of a special issue of *ACM Transactions on Graphics* on the modeling of natural phenomena (July 1987), and he is currently an associate editor of *ACM Transactions on Graphics*.

Roy Hall

Roy Hall graduated from Rensselaer Polytechnic Institute in 1976 with a B. Architecture and a B.S. Civil Engineering. He was introduced to computer graphics as a design tool for finite element analysis of large deflection tensile and inflated structures. He graduated from Cornell in 1983 with an M.S. from the Program of Computer Graphics, where he concentrated on realistic image synthesis. Roy Hall has written image generation systems for Robert Abel & Associates, Vertigo Computer Imagery, and Wavefront Technologies, where he was Director of Software Development. He has published in *IEEE Computer Graphics and Applications* and in *The Visual Computer*, and is a member of ACM and IEEE. He has lectured at numerous conferences on the subjects of rendering, realism, illumination models, and color science as applied to computer graphics. He has recently published a book, *Illumination and Color in Computer Generated Imagery*, Springer-Verlag, 1989. He is currently on the faculty at Cornell University in Ithaca, New York.

Paul Heckbert

Paul Heckbert has been doing research and development in computer graphics and image processing since 1977. At MIT's Architecture Machine Group (now the Media Lab), he investigated algorithms for color image quantization. As Software Manager at New York Institute of Technology Computer Graphics Lab, and later at Pixar, he developed rendering software and participated in animation projects for television and film. Paul has consulted at Pacific Data Images,

Xerox PARC, Lawrence Berkeley Lab, and Apple Computer, on topics including graphics software engineering, image filtering, and ray tracing. He has presented his work in numerous SIGGRAPH papers and tutorials.

Michael J. Muuss

Michael Muuss has 15 years of experience in working with advanced computer systems. Since 1981, he has been leading the Ballistic Research Laboratory's (BRL) Advanced Computer Systems Team in research projects concerning networking, graphics, CAD/CAE, operating systems, parallel architectures, and command and control. He is the principal architect of BRL's second-generation constructive solid geometry-based CAD system, which is now in use at over 150 sites, and the primary author of the model editor 'MGED' and the advanced ray-tracing package 'RT'. He is the architect for both processing and communications within BRLNET, BRL's extensive campus network of computers ranging from workstations through super-minicomputers up to a Cray X-M/P48 and Cray-2.

Leslie A. Piegl

Leslie Piegl is Professor in the Department of Computer Science and Engineering of the University of South Florida, Tampa, Florida. He has been a software consultant to Structural Dynamics Research Corporation, where he developed, designed and coded software in the areas of rational B-splines (NURBs), geometry processing, computer graphics, surface modeling and shaping, and numerical analysis; an Alexander von Humboldt Research Fellow and Professor of Mathematics and Computer Science at the Technical University Braunschweig; and Assistant Professor of Mathematics at the Technical University Budapest. His research interests include geometric modeling, computer aided geometric design, computer graphics, data structures, rational B-splines, the mathematical aspects of CADCAM, and applied computing.

Turner Whitted

Turner Whitted is co-founder and technical director of Numerical Design Limited, a company that produces image synthesis software. He is also research professor of computer science at the University of North Carolina at Chapel Hill, where he directs student research on geometric modeling and volumetric rendering. From 1978 to 1983 Whitted was a member of the Computer Systems Research Laboratory at Bell Labs, where he developed rendering systems and algorithms. He is best known for devising the widely-used technique of recursive ray tracing. For several years he has served as a member of the SIGGRAPH conference technical program committee and as an associate editor of *ACM Transactions on Graphics*. He also served as a member of the National Science Foundation's Panel on Scientific Visualization. He received BS and MS degrees from Duke University and a Ph.D. in electrical engineering from North Carolina State University.

Craig Upson

Craig Upson is currently with Silicon Graphics Inc. Formerly he was Visualization Scientist at Stardent Computer. His academic background is in numerical mathematics for the University of New Mexico. He worked at Lawrence Livermore National Laboratory for seven years, performing three-dimensional computational fluid dynamics research. After leaving LLNL he worked in the film industry in Los Angeles at Digital Productions. His film credits include 2010, The Last Starfighter, and animations for several world's fairs, as well as television commercials and scientific films. After leading the Scientific Visualization effort at Digital Productions, a phase-1 National Science Foundation Supercomputing Center, Upson left to work as a research scientist at the National Center for Supercomputing Applications at the University of Illinois. At NCSA he organized the Scientific Visualization project. While at Stardent Computer he was involved in the design of AVS, a visualization environment for computational scientists and engineers.

Index

Index